INTERNATIONAL REFUGEE LAW AND THE PROTECTION OF STATELESS PERSONS

International Refugee Law and the Protection of Stateless Persons

MICHELLE FOSTER

and

HÉLÈNE LAMBERT

OXFORD

UNIVERSITY PRESS

OXFORD
UNIVERSITY PRESS

Great Clarendon Street, Oxford, OX2 6DP,
United Kingdom

Oxford University Press is a department of the University of Oxford.
It furthers the University's objective of excellence in research, scholarship,
and education by publishing worldwide. Oxford is a registered trade mark of
Oxford University Press in the UK and in certain other countries

Published in the United States of America by Oxford University Press
198 Madison Avenue, New York, NY 10016, United States of America

British Library Cataloguing in Publication Data
Data available

Library of Congress Control Number: 2018967680

ISBN 978–0–19–879601–5

Acknowledgements

This book is the result of several wonderful years of collaboration. Cathryn Costello, whose invitation to Michelle to participate in the Oxford Refugee Studies Centre's Short Course on Statelessness and International Law in May 2014, was the catalyst for our collaboration on this project. We are indebted to Cathryn for her ongoing interest and support of our project. Over the years we have also benefitted enormously from discussions with other colleagues and friends. We wish in particular to thank Matthew Albert (Victorian Bar), Adrienne Anderson (PhD candidate, Melbourne Law School), Timnah Baker (Research Fellow, Peter McMullin Centre on Statelessness, Melbourne Law School), Claudia Barbarano (Community Engagement Coordinator, DLA Piper Rome), Bruce Burson (Immigration and Protection Tribunal, New Zealand), Judith Carter (Liverpool Law Clinic), Karen Hamann (Swiss State Secretariat for Migration), Erika Feller (Professorial Fellow, Melbourne School of Government), Guy S. Goodwin-Gill (UNSW and All Souls College Oxford), Radha Govil, (Senior Legal Officer (Statelessness), UNHCR), Gabor Gyulai (Hungarian Helsinki Committee and European Network on Statelessness), Susan Kneebone (Professorial Fellow, MLS), Cynthia Orchard and Ian Kane (Asylum Aid UK), Mark Manly (UNHCR), Hugo Storey (judge of the UK Upper Tribunal and former President of the IARMJ-Europe), Inge Sturkenboom (UNHCR), and Laura van Waas (Tilburg University and Institute on Statelessness and Inclusion) for their generous comments, feedback and encouragement.

We benefitted also from opportunities to present our ideas and receive valuable feedback at various fora. Hélène wishes to thank fellow participants from the Institute on Statelessness and Inclusion and the European Network on Statelessness (Scoping Meeting - European Context), the Institute on Statelessness and Inclusion and the Norwegian Refugee Council (Regional Expert Meeting - Syrian Context), and the UNHCR and Tilburg University (First Global Forum on Statelessness), as well as fellow academics at the University of Wollongong, the University of Reading, and the University of London to whom aspects of the research was presented, for their constructive feedback over the past six years. Michelle wishes to thank Professor Gregor Noll for the invitation to present our ideas to the Lund/Uppsala Migration Law Network at the University of Lund, to the International Association of Refugee and Migration Judges, Asia-Pacific Chapter, for the opportunity to test our ideas before a body of judicial experts, and to colleagues at the University of Melbourne Law School and Melbourne Social Equity Institute who provided feedback at various public seminars and lectures.

We also acknowledge the financial support of the University of Melbourne. The University's Dyason fellowship (2015) funded a research visit for Hélène to Melbourne at a crucial stage in the project, and the award of the International Collaboration Fund (ICF) grant over two years from Melbourne Law School funded much-needed research assistance. We also acknowledge the UNHCR for engaging

Hélène as a consultant on a project on claims to refugee status based on arbitrary deprivation of nationality that eventually led to this book. We benefitted from excellent research assistance over several years. Most importantly Rebecca Dowd took on the role of research fellow on this project, and undertook the identification and synthesis of the bulk of the case-law research. We are indebted to her for her efficiency, acuity and insightfulness. We also wish to thank the Melbourne Law School Academic Research Service for initial literature reviews, Grace Duncan, JD, MLS for important historical research, Anna Saunders, MPhil candidate, MLS for editorial assistance and Henry Bantick, JD MLS for research and editorial work. Mimi Oorloff, JD, MLS deserves particular mention as she undertook the enormous task of cite-checking and copy-editing the entire manuscript- all with good humour, efficiency and patience. We are very grateful to the generous and infallible support of our respective institutions, the University of Melbourne and the University of Westminster during the past six years.

Furthermore, we are grateful to Oxford University Press for their tremendous support and patience! In particular, Merel Alston sourced extremely helpful anonymous reviews of our book proposal and we benefitted significantly from that feedback in our shaping of the book's scope and focus.

It goes without saying that the work is our own, as are any errors within it.

Michelle and Hélène

February 2019

Contents

Table of Cases

Table of Cases

NATIONAL CASE LAW

Table of Legislation

Table of Treaties and International and Regional Instruments

1

Statelessness through the Prism of International Refugee Law

The Revival of a Protection Issue

Part 1: Introduction

The protection of refugees and stateless persons has long been understood as a challenge for the international community. However, for decades a focus on refugees has dominated, indeed overshadowed, the plight and protection needs of stateless persons. Yet, as observed by Guy Goodwin-Gill, 'refugees and stateless persons once walked hand in hand'.[1] Indeed, after the First World War 'their numbers and condition were almost coterminous'[2] and in the wake of the Second World War the intention had been to draft a single convention for the protection of both stateless persons and refugees. This historical interlacing is fully captured in Hannah Arendt's writing on the refugee in *The Origins of Totalitarianism*, which refers almost entirely to denationalized people, and thus to the de jure stateless.[3] However, the consignment of a protection regime for *non-refugee* stateless persons first to an annex and ultimately to excision from the 1951 *Convention relating to the Status of Refugees* ('*Refugee Convention*') undoubtedly contributed to a lack of concentrated effort to address the plight and protection needs of this category of 'unprotected persons'[4] notwithstanding the subsequent formulation of the *Convention relating to the Status of Stateless Persons* in 1954 ('*1954 Convention*')[5] and the *Convention on the Reduction of Statelessness* in 1961 ('*1961 Convention*').[6]

The separation of the international regime for the protection of refugees and stateless persons respectively into two distinct instruments did not, of course, mean that there was no relationship between stateless persons and refugees as a matter of

---

[1] Guy S Goodwin-Gill, 'The Rights of Refugees and Stateless Persons' in K P Saksena (ed), *Human Rights Perspective and Challenges* (Lancers Books 1994) 389.
[2] ibid.   [3] Hannah Arendt, *The Origins of Totalitarianism* (Schocken Books 1951).
[4] See the British delegate's suggestion for the definition of refugee and stateless persons to simply refer to 'unprotected persons': Ad Hoc Committee on Statelessness and Related Problems, 'United Kingdom: Draft Proposal for Article 1' (17 January 1950) UN Doc E/AC.32/L.2.
[5] *Convention relating to the Status of Stateless Persons* (adopted 28 September 1954, entered into force 6 June 1960) 360 UNTS 117 (hereafter *1954 Convention*).
[6] *Convention on the Reduction of Statelessness* (adopted 30 August 1961, entered into force 13 December 1975) 989 UNTS 175.

International Refugee Law and the Protection of Stateless Persons. Michelle Foster and Hélène Lambert.
© Michelle Foster and Hélène Lambert 2019. Published 2019 by Oxford University Press.

international law. On the contrary, it was recognized in the very text of the *Refugee Convention* that stateless persons might be entitled to refugee protection. Article 1A(2) of the 1951 *Refugee Convention* contemplates a refugee as someone with *or without* a nationality,[7] and provides that the country of reference for a person without a nationality is the place of '*former habitual residence*'. Hence, from the outset, stateless persons who are also refugees have been entitled to refugee protection as a matter of international law. Such protection includes the supervisory oversight and guidance provided by the United Nations High Commissioner for Refugees ('UNHCR').

Yet the relationship between the 1951 *Refugee Convention* and the *1954 Convention* is radically underexplored and indeed there is scarce scholarly analysis of the capacity of the *Refugee Convention* to accommodate the subset of stateless persons who are also refugees. To date, statelessness has been examined by law academics through the framework of international statelessness law,[8] international human rights law, nationality/citizenship law, and human security.[9] Despite a renewed impetus over the past decade in the international community's focus on stateless persons, attention to the phenomenon of *stateless refugees* remains inadequate. Although it has had responsibility for stateless refugees since 1950,[10] the UNHCR has dedicated very little attention to stateless refugees, at least as a matter of doctrine and international protection.[11] Indeed, no systematic argument has been made to date on the application

---

[7] *Convention relating to the Status of Refugees* (adopted 28 July 1951, entered into force 22 April 1954) 189 UNTS 137, art 1A(2) (hereafter *Refugee Convention*); *Protocol relating to the Status of Refugees* (signed 31 January 1967, entered into force 4 October 1967) 606 UNTS 267, art 1A(2).

[8] General texts on statelessness scarcely refer to refugee law. For example, a recent monograph by William E Conklin, *Statelessness: The Enigma of the International Community* (Hart 2014) dedicates half a page to the *Refugee Convention*: at 143.

[9] For a comprehensive review of the literature, see Brad K Blitz and Maureen Lynch (eds), 'Statelessness and the Benefits of Citizenship: A Comparative Study' (Geneva Academy of International Humanitarian Law and Human Rights and the International Observatory on Statelessness 2009) https://s3.amazonaws.com/academia.edu.documents/35024663/Blitz_Lynch_FINAL_08_Oct_ 2009.pdf?AWSAccessKeyId=AKIAIWOWYYGZ2Y53UL3A&Expires=1544145830&Signatu re=E81KW9fqjAH9jEJLPiZ2UMVidIE%3D&response-content-disposition=inline%3B%20 filename%3DStatelessness_and_the_Benefits_of_Citize.pdf> accessed 9 December 2018. See also Alison Kesby, *The Right to Have Rights: Citizenship, Humanity, and International Law* (OUP 2012); Alice Edwards and Carla Ferstman (eds), *Human Security and Non-Citizens: Law, Policy and International Affairs* (CUP 2010); Laura van Waas, *Nationality Matters: Statelessness under International Law* (Intersentia 2008); Alice Edwards and Laura van Waas (eds), *Nationality and Statelessness under International Law* (CUP 2014); Rhoda E Howard-Hassmann and Margaret Walton-Roberts (eds), *The Human Right to Citizenship: A Slippery Concept* (University of Pennsylvania Press 2015).

[10] The Statute of the Office of the United Nations High Commissioner for Refugees ('UNHCR') defines the 'competence of the High Commissioner' in art 6, and it includes, in A(i), any person who 'not having a nationality and being outside the country of his former habitual residence, is unable or, owing to such fear or for reasons other than personal convenience, is unwilling to return to it': UN General Assembly (UNGA), 'Statute of the Office of the United Nations High Commissioner for Refugees' (14 December 1950) UN Doc A/RES/428(V).

[11] There are no specific guidelines issued by the UNHCR relating to stateless refugees and very few of the existing Guidelines on International Protection mention issues particularly pertinent to stateless persons or indeed stateless persons at all as refugees. For example, the 'Guidelines on International Protection: Gender-Related Persecution within the Context of Article 1A(2) of the 1951 Convention and/or its 1967 Protocol relating to the Status of Refugees' mention 'nationality' as a protected ground but do not discuss gender discrimination in relation to citizenship: (7 May 2002) UN Doc HCR/GIP/ 02/01, para 27. However, more recent Guidelines have begun to address this. The most comprehensive

of the refugee definition in Article 1A(2) of the 1951 *Refugee Convention* to stateless refugees, in contrast to refugees with a nationality.[12]

As Maryellen Fullerton observes, the 'crossroads of statelessness and international refugee law is uncharted territory, and the need for exploring it is urgent'.[13]

This book thus addresses a critical gap in existing scholarship by examining statelessness through the prism of international refugee law, in particular by examining the extent to which the 1951 *Refugee Convention* protects de jure stateless persons. It responds to the need for a 'comprehensive legal framework ... to ensure that refugee law fully addresses the plight of stateless individuals who fear persecution'.[14] The central hypothesis of this book is that the capacity and potential of the 1951 *Refugee Convention* to protect stateless persons has been inadequately developed and understood. This is particularly so when we consider the significant transformation that has occurred over the past sixty years in delimiting state discretion in matters of nationality, including in relation to the acquisition and deprivation of nationality and the treatment of non-nationals. While it may once have been correct to assume that matters of nationality were outside the realm of international law, the advent of international human rights law in particular has limited sovereignty in this respect. Accordingly, whether a stateless person is also a refugee potentially admits of a very different answer in light of modern international human rights law as compared to 1951.

treatment of the issue is in 'Guidelines on International Protection: The Application of Article 1A(2) of the 1951 Convention and/or 1967 Protocol relating to the Status of Refugees to Victims of Trafficking and Persons at Risk of being Trafficked': see (7 April 2006) UN Doc HCR/GIP/06/07, pt III. See also UNHCR, 'Guidelines on International Protection: Child Asylum Claims under Articles 1(A)2 and 1(F) of the 1951 Convention and/or 1967 Protocol relating to the Status of Refugees' (22 December 2009) UN Doc HCR/GIP/09/08, paras 18, 35. Hélène Lambert's study, commissioned by the UNHCR, would appear to be the first work on this issue: 'Refugee Status, Arbitrary Deprivation of Nationality, and Statelessness within the Context of Article 1A(2) of the 1951 Convention and its 1967 Protocol relating to the Status of Refugees' (UNHCR Legal and Protection Policy Research Series PPLA/2014/01, October 2014) 58.

[12] With the exception of a few country-specific articles and one book written by a practitioner that analyses some components of art 1 of the *Refugee Convention* as it applies to stateless refugees: Eric Fripp, *Nationality and Statelessness in the International Law of Refugee Status* (Hart 2016). See also James Hathaway and Michelle Foster, *The Law of Refugee Status* (2nd edn, CUP 2014) 64–75 (hereafter Hathaway and Foster, *The Law of Refugee Status 2*); Guy S Goodwin-Gill, 'Nationality and Statelessness, Residence and Refugee Status: Issues Affecting Palestinians' (March 1990) <http://repository.forcedmigration.org/show_metadata.jsp?pid=fmo:567>; Kate Darling, 'Protection of Stateless Persons in International Asylum and Refugee Law' (2009) 21 IJRL 742; Maryellen Fullerton, 'Without Protection: Refugees and Statelessness—A Commentary and Challenge' (Brooklyn Law School Legal Studies Paper No 351, 8 August 2013) (hereafter Fullerton, 'Without Protection'); Maryellen Fullerton, 'The Intersection of Statelessness and Refugee Protection in US Asylum Policy' (2014) 2 JMHS 144; Stewart E Forbes, ' "Imagine There's No Country": Statelessness as Persecution in Light of *Haile II*' (2013) 61 BuffLR 699. See also Audrey Macklin, 'Who Is the Citizen's Other? Considering the Heft of Citizenship' (2007) 8 Theo Inq Law 333.

[13] Fullerton, 'Without Protection' (n 12) 29. Now appears in Maryellen Fullerton, 'Comparative Perspectives on Statelessness and Persecution' (2015) 63 UKanLRev 863, 902 (hereafter Fullerton, 'Comparative Perspectives on Statelessness and Persecution').

[14] Fullerton, 'Comparative Perspectives on Statelessness and Persecution' (n 13) 902.

Part 2: Context and Relevance

This book is primarily concerned with stateless persons on the move between states, or stateless persons who have already moved (and not with the stateless *in situ*), because it is members of this group who require recognition of their status in order to establish themselves in a new country following a decision to flee. In focusing on this group, we are not attempting to address the plight of the totality of the world's stateless persons—currently estimated at around ten million[15]—but rather we examine the potential of stateless persons who are outside their country of former habitual residence to obtain protection as refugees in international law. The total estimated number of this subset of persons affected by statelessness currently stands at over 1.5 million.[16] These figures are of course based on conservative estimates given the inherent challenges of identifying and accounting for a group of persons who are sometimes described as 'invisible'.[17] What is clear is that despite recent concerted efforts to respond to the challenge of statelessness, it remains an ongoing problem, with the UNHCR estimating that a child is born into statelessness every ten minutes.[18] States continue to invoke denationalization in the 'war on terror',[19] and to create 'pockets of populations invisible in the state's legal self image',[20] particularly in relation to ethnic minorities.[21] Further, the potentially devastating consequences of statelessness, particularly for children, are now well documented and understood. These developments are all highly pertinent to an assessment of whether stateless persons can and should be protected within the international refugee regime and

---

[15] The UNHCR estimates that there are at least ten million stateless persons today in the world: Institute on Statelessness and Inclusion, *The World's Stateless* (Wolf Legal Publishers 2014) 35, ch 3 (hereafter ISI, *The World's Stateless*).

[16] ibid, 10.

[17] See e.g., Nicoletta Policek, 'Turning the Invisible into the Visible: Stateless Children in Italy' in Marisa O Ensor and Elżbieta M Goździak (eds), *Children and Forced Migration* (Springer 2017) 79. On the challenge of mapping statelessness, see ISI, *The World's Stateless* (n 15) 37. The same concept has been applied to statelessness in international law scholarship, see e.g., Will Hanley, 'Statelessness: An Invisible Theme in the History of International Law' (2014) 25 EJIL 321.

[18] UNHCR, 'I Am Here, I Belong: The Urgent Need to End Childhood Statelessness' (November 2015) 1 (hereafter UNCHR, 'I Am Here, I Belong').

[19] As Matthew Gibney observes, 'in recent years, denationalization powers have gained increasing intellectual and political attention as many liberal states have created new laws or enforced old ones to strip citizenship from individuals involved with terrorism': Matthew J Gibney, 'Denationalization' in Ayelet Shachar, Rainer Bauböck, Irene Bloemraad, and Maarten Vink (eds), *The Oxford Handbook of Citizenship* (OUP 2017) 358, 359.

[20] Noora A Lori, 'Statelessness, "In-Between" Statutes and Precarious Citizenship' in Ayelet Shachar, Rainer Bauböck, Irene Bloemraad, and Maarten Vink (eds), *The Oxford Handbook of Citizenship* (OUP 2017) 743, 748.

[21] See UNHCR, '"This is Our Home": Stateless Minorities and their Search for Citizenship' (November 2017). In July 2018 it was reported that, '[a]bout 4 million people who live in the Indian border state of Assam have been excluded from a draft list of citizens, as Bengali-speaking Muslims fear they will be sent to detention centres or deported': Amrit Dhillon, 'India: 4 Million Excluded from Assam's Draft List of Citizens' *The Guardian* (London, 30 July 2018) <www.theguardian.com/world/2018/jul/30/four-million-excluded-from-indian-states-assam-draft-list-of-citizens> accessed 4 August 2018.

attest to the growing practical significance of the connection between the international regimes for stateless persons and refugees.[22]

This book is timely for several reasons. First, there is a growing body of jurisprudence by domestic courts exploring the capacity of the refugee definition in the *Refugee Convention* to accommodate stateless persons, yet there has been comparatively little scholarship exploring this issue. As will be examined in later chapters, refugee decision-makers are grappling with key issues relating to nationality, discrimination, and return. Being stateless often raises important issues relating to arbitrary deprivation of nationality, freedom of movement, and equality in the enjoyment of civil, political, and socio-economic rights, and international and domestic courts are increasingly called upon to interpret and protect those rights in the refugee setting. It is therefore timely to offer a human rights approach to assessing the refugee claims of de jure stateless persons in light of modern international human rights law.

The second reason why this book is timely is the significant transformation of the landscape due to the impetus given to statelessness as an issue of study and focus by the UNHCR over the past decade. This is most clearly highlighted by the pledges on statelessness made by over sixty states during a ministerial conference organized by the UNHCR in Geneva to celebrate the fiftieth anniversary of the *1961 Convention* in 2011. Three years later, at the sixtieth anniversary of the *1954 Convention* in 2014, the UNHCR launched a ten-year campaign to eradicate statelessness by 2024.[23] This campaign has already made concrete progress in increasing ratifications of both the 1954 and 1961 Conventions,[24] and mobilizing action particularly concerning the ten key priorities of action identified by the UNHCR as crucial to the reduction and elimination of statelessness.[25] The recognition of statelessness as an integral component of the broader debate concerning refugees is embodied in the 2016 *New York Declaration for Refugees and Migrants*,[26] which states:

> We recognize that statelessness can be a root cause of forced displacement and that forced displacement, in turn, can lead to statelessness. We take note of the campaign of the Office of the United Nations High Commissioner for Refugees to end statelessness within a decade and we encourage States to consider actions they could take to reduce the incidence of statelessness. We encourage those States that have not yet acceded to the 1954 Convention relating to the Status of Stateless Persons and the 1961 Convention on the Reduction of Statelessness to consider doing so.[27]

---

[22] We are grateful to one of the anonymous reviewers of our book manuscript (commissioned by OUP) for this observation.

[23] UNHCR, 'Global Action Plan to End Statelessness 2014–24' (November 2014).

[24] See Michelle Foster and Hélène Lambert, 'Statelessness as a Human Rights Issue: A Concept Whose Time Has Come' (2016) 28 IJRL 564, 571.

[25] See Executive Committee of the High Commissioner's Programme, 'Update on Statelessness' (7 June 2017) UN Doc EC/68/SC/CRP.13.

[26] UNGA Res 71/1 (3 October 2016) UN Doc A/RES/71/1 (hereafter *New York Declaration*).

[27] ibid, para 72 (citations omitted). This language is replicated in the 2018 Global Compact on Refugees: see UNHCR, Report of the United Nations High Commissioner for Refugees, Part II, Global Compact on Refugees, General Assembly Official Records, Seventy-third Session, A/73/12 (Part II), para 83 <https://www.unhcr.org/gcr/GCR_English.pdf> accessed 12 February 2019.

In addition to increasing state ratifications of the core statelessness treaties, there has been an increased focus on implementing the *1954 Convention* in the form of domestic statelessness status resolution systems. This has been supported by the normative guidance provided by the UNHCR in its 2014 Handbook on Protection of Stateless Persons under the *1954 Convention*. The Handbook consolidates guidelines adopted following a series of expert consultations; it also takes account of (albeit limited) state practice, including jurisprudence of national courts, on the application of the *1954 Convention*.

While there can be no question of the importance of these developments and recent achievements, it must be highlighted that these have focused solely on statelessness and non-refugee stateless persons, and that there is very little on stateless refugees, at least by way of principled guidance to support and strengthen the protection of an estimated 1.5 million stateless persons in a refugee-like situation. Hence, there is a genuine need for a comprehensive analysis of the interaction between statelessness and refugee law that could inform the work of scholars, advocates, and the UNHCR (including its Campaign to End Statelessness by 2024) through a greater understanding and use of refugee law in the statelessness context. Indeed, one should not forget the longstanding historical overlap between the two protection regimes (i.e. the 1951 *Refugee Convention* and the *1954 Convention*).

Part 3: Scope

The *1954 Convention* and the *1961 Convention*, together with UN human rights treaties and regional conventions, form the foundation of the international legal framework to address statelessness. While de jure stateless persons are clearly protected by the *1954 Convention*, this book explores the extent to which such persons are also entitled to refugee status under the 1951 *Refugee Convention*. Hence, this is a book about refugee law; it is concerned with the immediate protection of stateless persons who are on the move, and not with the prevention and reduction of statelessness in countries of origin or indeed in countries of refuge. The key instrument of relevance to this book is therefore the *Refugee Convention*; although the *1954 Convention* and the *1961 Convention* are considered where relevant.

The 1951 *Refugee Convention* is widely acknowledged to constitute the 'cornerstone of international protection',[28] and hence is the key focus of our examination of international refugee law. There have, of course, been vital regional developments, most notably in the form of the Organisation of African Unity *Convention Governing the Special Aspects of Refugee Problems in Africa*, which explicitly accommodates stateless persons within its 'extended definition' by referring to 'every person', 'place of habitual residence' and 'outside his country of origin or nationality'.[29] In addition, the

[28] UNHCR, 'Conclusion on the Provision on International Protection Including through Complementary Forms of Protection No. 103 (LVI)—2005' (7 October 2005) UN Doc A/AC.96/1021.
[29] *Convention Governing the Special Aspects of Refugee Problems in Africa* (adopted 10 September 1969, entered into force 20 June 1974) 1001 UNTS 45, art 1(2).

emergence of regimes providing for complementary protection, that is, implementation of *non-refoulement* obligations derived from other international and regional human rights treaties, have expanded the protective capabilities of international law. Such developments are also considered where relevant throughout the book.

It is important to acknowledge at the outset that an examination of the relationship between the 1951 *Refugee Convention* and the *1954 Convention* does not exhaust the connection between refugeehood and statelessness. Rather, there is increasing awareness of the manner in which refugeehood itself can give rise to statelessness. The renewed attention to statelessness as an issue has highlighted the way in which contemporary refugee flows, as well as certain restrictive policies such as offshore processing, can lead to statelessness or a risk of statelessness.[30] In the context of the Syrian conflict, for example, refugee children are born in neighbouring countries including Turkey, Lebanon, Jordan, and (the Kurdistan Region of) Iraq. These states are parties to international treaties (including the *Convention on the Rights of the Child, Convention on the Elimination of All Forms of Discrimination Against Women*, and the *International Covenant on Civil and Political Rights*),[31] which protect the right of a child to acquire a nationality and the right of women to be protected against discrimination in nationality laws. However, in reality, the situation is far from satisfactory. In all four countries, Syrian refugees may be reluctant to apply for a birth certificate for their new-born babies through the Syrian consulate for fear of retaliation by the Assad regime.[32] Even if they decide to apply, because of gender discrimination in Syria's nationality law (Syrian children can only acquire nationality through their fathers), both parents must be present, or if only the mother, she must provide a marriage certificate and the father's birth certificate.[33] In Turkey for

---

[30] On the topic of offshore processing, see Michelle Foster, Jane McAdam, and Davina Wadley, 'Part Two: The Prevention and Reduction of Statelessness in Australia—An Ongoing Challenge' (2017) 40 MULR 456. On the connection between refugeehood and citizenship, see Cathryn Costello, 'On Refugeehood and Citizenship' in Ayelet Shachar, Rainer Bauböck, Irene Bloemraad, and Maarten Vink (eds), *The Oxford Handbook of Citizenship* (OUP 2017) 717.

[31] Note that Turkey has made the following declarations and reservation to the International Covenant on Civil and Political Rights: 'The Republic of Turkey declares that; it will implement its obligations under the Covenant in accordance to the obligations under the Charter of the United Nations (especially Article 1 and 2 thereof). The Republic of Turkey declares that it will implement the provisions of this Covenant only to the States with which it has diplomatic relations. The Republic of Turkey declares that this Convention is ratified exclusively with regard to the national territory where the Constitution and the legal and administrative order of the Republic of Turkey are applied. The Republic of Turkey reserves the right to interpret and apply the provisions to Article 27 of the International Covenant on Civil and Political Rights in accordance with the related provisions and rules of the Constitution of the Republic of Turkey and the Treaty of Lausanne of 24 July 1923 and its Appendixes': UN Treaty Collection, 'Chapter IV: Human Rights, 4. International Covenant on Civil and Political Rights' (*UN Treaty Collection*, 10 August 2018) <https://treaties.un.org/Pages/ViewDetails.aspx?chapter=4&clang=_en&mtdsg_no=IV-4&src=IND> accessed 12 November 2018.

[32] Elizabeth Ferris, 'Displacement and Statelessness' in *A World on the Move: Migration and Statelessness*, vol 1 (International Affairs Forum 2016) 79, 80. See also Sarnata Reynolds and Tori Duoos, 'A Generation of Syrians Born in Exile Risk a Future of Statelessness' (*European Network on Statelessness*, 15 July 2015) <http://www.statelessness.eu/blog/generation-syrians-born-exile-risk-future-statelessness> accessed 12 November 2018 (hereafter Reynolds and Duoos, 'A Generation of Syrians Born in Exile').

[33] UNHCR, 'I Am Here, I Belong' (n 18) 23.

instance, possibilities to apply for an international birth certificate exist but there are clear obstacles: a time-limit of thirty days from the birth or, if later, subject to a fee; both parents must be present, or if only the mother, she must provide a marriage certificate and the father's birth certificate; and total lack of awareness that such opportunity exists.[34] Finally, statelessness may also occur amongst Syrian adults who may have left Syria following the destruction of their homes and identity documents and who can no longer prove their nationality.[35] Such situations of statelessness, or being at risk of statelessness, renders these individuals more vulnerable to harm, detention, and lack of resources, and may even prevent them from seeking refuge outside Syria because of lack of documentation or states' unwillingness to allow stateless persons to enter their territory (e.g. Palestinian refugees from Syria refused entry into Jordan).[36] These issues are ultimately about the interaction between the *Refugee Convention* and the *1961 Convention*, and hence are beyond the scope of this book. However, this indicates the scope for further research and analysis in this important and historically overlooked area of international protection.

As mentioned above, the *Refugee Convention*'s definition of 'refugee' makes clear that, from the advent of modern refugee law, it has always been understood that de jure stateless persons could claim protection under its ambit. For instance, Article 33 of the *Refugee Convention* (*non-refoulement*) is absent from the *1954 Convention* because it was assumed that a stateless person in a position of being *refoulé(e)* would be treated as a potential refugee and protected against *refoulement* under the *Refugee Convention*.

Of course, not all stateless persons are refugees, hence the need for a specific instrument in international law for the protection of persons who are not considered as a national of any state and who are not refugees. In many respects the *1954 Convention* mirrors the terms of the 1951 *Refugee Convention*, hence refugees and stateless persons, who find themselves outside their country of nationality or former habitual residence, are entitled to a similar level of protection under international law. As such, it might be questioned whether it matters if a person, who is both de jure stateless and a refugee, obtains protection under either the 1951 *Refugee Convention* or the *1954 Convention*.

However, there are significant differences in principle and practice, which render stateless persons less likely to be protected by international law. First, there are discrepancies between the rights listed in the *Refugee Convention* and the *1954 Convention*, such as Articles 15 (freedom of association), 17 (right to work), 31 (right to non-penalization for unauthorized entry), 33 (*non-refoulement*), and 35 (UNHCR supervision) which are either formulated less favourably for stateless persons (Articles 15 and 17)[37] or absent from the *1954 Convention* (in the case of

---

[34] Reynolds and Duoos, 'A Generation of Syrians Born in Exile' (n 32).   [35] ibid.

[36] Zahra Albarazi and Laura van Waas, 'Statelessness and Displacement: Scoping Paper' (Norwegian Refugee Council and Tilburg University 2016) 25.

[37] In the *Refugee Convention* (n 7) art 15, refugees are to enjoy 'the most favourable treatment accorded to nationals of a foreign country' in relation to these rights, whereas in the *1954 Convention* (n 5) those rights are delivered only at the same level as for 'aliens generally'.

Articles 31, 33 and 35).[38] It is worth emphasizing the significance of the omission of Article 33 from the *1954 Convention*. The practical consequence is that even where there is protection under both the refugee and statelessness regimes within one domestic jurisdiction,[39] careful attention should nonetheless be given in the first instance to the applicability of the *Refugee Convention*, given that the statelessness regime does not prohibit return.[40] In other words, the *1954 Convention* cannot provide adequate protection for a stateless individual fleeing persecution,[41] as it does not contain protection from *refoulement*.[42] Second, despite significant increases in state ratification of the *1954 Convention* in recent years, the *1954 Convention* enjoys far fewer ratifications than the 1951 *Refugee Convention* (ninety-one versus 146).[43] Third, even in those states that have ratified the *1954 Convention*, very few have implemented a procedure in domestic law for assessing and according a specific status under the *1954 Convention*.[44] Finally, even in countries that have a stateless status determination procedure, there remain significant concerns in terms of both the process of status determination[45] and full access to rights for stateless persons.[46]

---

[38] Regarding art 33, the *travaux préparatoires* to the *1954 Convention* reveal that the reason why *non-refoulement* was not included in this *Convention* was because it was assumed that 'any stateless person in such a position [needing to be protected against return to the frontiers of territories where their life or freedom would be threatened] would be treated as a potential refugee and given the status of a *réfugié sur place*': Conference of Plenipotentiaries on the Status of Stateless Persons, 'Summary Record of the Eighth Meeting' (29 September 1954) UN Doc E/CONF.17/SR.8 (The President, speaking as representative of Denmark). Regarding art 35, the UNHCR became responsible for stateless persons through an extension of its mandate: see Mark Manly, 'UNHCR's Mandate and Activities to Address Statelessness' in Alice Edwards and Laura van Waas (eds), *Nationality and Statelessness under International Law* (CUP 2014) 88.

[39] We note that this is quite rare: see generally Katia Bianchini, *Protecting Stateless Persons: The Implementation of the Convention relating to the Status of Stateless Persons Across EU States* (Brill Nijhoff 2018).

[40] See New Zealand decision *Refugee Appeal No 73861* [2005] NZRSAA 228 (30 June 2005) [110] for recognition of this point.

[41] ibid, [111].

[42] However, it should be acknowledged that it is now accepted that *non-refoulement* has attained the status of customary international law; nonetheless, this is still debated by some states and hence a less secure footing on which to base a protection need: see Cathryn Costello and Michelle Foster, 'Non-Refoulement as Custom and Jus Cogens? Putting the Prohibition to the Test' (2015) 46 NYIL 273.

[43] UN Treaty Collection, 'Chapter V: Refugees and Stateless Persons: 3. Convention relating to the Status of Stateless Persons' (*UN Treaty Collection*, 21 January 2019) <http://treaties.un.org/Pages/ViewDetailsII.aspx?src=TREATY&mtdsg_no=V-3&chapter=5&Temp=mtdsg2&clang=_en> accessed 22 January 2019; UN Treaty Collection, 'Chapter V: Refugees and Stateless Persons: 2. Convention relating to the Status of Refugees' (*UN Treaty Collection*, 21 January 2019) <https://treaties.un.org/Pages/ViewDetailsII.aspx?src=TREATY&mtdsg_no=V-2&chapter=5&Temp=mtdsg2&clang=_en> accessed 22 January 2019.

[44] Nineteen countries currently operate a full or partial statelessness-specific protection regime, see European Network on Statelessness, 'Amicus Curiae Submitted by the European Network on Statelessness to the Borgating Court of Appeal in Norway, in Case Number 17-073503ASD-BORG/01' (25 May 2018) <https://www.refworld.org/docid/5b361e374.html> accessed 9 December 2018.

[45] For instance, Katia Bianchini's important 2018 book, *Protecting Stateless Persons: The Implementation of the Convention relating to the Status of Stateless Persons Across EU States* (Brill Nijhoff 2018) undertook a comprehensive examination of ten European Union States that have ratified the *1954 Convention* and found that 'they are all in breach of their international obligations': at 291. She observed, that in most states there were common problems: 'poor decision-making; lengthy proceedings and lack of status for applicants while their cases are pending': at 291.

[46] See e.g., Hungary: Hélène Lambert, 'Comparative Perspectives on Arbitrary Deprivation of Nationality and Refugee Status' (2015) 64 ICLQ 1, n 3.

This book does not seek to undermine the importance of the *1954 Convention* to the de jure stateless, but rather to ensure that those persons who are both refugees and stateless persons receive the full protection to which they are entitled under international law. In this way, the 1951 *Refugee Convention* and the *1954 Convention* should be understood as complementary rather than mutually exclusive.

Part 4: Method and Outline of Book

This book draws on historical and contemporary interpretation of international law based on the *travaux préparatoires* to the 1951 *Refugee Convention* and its antecedents, the *travaux* of the *1954 Convention*, academic writing, UNHCR policy and legal documents, UN Human Rights Council resolutions, UN Human Rights Committee general comments, UN Secretary General reports, and UN General Assembly resolutions (Chapters 2 and 3). It is also based on original comparative case law analysis of existing jurisprudence globally relating to claims to refugee status connected with statelessness (Chapters 4, 5, and 6).

The chapters concerned primarily with interpretation of the *Refugee Convention*'s definition of 'refugee', namely Chapters 4, 5, and 6, are predicated on the need for a principled approach to such interpretation governed by the rules of treaty interpretation set by the *Vienna Convention on the Law of Treaties* ('*VCLT*'). In particular, it is well accepted that Article 31 *VCLT*'s requirement that the text of a treaty is to be interpreted in good faith in accordance with the ordinary meaning to be given to the terms of a treaty, 'in their context and in the light of its object and purpose', means that the terms of the definition should be informed by developments in relevant and cognate areas of international law, especially human rights law. This ensures that the open-ended *Convention* terms are permitted to evolve, in a principled manner, to ensure the continued relevance and efficacy of the 1951 *Refugee Convention*.[47] The *VCLT* also acknowledges the relevance of the drafting history,[48] and hence our analysis of the refugee definition considers, where relevant, what, if any, insight can be gleaned as to key concepts in relation to stateless persons *as refugees,* including 'not having a nationality', 'former habitual residence', 'unable or . . . unwilling to return', as well as the meaning of Article 1E (exclusion for those enjoying de facto nationality) and Article 1D (exclusion of Palestinians).

Chapter 2 sets the context for the book by examining the history and background to the formulation of two distinct regimes for refugees and stateless persons, respectively: the 1951 *Refugee Convention* and the *1954 Convention*. A re-examination of the relationship between the treatment in international law of refugees and stateless

---

[47] For a comprehensive treatment of the rules of treaty interpretation in this context, see Michelle Foster, *International Refugee Law and Socio-Economic Rights: Refuge from Deprivation* (CUP 2007) ch 2; Hathaway and Foster, *The Law of Refugee Status 2* (n 12) ch 1.

[48] *Vienna Convention on the Law of Treaties* (adopted 22 May 1969, entered into force 27 January 1980) 1155 UNTS 331, art 32.

persons must begin with the development of positive international law in this field in the early twentieth century. Accordingly, this chapter briefly reviews the pre-Second World War position, and then examines in depth the UN's seminal 1949 Study on Statelessness, which was the precursor to the formulation of the 1951 *Refugee Convention*. We analyse the extensive debate by the Ad Hoc Committee on Statelessness and Related Problems as to whether to separate issues relating to statelessness from the *Refugee Convention*. The drafting history reveals that despite ultimately developing separate regimes, stateless persons and refugees have always been understood to suffer a similar predicament and hence to present similar protection needs. The point of departure for our analysis, however, is that the drafting history reveals that the sense of similarity between the two 'categories' (refugees and stateless) was connected to their predicament—namely a lack of protection. However, the causes of the two predicaments were thought to be distinct: while the predicament of stateless de jure was thought to be more the result of technical, legal problems, the predicament of de facto stateless (refugees) was understood in more humanitarian terms. Given that the modern human rights regime was in its infancy, it is not surprising that the causes of statelessness were not fully understood in human rights terms. This sets the scene for our later contention that with the benefit of sixty years of evolution in human rights law we can now see that in many instances the causes and effects of statelessness are rooted in human rights violations which may in fact amount to persecution.

Second, while the focus of the book is very much on the 1951 *Refugee Convention*, important insight into the contemporaneous understanding of the connection between stateless persons and refugees is provided in the drafting history of the *1954 Convention*—given its proximity to the 1951 *Refugee Convention*. We therefore also analyse this history in order to assess whether it provides further insight into the scope, as understood at the time, of the 1951 *Refugee Convention* vis-à-vis stateless persons.

Chapter 3 turns to the role of nationality in the protection and enjoyment of human rights. It examines the history of international law's involvement in and regulation of matters concerning nationality, thereby providing a crucial link between Chapter 2 and Chapters 4, 5, and 6. It begins by reviewing the traditional position whereby considerations of nationality (and statelessness), including the practice of re-admission for non-nationals, fell within the reserved domain of states through their own nationality laws. According to this understanding, a lack of nationality could hardly be understood in human rights terms; hence statelessness de jure was an anomaly or aberration due to technical legal issues.[49] However as the chapter reveals, the advent of international human rights law has slowly but consistently

---

[49] Carol A Batchelor, 'Transforming International Legal Principles into National Law: The Right to a Nationality and the Avoidance of Statelessness' (2006) 25 Refugee Survey Quarterly 8; Carol A Batchelor, 'Stateless Persons: Some Gaps in International Protection' (1995) 7 IJRL 232, 235, citing Paul Weis, 'The United Nations Convention on the Reduction of Statelessness, 1961' (1962) 11 ICLQ 1073. See also Gerard D Cohen, *In War's Wake—Europe's Displaced Persons in the Postwar Order* (OUP 2012).

intruded into state discretion such that we can now see that in many instances deprivation of nationality (i.e. denial of nationality and/or withdrawal of nationality) may well violate norms of international law. The chapter therefore examines deprivation of nationality, and the consequences for the persons concerned, in treaty law, UN documents, and the jurisprudence of international and regional courts. For example, the Inter-American Court of Human Rights, the African Commission on Human and Peoples' Rights, the African Committee of Experts on the Rights and Welfare of the Child, and the European Court of Human Rights (ECtHR) have all issued important judgments, decisions, or opinions on nationality-related issues. The chapter also highlights gaps in the existing international jurisprudence (and litigation strategy), in particular the absence of judgments from the ECtHR on whether an arbitrary act of deprivation of nationality or statelessness per se constitutes inhuman and degrading treatment. Further, the chapter analyses the evolution in international law in respect of the right of stateless persons to enjoy fundamental human rights regardless of whether they are also entitled to nationality. Indeed, the contemporary human rights framework is premised on the notions of equality, liberty, and dignity, and on the idea that we hold basic rights because we are human beings.[50] Through the norms of anti-discrimination and equal protection, human rights law now imposes obligations on states to provide a range of civil, political, and socio-economic rights to stateless persons. These developments in international law are essential to a contemporary and principled understanding of the key definitional elements of the refugee definition. For example, given that it is now widely accepted that a denial of human rights can amount to persecution in international refugee law, it is crucial that refugee lawyers and decision-makers take account of the human rights context of the position of stateless persons in assessing their refugee claims.

Chapters 4, 5 and 6 turn to an examination of the key elements of the refugee definition as they pertain to stateless persons. Chapter 4 discusses preliminary issues relating to access to refugee status for stateless persons. It begins by considering the fundamental question of whether stateless persons should be protected per se under the 1951 *Refugee Convention* or whether they must meet the same criteria as those with a nationality, namely, well-founded fear of being persecuted on a *Convention* ground. We note the academic and judicial debate surrounding this issue but conclude that in all cases a well-founded fear of being persecuted is a prerequisite to refugee protection. In this respect, we posit that nationality is not determinative in claims for refugee status applications; rather, the need to establish a well-founded fear is key. Chapter 4 then continues to explain that nationality is nevertheless relevant because establishing an applicant's nationality (or lack of) is key in determining the 'country of nationality' or 'of former habitual residence', i.e. the country of reference.[51]

[50] Article 1 of the Universal Declaration of Human Rights states that 'All human beings are born free and equal in dignity and rights.' See also Rosalyn Higgins, *Problems and Process: International Law and How We Use It* (Clarendon Press 1994) 96.
[51] International Association for Refugee Law Judges European Chapter, 'Qualification for International Protection (Directive 2011/95/EU: A Judicial Analysis' (December 2016) <https://www.easo.europa.eu/sites/default/files/QIP%20-%20JA.pdf.

The chapter contends that 'not having a nationality' in Article 1A(2) of the 1951 *Refugee Convention* is the same as 'not being considered a national by any state under the operation of its law' in Article 1(1) of the *1954 Convention*, that is, it is only concerned with whether a person currently has a de jure nationality—under the law. Thus, we argue that there is no room for the concept of inchoate or discretionary nationality. The chapter provides guidance on establishing lack of nationality in the refugee status determination context, and considers questions such as voluntary renunciation and the imposition of nationality without consent, concluding with an examination of the meaning and interpretation of 'country of former habitual residence'.

In Chapter 5, we analyse the meaning of 'being persecuted' for a *Convention* reason as it applies to stateless persons, by examining its interpretation and application in the case law of the leading common law and civil law jurisdictions. The chapter first addresses deprivation of nationality (namely, denial of nationality and active withdrawal of nationality) and denial of the right to enter one's country. The chapter then considers other forms of harm related to an absence of nationality such as the right to education, right to work, right to health, right to liberty, right to an effective remedy, and right to family and private life. Thus, in this chapter, we consider various specific manifestations of harm faced by stateless persons in the context of the persecution inquiry. The chapter then concludes by examining instances where refugee protection failed but complementary protection may nevertheless be relevant. This may be the case where, for instance, no nexus exists between persecution and the *Convention* reasons, where the level of harm was not sufficient to constitute persecution, or where Article 1F applied to exclude a stateless (refugee) person from protection. With regard to the level of harm, the chapter examines why statelessness per se is not generally considered to be inhuman and degrading treatment by courts and tribunals, but instead in some cases is considered a violation of the right to private life.

In Chapter 6 we consider in what circumstances a stateless person may cease to be entitled to protection or indeed excluded from refugee protection. We begin by examining in what situations Article 1C of the 1951 *Refugee Convention* may apply to a stateless person, before turning to consider the application of Article 1D (in relation to Palestinians) and Article 1E (de facto nationality) to refugee claims by stateless persons. In the final part of the chapter we examine the application of Article 1F to stateless persons. This issue is particularly pertinent given a renewed focus by states on the invocation of citizenship laws, and in particular the withdrawal of citizenship, to respond to the threat of so-called 'home grown' terrorists.

In Chapter 7 we conclude by drawing together the analysis in previous chapters which cumulatively supports our hypothesis that a reconsideration of the relationship between stateless persons and the 1951 *Refugee Convention*, in the context of sixty years of doctrinal development in human rights law, suggests far greater capacity for the protection of stateless persons pursuant to the 1951 *Refugee Convention*. We reflect briefly on the practical issues raised by this conclusion, particularly in those states that have a domestic procedure under both the 1951 *Refugee Convention* and the *1954 Convention*. Finally, we reflect on the need for future research and scholarship on distinct but related issues, suggesting scope for a rich scholarship to develop which will complement and support the international community's efforts to resolve, protect, and ultimately eliminate statelessness.

2

A Tale of Two Conventions

The History of International Law's Protection of Stateless Persons and Refugees

This chapter examines the history and background to the formulation of two distinct regimes for refugees and stateless persons, respectively: the 1951 *Convention relating to the Status of Refugees* ('*Refugee Convention*')[1] and the 1954 *Convention relating to the Status of Stateless Persons* ('*1954 Convention*').[2] This is important because this book analyses the extent to which the central regime for the protection of refugees—the 1951 *Refugee Convention*—is capable of accommodating the claims of stateless persons. Hence, a key starting point for the book is an examination of the contemporaneous understanding of the drafters of the *Refugee Convention* in relation to stateless persons. The history of international refugee law has been analysed by many scholars,[3] yet there is little in-depth analysis focusing particularly on the relationship between refugees and stateless persons.[4] This chapter therefore offers a

---

[1] *Convention relating to the Status of Refugees* (adopted 28 July 1951, entered into force 22 April 1954) 189 UNTS 137 (hereafter *Refugee Convention*).

[2] *Convention relating to the Status of Stateless Persons* (adopted 28 September 1954, entered into force 6 June 1960) 360 UNTS 117, art 1 (hereafter *1954 Convention*).

[3] See Claudena M Skran, 'Historical Development of International Refugee Law' in Andreas Zimmermann (ed), *The 1951 Convention relating to the Status of Refugees and its 1967 Protocol: A Commentary* (OUP 2011) 2 (hereafter Skran, 'Historical Development'); Terje Einarsen, 'Drafting History of the 1951 Convention and the 1967 Protocol' in Andreas Zimmermann (ed), *The 1951 Convention relating to the Status of Refugees and its 1967 Protocol: A Commentary* (OUP 2011) 37 (hereafter Einarsen, 'Drafting History').

[4] In the modern refugee law scholarship that surveys or examines the history of the development of international refugee law, the issue of statelessness is generally not a focus.. For instance, in his classic piece, James Hathaway mentions statelessness but the core of the article is the characterization of phases of the development of refugee law: James C Hathaway, 'The Evolution of Refugee Status in International Law: 1920–1950' (1984) 33 ICLQ 348 (hereafter Hathaway, 'Evolution of Refugee Status'). In the more recent Commentary on the *Refugee Convention*, Einarsen notes that the Ad Hoc Committee 'decided to distinguish between refugees and stateless persons who were not also refugees', but there is no further explanation or analysis: Einarsen, 'Drafting History' (n 3) 54. In the later chapter by Zimmermann and Mahler, the history is again canvassed in some depth yet no mention is made of the decision to exclude de jure stateless persons: see Andreas Zimmermann and Claudia Mahler, 'Article 1 A, Para 2' in Andreas Zimmermann (ed), *The 1951 Convention relating to the Status of Refugees and its 1967 Protocol: A Commentary* (OUP 2011) 280, 308–11 (hereafter Zimmermann and Mahler, 'Article 1 A, Para 2'). Some exceptions in the literature are: Carol A Batchelor, 'Stateless Persons: Some Gaps in International Protection' (1995) 7 IJRL 232, 245–47 (hereafter Batchelor, 'Stateless Persons'); Guy S Goodwin-Gill, 'Convention relating to the Status of Stateless Persons' (United Nations Audiovisual Library of International Law 2010). Importantly, Paul Weis's early work was at the intersection of

---

International Refugee Law and the Protection of Stateless Persons. Michelle Foster and Hélène Lambert.
© Michelle Foster and Hélène Lambert 2019. Published 2019 by Oxford University Press.

fresh perspective on the historical material by focusing specifically on the emergence of the international law protecting stateless persons in order to explore and understand its modern relationship to international refugee law.

Guy Goodwin-Gill has observed that 'refugees and stateless persons once walked hand in hand, and after the First World War, their numbers and condition were almost coterminous'.[5] However, it is now well understood that following the Second World War 'their paths diverged',[6] most notably by the promulgation of distinct legal instruments in the form of the 1951 *Refugee Convention* on the one hand, and the *1954 Convention* on the other. Although identical in many respects, there are key substantive distinctions between the two regimes,[7] a lack of clear supervisory authority, at least historically, in relation to the *1954 Convention*,[8] and vital differences in state ratification and implementation that have together resulted in a significantly inferior system of protection for a person who 'is not considered as a national by any State' as compared to refugees.[9] This is not to deny the very great importance of the *1954 Convention* and the need for continued work on securing its wider ratification and attention; however, it does highlight the limits and the concomitant need for thorough consideration of the possibilities for protection under other instruments, namely, the *Refugee Convention*.

In this chapter, we trace the drafting history and background to the formulation of the two regimes in order to set the context for our later contention that the *Refugee Convention* has a greater capacity to accommodate stateless persons than has traditionally been assumed. International refugee law is most accurately understood as a regime,[10] rather than being constituted by a single treaty,[11] and this is certainly true in the case of stateless refugees, given the multiple treaties pertinent to this category of persons. The regime also incorporates the role of any institutional oversight or supervisory mechanism. This chapter accordingly considers the history of international law's regulation of stateless refugees from the perspective of all the components of the regime. In our view this holistic analysis is necessary in

---

refugees and stateless persons: see e.g., Paul Weis, 'Statelessness as a Legal-Political Problem' in Paul Weis and Rudolf Graupner, *The Problem of Statelessness* (British Section of the World Jewish Congress 1944).

[5] Guy Goodwin-Gill, 'The Rights of Refugees and Stateless Persons' in K P Saksena (ed), *Human Rights Perspective and Challenges (in 1990 and Beyond)* (Lancers Books 1994) 378, 389 (hereafter Goodwin-Gill, 'The Rights of Refugees and Stateless Persons').

[6] ibid.

[7] For e.g., the absence of arts 31 and 33 in the *1954 Convention* (n 2): see discussion in Chapter 1, n 37–42.

[8] See Mark Manly, 'UNHCR's Mandate and Activities to Address Statelessness' in Alice Edwards and Laura van Waas (eds), *Nationality and Statelessness under International Law* (CUP 2014) 88 (hereafter Manly, 'UNHCR's Mandate').

[9] *1954 Convention* (n 2) art 1.

[10] As Skran observes, in international relations theory, the term 'international regime' 'refers to the governing arrangements created by a group of countries to deal with a particular issue in world politics': Claudena M Skran, *Refugees in Inter-War Europe: The Emergence of a Regime* (Clarendon Press 1995) 65 (hereafter Skran, *Refugees in Inter-War Europe*).

[11] Guy Goodwin-Gill characterizes international refugee law as a regime: see Guy S Goodwin-Gill, 'International Refugee Law: Yesterday, Today, but Tomorrow?' (January 2017) (paper on file with authors).

order to understand fully the context and background to the key issues considered in this book.

The chapter begins in Part 1 by examining the inter-war position. Of course it must be acknowledged that statelessness did not begin with the inter-war period.[12] Rather, statelessness occurred prior to the First World War following both individual cases of loss of or failure to acquire nationality,[13] mainly due to a conflict of nationality laws which was particularly acute prior to the *1930 Hague Convention*,[14] as well as (albeit less commonly) more widespread measures, for example the mass expulsion of Danish nationals from Northern Schleswig in 1865.[15] However, we begin with the inter-war period in light of its relevance as background to the major international treaties that today comprise the international legal framework for the prevention and regulation of statelessness. As this book is concerned with the protection of the stateless in international refugee law, our historical analysis is focused not on the history of statelessness as a phenomenon, but on its regulation as a matter of international law. In any event, it is no coincidence that the first 'real appearance' of mass statelessness in Europe at the end of the First World War[16] coincided with the emergence of the first tentative steps towards the international regime of protection for stateless persons and refugees in place today.

In Part 2 we turn to the post-Second World War era, briefly reviewing the institutional context before turning in more depth to the progressive development of international law. We analyse in detail the UN's seminal 1949 Study on Statelessness, which was the precursor to the formulation of the *Refugee Convention*.

In Part 3 we analyse the extensive debate by the Ad Hoc Committee on Statelessness and Related Problems on whether to separate issues relating to statelessness from the *Refugee Convention*. The drafting history reveals that despite ultimately developing separate regimes, stateless persons and refugees have always been understood to suffer a similar predicament and hence to present similar protection needs. However our examination of the drafting history reveals that the sense of similarity between the two 'categories' (refugees and stateless) was confined to their predicament—namely a lack of protection. Statelessness de jure was thought to be primarily the result of technical, legal problems, whereas the causes of de facto statelessness (refugees) was understood in more humanitarian terms. This is not surprising when we consider that, in the words of Goodwin-Gill, 'the individual was only then beginning to be seen as the beneficiary of human rights in international law'.[17]

---

[12] William Conklin, e.g., identifies instances of statelessness in the sixth century BC: William E Conklin, *Statelessness: The Enigma of the International Community* (Hart 2014) 5.

[13] A Peter Mutharika, *The Regulation of Statelessness under International and National Law* (Oceana Publications 1977) 5 (hereafter Mutharika, *Regulation of Statelessness*). He states that up until the First World War 'most cases of statelessness were the result of individual losses of nationality'.

[14] ibid, 3–5.   [15] ibid, 5–6.

[16] ibid, 6. Mutharika's assertion that mass statelessness 'made its real appearance in Europe at the end of the First World War' (at 6) is borne out by the discussion below.

[17] Guy S Goodwin-Gill, 'Convention relating to the Status of Refugees; Protocol relating to the Status of Refugees' (United Nations Audiovisual Library of International Law 2008) 1 (hereafter Goodwin-Gill, 'Convention relating to the Status of Refugees').

In Part 4, the drafting history of the *1954 Convention* is examined, in order to assess whether it provides further insight into the scope, as understood at the time, of the *Refugee Convention* vis-à-vis stateless persons.

Finally, in Part 5 we consider the history of institutional governance in relation to stateless persons and refugees, highlighting both the significant recent developments and acknowledging continuing gaps in supervisory guidance.

Part 1: The Inter-War Period

While the phenomenon of statelessness and refugeehood did not emerge from a vacuum following the First World War,[18] the liberal approach to freedom of movement that had marked pre-First World War practice in Europe, and hence had ameliorated many of the disadvantages of refugeehood and statelessness,[19] 'came to an abrupt halt' following the War.[20] As James Hathaway has observed, this led to the need for international instruments to provide at least limited support for those who might otherwise find themselves adrift and unable to access protection in the era of more tightly constrained immigration control post-War.[21]

It is well accepted and understood that this era witnessed the birth of modern refugee law,[22] yet what is less frequently acknowledged is that it effectively witnessed the advent of an international regime for the protection of stateless persons as well.[23] An analysis of the instruments promulgated under the auspices of the League of Nations during this period reveals that there was no meaningful distinction in legal terms between the two groups, in that their protection needs were understood as equally compelling, of the same nature, and hence appropriately addressed through a single instrument.

There was, of course, some factual distinction between stateless persons and refugees. Following the First World War, some stateless populations were created 'as a consequence of the Treaties of Peace' and the creation of new state boundaries.[24] Yet others became stateless by operation of municipal law, for example, by discriminatory laws regarding loss of nationality for women on marriage.[25] However, this was significantly overshadowed by the millions affected by denationalization measures that led to (or in some cases followed from) a decision to flee their country of origin. Such persons on the move, whether technically stateless or not, were largely

---

[18] For an overview of the ancient roots of the tradition of providing asylum and the views of the 'theoretical founders of modern international law', see Einarsen, 'Drafting History' (n 3) 41–43.

[19] See Mutharika, *Regulation of Statelessness* (n 13) 22–23.

[20] Hathaway, 'Evolution of Refugee Status' (n 4) 348.

[21] See also Skran, 'Historical Development' (n 3) 6.   [22] ibid, 6.

[23] Batchelor is one of the few scholars to have discussed the interconnection of stateless persons and refugees through this period: see Batchelor, 'Stateless Persons' (n 4) 239–41.

[24] John Hope Simpson, *The Refugee Problem: Report of a Survey* (OUP 1939) 231 (hereafter Simpson, *The Refugee Problem*). See also Intergovernmental Committee on Refugees, 'Statelessness and Some of Its Causes: An Outline '(IGCR1946) 6–9 (hereafter IGCR, 'Statelessness and Some of Its Causes'). See also Mutharika, *Regulation of Statelessness* (n 13) 6–7.

[25] Simpson, *The Refugee Problem* (n 24) 231.

understood to be in an identical predicament. Indeed, some contemporary scholars viewed the problem as primarily one of statelessness on the basis that all 'refugees are stateless, whether it be *de jure* . . . or *de facto*'.[26] In summarizing the legal status of refugees throughout this period, Louise Holborn explained that the term refugee 'includes those from whom the state has taken away protection and assistance but without suppressing juridically their nationality, and those whom the state has deprived of their nationality, thus making them stateless', describing the position of the two categories as 'identical' in practice.[27] Accordingly, the instruments formulated during this period in their terms protected both refugees and stateless persons, usually without distinguishing between them.[28]

The first instruments emanating from the League of Nations dealt with Russian and Armenian refugees, respectively. In 1921, the League of Nations appointed Fridtjof Nansen as High Commissioner for Refugees. An immediate challenge for the new High Commissioner was to respond to the predicament of the 'over one million Russian refugees then spread out along the border of the former Russian empire'.[29] A 1921 Russian decree had exacerbated their situation by effectively rendering stateless the Russian émigrés who had fled the Revolution.[30] While denationalization has been described as 'a very old form of punishment for antisocial conduct',[31] tracing its origins to ancient Rome while its modern manifestation can be traced to France during the French revolution,[32] Williams accurately observed that no denationalization 'on any such scale as this ha[d] hitherto been known to history', affecting as it did 'some 2,000,000 people'.[33] Yet international law did not 'forbid a state unilaterally to sever the relationship of nationality so far as the individual is concerned, even if the person affected possesses or acquires no other nationality'.[34] It is true that consequences could follow for a state vis-à-vis its relationship with other states,[35] but the notion that states may have duties to individuals and hence that individuals could be rights-holders in international law had not yet

---

[26] M J L Rubinstein, 'The Refugee Problem' (1936) 15 International Affairs 716, 721.

[27] Louise W Holborn, 'The Legal Status of Political Refugees, 1920–1938' (1938) 32 AJIL 680 (hereafter Holborn, 'Legal Status of Political Refugees').

[28] See Batchelor, 'Stateless Persons' (n 4) 240.

[29] Skran, 'Historical Development' (n 3) 7. See also Holborn, 'Legal Status of Political Refugees' (n 27) 681–82.

[30] Hathaway, 'Evolution of Refugee Status' (n 4) 351. See Williams, which sets out the legislation: John Fischer Williams, 'Denationalization' (1927) 8 BYBIL 45 (hereafter Williams, 'Denationalization'). It deprived the right of Russian citizenship to all persons who remained outside Russia and fell under certain categories, including 'persons who left Russia after the 7th November 1917, without the authorization of the Soviet authorities': Williams, 'Denationalization' at 45.

[31] Mutharika, *Regulation of Statelessness* (n 13) 8–9.   [32] ibid, 8–9.

[33] See Williams, 'Denationalization' (n 30) 46. See also Mutharika, concurring that it is only after the First World War that denationalization 'was used as a means of punishing large masses of people for political and other assorted offences': *Regulation of Statelessness* (n 13) 8–9.

[34] Williams, 'Denationalization' (n 30) 61.

[35] See ibid, 61; see also R Y Jennings, 'Some International Law Aspects of the Refugee Question' (1939) 20 BYBIL 98, 111–13 (hereafter Jennings, 'Some International Law Aspects of the Refugee Question').

emerged.[36] Hence any remedy for the predicament of such stateless persons needed to be formulated via positive law.

One of the key challenges for the newly stateless Russians was their lack of identity papers,[37] which in turn restricted their freedom of movement between countries and hence ability to resettle. In response, the High Commissioner formulated a proposal for the issue of identity certificates in a report to the Council of the League of Nations, which was subsequently adopted at the Conference on Russian Refugees.[38] The agreed *Arrangement with respect to the Issue of Certificates of Identity to Russian Refugees* in 1922,[39] adopted Nansen's sample certificate of identity which did not guarantee the grant of a visa,[40] but 'would provide refugees with a more secure legal status'.[41]

The renewal of persecution against Armenians in Turkey following the end of Allied occupation led to a mass exodus of Armenians to neighbouring countries,[42] and a consequential loss of nationality leading to statelessness.[43] Hence there was a need, again identified by the High Commissioner for Refugees, for approximately 320,000 Armenians to be granted identity certificates.[44] The League of Nations responded in 1924 by adopting a *Plan for the Issue of a Certificate of Identity to Armenian Refugees*, by which thirty-nine states in adhering to the *Plan* agreed to provide Armenian refugees with an emergency certificate in a similar vein to those granted to Russian refugees.[45]

While neither of these pioneering instruments further elaborated on the meaning of 'Russian refugee' or 'Armenian refugee', it was clear that they viewed a refugee as a person without protection regardless of whether this was due to de jure or de facto status. For example, the 'certificate of identity' appended to the 1922 Arrangement

---

[36] As R Y Jennings acknowledged in 1939, '[c]ustomary international law has little, if anything, to say concerning the individual refugee as such', and later, '[p]*rima facie* the treatment accorded by a state to its own subjects, including the conferment or deprivation of nationality, is a matter of purely domestic concern': Jennings, 'Some International Law Aspects of the Refugee Question' (n 35) 110. Although he acknowledges that there is some authority for an alternative view, he ultimately declares this line of argument 'dangerous for the practical lawyer' and 'wishful thinking': at 111. Cf Andrew Clapham, *Brierly's Law of Nations* (7th edn, OUP 2012). Clapham reflects that as early as 1936, Brierly 'foresaw other entities becoming subjects of international law', just as 'the law of any state has for its subjects both individuals and institutions': at (n 1) xv.

[37] Skran, *Refugees in Inter-War Europe* (n 10) 7.

[38] The background to the Arrangement is set out in its preamble: *Arrangement with respect to the Issue of Certificates of Identity to Russian Refugees* (signed 5 July 1922) 355 LNTS 238 (hereafter *1922 Arrangement*).

[39] ibid. Sixteen states adhered to the *1922 Arrangement*: see at 242.

[40] The arrangement explicitly stated that '[t]he grant of the certificate does not in any way imply the right for the refugee to return to the State in which he has obtained it without the special authorisation of the state': ibid, at 238–39, para 3.

[41] Skran, *Refugees in Inter-War Europe* (n 10) 7.

[42] Hathaway, 'Evolution of Refugee Status' (n 4) 352. For an in-depth account of the experience of the Armenians, see C A Macartney, *Refugees: The Work of the League* (League of Nations Union 1931) 46–73 (hereafter Macartney, *The Work of the League*).

[43] Mutharika, *Regulation of Statelessness* (n 13) 11–12.

[44] Hathaway, 'Evolution of Refugee Status' (n 4) 352.

[45] See League of Nations, 'Armenian Refugees: Report by Dr Fridtjof Nansen High Commission for Refugees' (31 May 1924) LN Doc C 237 1924, Annex, 6. See also Macartney, *The Work of the League* (n 42) 28.

referred to a 'person of Russian origin not having acquired another nationality',[46] suggesting that the focus was not on the precise reasons for the individual's predicament but only on whether he or she belonged to the relevant ethnic group, and had not acquired a new source of protection in the form of another nationality which would presumably render international assistance obsolete.

Indeed, a *1926 Arrangement* made this explicit in formulating a definition of both Russian and Armenian refugees that referred respectively to any person of Russian or Armenian origin 'who does not enjoy or who no longer enjoys the protection of the Government'[47] of the USSR (Russian) or Turkish Republic (Armenians formerly subjects of the Ottoman Empire), and has 'not acquired another nationality'.[48] Hence, it was lack of protection—not nationality or fear of persecution—that was determinative.[49]

Similarly, a *1928 Arrangement*, which extended the favourable protection measures granted to Russian and Armenian Refugees to 'other categories of refugees', adopted a definition of 'Assyrian, Assyro-Chaldean and assimilated refugee' and 'Turkish refugee' that relied on lack of national protection as its central tenet.[50]

In each of the *1926* and *1928 Arrangements*, the underlying reason for lack of protection was ostensibly irrelevant. In other words, whether the lack of national protection was due to a lack of legal entitlement 'to claim the protection of any state'[51] (in the case of a stateless person) or that the person did not in fact 'enjoy the protection of the government of his state of origin' (in the case of a refugee),[52] the predicament was the same. The only legally relevant issue was whether the individual was of the requisite national or ethnic origin and had 'acquired another nationality',[53] because in such a case protection could be expected to be forthcoming from the new country of nationality rather than the signatories to these *Arrangements*.[54]

---

[46] See *1922 Arrangement* (n 38), Annex, 'Certificate of Identity'.

[47] *Arrangement relating to the Issue of Identity Certificates to Russian and Armenian Refugees, Supplementing and Amending the Previous Arrangements dated July 5, 1922, and May 31, 1924* (signed 12 May 1926) 89 LNTS 47, para 2 (hereafter *1926 Arrangement*).

[48] ibid. See also *Arrangement relating to the Legal Status of Russian and Armenian Refugees* (signed 30 June 1928, entered into force 5 March 1929) 89 LNTS 53, 55.

[49] See the comprehensive outline of pre-Second World War developments in the Study on Statelessness: Ad Hoc Committee on Refugees and Stateless Persons, 'A Study of Statelessness' (1949) UN Doc E/1112, 34 (hereafter UN, 'Study of Statelessness').

[50] See *Arrangement Concerning the Extension to Other Categories of Certain Measures Taken in Favour of Russian and Armenian Refugees*, 30 June 1928, League of Nations, Treaty Series, 1929; 89 LNTS 63. Resolution (2) referred to the first category as any person of 'Assyrian or Assyro-Chaldaean origin, and also by assimilation any person of Syrian or Kurdish origin, who does not enjoy or who no longer enjoys the protection of the State to which he previously belonged and who has not acquired or does not possess another nationality'. The definition of 'Turkish refugee' was any person 'of Turkish origins, previously a subject of the Ottoman empire, who ... does not enjoy or no longer enjoys the protection of the Turkish Republic and who has not acquired another nationality'.

[51] Jennings, 'Some International Law Aspects of the Refugee Question' (n 35) 99.

[52] ibid, 99.   [53] *1926 Arrangement* (n 47) Resolution (2).

[54] Although it must be acknowledged that the numbers of signatories to these arrangements was quite limited. See Hathaway, who explains that the reference to acquiring another nationality related to the 'theory that such individuals would no longer be legally unprotected': 'Evolution of Refugee Status' (n 4) 358.

This approach to defining the beneficiaries of international protection subsequently delimited the ambit of protection provided by the first comprehensive refugee convention,[55] the *Convention relating to the International Status of Refugees* ('*1933 Convention*').[56] In its Article 1 'definition' it provided that the present *Convention* is 'applicable to Russian, Armenian and assimilated refugees, as defined by the *Arrangements* of May 12th, 1926, and June 30th, 1928', although this was subject to 'such modifications or amplifications as each Contracting Party may introduce into this definition at the moment of signature of accession'.[57]

It soon became clear that the narrow definition adopted in the *1933 Convention*, applying as it did only to defined ethnicities, and pre-existing refugee groups,[58] was not capable of responding to an emerging problem in Germany.[59] Following the assumption of power by the Nationalist Socialist Party in January 1933, legislative and administrative and Party action against 'non-Aryans' steadily intensified.[60] In September 1935, the Reichstag met in an extraordinary session at Nuremberg and approved legislation which, inter alia, withdrew civic citizenship from persons of 'non-German blood'.[61] While these laws did not provide for the automatic en masse denationalization of German Jews,[62] the effect was that German Jews became 'mere nationals with no civic rights',[63] and were ultimately denationalized following a 1941 decree.[64] As was observed at the time of the Nuremberg Laws by the High Commissioner for Refugees (Jewish and Other) Coming from Germany,[65] James G McDonald, the policy of denationalization was 'not a passing phenomenon'.[66] Rather, the Nationalist Socialist Party had proposed as far back as February 1920 that '[n]one but those of German blood, whatever their creed, may be members of the nation. No Jew, therefore, may be a member of the nation.'[67] By December 1935, more than 80,000 refugees had already fled Germany,[68] and it became clear

---

[55] As described by Skran: *Refugees in Inter-War Europe* (n 10) 14. It had only nine ratifications but was comprehensive in the nature of rights accorded.
[56] *Convention relating to the International Status of Refugees* (signed 28 October 1933, entered into force 13 June 1935) 159 LNTS 3663 (hereafter *1933 Convention*).
[57] There were few such modifications, although Egypt reserved 'the right to extend or limit the said definition in any way'. For a thorough examination of the political context, particularly from a British perspective, see Robert J Beck, 'Britain and the 1933 Refugee Convention: National or State Sovereignty?' (1999) 11 IJRL 597 (hereafter Beck, 'Britain and the 1933 Refugee Convention').
[58] As Beck observes, the *1933 Convention* was confined to those 'already under League of Nations protection': Beck, 'Britain and the 1933 Refugee Convention' (n 57) 603.
[59] See Holborn, 'Legal Status of Political Refugees' (n 27) 690–92.
[60] 'Letter of Resignation of James G McDonald, High Commissioner for Refugees (Jewish and Other) Coming from Germany addressed to the Secretary General of the League of Nations' (27 December 1935) LN Doc C.13.M.12.1936.XII, v.
[61] This legislation is known as the Nuremberg Laws and comprises two decrees made on 15 September 1935: the *Reich Citizenship Law* and the *Law for the Protection of German Blood and German Honor*. See Greg Bradsher, 'The Nuremberg Laws: Archives Receives Original Nazi Documents that "Legalized" Persecution of Jews' (2010) 42 *Prologue Magazine* <https://www.archives.gov/publications/prologue/2010/winter/nuremberg.html> accessed 12 November 2018.
[62] IGCR, 'Statelessness and Some of Its Causes' (n 24) 14.   [63] ibid, 14.
[64] ibid, 15.
[65] This post was initially established outside the League of Nations owing to Germany's membership at the time.
[66] Letter of Resignation (n 60) Annex, 2.   [67] ibid, Annex, 2.   [68] ibid, vi.

that the objective of the Nationalist Socialist Party was not only to deprive Germans of Jewish ancestry of citizenship and to 'eliminate them from the political, cultural, social and economic life of the country',[69] but also to 'force them to emigrate'.[70] McDonald's letter of resignation from the post of High Commissioner for Refugees (Jewish and Other) Coming from Germany addressed to the Secretary General of the League of Nations in December 1935, was born of his frustration at the failure of the League to tackle the problems for German Jews 'at its source'.[71] It outlines in detail the extent of the measures taken in just two years by the Nazi government which had created a 'reservoir from which more and ever more refugees will flow into neighbouring lands'.[72]

The instruments developed to respond to the 'critical situation'[73] of refugees coming from Germany—both in the form of a Provisional Arrangement and subsequently a Convention—focused, like previous instruments, on a lack of protection rather than the reasons underlying such a predicament. For example, the 1936 *Provisional Arrangement concerning the Status of Refugees Coming from Germany* applied to 'any person who was settled in [Germany], who does not possess any nationality other than German nationality, and in respect of whom it is established that in law or in fact he or she does not enjoy the protection of the Government of the Reich'.[74] While there is some ambiguity as to the scope of the definition to include the stateless,[75] the 1938 *Convention concerning the Status of Refugees Coming from Germany* was unambiguous in including persons not enjoying the protection of the German government in law or in fact, as well as providing explicitly for 'stateless persons not covered by previous Conventions or Agreements who have left Germany [sic] territory after being established therein and who are proved not to enjoy, in law or in fact, the protection of the Germany [sic] government'.[76] While constituting one of the first explicit references to stateless persons in an international instrument, it is significant that this convention, like similar arrangements and conventions for international protection that predated it, understood stateless persons and refugees as effectively indistinguishable, an unsurprising development given that the use of denationalization as a method of persecution by the Nazis made stark the connection between refugees and stateless persons. The *1938 Convention* provided identical rights for all those who came within the broad definitional ambit, regardless of whether they were technically stateless or not. In other words, there continued to be no distinction made between refugees and stateless persons in terms of understanding their predicament and protection needs.

---

[69] ibid, Annex, 2.   [70] ibid.   [71] ibid, ix.   [72] ibid, Annex, 1.

[73] Holborn, 'Legal Status of Political Refugees' (n 27) 692.

[74] *Provisional Arrangement concerning the Status of Refugees Coming from Germany* (signed 4 July 1936) 171 LNTS 75, art 1.

[75] Holborn explains that the 1936 instrument did not explicitly include stateless persons but the stateless may have been included in the notion of 'not enjoying [state] protection in law': Holborn, 'Legal Status of Political Refugees' (n 27) 695.

[76] *Convention concerning the Status of Refugees Coming from Germany* (signed 10 February 1938) 192 LNTS 59, arts 1 (a) and (b). See also *Additional Protocol to the Provisional Arrangement and to the Convention* (signed at Geneva on 4 July and 10 February 1938) and, respectively, *concerning the Status of Refugees Coming from Germany* (signed 14 September 1939) 198 LNTS 141, art 1(1).

With the refugee challenge continuing to intensify, in particular with a dramatic escalation from 1938 of the practice of forced mass deportation of German and then Austrian Jews by the Nazi regime,[77] the international community created a new refugee agency outside the League of Nations—the Intergovernmental Committee on Refugees (IGCR), which operated from 1938 until 1947.[78] For the first five years of its existence it was charged with responsibility for '1) persons in Germany and Austria who had to emigrate on account of political opinions, religious beliefs or racial origin and 2) persons in this category who had left their country of origin but had not yet settled permanently elsewhere'.[79] While this definition was innovative in adverting to the particular reasons for flight rather than merely the predicament of being without protection,[80] the Committee's work embraced 'stateless persons denationalized by action of their home governments',[81] and was later enlarged to include displaced persons who were unwilling or unable to return to their home countries.[82] The continued interconnection between statelessness and refugeehood was made explicit in the conditions set for grant of an international travel document by states party to the *1946 London Agreement*, which included the requirement that 'the said refugees are stateless or do not in fact enjoy the protection of any Government'.[83]

Part 2: Post Second World War

2.1 Institutional: The International Refugee Organization 1947–52

The International Refugee Organization ('IRO'), formed in 1947,[84] was the first international agency created by the new United Nations Organization.[85] This is not

---

[77] Tommie Sjöberg, *The Powers and the Persecuted: The Refugee Problem and the Intergovernmental Committee on Refugees (IGCR), 1938–1947* (Lund University Press 1991) 30 (hereafter Sjöberg, *The Powers and the Persecuted*).

[78] ibid, 23. We note that the United Nations Relief and Rehabilitation Administration (UNRRA), which operated from 1943 to 1946, also undertook work to repatriate displaced persons, and hence interacted with the IGCR. See generally Sjöberg, *The Powers and the Persecuted* (n 77) 153–55. However, a discussion of UNRRA is beyond the scope of the present book.

[79] 'Intergovernmental Committee on Refugees' (1947) 1 Int'l Org 144, 144 (hereafter 'Intergovernmental Committee on Refugees').

[80] Hathaway, 'Evolution of Refugee Status' (n 4) 371.

[81] 'Intergovernmental Committee on Refugees' (n 79) 144. See also Louise Holborn, *The International Refugee Organization: A Specialized Agency of the United Nations, Its History and Work, 1946 1952* (OUP 1956) 58 (hereafter Holborn, *The International Refugee Organization*); IGCR, 'Statelessness and Some of Its Causes' (n 24) 9–10.

[82] Holborn, *The International Refugee Organization* (n 81) 58. See also 'Intergovernmental Committee on Refugees' (n 79) 144, referring to 'emigration services on behalf of non-repatriable refugees of Germany, Austria and Italy'.

[83] The 1946 *Final Act of the Intergovernmental Conference on the Adoption of a Travel Document for Refugees and Agreement relating to the Issue of a Travel Document to Refugees Who Are the Concern of the Intergovernmental Committee on Refugees* provided (inter alia) for the issue of a travel document to refugees 'provided that the said refugees are stateless or do not in fact enjoy the protection of any Government': (signed 15 October 1946) 150 UNTS 73, art 1.

[84] UNGA Res 62(1) (15 December 1946).

[85] Holborn, *The International Refugee Organization* (n 81) 1.

surprising when we consider that the Second World War had 'caused the most for-
midable displacements of population ever experienced';[86] hence the most pressing
priority for the international community was to develop a feasible solution to this
unprecedented challenge. Unlike the inter-war instruments, the IRO Constitution
attempted a more inclusive definition of the beneficiaries of its protection, albeit
it still referred to particular populations. The definition of refugee in the IRO
Constitution applied to a person who was (a) outside his or her country of nationality or former habitual residence, regardless of whether he or she had retained their
nationality; and (b) belonged to a specified category.[87] The listed categories included
both broadly defined groups such as 'victims of the nazi or fascist regimes or ... of
the quisling or similar regimes',[88] and 'Spanish Republicans and other victims of the
Falangist regime in Spain',[89] as well as more individualized criteria that referred to
'persons who were considered refugees before the outbreak of the second world war,
for reasons of race, religion, nationality or political opinion'.[90] The term 'refugee'
also applied to a person who 'is outside of his country of nationality or former habitual residence, and who, as a result of events subsequent to the outbreak of the
second world war, is unable or unwilling to avail himself of the protection of the
Government of his country of nationality or former nationality'.[91] The IRO was also
concerned with 'displaced persons' which were defined as persons who as a result of
the actions of the Nazi, fascists, or quisling regimes already mentioned have 'been
deported from, or ha[ve] been obliged to leave [their] country of nationality or of
former habitual residence'.[92] Despite a greater degree of specification than previous
instruments,[93] the IRO definitions remained broad and encompassed both de facto
and de jure stateless persons, who received legal assistance and protection from the
IRO during its operation,[94] including benefitting from resettlement.[95]

Notwithstanding the existence of the IRO, the fact remained that there was still no
international comprehensive legal framework in place for the protection of stateless
persons and refugees. Both the IGCR and the IRO were principally concerned with
providing material assistance,[96] and identifying and negotiating political solutions

---

[86] ibid, 15.
[87] *Constitution of the International Refugee Organization* (opened for signature 15 December 1946,
entered into force 20 August 1948) 18 UNTS 3, Annex I, Part 1, Section A, art 1 (hereafter *IRO
Constitution*).
[88] ibid, pt I, s A art 1(a).   [89] ibid, pt I, s A art 1(b).   [90] ibid, pt I, s A art 1(c).
[91] ibid, pt I, s A art 2.   [92] ibid, pt I, s B.
[93] For a discussion of the eligibility policies and procedures of the IRO, see Kim Salomon, *Refugees
in the Cold War: Toward a New International Refugee Regime in the Early Postwar Era* (Lund University
Press 1991) 60–66 (hereafter Salomon, *Refugees in the Cold War*).
[94] Holborn, *The International Refugee Organization* (n 81) 189; see also at 311 describing a refugee as
a 'stateless person, either de facto or de jure'; at 154, describing the situation of refugees in France, and
noting the assistance given to stateless persons. See further at 322–23 for discussion of aid in the form
of travel documents for stateless persons.
[95] See ibid, 390, citing statistics from the United Kingdom stating that 22,062 stateless persons were
settled in the United Kingdom between the end of the war and 31 March 1952.
[96] Holborn describes the IRO as a 'welfare organization on a world-wide scale': ibid, 2. See also
Salomon, *Refugees in the Cold War* (n 93) 53–54.

such as repatriation or resettlement,[97] not with creating a legal framework to impose legal obligations on states vis-à-vis refugees and stateless persons.[98]

Yet a study undertaken by the IGCR in 1946 on statelessness had revealed that at the end of the Second World War the problem of statelessness was widespread. Moreover, the predicament of those displaced without a nationality required international action,[99] since it could not be assumed that their legal status would be resolved by national action alone.[100] In part this was due to much of the post-War remedial legislation, where present,[101] having only prospective effect.[102]

While not designed as a 'definitive treatment of the subject of statelessness',[103] the IGRC study indicated the scope of the problem of statelessness in Europe at the end of the Second World War. The causes included German measures which had denationalized Jews (e.g. in Austria[104] and Germany[105]), German laws implemented in annexed territory which had denationalized Jews (in Czech territory and Slovakia[106]), as well as those 'who have committed acts prejudicial to the interests and prestige of the Reich',[107] (Czech territory and Poland[108]), Hungarian anti-Jewish legislation that resulted in many persons becoming stateless,[109] and Romanian laws that had denationalized Jews and Christians whose fathers were Jews.[110] Additional measures were already being implemented at the end of the War, including to denationalize and expel persons of specific ethnicities, for example, Sudeten Germans and Hungarians from a reconstituted Czechoslovakia.[111] It was thus evident that international action was required to formulate a comprehensive legal, rather than merely institutional, response to the ongoing challenges of both de jure and de facto statelessness.

[97] The work of the Director of the IGCR was to negotiate solutions to the tens of thousands of victims fleeing Nazi persecution: see Holborn, *The International Refugee Organization* (n 81) 11. The functions of the IRO were to 'care for, protect and re-establish refugees in a normal life': at 50. It was empowered to 'conduct negotiations and conclude agreements with governments': at 50. The *IRO Constitution*'s Preamble did refer to the need for 'genuine refugees and displaced persons' to be 'protected in their rights and legitimate interests', but the 'main task to be performed is to encourage and assist in every possible way their early return to their country of origin': *IRO Constitution* (n 87) Preamble. See also Annex I, 'General Principles' which stated that the 'main object of the organization will be to bring about a rapid and positive solution of the problem of bona fide refugees and displaced persons, which shall be just and equitable to all concerned': at Annex I, art 1(a).
[98] See generally Holborn, *The International Refugee Organization* (n 81) 11–23. One exception is the intergovernmental agreement on the issue of travel documents, October 1946, mentioned above at n 83.
[99] IGCR, 'Statelessness and Some of Its Causes' (n 24) 11, observing that international authorities aim 'at a radical and complete solution of statelessness'. These authorities included the League of Nations, the High Commissioner for Refugees and the IGCR: see at 9.
[100] See ibid, 15–16 discussing German laws; at 17–18 discussing Hungary; at 18 regarding Poland.
[101] The IGCR report suggests that some nations did not attempt to implement remedial legislation. See, e.g., ibid, 19–20 (Rumania).
[102] See ibid, 15–16 discussing German laws; 17–18 discussing Hungary. [103] ibid, 1.
[104] ibid, 11, discussing the extension of the Nuremberg laws to Austria in 1938.
[105] ibid, 13–17. [106] ibid, 12–13. [107] ibid, 12, referring to Czech territory.
[108] ibid, 18. [109] ibid, 17. [110] ibid, 19–20. [111] ibid, 12–13.

2.2 Progressive development of international law

In 1948 the Economic and Social Council requested the Secretary General to 'undertake a study of the existing situation in regard to the protection of stateless persons',[112] including 'a study of national legislation and international agreements and conventions relevant to statelessness, and to submit recommendations to the Council as to the desirability of concluding a further convention on this subject'.[113] This request had in turn been inspired by a resolution of the Commission on Human Rights in which it had expressed its wish that 'early consideration be given by the United Nations to the legal status of persons who do not enjoy the protection of any government, in particular pending the acquisition of nationality as regards their legal and social protection and their documentation'.[114]

After the Council's Resolution, and prior to the Study on Statelessness being concluded in 1949, the General Assembly of the United Nations adopted the *Universal Declaration of Human Rights* ('*UDHR*'). The drafting history of the *UDHR* reveals that the issue of statelessness was considered. While it was not discussed in any great depth, it is significant that some delegates were beginning to view statelessness as a human rights issue. For example, in the first Draft Declaration of Human Rights prepared by the Drafting Committee, Article 2 stated that every state is 'by international law, under an obligation to ensure (a) that its laws secure to all persons under its jurisdictions, whether citizens, persons of foreign nationality or *stateless persons*, the enjoyment of these human rights and fundamental freedoms'.[115] The final text referred only to 'everyone' being entitled to 'all the rights and freedoms set forth in this Declaration, without distinction of any kind', listing grounds that include 'national or social origin' and 'other status'. Although statelessness was not explicitly mentioned as a protected ground, 'national or social origin' and 'other status' have been interpreted to include statelessness by international human rights bodies.[116]

Of more direct relevance for present purposes was the debate concerning the formulation of what was ultimately adopted in Article 15 of the *UDHR*. An early

---

[112] UNESC Res 116 D (VI) (1–2 March 1948) UN Doc E/777; UN, 'Study of Statelessness' (n 49) 3.

[113] UN, 'Study of Statelessness' (n 49) 3.

[114] ibid. See also the Report of the Working Party on an International Convention on Human Rights, in which the Commission had stated that it 'is of the opinion that it is desirable that the United Nations should give early consideration to the position of persons who do not enjoy the protection of any State': Commission on Human Rights, 'Report of the Working Party on an International Convention on Human Rights' (11 December 1947) UN Doc E/CN.4/56, 15. In a separate paragraph, the Working Party recommended that the Commission on Human Rights 'should examine at an early opportunity the question of the inclusion of the right of asylum of refugees from persecution in the Bill of Human Rights or in a special Convention for that purpose': at 15.

[115] See Commission on Human Rights, 'Report of the Working Party on an International Convention on Human Rights (11 December 1947) UN Doc E/CN.4/56, 5 (emphasis added).

[116] The *UDHR* was translated into binding form in both the *International Covenant on Civil and Political Rights* ('*ICCPR*') and the *International Covenant on Economic, Social and Cultural Rights* ('*ICESCR*'). See e.g., the Economic and Social Council, 'General Comment No. 20: Non-Discrimination in Economic, Social and Cultural Rights (Art. 2, Para. 2, of the International Covenant on Economic, Social and Cultural Rights)' (2 July 2009) UN Doc E/C.12/GC/20, para 30.

draft of Article 15 provided simply that '[e]veryone has the right to a nationality'.[117] In the Commission on Human Rights' debate on this draft, some delegates raised the question of statelessness and its relevance to Article 15. The French delegation highlighted the importance of prevention in its proposed amendment to Article 15 that stated '[i]t is the duty of the United Nations and the Member States to prevent statelessness'.[118]

Other delegates focused on protection, including the French, Lebanese, and Egyptian representatives, who advocated for 'some mention … in Article 15 of the responsibilities of the United Nations in connection with those persons who did not enjoy the protection of any Government'.[119] While acknowledging that the Economic and Social Council was 'studying the question of drawing up a special convention on statelessness',[120] some delegates argued that the *UDHR* should recognize that the United Nations has 'responsibility for the protection of persons who had been deprived of their nationality'.[121] The representative of the International Refugee Organization felt that the *UDHR* 'should contain a statement recognising the fundamental need of protection of thousands of people who were stateless either in law or in fact'.[122] The French delegate, René Cassin, argued that the Commission 'would be taking a backward step' if it neglected stateless persons, especially since the Economic and Social Council had 'already recognized its duty in that field'.[123] Hence in his view the 'United Nations must accept responsibility and protect those who did not enjoy the protection of any government'.[124] The overarching concern was the stateless, with refugees apparently assumed to constitute a subset of stateless persons.

On the other hand, others, including the representative of the United Kingdom, preferred to defer to the work of the Economic and Social Council, which was carrying out a study on statelessness to 'see what positive steps could be taken to relieve all the problems arising from statelessness'.[125] Such views prevailed so that despite strong sentiment in support, when an amendment was proposed to Article 15 to include: '[a]ll persons who do not enjoy the protection of any Government shall be the concern of the United Nations',[126] it was defeated by nine votes to six.[127] The French delegate's proposal regarding prevention was also defeated by nine votes to three.[128]

Ultimately, the text finally agreed upon was as follows:

(1) Everyone has the right to a nationality.

(2) No one shall be arbitrarily deprived of his nationality nor denied the right to change his nationality.

---

[117] Commission on Human Rights, 'Report of the Drafting Committee to the Commission on Human Rights' (21 May 1948) UN Doc E/CN.4/95, 8.
[118] Commission on Human Rights, 'Summary Record of the Fifty-Ninth Meeting' (10 June 1948) UN Doc E/CN.4/SR.59, 12.
[119] ibid, 11 (Lebanon).   [120] ibid, 6 (American Federation of Labor).   [121] ibid.
[122] ibid, 7 (International Refugee Organization). See also at 8 (Lebanon).
[123] ibid, 8 (France).   [124] ibid, 9 (France).   [125] ibid, 9 (United Kingdom).
[126] ibid, 11 (Egypt).   [127] ibid, 11.   [128] ibid, 12.

The task of addressing statelessness in all its facets was hence left to the Secretary General's 'A Study of Statelessness'. The authors of the Study viewed the Council's resolution as dealing with the means of implementation of Article 15, namely, 'the adoption of interim measures to afford protection to stateless persons' and action 'to ensure that everyone shall have an effective right to a nationality'.[129] The report was accordingly divided into two parts: the status of stateless persons and the longer-term goal of its elimination.

Although the Council Resolution referred only to stateless persons, the Secretary General took the view that 'the fact that refugees are not mentioned does not mean that they must be excluded from the scope of the present study',[130] since it was understood that 'a considerable majority of stateless persons are at present refugees'.[131] Refugees were either de jure or de facto stateless which in practice, according to the Study, resulted in a similar predicament for those concerned.[132] Indeed, while the Study did not exclude stateless persons who were not also refugees, it considered that that group was 'much less numerous' and that 'its position is in certain respects more favourable than that of stateless refugees', as a stateless person who is not a refugee could 'obtain documents establishing his civil status from the authorities of the countries where these documents were originally issued, because these authorities have no reason to refuse them to him'.[133] Of course, this was rather contradicted by the study's later discussion of the key disabilities for stateless persons in countries of reception, which applied in practice equally to refugees and non-refugee stateless persons alike.

The focus of the Study was very much on the displaced, as indicated by the Study's identification of the difficulties arising from statelessness as follows: difficulties for the reception country, the country of origin, and the stateless person herself.[134] Moreover, the Study recognized that the difficulties for stateless persons had increased exponentially since the First World War with the 're-establishment of the passport and visa system, the increased control over foreigners, [and] the regulations governing all aspects of social life',[135] again indicating the focus on displacement rather than stateless persons *in situ*.

The Study considered in depth the means of improving the position of stateless persons, focusing on the need for a status 'which will ensure their enjoyment of the rights necessary to enable them to lead an existence worthy of human beings', and on the need for 'adequate international protection'.[136] After considering the principal elements of an adequate status,[137] the Secretary General then explained why it was essential to embody these elements in convention form.[138] Some measures, such

---

[129] UN, 'Study of Statelessness' (n 49) 4.   [130] ibid, 9.   [131] ibid.   [132] ibid.
[133] ibid, 10.   [134] ibid.   [135] ibid, 11.   [136] ibid, 53.
[137] In the Recommendation to the United Nations Economic and Social Council (ECOSOC), the Secretary-General recommended that a draft convention include provisions concerning the following subjects: 'personal status, rights formerly acquitted, property rights, the exercise of trades and professions, education, relief, social security, the right to appear before the courts as plaintiff or defendant, exemption from reciprocity, taxation, military service, travel documents, documents necessary to perform acts of civil and administrative life, entry, sojourn, expulsion and reconduction': ibid, 73–74.
[138] ibid, 63.

as the provision of a document to take the place of passports, necessitated a formal international agreement.[139]

On a more fundamental level, it was thought that a multilateral convention was essential to encourage simultaneous action by states to adopt such favourable provisions, and that a convention would provide 'a lasting international structure'.[140] The view was taken that the optimal solution was to conclude a general convention which would not entail abrogation of existing agreements and which would 'apply in principle to all stateless persons' (except war criminals and the like).[141] The reference to both de jure and de facto stateless persons clearly included refugees within its scope, since refugees were understood to be in the position of de facto statelessness. As the Secretary General noted in his recommendation to the Economic and Social Council, 'the fact of not having a nationality or not enjoying in practice the protection of a State places stateless persons, de jure or de facto, in a position of inferiority incompatible with the respect of human rights'.[142] It was therefore the lack of national protection abroad, which impacted on stateless persons and refugees equally, that unified the position of the stateless and refugees and indicated the need for a universal single instrument.

While the first part of the Secretary General's study on statelessness concerned the securement of an adequate status for stateless persons abroad, the second part addressed the longer-term problem of the causes of statelessness. Here again the connection between statelessness and refugeehood was made clear in the discussion of racial, religious, or political persecution as underlying causes of statelessness.[143] As the study noted, measures for the deprivation of nationality applied by the Nazi and Fascist regimes against opponents of the regime, most notably Jews, 'constituted a part of the body of the measures of racial, religious or political persecution'.[144] Denationalization as persecution is hence not a modern concept, although the study assumed that this particular cause of statelessness had disappeared with the fall of the Nazi and Fascist regimes.[145] As we explore further in Chapter 5, denationalization as persecution is still very much prevalent, albeit historically underexplored, and indeed misunderstood at times in the refugee jurisprudence.

Much of the analysis in the study of the other causes of statelessness—for example, the impact of nationality laws on married women—lacks a human rights dimension because the *UDHR* was new and the specialized instruments were still decades away. Thus, to a large extent, much of the early understanding of the difference between statelessness de jure and statelessness as persecution was anchored in pre-human-rights thinking. Yet, as Goodwin-Gill has observed, statelessness is 'a broad human rights issue, even as it retains a distinct technical dimension'.[146]

---

[139] ibid.   [140] ibid, 64.   [141] ibid, 67.   [142] ibid, 72.   [143] ibid, 141.
[144] ibid.
[145] ibid, 150. Indeed, in the subsequent discussion of methods of eliminating statelessness, denationalization as a persecution subcategory is ignored altogether. See, e.g., at 161–62.
[146] Goodwin-Gill, 'The Rights of Refugees and Stateless Persons' (n 5) 390. See Michelle Foster and Hélène Lambert, 'Statelessness as a Human Rights Issue: A Concept Whose Time has Come' (2016) 28 IJRL 564. It has been famously said that citizenship is the 'right to have rights': Hannah Arendt, *The Origins of Totalitarianism* (Allen & Unwin 1958) 296. See also Batchelor, 'Stateless Persons' (n 4) 235, and Mark Manly and Laura van Waas, 'The Value of the Human Security Framework in Addressing

This underlines the importance of revisiting the connection between stateless persons and refugees, with the benefit of sixty years of more developed thinking from a human rights perspective.

Part 3: Drafting the *Refugee Convention*

On 8 August 1949, the Economic and Social Council adopted Resolution No 248 (IX) in which it referred to the study of statelessness as the 'study relating to the question of displaced persons, refugees and stateless persons',[147] again underlining the perceived interconnectedness of these categories at the time. The resolution appointed

an *ad hoc* Committee consisting of representatives of thirteen Governments, who shall possess special competence in this field and who, taking into account comments made during the discussions on the subject at the ninth session of the Council, in particular as to the distinction between displaced persons, refugees and stateless persons, shall:
(a) Consider *the desirability of preparing a revised and consolidated convention* relating to the international status of refugees and stateless persons and, if they consider such a course desirable, draft the text of such a convention;
(b) Consider *means of eliminating the problem of statelessness*, including the desirability of requesting the International Law Commission to prepare a study and make recommendations on this subject;
(c) Make *any other suggestions* they deem suitable for the solution of these problems, taking into consideration the recommendations of the Secretary-General referred to above.[148]

In a memorandum from the Secretary General to the Ad Hoc Committee on Statelessness and Related Problems, the Secretary General provided a preliminary draft convention, dealing exclusively with question (a), which had been prepared in consultation with the IRO, 'as a basis for discussion' for the Ad Hoc Committee.[149] The draft contained the following relevant sections in the Preamble:

Considering that Article 6 of the Universal Declaration of Human Rights lays down that: 'Everyone has the right to recognition everywhere as a person before the law' and that Article 15(1) lays down that: 'Everyone has the right to a nationality' ...
Considering that stateless persons other than refugees *are in the same unfavourable position* [as refugees]
Considering that until a refugee has been able either to return to his country of origin or to acquire the nationality of the country in which he has settled, he must be granted juridical status that will enable him to lead a normal and self-respecting life,
Considering that the same should be given to stateless persons other than refugees.[150]

Statelessness' in Alice Edwards and Carla Ferstman (eds), *Human Security and Non-Citizens: Law, Policy and International Affairs* (CUP 2010) 49, 66–68.

[147] UNESC Res 248 (IX) (6 August 1949).   [148] ibid, 60 (emphasis added).

[149] Ad Hoc Committee on Statelessness and Related Problems, 'Status of Refugees and Stateless Persons: Memorandum by the Secretary-General' (3 January 1950) UN Doc E/AC.32/2, [5](g).

[150] ibid, 13 (emphasis added).

Draft Article 2 accordingly provided that the provisions of the present *Convention* 'shall apply to the refuges [sic] referred to in Article 1 and also to persons who are stateless de jure, either because they did not obtain a nationality at birth or because they lest [sic] the nationality which they possessed without acquiring a new nationality'.[151] In the accompanying commentary, the Secretary-General observed that there were 'very compelling reasons why the Ad Hoc Committee should consider the case of stateless persons who are not refugees', but accepted that the Committee might adopt one of three different approaches (including drafting separate conventions for refugees and de jure stateless, respectively), with a 'single convention for stateless refugees and non-refugee stateless persons' the 'simpler' solution.[152]

The Secretary General supplemented this Memorandum several weeks later with a second that dealt exclusively with the Economic and Social Council's request that the Ad Hoc Committee also consider the 'means of eliminating the problem of statelessness'.[153] This second memorandum highlighted both the technical and political nature of the problem of statelessness, observing that even where technical solutions could be identified, 'the real difficulties are political',[154] given that many of the solutions to statelessness involve changes to domestic nationality laws that 'affect[] the State's conception of nationality'.[155]

In its first session, the Ad Hoc Committee on Statelessness and Related Problems in January 1950 quickly turned to the question of scope,[156] and in particular, whether the proposed Convention should include stateless persons who were *not* also refugees.

Part of the problem was clearly related to the Economic and Social Council's inclusion of the challenge of *eliminating* statelessness, in addition to the question of the *status* of stateless persons, in the Committee's terms of reference.[157] It has been observed by other scholars that the key reason for the exclusion of the status of de jure stateless persons from the ambit of the ultimate draft Convention was that the plight of refugees was perceived as more urgent than the stateless.[158] However, a close reading of the drafting history indicates that, at least for some participants, the question of imminence or need was not so much drawn in relation to stateless persons versus refugees but more in the context of *remedy vs cure*. For example, the French representative, Mr Rain, the first to suggest that the questions of refugees and stateless persons were distinct, opined that:

---

[151] ibid, 5.   [152] ibid, 5 6.
[153] UNESC Res 248 (IX) (n 147); Ad Hoc Committee on Statelessness and Related Problems, 'Elimination of Statelessness: Memorandum Prepared by the Secretary-General' (17 January 1950) UN Doc E/AC.32/ 4 (hereafter Ad Hoc Committee, 'Elimination of Statelessness').
[154] Ad Hoc Committee, 'Elimination of Statelessness' (n 153) 8.   [155] ibid, 8.
[156] Indeed, the relevant discussion began on the second day of meetings: Ad Hoc Committee on Statelessness and Related Problems, 'Summary Record of the First Meeting' (23 January 1950) UN Doc E/AC.32/SR.1 (hereafter UN Doc E/AC.32/SR.1).
[157] Although we note that the Secretary General envisaged that the Committee may merely recommend further study in relation to elimination.
[158] See Batchelor, 'Stateless Persons' (n 4) 243; James Hathaway and Michelle Foster, *The Law of Refugee Status* (2nd edn, CUP 2014) 65.

The question of the *elimination* of statelessness was basically different from that of the *status* of refugees. It was rather a continuing concern of the world community than an acute situation which required immediate remedial measures. It could only be resolved after a thorough study of national legislation on stateless persons by specially qualified experts and by the long process of reconciling those various bodies of law.[159]

The Israeli delegate concurred, observing that 'the Committee could not hope to solve the problem of statelessness'.[160] This discussion was initially related to a question, raised by the Israeli delegate, as to whether the Committee could accomplish its work in a single session.[161] The Chairman felt that the Committee could 'attempt to draft a new convention on the status of refugees and stateless persons in five weeks or less',[162] but the French delegate argued that whereas it 'seemed perfectly feasible for the Committee to draft a convention on refugees in general terms within a two-week period',[163] in relation to the question of elimination of statelessness the Committee 'could not presume to do more than lay down the broad lines of an international policy regarding stateless persons'.[164]

Debate in subsequent meetings of the Ad Hoc Committee and indeed in the later Conference of Plenipotentiaries reveals that other delegates also saw the distinction as being between a convention dealing with the protection of refugees on the one hand and one that also dealt with the elimination of statelessness on the other.[165] For example, in the Ad Hoc Committee, the Venezuelan delegate felt that it 'would be preferable for the convention to deal with the question of refugees' and that the 'question of statelessness should temporarily be left in abeyance', as the question of statelessness 'should be studied in connexion with the problem of nationality'.[166] Other delegates observed that addressing statelessness involved a 'much wider question'.[167]

In this regard, the drafters were cognizant of simultaneous activity related to the elimination of statelessness, in particular, the fact that the Secretary General was working on a final report on the nationality of married women.[168] As the Israeli representative noted, the status of married women could not be ignored in a discussion of the elimination of statelessness and it 'might therefore become necessary to defer consideration of that question'.[169] Reference was also made to the fact that the United Nations intended to consider 'the problem of nationality',[170] and hence

[159] UN Doc E/AC.32/SR.1 (n 156) para 8 (emphasis added).   [160] ibid, para 9.
[161] ibid, paras 2–4.   [162] ibid, para 5 (Canada).   [163] ibid, para 8.   [164] ibid.
[165] In the short debate in the Conference of Plenipotentiaries concerning the Protocol relating to the Status of Stateless Persons, the Belgian delegate recalled that, 'it had been the [Ad Hoc] Committee's task to consider means whereby statelessness might be abolished, and to study the desirability of requesting the International Law Commission to prepare a study and make appropriate recommendations': Conference of Plenipotentiaries on the Status of Refugees and Stateless Persons, 'Summary Record of the Thirty-First Meeting' (29 November 1951) UN Doc A/CONF.2/SR.31, 19 (hereafter UN Doc A/CONF.2/SR.31).
[166] Ad Hoc Committee on Statelessness and Related Problems, 'Summary Record of the Third Meeting' (26 January 1950) UN Doc E/AC.32/SR.3, para 18 (hereafter UN Doc E/AC.32/SR.3).
[167] ibid, para 32 (Canada).
[168] Ad Hoc Committee on Statelessness and Related Problems, 'Summary Record of the Second Meeting' (26 January 1950) UN Doc E/AC.32/SR.2, para 2 (hereafter UN Doc E/AC.32/SR.2).
[169] ibid, para 2 (Israel). See also at para 9.
[170] UN Doc E/AC.32/SR.3 (n 166) para 18 (Venezuela).

there was a sense that addressing statelessness was a far more complex challenge that would need to be addressed in conjunction with work on associated topics.

It is not surprising that the delegates took this position. Indeed, had the Secretary General requested the Committee to consider both the *status* of refugees and the ultimate elimination of the *causes* of refugeehood, the Committee would undoubtedly have suggested a similarly dichotomous approach, since the ultimate elimination of a problem is both technically distinct from, and involves an entirely different level of feasibility to, the formulation of an immediate remedy.[171] Indeed, the Secretary General's Memorandum to the Ad Hoc Committee dealing with the elimination of statelessness observed that the 'technical' cause of statelessness 'may be removed by the concerted revision of national legislations', and that 'this would be the purpose of international conventions'.[172] By contrast, 'it is not easy to see how international conventions or recommendations can be used to put an end to the exodus of refugees'.[173] This sense of the enormous scope of the challenge of elimination pervades the drafting history. In presenting the proposed *Protocol Concerning Stateless Persons* to the twenty-sixth meeting of the first session of the Ad Hoc Committee, the Chairman explained that the protocol was 'a temporary solution by which the position of stateless persons could be improved, *pending a settlement of the problem of statelessness as a whole*'.[174]

Another dominant theme to emerge from the meetings was the viewpoint that the nature of the underlying problem was distinct vis-à-vis the two groups. The US representative emphasized that the Committee should not confuse the 'humanitarian problem of refugees and the primarily legal problem of stateless persons which should be dealt with by a body of legal experts'.[175] Although he later conceded that '[a]ll stateless persons, whatever the reason for their status, represented a humanitarian problem',[176] there was nonetheless persistent argument that the plight of refugees was more urgent than that of stateless persons,[177] and hence the formulation of an instrument regulating status was more urgent in relation to refugees as compared to stateless persons. The French representative insisted, for example, that '[a]lmost

---

[171] Indeed, this was observed by the UK delegate: ibid, para 6: '[m]eans of eliminating statelessness should not be confused with measures taken to protect existing stateless persons until such time as their position had been regularized'. Mr Rain (France) agreed with this distinction, but the confusion still prevailed: at para 9. For example, immediately after that discussion, the Venezuelan representative argued that 'it would be preferable for the convention to deal with the question of refugees and that the question of statelessness should temporarily be left in abeyance. That question should be studied in connexion with the problem of nationality': at para 18.

[172] Ad Hoc Committee on Statelessness and Related Problems, 'Summary Record of the Fourth Meeting' (26 January 1950) UN Doc E/AC.32/SR.4 (hereafter UN Doc E/AC.32/SR.4); Ad Hoc Committee, 'Elimination of Statelessness' (n 153) 6–7.

[173] Ad Hoc Committee, 'Elimination of Statelessness' (n 153) 7.

[174] Ad Hoc Committee on Statelessness and Related Problems, 'Summary Record of the Twenty-Sixth Meeting' (23 February 1950) UN Doc E/AC.32/SR.26, para 61 (emphasis added).

[175] UN Doc E/AC.32/SR.2 (n 168) para 19 (United States).

[176] UN Doc E/AC.32/SR.4 (n 172) para 6.

[177] See e.g., ibid, para 11 (Brazil): 'refugees were in much more urgent need of immediate protection'. See also at para 13 (Denmark).

all refugees were in need, a fact which gave the problem its special urgency. The same could not be said of stateless persons who were not also refugees.'[178]

The US representative's argument that 'the problem of refugees differed from that of stateless persons and ought to be considered separately'[179] was largely related to his perspective that the object of the Convention was to identify those in need of protection *by the UN,* and in particular the High Commissioner.[180] In his view there 'were doubtless stateless persons who were in no need of protection by the United Nations'.[181] Rather than focusing on legal protection, some of the argument by the US representative on this question seemed more focused on the implications for the UN, and in particular, 'administrative and financial problems' that would ensue if too broad a definition were adopted.[182]

On the other hand, some delegates observed that once attention was confined to the question of status, there were 'several points of similarity'.[183] The UK representative, for example, argued that in matters such as personal status, property rights, social security, and the right of association, 'the same principle should apply to both stateless persons and refugees'.[184] The difference between refugees and stateless persons was, in his view, 'quantitative rather than qualitative';[185] '[t]heoretically, hardly any distinction could be drawn between the treatment to be applied to refugees and to stateless persons who were not refugees'.[186] The Chinese delegate agreed, observing that *UDHR* Article 15's 'right of everyone to a nationality' lacked legal protection—a defect that could be remedied by 'including [the stateless] within the purview of the proposed convention'.[187]

The UK delegate proposed that Article 1 of the draft *Refugee Convention* provide:

(1) The provisions of this *Convention* shall, except where otherwise provided, apply to unprotected persons.
(2) In this *Convention*, the expression 'unprotected persons' means:
    (a) persons who are not nationals of any State; and
    (b) persons who, being outside the territory of the State of which they are nationals, do not enjoy the protection of the State either because that State refuses them protection or because for good reasons (such as, for example, serious apprehension based on reasonable grounds, of political, racial or religious persecution in the event of their going to that State) they do not desire the protection of that State.[188]

This was consistent with the UN's 1949 Study on Statelessness, which as described above, had identified a lack of protection as the unifying theme and problem to be

---

[178] UN Doc E/AC.32/SR.2 (n 168) para 22 (France).   [179] ibid, para 15.

[180] This is discussed in several places, beginning in the second meeting: ibid, para 18; see also at para 28.

[181] ibid, para 28.

[182] UN Doc E/AC.32/SR.3 (n 166) paras 37–39. See the French delegate's critique of this position at para 51.

[183] UN Doc E/AC.32/SR.2 (n 168) para 20 (United Kingdom).   [184] ibid, para 20.

[185] UN Doc E/AC.32/SR.3 (n 166) para 34.   [186] ibid, para 34.

[187] UN Doc E/AC.32/SR.2 (n 168) para 24. The Belgian representative also agreed: see UN Doc E/AC.32/SR.4 (n 172) para 17.

[188] Ad Hoc Committee on Statelessness and Related Problems, 'United Kingdom: Draft Proposal of Article 1' (17 January 1950) UN Doc E/AC.32/L.2.

addressed in relation to both stateless persons and refugees. The British delegate's focus was firmly on the notion that the convention should concern *status* and thus he did not allow issues such as prevention and elimination to complicate his analysis.[189] As he explained, in his view 'the status of both refugees and stateless persons was that of unprotected persons in need of international protection, and the convention should therefore apply equally to both groups'.[190] The Belgian representative agreed with the UK representative that the Convention should deal with the status of both refugees and stateless persons.[191]

At one point, the Israeli delegate drew a distinction between 'persons who had lost their nationality by their own acts and in full knowledge of the consequences, and those who had lost it owing to circumstances beyond their control'.[192] It was the second group that in his view 'had a far better claim on humanitarian grounds to the protection of the United Nations'.[193] He therefore proposed that the Committee include in Article 2 of the draft Convention 'a statement to the effect that the convention should apply to stateless persons who had lost their nationality for reasons beyond their control'.[194] Although this was not adopted, as we later argue, international law has now evolved to this point by virtue of the contemporary understanding of denationalization amounting, in some circumstances, to persecution.[195]

A final key theme to emerge was a concern about feasibility and political expediency: it was assumed that states were far more likely to agree to a more circumscribed instrument which applied to a more limited and specific group, and that an obvious method of limiting scope was to eliminate stateless de jure from its ambit.[196] In the words of the Chairman, 'a limited convention that was generally acceptable was worth more than one which aimed at impossible ideals and was not ratified by Member States'.[197]

Ultimately the Committee separated the issues by preparing a Draft Convention relating to the Status of Refugees and attaching to that Draft Convention a Protocol Concerning Stateless Persons ('Draft Protocol'). The Draft Protocol made clear that stateless refugees were protected within the ambit of the *Refugee Convention*,[198] and indeed it is important to emphasize that the notion that stateless refugees should

---

[189] Indeed, he argued that '[m]eans of eliminating statelessness should not be confused with measures taken to protect existing stateless persons': UN Doc E/AC.32/SR.3 (n 166) para 6.

[190] UN Doc E/AC.32/SR.4 (n 172) para 8.   [191] ibid, paras 16–17.

[192] ibid, para 3.   [193] ibid.

[194] ibid, para 3. We note that was in fact in response to a concern that excluding stateless persons altogether may have violated the Ad Hoc Committee's terms of reference: see at para 2. The Israeli delegate later sought to summarize the views of the delegates at the end of the fourth meeting, and noted that 'the Israel delegation had explicitly stated that the question of statelessness and stateless persons should be dealt with': at para 28.

[195] See Chapter 5.

[196] See e.g., the views of Mr Guerreiro (Brazil), Mr Perez Perozo (Venezuela), and Mr Kual (Turkey): UN Doc E/AC.32/SR.3 (n 166) paras 14–15 (Brazil), 17 (Venezuela), and 22 (Turkey).

[197] UN Doc E/AC.32/SR.2 (n 168) para 29.

[198] The Preamble began 'Considering that the Convention relating to the status of refugees ... deals only with refugees, whether stateless or not': UN Economic and Social Council, 'The Draft Protocol relating to the Status of Stateless Persons: Memorandum by the Secretary-General' (6 August 1954) UN Doc E/CONF.17/3, 7 (hereafter UN Doc E/CONF.17/3).

be protected by the *Refugee Convention* was never contested by any of the delegates, even those who thought that non-refugee stateless persons were outside the ambit of the *Refugee Convention*.[199] The French delegate, for example, affirmed that 'there was obviously no question of depriving refugees who were stateless of the protection of the convention'.[200] The draft definition prepared by the relevant working group established during the course of the work of the Ad Hoc Committee on Statelessness and Related Problems included from the outset reference to a person being outside the country of 'nationality, former nationality or former habitual residence owing to persecution, or well-founded fear of persecution',[201] clearly envisaging that stateless refugees were within the ambit of the Convention, an issue that was never questioned or critiqued in later discussions of the refugee definition.[202]

The Protocol stated that 'there are many stateless persons not covered by the [draft Refugee] Convention who do not enjoy any national protection and, pending a more special solution of the problem of such persons, it appears desirable to improve the status of these persons'.[203] While the Ad Hoc Committee's Draft Protocol did not attempt to define 'stateless person', but referred simply to 'stateless persons to whom the Convention did not apply',[204] it proposed to apply, *mutatis mutandis*, most of the provisions in the Draft Convention to stateless persons.[205] In doing so it implicitly acknowledged that stateless persons who were not refugees effectively had the same protection needs as refugees—a concession replicated in the *1954 Convention* in its direct transplantation of most of the rights from the *Refugee Convention*.

Following adoption of the Draft Convention and Protocol, the Ad Hoc Committee debated at some length the question of the appropriate response to the Economic and Social Council's request that it '*consider means of eliminating the problem of statelessness*, including the desirability of requesting the International Law Commission to prepare a study and make recommendations on this subject'.[206] It

---

[199] See e.g., UN Doc E/AC.32/SR.2 (n 168) para 27 (United States); UN Doc E/AC.32/SR.4 (n 172) para 11 (Brazil).
[200] UN Doc E/AC.32/SR.3 (n 166) para 10.
[201] See Ad Hoc Committee on Statelessness and Related Problems, 'Provisional Draft of Parts of the Definition: Article of the Preliminary Draft Convention relating to the Status of Refugees, Prepared by the Working Group on this Article' (23 January 1950) UN Doc E/AC.32/L.6, art I (A)(2).
[202] For instance, the *Refugee Convention*, adopted by the First Session, similarly referred to the person being 'outside the country of his nationality, or if he has no nationality, the country of his former habitual residence': art 1 (A)(1)(b): Ad Hoc Committee on Statelessness and Related Problems, 'Draft Convention relating to the Status of Refugees: Decisions of the Working Group Taken on 9 February 1950' (9 February1950) UN Doc E/AC,32/L.32 (hereafter UN Doc E/AC.32/L.32).
[203] ibid, 18.
[204] UN Economic and Social Council, 'Report of the Ad Hoc Committee on Refugees and Stateless Persons' (25 August 1950) UN Docs E/1850, E/AC.32/8 (hereafter 'Report of the Ad Hoc Committee on Refugees and Stateless Persons').
[205] The Protocol adopted by the Ad Hoc Committee at the end of the First Session is contained in UN Doc E/AC.32/L.32 (n 202). It applied the following to stateless persons: arts 2–4, 6–11, 12(1), 13, 14(1), 15–23, 24(1) and (2), 27, 29. This was adopted in the Twenty-Seventh Meeting: see Ad Hoc Committee on Statelessness and Related Problems, 'Summary Record of the Twenty-Seventh Meeting' (23 February 1950) UN Doc E/AC.32/SR.27, para 4 (hereafter UN Doc E/AC.32/SR.27).
[206] See UN Doc E/AC.32/SR.27 (n 205); Ad Hoc Committee on Statelessness and Related Problems, 'Summary Record of the Twenty-Eighth Meeting' (23 February 1950) UN Doc E/AC.32/

ultimately concluded that it was 'not practicable at this stage for it to examine this complex problem in great detail or to draft a convention on the subject'.[207]

The Draft Convention and Protocol were transmitted to governments for comment.[208] Following a consideration of the Ad Hoc Committee's report, and the comments received from governments, the Economic and Social Council requested the Secretary General to reconvene the Ad Hoc Committee 'in order that it may prepare revised drafts of these agreements in the light of comments of Governments and of specialised agencies'.[209] However there was little attention given in either the comments of government, or more relevantly, in the second session of the Ad Hoc Committee—which was renamed the Ad Hoc Committee on Refugees and Stateless Persons and met from 14–25 August 1950—to the issue of de jure stateless persons or to the proposed protocol, although the Committee did formally vote to retain the Draft Protocol relating to the Status of Stateless Persons.[210]

The recommendations of the Ad Hoc Committee on Refugees and Stateless Persons were referred by the General Assembly to the United Nations Conference of Plenipotentiaries on the Status of Refugees and Stateless Persons. The Conference of Plenipotentiaries was asked to 'complete the drafting of and to sign both the Convention relating to the Status of Refugees and *the Protocol relating to the Status of Stateless Persons*'.[211] The Conference of Plenipotentiaries held in Geneva from 2–25 July 1951 considered the two instruments prepared by the Ad Hoc Committee, but spent relatively little time on the Protocol. The debate such as it was focussed primarily on the suitability and applicability of certain rights in the *Refugee Convention* to stateless persons. There was general recognition of the need for legal protection for stateless persons, and indeed the Israeli delegate argued that at least in respect of protection against expulsion, 'the case of the stateless person was much more serious than that of the refugee'.[212]

However, other delegates put forward a number of reasons for deferring the issue of the formulation of a legal status of stateless persons, ranging from concern that the

---

SR.28; Ad Hoc Committee on Statelessness and Related Problems, ' Summary Record of the Twenty-Ninth Meeting' (23 February 1950) UN Doc E/AC.32/SR.29.

[207] UN Economic and Social Council, 'Report of the Ad Hoc Committee on Statelessness and Related Problems' (17 February 1950) UN Docs E/1618, E/AC.32/5, para 18.

[208] UN Economic and Social Council, 'Compilation of the Comments of Governments and Specialized Agencies on the Report of the Ad Hoc Committee on Statelessness and Related Problems' (10 August 1950) UN Doc E/AC.32/L.40 (hereafter UN Doc E/AC.32/L.40).

[209] UN Economic and Social Council, 'Refugees and Stateless Persons: Resolutions Adopted by the Economic and Social Council on 11 August 1950' (12 August 1950) UN Doc E/1818.

[210] For the minimal discussion that took place, and the formal vote to retain the Protocol, in the Forty-Third Meeting of the Second Session of the Ad Hoc Committee: see Ad Hoc Committee on Refugees and Stateless Persons, 'Summary Record of the Forty-Third Meeting' (28 September 1950) UN Doc E/AC.32/SR.43, 3–4. 'Report of the Ad Hoc Committee on Refugees and Stateless Persons' (n 204) Annex II.

[211] UNGA Res 429 (V) (14 December 1950) UN Doc A/RES/429 (emphasis added). Note that the Ad Hoc Committee's Draft Protocol did not attempt to define 'stateless person', but referred simply to 'stateless persons to whom that Convention does not apply', while also acknowledging that there are 'many stateless persons ... who do not enjoy any national protection': 'Report of the Ad Hoc Committee on Refugees and Stateless Persons' (n 204) 33.

[212] UN Doc A/CONF.2/SR.31 (n 165) 19.

definition of 'stateless person' in the Protocol was not constrained by the same geographical and temporal restrictions as the refugee definition,[213] and a question about the suitability of protecting stateless persons who had been deprived of nationality due to criminal activity,[214] to the view that domestic law in some countries already arguably provided adequate,[215] or in the case of Italy,[216] greater protection than that envisaged in the Protocol. There was also a concern that the High Commissioner for Refugees may not have the authority to protect stateless persons.[217] Ultimately, the main theme appeared to be one of lack of time to examine the issue in detail; the Netherlands' proposal to refer the Protocol for further study was adopted by thirteen votes to two, with eight abstentions.[218]

Hence while the Conference adopted and opened for signature the *Refugee Convention*, it decided not to take a decision on the Draft Protocol relating to the Status of Stateless Persons, but rather to refer it 'back to the appropriate organs of the United Nations for further study'.[219] In its Final Act, it noted that the Committee had concluded, in relation to the Protocol, that 'the subject still requires more detailed study'.

What can we conclude from this reconsideration of the drafting history? First, the decision to excise statelessness was not as clear-cut as may sometimes be assumed or implied in the scholarship. In fact, there was very strong support for including de jure statelessness in the ambit of the draft Convention, most notably from the UK representative in the Ad Hoc Committee, but also from China and Belgium. Second, the key arguments against inclusion were largely practical rather than principled, it being accepted by most that stateless persons were in need of status resolution. Indeed, the nature of the protocol and subsequent *1954 Convention* supports this.

However, despite these observations, it remains the case that even for those delegates who perceived the similarity in *predicament* for stateless persons and refugees (namely being outside their country and in need of protection), they understood the *source of the problem* as being distinct. Statelessness was understood primarily as a legal problem, different from the so-called 'humanitarian' problem of refugeehood. Our contention is that with the benefit of sixty years of an evolution in human rights law it is in fact more than the predicament that they have in common. Indeed, often (albeit not always) the reason for the predicament for stateless persons and refugees is the same—discrimination sufficient to amount to persecution, coupled with the non-enjoyment of state protection.

---

[213] ibid, 20 (Sweden), 22 (United Kingdom).   [214] ibid, 19–20 (Belgium).
[215] ibid, 21 (Netherlands), 21 (Sweden).   [216] ibid, 20–21.
[217] ibid, 22–23 (France).   [218] ibid, 24.
[219] Conference of Plenipotentiaries on the Status of Refugees and Stateless Persons, 'Final Act and Convention relating to the Status of Refugees' (2–25 July 1951) UN Doc A/CONF.2/108, s III.

Part 4: The Drafting of the *1954 Convention*

Following the Conference of Plenipotentiaries' decision not to adopt the Protocol in 1951, the General Assembly requested that the Secretary General communicate the provisions of the Draft Protocol relating to the Status of Stateless Persons to all the governments invited to attend the Conference of Plenipotentiaries with a request for comments.[220] Fifteen states provided comments on those provisions of the *Convention* that they would be prepared to apply to the various categories of stateless persons.[221] These governments were largely supportive of the development of a legal instrument for the protection of stateless persons, and of the application of many of the provisions in the *Refugee Convention* to stateless persons,[222] in some cases expressing a willingness to apply additional provisions to those set out in the protocol.[223] However some different views were expressed about the relationship between refugees and stateless persons. On one hand, the Belgian government stated that it considered that 'the problem of statelessness is essentially different from that of refugees' on the basis that while 'refugees are the victims of political regimes which violate freedom and human dignity, the fact that non-refugee stateless persons have no nationality is in most cases the result either of their own express wishes or of their negligence'.[224] On the other hand, the Swiss government viewed favourably the notion that the application of the *Refugee Convention* to stateless persons would 'represent a certain extension of the concept of refugee', stating that there

---

[220] UNGA Res 629 (VII) (6 November 1952) UN Doc A/RES/629.

[221] UN Doc E/CONF.17/3 (n 198) 7.

[222] See e.g., UN Economic and Social Council, 'Comments Received from Governments on the Subject of the Draft Protocol relating to the Status of Stateless Persons: Netherlands' (26 January 1954) UN Doc E/2373/Add.13 (hereafter 'UN Doc E/2373/Add.13'); UN Economic and Social Council, 'Comments Received from Governments on the Subject of the Draft Protocol relating to the Status of Stateless Persons: United Kingdom of Great Britain and Northern Ireland' (3 August 1953) UN Doc E/2373/Add.11; UN Economic and Social Council, 'Comments Received from Governments on the Subject of the Draft Protocol relating to the Status of Stateless Persons: Pakistan' (3 August 1953) UN Doc E/2373/Add.10; UN Economic and Social Council, 'Comments Received from Governments on the Subject of the Draft Protocol relating to the Status of Stateless Persons: France' (27 April 1953) UN Doc E/2373/Add.4; UN Economic and Social Council, 'Comments Received from Governments on the Subject of the Draft Protocol relating to the Status of Stateless Persons: Finland' (15 April 1953) UN Doc E/2373/Add.2. But note that the government of the Union of South Africa did not agree: see UN Economic and Social Council, 'Comments Received from Governments on the Subject of the Draft Protocol relating to the Status of Stateless Persons: South Africa' (14 July 1953) UN Doc E/2373/Add.9. The United States stated it did not intend to ratify because stateless persons were already protected: UN Economic and Social Council, 'Comments Received from Governments on the Subject of the Draft Protocol relating to the Status of Stateless Persons: United States' (5 May 1953) UN Doc E/2373.Add.5.

[223] See e.g., the response of Norway: UN Economic and Social Council, 'Comments Received from Governments on the Subject of the Draft Protocol relating to the Status of Stateless Persons: Norway' UN Doc E/2372/Add.14, 2.

[224] UN Economic and Social Council, 'Comments Received from Governments on the Subject of the Draft Protocol relating to the Status of Stateless Persons: Belgium' (27 February 1953) UN Doc E/2373.

was no reason 'why this concept should not also be applied to stateless persons',[225] and the Netherlands was in favour of treating stateless persons 'in the most liberal manner'.[226]

Following a consideration of these largely supportive submissions, the Economic and Social Council adopted a resolution that decided that 'a second conference of plenipotentiaries should be convened' with the task of revising the draft protocol relating to the Status of Stateless persons, and adopting the revised Protocol and opening it for signature by all Members States.[227] The Conference of Plenipotentiaries on the Status of Stateless Persons was convened and met in New York in September 1954, during which it decided to finalize and open the revised protocol as an independent Convention.

For present purposes the most relevant discussion during the drafting debates centred on certain aspects of the relationship between the new instrument and the existing *Refugee Convention*. First, the conference considered immediately the question whether the new instrument should take the form of a Protocol to the *Refugee Convention* or an independent treaty. Many of the delegates believed the definition of stateless person and refugee to be sufficiently different that they should not be 'lump[ed] together',[228] and hence an independent convention was preferable. Yet others relied on the notion that previous studies had 'taken the view that the problem of refugees and that of stateless persons constituted a single problem and that it was merely a matter of protecting certain persons who found themselves in a difficult situation as a result of certain events'.[229] While ultimately the decision was taken to formulate an independent convention,[230] the debate concerning its substantive content used the *Refugee Convention* as a template,[231] and there was little if any debate in relation to the adoption of many of the rights contained in the *Refugee Convention* to stateless persons,[232] revealing that most delegates understood the similar protection needs of stateless persons and refugees.

[225] UN Economic and Social Council, 'Comments Received from Governments on the Subject of the Draft Protocol relating to the Status of Stateless Persons: Switzerland' (10 August 1953) UN Doc E/2372/Add.12, 2.

[226] UN Doc E/2373/Add.13 (n 222).   [227] UNESC Res 526 A (XVII) (26 April 1954).

[228] Conference of Plenipotentiaries on the Status of Refugees and Stateless Persons, 'Summary Record of the Second Meeting' (29 September 1954) UN Doc E/CONF.17/SR.2, 7 (Belgium).

[229] Conference of Plenipotentiaries on the Status of Refugees and Stateless Persons, 'Summary Record of the Third Meeting' (29 September 1954) UN Doc E/CONF.17/SR.3, 14 (Australia) (hereafter 'UN Doc E/CONF.17/SR.3').

[230] It was decided by 12 to 0 with three abstentions that the international instrument should be an independent document: see Conference of Plenipotentiaries on the Status of Refugees and Stateless Persons, 'Summary Record of the Twelfth Meeting' (12 October 1954) UN Doc E/CONF.17/SR.129.

[231] The Conference of Plenipotentiaries on the Status of Stateless Persons took as the basis of its work the Secretary General's Memorandum on the Draft Protocol relating to the Status of Stateless Persons, which set out both the provisions of the Draft Protocol relating to the Status of Stateless Persons (as prepared by the Ad Hoc Committee in 1950) and the articles of the 1951 *Refugee Convention*, with annotations to guide the Conference's work in drafting a new instrument on the status of stateless persons: UN Doc E/CONF.17/3 (n 198) paras 19–21.

[232] See e.g., the debate concerning the adoption of arts 9–15, where the only substantive discussion concerned art 15: Conference of Plenipotentiaries on the Status of Refugees and Stateless Persons, 'Summary Record of the Sixth Meeting' (29 November 1954) UN Doc E/CONF.17/SR.6 (hereafter UN Doc E/CONF.17/SR.6).

In terms of the text of the new *Convention* the first item to be debated was the definition.[233] What was clear was that there was an understanding that stateless persons could be 'covered by the provisions of the Convention relating to the Status of Refugees'.[234] Some delegates concluded hence that such stateless refugees 'should not also be protected by the protocol'.[235] However, this suggestion, as well as the Australian suggestion that a temporal restriction identical to the *Refugee Convention* be imposed,[236] was strongly resisted by others. The President, speaking as representative of Denmark, explained in relation to the temporal issue that '[s]tatelessness was not a problem relating to a specific group of persons at a given moment, but a problem that had always existed'.[237] Responding to the issue of whether access to protection for stateless persons needed to be exclusively available under this new treaty to the exclusion of the *Refugee Convention*, the Danish representative made the logical point that it was

unlikely that the protocol would grant stateless persons privileges or rights more extensive than those which the *Convention relating to the Status of Refugees* granted to refugees. It was therefore of little consequence whether the protocol applied to persons who were already protected by the Convention relating to the Status of Refugees.[238]

He later explained further that in domestic law,

[i]t was generally accepted that when a person might invoke two provisions, one of which was more favourable to him than the other, the more favourable should be applied, and that the person concerned was not obliged to state once and for all which of the two provisions he preferred to come under.[239]

There was, he explained, 'no reason why the same principle should not hold good at the international level'.[240] This approach was ultimately accepted in that any limiting amendments were rejected. Indeed, the Preamble of the *1954 Convention* states that 'those stateless persons who are also refugees are covered by the *Convention relating to the Status of Refugees*'.[241] As explained above, the more generous provisions of the *Refugee Convention* vis-à-vis the *1954 Convention*, and the greater accessibility and enforcement of the *Refugee Convention* in domestic law means that stateless persons who qualify for refugee status should benefit from refugee protection.

Importantly, in addition to a recognition that stateless persons may qualify as refugees, some delegates understood that the predicament of statelessness *itself* may constitute a basis for refugee status in certain circumstances. It was observed by the Yugoslavian representative, for example, that '[i]f persons become stateless for political reasons, they should be treated as refugees'.[242]

---

[233] Delegates could not agree on a definition in the first meeting, hence the matter was referred to a drafting sub-committee and reappeared in the Tenth Meeting: Conference of Plenipotentiaries on the Status of Refugees and Stateless Persons, 'Summary Record of the Tenth Meeting' (6 October 1954) UN Doc E/CONF.17/SR.10 (hereafter UN Doc E/CONF.17/SR.10).

[234] UN Doc E/CONF.17/SR.3 (n 229), 3 (United Kingdom).

[235] ibid. See also at 4 (Australia).   [236] ibid, 4–5.   [237] ibid, 9.   [238] ibid, 9.

[239] Conference of Plenipotentiaries on the Status of Refugees and Stateless Persons, 'Summary Record of the Third Meeting' (12 October 1954) UN Doc E/CONF.17/SR.13, 11.

[240] ibid.   [241] *1954 Convention* (n 2) Preamble, para 3.

[242] UN Doc E/CONF.17/SR.10 (n 233) 11.

Undoubtedly the bulk of the discussion relating to the definition of 'stateless person' was devoted to the question whether to confine the definition to de jure stateless persons—as was ultimately agreed—or to expand the definition to encompass de facto stateless persons. There was no consideration of the relationship between the adopted definition, namely, 'a person who is not considered as a national by any state under the operation of its law' and the similar but not necessarily identical requirement for qualification of refugee status for stateless persons in the refugee definition, namely, 'not having a nationality'. This is an issue that is explored further in Chapter 4.

In terms of the rights regime, it was observed in Chapter 1 that while the *1954 Convention* and *Refugee Convention* are in many respects identical in the scope and content of protection, there are nonetheless some significant differences. The Draft Protocol relating to the Status of Stateless Persons prepared by the Ad Hoc Committee had omitted reference to a number of the articles of the *Refugee Convention*.[243] However, most of these were re-inserted into the *1954 Convention* by the Conference of Plenipotentiaries. As mentioned, most of the articles that were ultimately included in the *1954 Convention* were transposed directly from the *Refugee Convention* and generated very little, if any, debate by the Conference of Plenipotentiaries on the Status of Stateless Persons. It is unsurprising that it is some of the articles that were modified or even omitted altogether in the *1954 Convention* that produced more comprehensive debate, although this is not uniformly the case.

Two articles—dealing with rights of association and to wage-earning employment, respectively—appear in both conventions but are guaranteed to a less advantageous standard in the case of stateless persons (*1954 Convention*) as compared with refugees (*Refugee Convention*). While the *Refugee Convention* guarantees in relation to those rights, 'the most favourable treatment accorded to nationals of a foreign country in the same circumstances',[244] the *1954 Convention* guarantees in relation to the same rights treatment 'as favourable as possible, and in any event, not less favourable than that accorded to aliens generally in the same circumstances'.[245] This modification was made by the Conference in order to avoid a large number of reservations that may have ensued should the higher standard have been adopted in relation to these articles.[246]

More significantly, two key articles of the *Refugee Convention* were omitted altogether from the *1954 Convention*, namely the protection against penalization found in Article 31 of the *Refugee Convention* and the obligation of *non-refoulement*

---

[243] See at n 205, where those rights that were included are mentioned. There was little discussion as to why these rights were selected and others were not.

[244] *Refugee Convention* (n 1) arts 15, 17.   [245] *1954 Convention* (n 2) arts 15, 17.

[246] The debate on art 15 began at the Sixth Meeting, and continued into the Seventh: UN Doc E/CONF.17/SR.6 (n 232); Conference of Plenipotentiaries on the Status of Refugees and Stateless Persons, 'Summary Record of the Seventh Meeting' (29 September 1954) UN Doc E/CONF.17/SR.7. When the Conference discussed art 17, it was observed that it should adopt the same language as Article 15: UN Doc E/CONF.17/SR.7. These two articles were then revisited at the Ninth Meeting, where the Conference adopted the modification to the level of rights guarantee: see Conference of Plenipotentiaries on the Status of Refugees and Stateless Persons, 'Summary Record of the Ninth Meeting' (30 September 1954) UN Doc E/CONF.17/SR.9, 8 art 15, 10–12 art 17 (hereafter 'UN Doc E/CONF.17/SR.9').

found in Article 33 of the *Refugee Convention*. In relation to non-penalization, the debate was cursory and swift, with delegates apparently accepting the French observation that Article 31 was applicable only to refugees because a 'stateless person would not be under the pressures described in the article',[247] presumably referring to the need to enter territory without prior authorization having come directly from a place where 'their life or freedom was threatened'.[248]

In relation to Article 33, protection against *refoulement*, there was virtually no discussion directed precisely to this issue as it had not been included in the draft Protocol and there was no attempt to introduce a comparable provision into the *1954 Convention*.[249] During the debate relating to Article 32 (protection against expulsion), the Yugoslavian delegate noted that Article 33 had not been included in the Draft Protocol and 'wondered whether some of the essential ideas in article 33 might not somehow be combined with those in article 32',[250] since it would be 'intolerable that a stateless person should be returned to the frontiers of territories where his life or freedom would be threatened'.[251] The President, speaking as representative of Denmark, replied that in Denmark 'any stateless person in such a position would be treated as a potential refugee and given the status of a refugié sur place'.[252] In a later session, he reiterated this point, observing that while Article 33 'had been necessary in respect of refugees, the principle applied to all aliens and no special reference to stateless persons was required'.[253] There was no formal proposal put forward to include reference to Article 33, nor any further debate.[254] In the Final Act of the United Nations Conference on the Status of Stateless Persons it was stated

[b]eing of the opinion that Article 33 of the Convention Relating to the Status of Refugees of 1951 is an expression of the generally accepted principle that no State should expel or return a person in any manner whatsoever to the frontiers of territories where his life or freedom would be threatened on account of his race, religion, nationality, membership of a particular social group or political opinion,

Has not found it necessary to include in the Convention Relating to the Status of Stateless Persons an article equivalent to Article 33 of the Convention Relating to the Status of Refugees of 1951.[255]

This suggests that the drafters considered the principle to be at least a general principle, if not already part of customary international law, and hence unnecessary to

---

[247] Conference of Plenipotentiaries on the Status of Refugees and Stateless Persons, 'Summary Record of the Eighth Meeting' (29 September 1954) UN Doc E/CONF.17/SR.8, 8 (hereafter UN Doc E/CONF.17/SR.8).

[248] *Refugee Convention* (n 1) art 31.

[249] During the Tenth Meeting, the President noted that 'no formal proposal [had been made] for the inclusion of or reference to [the article] in the future instrument': UN Doc E/CONF.17/SR.10 (n 233) 8.

[250] UN Doc E/CONF.17/SR.8 (n 247) 10 (Yugoslavia) (Mr Bozovic).   [251] ibid.

[252] ibid, 10.   [253] UN Doc E/CONF.17/SR.10 (n 233) 8.   [254] See ibid, 8.

[255] *Final Act of the United Nations Conference on the Status of Stateless Persons* (signed 28 September 1954, entered into force 6 June 1960) 360 UNTS 117.

include in the *1954 Convention*. In any event, there was no suggestion that stateless persons would not be entitled to its protection.

The final provision to consider is the only Article in both the 1951 *Refugee Convention* and the *1954 Convention* that is directly pertinent to the prevention or elimination of statelessness, namely, Article 34 of the *Refugee Convention* (and its equivalent in identical terms in Article 32, the *1954 Convention*) which provides: 'The Contracting States shall as far as possible facilitate the assimilation and naturalization of refugees. They shall in particular make every effort to expedite naturalization proceedings and to reduce as far as possible the charges and costs of such proceedings.'[256]

In the Draft Convention provided in the Memorandum by the Secretary General to the Ad Hoc Committee in January 1950, we see the antecedents of Article 34 of the *Refugee Convention* (and the *1954 Convention*), namely, that the 'High Contracting Parties shall facilitate the assimilation and naturalization of refugees (and stateless persons) to the fullest possible extent'.[257] The Commentary accompanying this draft provision observed that 'decisions of the State granting naturalization is, in this respect, absolute. It cannot be compelled to grant its nationality, even after a long waiting period, to a refugee settled in its territory since naturalization confers on the naturalized citizen a series of privileges, including political rights.'[258] This was entirely consistent with the prevailing dominant view of state sovereignty, as is further explored in Chapter 3. As Goodwin-Gill has observed, the *Charter of the United Nations*, concluded in June 1945 and hence just five years prior to the Memorandum, had identified 'the principles of sovereignty, independence, and non-interference within the reserved domain of domestic jurisdiction as fundamental to the success of the Organization'.[259]

The debate by the Ad Hoc Committee on Refugees and Stateless Persons on Draft Article 28/29 did not in any way question this assumption about sovereignty,[260] nor did the discussion within the Conference of Plenipotentiaries on the Status of Refugees and Stateless Persons.[261] None of the delegates suggested that the Article might be recast such that a state could be *required* to naturalize refugees within its

---

[256] *Refugee Convention* (n 1) art 34; *1954 Convention* (n 2) art 32.   [257] Draft art 28.

[258] See the commentary on art 28 in Ad Hoc Committee on Statelessness and Related Problems, 'Status of Refugees and Stateless Persons: Memorandum by the Secretary General' (3 January 1950) UN Doc E/AC.32/2, 50. Although see following section headed 'Observation on Article 28' where the Secretary General sets out arguments for and against a more robust provision whereby the state could offer citizenship after a 'fairly long lapse (eg fifteen years)' and if not taken up the contracting party 'would be entitled to consider itself as released from the obligations of the Convention': at 50.

[259] Goodwin-Gill, 'Convention relating to the Status of Refugees' (n 17) 1, citing art 2 of the *UN Charter*.

[260] We note that the Article moved position throughout the debates. For instance, at the end of the First Session it appeared in art 29: UN Doc E/AC.32/L.32 (n 202). The Draft Convention was adopted at the twenty-fifth meeting of the Committee: Ad Hoc Committee on Statelessness and Related Problems, 'Summary Record of the Twenty-Fifth Meeting' (17 February 1950) UN Doc E/AC.32/SR.25, para 53.

[261] The entire debate is contained in two paragraphs: Conference of Plenipotentiaries on the Status of Refugees and Stateless Persons, 'Summary Record of the Sixteenth Meeting' (23 November 1951) UN Doc A/CONF.2/SR.16, 18.

territory. Rather the debate in the Ad Hoc Committee turned on the degree of guidance to be included in the Article in terms of how and to what extent facilitation of naturalization should be conducted.[262] Indeed, in a response to the observation by Mr Weis of the IRO that the Ad Hoc Committee might consider the Secretary General's suggestion that a refugee may accrue a right to apply for naturalization after a 'fairly long period of residence',[263] the Chairman responded that he felt that 'that question was part of the problem of the elimination of statelessness, which did not fall within the scope of the convention'.[264] The identical provision was included in the *1954 Convention* with no debate or discussion.[265]

In Chapter 3 we revisit the core ideas underlying the framing of these provisions, and in particular, the degree to which the notion that states retain absolute sovereignty in relation to matters of nationality has been modified by subsequent developments in international law.

Part 5: Institutional Considerations—the Role of the UNHCR

A central issue in examining any regime in international law is the governance structure; hence a key question here is the institutional supervisory mechanisms envisaged for stateless refugees and refugees de jure from the inception of the modern international protection regime. It has been noted that several Articles included in the 1951 *Refugee Convention* were omitted from the Draft Protocol relating to the Status of Stateless Persons, and while many were re-inserted by the Conference of Plenipotentiaries on the Status of Stateless Persons, some key provisions were not. The provisions concerning the rights of stateless persons were considered above in Part 4, but here we briefly reflect on the role of the UNHCR in supervising stateless persons since 1950 and in particular on the final significant omission from the *1954 Convention*, namely, the lack of an equivalent provision to Article 35 of the *Refugee Convention*, which provides that: 'The Contracting States undertake to co-operate with the Office of the United Nations High Commissioner for Refugees ... in the exercise if its functions, and shall in particular facilitate its duty of supervising the application of the provisions of this Convention.'[266]

Article 35 was not included in the draft Protocol and a close reading of the Conference of Plenipotentiaries' debates reveals that there was no discussion relating to the possible inclusion of such an article whatsoever. Carol Batchelor suggests this may have been an oversight; specifically, it may have been a casualty of the transition from the original intention that the *1954 Convention* operate as a Protocol to the *Refugee Convention* to the decision during the Conference debate that it instead

---

[262] See Ad Hoc Committee on Statelessness and Related Problems, 'Summary Record of the Twenty-Second Meeting (14 February 1950) UN Doc E/AC.32/SR.22, paras 1–11.

[263] ibid, para 12.

[264] ibid, para 14. We note also that in the response by governments to the work of the Ad Hoc Committee, some governments questioned whether even the 'facilitation' language was too strong: see UN Doc E/AC.32/L.40 (n 208) 58.

[265] See UN Doc E/CONF.17/SR.8 (n 247) 13.   [266] *Refugee Convention* (n 1) art 35(1).

operate as an independent Convention.[267] On the other hand, the fact that the competence of the High Commissioner pursuant to the 1950 *Statute of the Office of the United Nations High Commissioner for Refugees* did not extend to stateless persons de jure may have been assumed to render UNHCR supervision irrelevant.[268]

Ultimately all that can be concluded is that the Conference did not at any stage discuss the possibility of inserting an obligation on state parties to co-operate with the UNHCR. This is not to say that the drafters considered the *Convention* outside the governance of international law; on the contrary the *Refugee Convention*'s dispute resolution clause was transposed without amendment into the *1954 Convention*, where it appears in Article 34 and provides, as does Article 38 of the *Refugee Convention*, for any dispute between the parties relating to interpretation or application to be referred to the International Court of Justice—a mechanism that has never been invoked in the context of either of these Conventions. In addition, the *Refugee Convention*'s Article 36—which requires contracting states to communicate to the Secretary General of the United Nations the laws and regulations which they may adopt to ensure the application of the *Convention*—was replicated in Article 33 of the *1954 Convention*.[269]

Notwithstanding this, however, it remained the case that for the first four decades of the *1954 Convention*'s operation it was without a clear supervisory mechanism, leading to calls from scholars for the 'effective protection of the rights of stateless persons [to be] entrusted to an appropriate international agency'.[270] The UNHCR was assigned a supervisory role in relation to the 1961 *Convention on the Reduction of Statelessness* ('*1961 Convention*') when it came into force in the mid 1970s,[271] and it has been argued that it had 'attempted to engage states on statelessness issues during the Cold War',[272] but it was not until 1995 that the UN General Assembly conferred upon the UNHCR the protection of stateless persons as part of its statutory function.[273] It has been acknowledged that this new authority to act did not 'immediately lead to global action on statelessness by UNHCR',[274] however, in the past decade the UNHCR's work in this area has grown exponentially, as have the number of ratifications of both the *1954* and *1961 Conventions*.

The UNHCR's contribution both to substantive issues of interpretation of the *1954 Convention*, and in motivating state action to ratify and implement core obligations, has been significant and important.[275] Moreover, this work is increasingly recognized by states, including the Executive Committee of the UNHCR.[276]

---

[267] Batchelor, 'Stateless Persons' (n 4) 245–47.

[268] This is the position taken by Hugh Massey, 'UNHCR and De Facto Statelessness' (UNHCR Legal and Protection Policy Research Series, April 2010) 16.

[269] There was some debate in relation to this article, but no one mentioned a potential role for the UNHCR in this context: see UN Doc E/CONF.17/SR.9 (n 246) 2–4.

[270] Goodwin-Gill, 'The Rights of Refugees and Stateless Persons' (n 5) 394.

[271] Matthew Seet, 'The Origins of the UNHCR's Global Mandate on Statelessness' (2016) 28 IJRL 7, 10.

[272] ibid, 8.   [273] See ibid, 11.   [274] Manly, 'UNHCR's Mandate' (n 8) 88.

[275] See Chapter 1 at n 23–27.

[276] We note that the Executive Committee has requested UNHCR to 'report regularly on its activities related to the Office's global statelessness mandate, as set out in relevant United Nations General

For example, in a 2016 Executive Committee conclusion, the Committee noted the 'progress made towards addressing statelessness in recent years, including through accession to stateless conventions and measures at regional and national levels', citing the UNHCR's Global Campaign to End Statelessness in particular, and encouraged 'continued efforts in this regard'.[277] In a second 2016 Executive Committee Conclusion on Youth, the members highlighted 'the urgent need to take further measures to prevent childhood statelessness and engage with and find solutions for stateless youth, including as reflected in UNHCR's Global Campaign to End Statelessness', and encouraged 'the continuation of efforts to promote adherence to the Conventions on Statelessness, where applicable, and the taking of measures at the global, regional and national level'.[278]

However, while recent significant achievements and developments are to be celebrated, we must remember that the UNHCR has been entrusted with authority in relation to stateless refugees since 1950. Indeed, its competence is defined in the Statute to extend to persons who 'not having a nationality and being outside the country of his former habitual residence, is unable or, owing to such fear or for reasons other than personal convenience, is unwilling to return to it'.[279] Yet the UNHCR has traditionally undertaken very little work, at least in respect of its international protection function, in relation to stateless refugees. For example, its classic mechanism for providing interpretative guidance, the Handbook on Procedures and Criteria for Determining Refugee Status, does not consider in any meaningful way the application of the definition to stateless persons, nor has there been any focused attention to this question in the more recent Guidelines on International Protection.[280] Indeed, a recent scholarly account of UNHCR's record pre-1995 in attempting to assist stateless persons does not point to any action in relation to stateless refugees.[281] Moreover, none of the renewed UNHCR focus has involved stateless refugees.[282] The one exception is a study commissioned by the UNHCR in 2014 entitled 'Refugee Status, Arbitrary Deprivation of Nationality, and Statelessness within the context of Article 1A(2) of the 1951 Convention and its 1967 Protocol

---

Assembly resolutions': see United Nations High Commissioner for Refugees, 'Note on International Protection: Report of the High Commissioner' (28 June 2011) UN Doc A/AC.96/1098, para 1.

[277] UN Executive Committee of the High Commissioner's Programme, 'Conclusion of the Executive Committee on International Cooperation from a Protection and Solutions Perspective' (6 October 2016) Conclusion No 112 (LXVII) 2016, para 16.

[278] UN Executive Committee of the High Commissioner's Programme, 'Conclusion of the Executive Committee on Youth' (6 October 2016) Conclusion No 113 (LXVII) 2016, para 8. See also the Global Compact on Refugees, discussed in Chapter 1, n 27.

[279] Statute of the Office of the United Nations High Commissioner for Refugees, UNGA Res 428 (V) (14 December 1950) ch II art 6(A)(ii). The reference to 'reasons other than personal convenience' is replicated in relation to those refugees with a nationality and hence does not appear to be intended to expand the scope of the definition.

[280] The exceptions are the UNHCR Guidelines on Victims of Trafficking, and a brief reference in the Guidelines on Children: see Chapter 1, n 11.

[281] Seet, 'Origins of the UNHCR's Global Mandate' (n 271).

[282] For instance, in work celebrating UNHCR's achievements, stateless refugees are not mentioned: see e.g., Manly, 'UNHCR's Mandate' (n 8).

relating to the Status of Refugees'.[283] While an extremely important development, this has not to date led to the development of relevant Guidelines on International Protection or other similar mechanisms for providing insight into the protection of stateless persons through international refugee law. It remains the case, therefore, that the protection of stateless refugees continues to be overlooked in UNHCR's supervisory responsibility under the 1951 *Refugee Convention* and the 1967 *Protocol*.

Part 6: Conclusion

This chapter has examined the emergence of the modern international regime for the protection of stateless persons, beginning with its origins in the concern of the international community to protect certain categories of 'unprotected persons' defined by ethnic or national group, rather than by a distinction between refugees and stateless persons. While the legal instruments ultimately diverged, resulting in the distinct legal regimes in place today, an analysis of the history of both the 1951 *Refugee Convention* and the *1954 Convention* highlights the longstanding recognition of the similar predicament and protection needs of refugees and stateless persons.

What is striking, however, is the rudimentary nature of the understanding of the root causes of statelessness revealed in much of the historical material, and the distinct lack of a human rights approach to identifying the reasons underlying the predicament of stateless persons. The extensive rights regime in both conventions operates as one of the earliest examples of the emerging modern human rights system, yet the notion that stateless persons deserved access to human rights and protection was not matched by a human rights understanding of the reasons underpinning their lack of nationality. This is largely explained on the basis that state sovereignty in relation to the grant and recognition of nationality was largely untrammelled; it was yet to be affected by the human rights regime.

It is hence against this historical background that the importance and significance of the extensive developments over the past sixty years can be understood and their relevance appreciated. It is to this issue that Chapter 3 turns.

---

[283] Hélène Lambert, 'Refugee Status, Arbitrary Deprivation of Nationality, and Statelessness within the Context of Article 1A(2) of the Refugee Convention and its 1967 Protocol relating to the Status of Refugees' (UNHCR Legal and Protection Policy Research Series, October 2014).

3

The Evolving Role of Nationality in the Protection and Enjoyment of Human Rights

In Chapter 2 we examined the history and development of the international legal framework for the protection of stateless persons and refugees respectively, tracking their early interconnectedness and subsequent reasons for divergence. As we observed, statelessness was largely considered a technical legal issue rather than one relating to human rights. In this chapter, we examine international law's evolution on this question, as this is foundational to the book's thesis that international refugee law, itself anchored in human rights, can and should accommodate a more sophisticated understanding of the connection between statelessness and refugeehood. According to the traditional understanding under international law, a lack of nationality could hardly be understood in human rights terms; hence statelessness de jure was an anomaly or aberration due to technical legal issues.[1] However, as this chapter reveals, the advent of international human rights has slowly but consistently intruded into state discretion such that we can now see that, in many instances, both a denial to grant nationality and a withdrawal of nationality violate norms of international law. In the latter part of the chapter we turn our attention to the rights of stateless persons, observing that international law has evolved such that stateless persons are entitled to equal access to most fundamental human rights in their country of habitual residence.

These developments in international law are essential to a contemporary and principled understanding of the key definitional elements of the refugee definition. Given that it is now widely accepted that a denial of human rights can amount to 'being persecuted' in international refugee law, it is crucial that refugee lawyers and decision-makers take account of the human rights context of the position of stateless persons in assessing their refugee claims. Refugee claims by stateless persons may be anchored in a denial or withdrawal of nationality; denial of the right to return; and/or denial of a

---

[1] Carol A Batchelor, 'Transforming International Legal Principles into National Law: The Right to a Nationality and the Avoidance of Statelessness' (2006) 25 Refugee Survey Quarterly 8 (hereafter Batchelor, 'Transforming International Legal Principles into National Law'); Carol A Batchelor, 'Stateless Persons: Some Gaps in International Protection' (1995) 7 IJRL 232, 235 (hereafter Batchelor, 'Stateless Persons: Some Gaps in International Protection') citing Paul Weis, 'The United Nations Convention on the Reduction of Statelessness, 1961' (1962) 11 ICLQ 1073. See also Jean-Pierre-Adrien François, 'Le problème des apatrides' in *Recueil des cours*, vol 53 (Académie de Droit International 1935) 283 (hereafter François, 'Le problème des apatrides'); Gerard D Cohen, *In War's Wake—Europe's Displaced Persons in the Postwar Order* (OUP 2012) (hereafter Cohen, *In War's Wake*).

International Refugee Law and the Protection of Stateless Persons. Michelle Foster and Hélène Lambert.
© Michelle Foster and Hélène Lambert 2019. Published 2019 by Oxford University Press.

range of other civil, political, social, and economic rights. Thus, this chapter provides vital context for the subsequent chapters, which draw on these developments, together with relevant refugee law jurisprudence, to argue for a contemporary and principled understanding of the role of refugee law in the protection of stateless persons.

Part 1 of the chapter begins by setting out the significance of nationality in international law. Nationality is the legal bond between an individual and the state; although nationality is determined by states internally, it creates rights and duties for states under international law. In Part 2 we examine the legal framework for the regulation of nationality and the constraints that human rights norms have imposed on state discretion in this area. This part of the chapter focuses on the right to a nationality, deprivation of nationality, and the prevention of statelessness, and the critical role of non-discrimination in treaty law, soft law, and the jurisprudence of international courts. The Inter-American Court of Human Rights, the African Commission on Human and Peoples' Rights, the African Committee of Experts on the Rights and Welfare of the Child (ACERWC), and the European Court of Human Rights (ECtHR) have all issued important judgments, decisions, or opinions on nationality-related issues. In Part 3, we discuss the evolution of international human rights norms that now provide equal access to fundamental rights for all those within a state's territory or jurisdiction regardless of nationality, in order to provide a critical foundation for the discussion of the 'being-persecuted' criteria in subsequent chapters.

At the outset it is important to clarify a point of terminology on the term 'deprivation' which can have different meanings depending on the context. Under the 1961 *Convention on the Reduction of Statelessness* ('*1961 Convention*'), the terms 'loss' and 'deprivation' are both used in the sense of withdrawal of nationality. Thus deprivation, in the *1961 Convention*, is used in its narrow sense, to mean an administrative act through which a state decides to exercise its power to withdraw a person's nationality. The concept of loss of nationality, in the *1961 Convention*, refers to a situation in which no administrative act is needed for withdrawal, but rather this happens by operation of the law because certain conditions have been met.

Under human rights law, the term 'deprivation' is most often used in the context of the norm prohibiting 'arbitrary deprivation' of nationality. This norm has come to be understood as prohibiting both arbitrary *withdrawal* of a nationality that a person already holds *and* arbitrary *denial* of a nationality that a person should be able to access. This meaning of the term 'deprivation' is best illustrated in the 2009 UN Secretary General report on arbitrary deprivation of nationality:

While the question of arbitrary deprivation of nationality does not comprise the loss of nationality voluntarily requested by the individual, it covers all other forms of loss of nationality, including those that arbitrarily preclude a person from obtaining or retaining a nationality, particularly on discriminatory grounds, as well as those that automatically deprive a person of a nationality by operation of the law, and those acts taken by administrative authorities that result in a person being arbitrarily deprived of a nationality.[2]

---

[2] United Nations Human Rights Council (UN HRC), 'Human Rights and Arbitrary Deprivation of Nationality' (14 December 2009) UN Doc A/HRC/13/34, para 23 (hereafter UN HRC, 'Human Rights and Arbitrary Deprivation of Nationality').

What this statement makes clear is that in the context of the norm prohibiting 'arbitrary deprivation' of nationality, the term 'deprivation' is used in a broad sense, to cover both 'loss' and 'deprivation' (two forms of withdrawal) as used in the *1961 Convention, as well as denial* of nationality.[3] It is this broader understanding of deprivation which is used in this book.

Part 1: The Significance of Nationality in International Law

Nationality is typically viewed as an essential link between individuals and international law;[4] it has 'origins in the notion of allegiance'.[5] In one of the most cited passages of the seminal *Nottebohm Case (Liechtenstein v Guatemala)* ('*Nottebohm*'), the facts of which are described in more detail below in Part 3, the International Court of Justice ('ICJ') defined nationality as the following: '[a]ccording to the practice of States, to arbitral and judicial decisions and to the opinions of writers, nationality is a legal bond having at its basis a social fact of attachment, a genuine connection of existence, interest and sentiments together with the existence of reciprocal rights and duties'.[6]

This conception of nationality is further embodied in Article 2 of the *European Convention on Nationality*, which defines nationality as 'the legal bond between a person and a State and does not indicate the person's ethnic origin'.[7]

In *Nottebohm*, the ICJ added:

It may be said to constitute the juridical expression of the fact that the individual upon whom it is conferred, either directly by the law or as the result of an act of the authorities, is in fact more closely connected with the population of the State conferring nationality than with that of any other State. Conferred by a State, it only entitles that State to exercise protection vis-à-vis another State, if it constitutes a translation into juridical terms of the individual's connection with the State which has made him its national.[8]

---

[3] We are grateful to Laura van Waas for clarification on this terminology, and we refer the reader to her book *Nationality Matters: Statelessness under International Law* (Intersentia 2008) (hereafter van Waas, *Nationality Matters*) at 101. In her book, van Waas makes a convincing argument for equating discriminatory deprivation of nationality to the denial of citizenship. See also *Modise v Botswana*: failure to recognize Mr Modise's citizenship by birth was implicitly recognized as deprivation of access to nationality, and *Yean and Bosico*, where it was held explicitly: African Commission on Human and Peoples' Rights, 'Communication No 97/93: *Modise v Botswana*' (6 November 2000) (hereafter *Modise v Botswana*); *Case of the Yean and Bosico Children v Dominican Republic* (Preliminary Objections, Merits, Reparations and Costs) Inter-American Court of Human Rights Series C No 130 (8 September 2005) (hereafter *Case of the Yean and Bosico Children*).

[4] Hersch Lauterpacht, *International Law Collected Papers: The Law of Peace Part I International Law in General*, vol 2 (CUP 1975) 284: 'an essential link between the individual and the League of Nations'.

[5] Robert Jennings and Arthur Watts (eds), *Oppenheim's International Law*, vol I ('Peace') (9th edn, Longman 1992) 851 (hereafter Jennings and Watts (eds), *Oppenheim's International Law*).

[6] *Nottebohm Case (Liechtenstein v Guatemala)* (Second Phase (Judgment)) [1955] ICJ Rep 4, 23 (emphasis added) (hereafter *Nottebohm Case*).

[7] *European Convention on Nationality* 1997, art 2 (hereafter *ECN*).

[8] *Nottebohm Case* (n 6) 23.

In principle, the regulation of nationality is not a matter for international law. Rather it is for each state to determine who is (and who is not) one of its nationals. With their nationality laws, states determine who their nationals are through a complex process of inclusion and exclusion. Most commonly, nationality is acquired by descent/parentage (*jus sanguinis* or law of the blood) or by birth on the territory (*jus soli* or law of the soil).[9] In addition, nationality can be acquired by way of naturalization (*jus domicile*, based on long-term residence or exceptionally also *by investment*).[10] Finally, nationality can be acquired through cession or annexation.[11] Withdrawal of nationality also can occur in a number of ways.[12] States' discretion in matters concerning nationality is nevertheless subject to certain limits imposed by international law, traditionally to be found in custom and general principles of international law, and later in international human rights treaties. The extent of the limits varies considerably based on whether nationality was acquired *jus sanguinis* or *jus soli* (where the limits imposed by international law are quite broad) or whether it was acquired by naturalization (where the state's discretion remains strong).[13]

From the perspective of international law, nationality is 'the medium' through which individuals enjoy protection in international law; nationality also secures re-entry into their state of nationality.[14] It is concerned with the rights and duties of the state of nationality in its relationship with other states to avoid *un abus des droits*. The rights and duties in question consist of the right to diplomatic protection (a right of the state of nationality) and the duty of states to re-admit their nationals from abroad. According to this perspective, nationality is essentially outward looking; it is an extension of the sovereignty of the state of nationality,[15] an element of international public order.[16]

---

[9] European Union Democracy Observatory ('EUDO') on Citizenship elaborates a typology of modes of acquisition of citizenship comprising of seven modes, sub-divided into twenty-seven target groups: Kristen Jeffers, Iseult Honohan, and Rainer Bauböck, 'Comparing Citizenship across Europe: Laws, Implementation and Impact, CITLAW Indicators: How to Measure the Purposes of Citizenship Laws' (EUDO 2012) Appendix, 60.

[10] Jules Lepoutre, 'Les États membres de l'Union peuvent-ils vendre la citoyenneté européenne?' (2015) 19 Petites affiches 6.

[11] Jennings and Watts (eds), *Oppenheim's International Law* (n 5) para 390.

[12] ibid, 877–81, lists release, renunciation, deprivation, expiration, or substitution as ways one can lose a nationality.

[13] Alice Edwards, 'The Meaning of Nationality in International Law in an Era of Human Rights: Procedural and Substantive Issues' in Alice Edwards and Laura van Waas (eds), *Nationality and Statelessness under International Law* (CUP 2014) 11, 18 (hereafter Edwards, 'The Meaning of Nationality').

[14] Jennings and Watts (eds), *Oppenheim's International Law* (n 5) 849 [376].

[15] 'Nationality' as 'nationalité formelle' (F de Castro, 'La nationalité' in *Recueil des cours*, vol 102 (Académie de Droit International 1961) 523, 552 (hereafter de Castro, 'La nationalité'), also referred to as a passive or a formal status, contrasted with the more dynamic concept of 'citizenship' whereby an individual exercises full political and civil rights (Alison Kesby, *The Right to Have Rights: Citizenship, Humanity, and International Law* (OUP 2012) 43–44 (hereafter Kesby, *The Right to Have Rights*)).

[16] Peter Spiro refers to 'order management': Peter J Spiro, 'A New International Law of Citizenship' (2011) 105 AJIL 694, 698 (hereafter Spiro, 'A New International Law of Citizenship'). See also Kay Hailbronner, 'Nationality in Public International Law and European Law' in Rainer Bauböck, Eva Ersbøll, Kees Groenendijk, and Harald Waldrauch (eds), *Acquisition and Loss of Nationality: Policies and Trends in 15 European Countries*, vol 1 (Amsterdam University Press 2006) 35, pt 1.1.4.

Thus, under (the traditional perspective of) international law, nationality and citizenship are viewed as two sides of the same coin, namely, state membership. While nationality is essentially outward looking, citizenship is concerned with the internal relationship between the individual and the state, namely, the rights attached to citizenship within a community, for example political and social rights. It is therefore essentially inward looking, a purely internal status.

Yet, there is another perspective, that of international human rights law, according to which nationality and citizenship 'can be used interchangeably' because the ability to access and exercise rights matters more than 'the label'.[17] For instance, according to Alison Kesby, 'the "right to a nationality" is perhaps best articulated as the "right to citizenship"', with citizenship meaning more than just legal and political inclusion, but also crucially social inclusion and integration.[18] This is the view adopted in this book, where both terms will be used interchangeably and the prime focus will be on rights.

Part 2: The International Legal Framework Governing Nationality

The focal point of this part of the chapter is on the evolution of the regulatory framework governing nationality and the constraints imposed by international law on state discretion in matters concerning nationality. With regard to the latter, we examine in particular deprivation of nationality (i.e. denial of access to a nationality and withdrawal of a nationality) and prevention of statelessness as issues of particular relevance to refugee law because of the strong links that exist between denial and deprivation of nationality and discrimination.

2.1 The right to a nationality in international law: the traditional approach

People have long travelled between countries.[19] However, when migration began to increase in the late nineteenth and early twentieth centuries, together with the desire of migrants to acquire membership in their new state of residence, nationality practices (such as, for instance, the refusal of many European states to recognize the validity of naturalization claims) became a source of serious tension.[20] Furthermore, at the time, both dual nationality and statelessness were viewed as anomalies.[21] Paul Weis, for instance, reminds us that '[a] stateless person—and this applies equally to

---

[17] Edwards, 'The Meaning of Nationality' (n 13) 14.

[18] Kesby, *The Right to Have Rights* (n 15) 64. See also Ernst Hirsch Ballin, *Citizens' Rights and the Right to Be a Citizen* (Brill Nijhoff 2014).

[19] Vincent Chetail, 'The Transnational Movement of Persons under General International Law—Mapping the Customary Law Foundations of International Migration Law' in Vincent Chetail and Céline Bauloz (eds), *Research Handbook on International Law and Migration* (Edward Elgar 2014) 1, 11 (hereafter Chetail, 'The Transnational Movement of Persons').

[20] Peter J Spiro, 'Citizenship, Nationality, and Statelessness' in Vincent Chetail and Céline Bauloz (eds), *Research Handbook on International Law and Migration* (Edward Elgar 2014) 281, 282.

[21] Batchelor, 'Transforming International Legal Principles into National Law' (n 1); Batchelor, 'Stateless Persons: Some Gaps in International Protection' (n 1) 235, citing Weis, 'The United Nations

refugees—has been compared to a vessel on the open sea, not sailing under any flag. He has been called flotsam, *res nullius*.'[22] In 1927, therefore, nationality was selected as a topic of importance for debate at the 1930 Hague Conference seeking to codify the rules of customary international law on nationality.[23]

The 1930 *Hague Convention on Certain Questions relating to the Conflict of Nationality Laws* ('*1930 Hague Convention*') succeeded in laying down some rules that states should adhere to in regulating access to nationality of children (e.g. Articles 14 and 15 of the *Convention*).[24] It also 'codified the first significant international rules regarding the avoidance of statelessness',[25] both in the *1930 Hague Convention* and through a *Protocol relating to a Certain Case of Statelessness*.[26] However, it retained the foundational principle of state sovereignty as the default position in relation to nationality.[27]

Thus, Article 1 provides: 'It is for each State to determine under its own law who are its nationals. This law shall be recognised by other States in so far as it is consistent with international conventions, international custom and the principles of law generally recognised with regard to nationality.'[28]

This power is further stated in Article 2: 'Any question as to whether a person possesses the nationality of a particular State shall be determined in accordance with the law of that State.'

This principle had already been stated by the Permanent Court of International Justice in its advisory opinion of 1923:

The question whether a certain matter is or is not solely within the jurisdiction of a State is an essentially relative question; it depends upon the development of international relations. Thus, in the present state of international law, questions of nationality are, in the opinion of the Court, in principle within this reserved domain. . . . it may well happen that, in a matter

Convention on the Reduction of Statelessness, 1961' (n 1) 1073. See also François, 'Le problème des apatrides' (n 1) 283; Cohen, *In War's Wake* (n 1).

[22] Paul Weis, 'The International Protection of Refugees' (1954) 48 AJIL 183, 193.

[23] François, 'Le problème des apatrides' (n 1) 343. See also Manley O Hudson and Richard W Flournoy Jr, 'The Law of Nationality' (1929) 23 AJIL Supplement: Codification of International Law 1 (hereafter Hudson and Flournoy, 'The Law of Nationality'); M Vichniac, 'Le statut international des apatrides' in *Recueil des cours*, vol 43 (Académie de Droit International 1933) 119 (hereafter Vichniac, 'Le statut international des apatrides') observing that, prior to the First World War, the Institute of International Law deliberately chose to consider these issues within the realm of *private* international law, and not as an issue of public law.

[24] *Convention on Certain Questions relating to the Conflict of Nationality Laws* (signed 12 April 1930, entered into force 1 July 1937) 179 LNTS 89 (hereafter *1930 Hague Convention*).

[25] Laura van Waas, 'The UN Statelessness Conventions' in Alice Edwards and Laura van Waas (eds), *Nationality and Statelessness under International Law* (CUP 2014) 64, 70.

[26] *Protocol relating to a Certain Case of Statelessness* (signed 12 April 1930, entered into force 1 July 1937) 179 LNTS 115, art 1: 'In a State whose nationality is not conferred by the mere fact of birth in its territory, a person born in its territory of a mother possessing the nationality of that State and of a father without nationality or of unknown nationality shall have the nationality of the said State.' See, Stephen Hall, 'The European Convention on Nationality and the Right to Have Rights' (1999) 24 ELRev 586, 589, 591.

[27] It also perpetuated the 'tie of allegiance' owed by the national person to the state: Hudson and Flournoy, 'The Law of Nationality' (n 23) 23.

[28] *1930 Hague Convention* (n 24) art 2.

which, like that of nationality, is not, in principle, regulated by international law, the right of a State to use its discretion is nevertheless restricted by obligations which it may have undertaken towards other States. In such case, jurisdiction which, in principle, belongs solely to the State, is limited by rules of international law.[29]

Hence, the *1930 Hague Convention* did not create an individual right to nationality. States alone remained competent *internally* to grant or withdraw someone's nationality. On the international plane, other states are obliged to recognize the effects of the power exercised internally *so long as* it conforms to international law.

In subsequent jurisprudence, the International Court of Justice continued to adopt this position, stating in *Nottebohm* in 1955 that:

It is for Liechtenstein, as it is for every sovereign State, to settle by its own legislation the rules relating to the acquisition of its nationality, and to confer that nationality by naturalization granted by its own organs in accordance with that legislation.... Furthermore, nationality has its most immediate, its most far-reaching and, for most people, its only effects within the legal system of the State conferring it.[30]

The traditional approach described above presages the beginning of the next path, namely the development of constraints on state discretion in matters of nationality, by the advent and proliferation of human rights standards. A new rights' conception of nationality began to emerge based on core principles that have come to frame nationality and combat exclusion from full membership in a community.

2.2 Constraints on state discretion in matters concerning nationality

The new era emerged in the aftermath of the Second World War and in particular in the context of the drafting of the *Universal Declaration of Human Rights* ('*UDHR*'). Peter Spiro explains that the *UDHR* was a turning point, as with its formulation, 'the discourse shifted away from an order-centred orientation and recognized, instead, the individual's interest in nationality to be a matter of international law'.[31]

2.2.1 The Universal Declaration of Human Rights

The 'rights perspective' of nationality or citizenship was made explicit in Article 15 of the 1948 *UDHR*, the history of which was considered briefly in Chapter 2. Described as 'a total innovation in the history of international law',[32] Article 15 provides:

---

[29] *Nationality Decrees Issued in Tunis and Morocco (French Zone) Case* (Advisory Opinion) 1923 PCIJ Rep Series B No 4, 24. See also Lawrence Preuss, 'International Law and Deprivation of Nationality' (1935) 23 GeoLJ 250, 254; Jennings and Watts (eds), *Oppenheim's International Law* (n 5) 851–52 [378].

[30] *Nottebohm Case* (n 6) 20.

[31] Spiro, 'A New International Law of Citizenship' (n 16) 710.

[32] ibid, n 105, citing the words of Nehemiah Robinson, *The Universal Declaration of Human Rights: Its Origin, Significance, Application, and Interpretation* (Institute of Jewish Affairs 1958). This right has been said to be in line with Francisco de Vitoria's thinking, in de Castro, 'La nationalité' (n 15) 572.

1. Everyone has the right to a nationality.
2. No one shall be arbitrarily deprived of his nationality nor denied the right to change his nationality.[33]

Article 15(1) protects the right to a nationality, namely, the right of everyone to acquire, change, and retain a nationality. More specifically, the right to acquire and retain a nationality corresponds to the prohibition of arbitrary deprivation of nationality in Article 15(2).[34]

The significance of the reconceptualization of nationality as a human right in Article 15 *UDHR* is articulated by the Inter-American Court of Human Rights as follows:

It is generally accepted today that nationality is an inherent right of all human beings. Not only is nationality the basic requirement for the exercise of political rights, it also has an important bearing on the individual's legal capacity. Thus, despite the fact that it is traditionally accepted that the conferral and regulation of nationality are matters for each state to decide, contemporary developments indicate that international law does impose certain limits on the broad powers enjoyed by the states in that area, and that the manners in which states regulate matters bearing on nationality cannot today be deemed within their sole jurisdiction; those powers of the state are also circumscribed by their obligations to ensure the full protection of human rights.[35]

The Court then concluded that to arrive at a correct interpretation of the right to nationality (as embodied in Article 20 of the *American Convention*[36]), one must necessarily reconcile two principles:

the principle that the conferral and regulation of nationality fall within the jurisdiction of the state, that is, they are matters to be determined by the domestic law of the state, with the further principle that international law imposes certain limits on the state's power, which limits are linked to the demands imposed by the international system for the protection of human rights.[37]

Thus, with the *UDHR*, nationality has evolved from a state's attribute to a human right; both conceptions exist to strengthen the protection of individuals. For human rights scholars, such as Kesby, possessing a nationality means having 'a place in the world—namely a place of lawful residence';[38] as such it is 'amongst the most important rights a state can assign to individuals'.[39]

---

[33] *Universal Declaration of Human Rights* (adopted 10 December 1948) UNGA Res 217 A(III) art 15 (hereafter *UDHR*).

[34] UN HRC, 'Human Rights and Arbitrary Deprivation of Nationality' (n 2) para 23.

[35] *Proposed Amendments to the Naturalization Provision of the Constitution of Costa Rica*, Advisory Opinion OC-4/84, Inter-American Court of Human Rights Series A No 4 (19 January 1984) [32] (hereafter *Constitution of Costa Rica Case*).

[36] *American Convention on Human Rights* (adopted 22 November 1969, entered into force 19 July 1978) 1144 UNTS 123 (hereafter *American Convention*).

[37] *Constitution of Costa Rica Case* (n 35) [38].

[38] Kesby, *The Right to Have Rights* (n 15) 6.

[39] ibid, 51, citing International Law Association (ILA), 'Final Report on Women's Equality and Nationality in International Law' (2000) 69 ILA Rep Conf 257 (hereafter ILA, 'Final Report on Women's Equality'). See also Guy S Goodwin-Gill, 'The Rights of Refugees and Stateless Persons' in

It must be acknowledged, however, that not only is the *UDHR* not binding, the 'right to a nationality' does not necessarily entail a corresponding *obligation* on any particular state to grant this right. Thus, it is difficult to establish a binding obligation, based on the *UDHR* alone, on states to confer nationality on any particular individual. It is therefore necessary to consider the human rights treaties that were inspired by the *UDHR*.

2.2.2 Human rights treaties

The right to a nationality embodied in Article 15 *UDHR* is recognized in some form or another in a raft of international treaties. While these instruments are clearly binding, attention must be paid to the precise formulation in each case as they do not in the main universally guarantee a right to nationality. However, for the reasons explained below these instruments nonetheless represent vital and significant inroads into state discretion in the regulation of nationality.

The tension inherent in the recognition of a general right to nationality and the concomitant imposition of positive obligations on states required to give force to this right was clearly present during the drafting of the *International Covenant on Civil and Political Rights* ('*ICCPR*'). In 1963, it was remarked that 'no article on the right to a nationality had been included in the draft Covenant on Civil and Political Rights precisely because of the complexity of the problem',[40] and this was, 'despite the fact that such an article was contained in the Universal Declaration of Human Rights; and that attempts to solve the very difficult problem of statelessness had been made in several international instruments, particularly in the Convention on the Reduction of Statelessness'.[41]

Although some representatives regretted the absence of such provision,[42] strong resistance existed against incorporating a right to a nationality for everyone because nationality was governed by different constitutional rules in each state.[43] For instance, according to Mr Herndl (Austria), 'the problem of nationality ... was governed by national law and could not be solved in an instrument such as the draft Covenant'.[44] However, there was 'general agreement that children were entitled

---

K P Saksena (ed), *Human Rights: Perspective and Challenges* (Lancers Books 1994) 378, 392 (referring to 'an individual's belonging to a particular territorial community'); Sheila Keetharuth, 'The African Charter and the Right to a Nationality' (Report of a Meeting Held in Banjul, The Gambia, 14 May 2010) (referring to a 'sense of identity' or membership in a community).

[40] UN General Assembly (UNGA), 'Report of the Third Committee' (10 December 1963) UN Doc A/5655, para 76 (hereafter UN Doc A/5655). It is instructive that a Note by the UN Secretary General, 'Text of Articles Adopted by the Third Committee at the Tenth to Seventeenth Sessions of the General Assembly' (24 September 1963) UN Doc A/C.3/L.1062 does not mention nationality at all (nor any preceding documents).

[41] UNGA, 'Report of the Third Committee' (17 December 1962) UN Doc A/5365, para 25 (hereafter UN Doc A/5365).

[42] UN Doc A/5655 (n 40) para 76.

[43] See e.g., UNGA, 'Third Committee, 1262nd Meeting' (13 November 1963) UN Doc A/C.3/SR.1262, paras 42, 51 (hereafter UN Doc A/C.3/SR.1262).

[44] UNGA, 'Third Committee, 1265th Meeting' (15 November 1963) UN Doc A/C.3/SR.1265, para 14 (hereafter UN Doc A/C.3/SR.1265).

to special protection'.[45] Hence, discussion began on the inclusion of an article on the rights of the child to acquire a nationality in the draft Covenant on Civil and Political Rights.[46] The issue was not without controversy, with opinions divided as to the desirability of such a provision. However, after years of debate,[47] Article 24 was finally adopted as follows:[48]

1. Every child shall have, without any discrimination as to race, colour, sex, language, religion, national or social origin, property or birth, the right to such measures of protection as are required by his status as a minor, on the part of his family, society and the State.

2. Every child shall be registered immediately after birth and shall have a name.

3. Every child has the right to acquire a nationality.

Human Rights Committee General Comment No 17 explains that

While the purpose of this provision [Article 24(3)] is to prevent a child from being afforded less protection by society and the State because he is stateless, it does not necessarily make it an obligation for States to give their nationality to every child born in their territory. However, States are required to adopt every appropriate measure, both internally and in cooperation with other States, to ensure that every child has a nationality when he is born [in pursuance of the principle of non-discrimination].[49]

The right of every child *to acquire* a nationality (and the obligation on states to take measures where statelessness ensues) is further guaranteed in the *Convention on the Rights of the Child*,[50] and the *1961 Convention*.[51] It is also contained in some form or

---

[45] UN Doc A/5365 (n 41).

[46] Prompted by Poland, seven other delegations soon joined in this proposal: see ibid, paras 5–6.

[47] These can be read in the following documents (listed in chronological order): UN Commission on Human Rights, 'Report to the Economic and Social Council on the Seventh Session of the Commission, held at the Palais des Nations, Geneva, from 16 April to 19 May 1951' (24 May 1951) UN Doc E/1992; UNGA, 'Report of the Third Committee' (5 December 1957) UN Doc E/1992; UNGA, 'Report of the Third Committee' (10 December 1957) UN Doc A/364/Add.1; UN Doc A/5365 (n 41); UN Doc A/5655 (n 40); UNGA, 'Third Committee, 1261st Meeting' (12 November 1963) UN Doc A/C.3/SR.1261; UN Doc A/C.3/SR.1262 (n 43); UNGA, 'Third Committee, 1263rd Meeting' (14 November 1963) UN Doc A/C.3/SR.1263; UN Doc A/C.3/SR.1265 (n 44); UNGA, 'Third Committee, 1266th Meeting' (18 December 1963) UN Doc A/C.3/SR.1266.

[48] UNGA Res 2200A(XXI) (16 December 1966) UN Doc A/RES/2200A(XXI).

[49] Office of the High Commissioner for Human Rights, 'General Comment No 17: Article 24 (Rights of the Child)' (7 April 1989) UN Doc HRI/GEN/1/Rev.1, para 8.

[50] *Convention on the Rights of the Child* (adopted 20 November 1989, entered into force 2 September 1990) 1577 UNTS 3, arts 7(1), 7(2) (hereafter *CRC*). Note that the *CRC* has very wide support from states (with 196 states parties). Article 3 *CRC*, in particular, when applied properly, provides perhaps one of the strongest legal bases to ground the right to a nationality of children. Indeed, can anyone argue that it is in the best interest of the child not to have a nationality? The Committee on the Rights of the Child has developed a broad understanding of the right to a nationality and the obligations of states to prevent childhood statelessness in several Concluding Observations and General Comments. For a useful discussion, see Institute on Statelessness and Inclusion, 'Addressing the Right to a Nationality through the Convention on the Rights of the Child: A Toolkit for Civil Society' <www.institutesi.org/children> accessed 12 November 2018.

[51] *Convention on the Reduction of Statelessness* (adopted 30 August 1961, entered into force 13 December 1975) 989 UNTS 175, arts 1–4 (hereafter *1961 Convention*). For many years, only a few states signed this *Convention* but this number almost doubled following the launch of UN High

another in several other treaties and soft law instruments. For example, the *Convention on the Elimination of All Forms of Discrimination Against Women* ('*CEDAW*') recognizes 'women['s] equal rights with men to acquire, change or retain their nationality' and in the transmission of their nationality to children;[52] the *Convention on the Rights of Persons with Disabilities* guarantees 'the right to acquire and change a nationality' to persons (including children) with disabilities;[53] and the *International Convention on the Protection of the Rights of All Migrant Workers and Members of their Families* also guarantees that '[e]ach child of a migrant worker shall have the right to a name, to registration of birth and to a nationality'.[54] In 2016, the Human Rights Council reaffirmed the right of every child to acquire a nationality and to be protected against arbitrary deprivation of nationality.[55] It further reiterated 'that the right to identity is intimately linked to the right of nationality', and urged states 'to register every child's birth ... and to ensure that proof of identity is available to all children'.[56] And in November 2017, the Committee on the Protection of the Rights of All Migrant Workers and Members of their Families and the Committee on the Rights of the Child clarified states' obligations under treaty law relating to statelessness and every child's right to a nationality in an international migration context (including protection against discrimination on grounds such as residence status or migration status).[57]

Commissioner for Refugee's ('UNHCR') campaign to promote accession to his treaty. This campaign resulted in an increase in state parties to the *1961 Convention* from thirty-seven to seventy-three: UN Treaty Collection, 'Chapter V: Refugees and Stateless Persons, 4. Convention on the Reduction of Statelessness' (*UN Treaty Collection*, 21 January 2019) <https://treaties.un.org/Pages/ViewDetails. aspx?src=IND&mtdsg_no=V-4&chapter=5&clang=_en> accessed 22 January 2019.

[52] *Convention on the Elimination of All Forms of Discrimination Against Women* (adopted 18 December 1979, entered into force 3 September 1981) 1249 UNTS 13, art 9 (hereafter *CEDAW*): '1. States Parties shall grant women equal rights with men to acquire, change or retain their nationality. They shall ensure in particular that neither marriage to an alien nor change of nationality by the husband during marriage shall automatically change the nationality of the wife, render her stateless or force upon her the nationality of the husband. 2. States Parties shall grant women equal rights with men with respect to the nationality of their children.' See also UN Committee on the Elimination of All Forms of Discrimination Against Women, 'General Recommendation No 21: Equality in Marriage and Family Relations' (1994) UN Doc A/49/38, para 6: 'Nationality is critical to full participation in society ... Nationality should be capable of change by an adult woman and should not be arbitrarily removed because of marriage or dissolution of marriage or because her husband or father changes his nationality.'

[53] *Convention on the Rights of Persons with Disabilities* (adopted 13 December 2006, entered into force 3 May 2008) 2515 UNTS 3 (hereafter *Convention on the Rights of Persons with Disabilities*), art 18: 'Liberty of movement and nationality. 1. States Parties shall recognize the rights of persons with disabilities ... to a nationality, on an equal basis with others, including by ensuring that persons with disabilities: a. Have the right to acquire and change a nationality and are not deprived of their nationality arbitrarily or on the basis of disability; ... 2. Children with disabilities shall be registered immediately after birth and shall have the right from birth to a name, the right to acquire a nationality and, as far as possible, the right to know and be cared for by their parents.'

[54] *International Convention on the Protection of the Rights of All Migrant Workers and Members of their Families* (adopted 18 December 1990, entered into force 1 July 2003) 2220 UNTS 3, art 29.

[55] UN Human Rights Council (UN HRC) Res 32/5 (15 July 2016) UN Doc A/HRC/RES/32/5, para 9 (hereafter UN HRC Res 32/5).

[56] ibid, paras 11, 12.

[57] Committee on the Protection of the Rights of All Migrant Workers and Members of their Families (CMW) and Committee on the Rights of the Child (CRC), 'Joint General Comment No 3 (2017) of the CMW and No 22 (2017) of the CRC on the General Principles regarding the Human Rights of Children in the Context of International Migration' (16 November 2017) UN Doc CMW/C/GC/ 3–CRC/C/GC/22 (hereafter CMW and CRC Joint General Comment No 3, 22 (2017)); CMW and

In contrast with universal instruments, regional human rights instruments have more effectively incorporated Article 15 of the *UDHR*. For instance, the *American Convention on Human Rights* ('*American Convention*'),[58] the *European Convention on Nationality* ('*ECN*'),[59] the *ASEAN Human Rights Declaration*,[60] the *Commonwealth of Independent States Convention on Human Rights and Fundamental Freedoms*,[61] and the *Arab Charter on Human Rights*[62] all provide the right of *everyone* to a nationality.[63] Some of these instruments also include provisions for the elimination of statelessness.[64] The *Covenant on the Rights of the Child in Islam* protects the right of a child 'to have his nationality determined' as part of his identity.[65] The *African Charter of the Rights and Welfare of the Child* guarantees every child the right to acquire a nationality, particularly the nationality of the country in which he was born.[66] Both instruments contain provisions for the reduction of statelessness.[67]

CRC, 'Joint General Comment No 4 (2017) of the CMW and No 23 (2017) of the CRC on State Obligations regarding the Human Rights of Children in the Context of International Migration in Countries of Origin, Transit, Destination and Return' (16 November 2017) UN Doc CMW/C/GC/4–CRC/C/GC/23 (hereafter CMW and CRC Joint General Comment No 4, 23 (2017)).

[58] *American Convention* (n 36) art 20: 'Right to nationality. 1. Every person has the right to a nationality. 2. Every person has the right to the nationality of the state in whose territory he was born if he does not have the right to any other nationality. 3. No one shall be arbitrarily deprived of his nationality or of the right to change it.'

[59] *ECN*, art 4: 'Principles. a. Everyone has the right to a nationality; b. Statelessness shall be avoided; c. No one shall be arbitrarily deprived of his or her nationality.... Article 6—Acquisition of nationality. 4. Each State Party shall facilitate in its internal law the acquisition of its nationality for the following persons: ... e. persons who were born on its territory and reside there lawfully and habitually; f. persons who are lawfully and habitually resident on its territory for a period of time beginning before the age of 18, that period to be determined by the internal law of the State Party concerned.' See also Council of Europe (COE) Parliamentary Assembly Res 1989 (9 April 2014); COE Recommendation 2042 (9 April 2014); COE Committee of Ministers' Rec (2000) 15 (13 September 2000).

[60] *ASEAN Human Rights Declaration 2012*, art 18 (hereafter *ASEAN Human Rights Declaration*): 'Every person has the right to a nationality as prescribed by law. No person shall be arbitrarily deprived of such nationality nor denied the right to change that nationality.'

[61] *Commonwealth of Independent States Convention on Human Rights and Fundamental Freedoms 1995* (hereafter *Commonwealth Convention on Human Rights*), art 24: '1. Everyone shall have the right to citizenship. 2. No one shall be arbitrarily deprived of his citizenship or of the right to change it.'

[62] *Arab Charter on Human Rights 2004*, art 29 (hereafter *Arab Charter 2004*): '1. Everyone has the right to nationality. No one shall be arbitrarily or unlawfully deprived of his nationality. 2. States parties shall take such measures as they deem appropriate, in accordance with their domestic laws on nationality, to allow a child to acquire the mother's nationality, having due regard, in all cases, to the best interests of the child. 3. No one shall be denied the right to acquire another nationality, having due regard for the domestic legal procedures in his country.'

[63] See also the *Arab Charter on Human Rights 1994*, art 24: 'No citizen shall be arbitrarily deprived of his original nationality, nor shall his right to acquire another nationality be denied without a legally valid reason.'

[64] *American Convention* (n 36) art 20(2); *ECN* (n 7) art 4(b); *Arab Charter 2004* (n 62) art 29(2).

[65] *Covenant on the Rights of the Child in Islam 2004*, art 7 (hereafter *Covenant on the Rights of the Child in Islam*).

[66] *African Charter on the Rights and Welfare of the Child* (adopted 1 July 1990, entered into force 29 November 1999) (hereafter *African Children's Charter*) art 6, entitled 'Name and Nationality', provides in full that: '1. Every child shall have the right from his birth to a name 2. Every child shall be registered immediately after birth. 3. Every child has the right to acquire a nationality. States Parties to the present Charter shall undertake to ensure that their Constitutional legislation recognize the principles according to which a child shall acquire the nationality of the State in the territory of which he has been born if, at the time of the child's birth, he is not granted nationality by any other State in accordance with its laws.'

[67] *Covenant on the Rights of the Child in Islam* (n 65) art 7; *African Children's Charter* (n 66) art 6.

Although some of these universal and regional instruments provide certain limitations on the right of a child to acquire nationality from the country in which he or she is born (e.g. residence requirements in the *1961 Convention* and the *1997 ECN*), these limitations have since been significantly curtailed (procedurally and substantively) by the application of the principle of the best interests of the child, including in the case of refugee children or children of refugee parents.[68]

Several of the instruments discussed above also embody a provision against arbitrary deprivation of nationality as stated in Article 15(2) *UDHR*, thereby reinforcing the right to retain one's nationality.[69] Although no explicit provision on arbitrary deprivation of nationality exists in the *ICCPR*, the latter indirectly enshrines Article 15(2) through its general clause on non-discrimination (Article 26) because 'a major element of the prohibition of arbitrary deprivation of nationality is the prohibition of *discriminatory* deprivation of nationality'.[70]

According to Article 26, 'the law shall prohibit any discrimination and guarantee to all persons equal and effective protection against discrimination on any ground such as race, colour, sex, language, religion, political or other opinion, national or social origin, property, birth or other status'.

This general provision applies to nationality laws, including laws denying or withdrawing citizenship to persons. Indeed, the *ICCPR*'s Preamble expressly refers to the *UDHR*, and therefore its provisions on nationality and non-discrimination.

Neither the *European Convention on Human Rights* ('*ECHR*') nor the *African Charter on Human and Peoples' Rights* ('*African Charter*') explicitly mention nationality. However the right to a nationality (including against arbitrary deprivation of nationality) is protected under both instruments as an element of one's legal identity (Article 8 *ECHR*—'[e]veryone has the right to respect for his private life'),[71] and as one's legal status (Article 5 *African Charter*—everyone has the 'right to the respect of the dignity inherent in a human being and to the recognition of his legal status').[72] Indeed, in a recent decision, the African Court on Human and Peoples' Rights noted that while 'neither the Charter nor the ICCPR contains an

---

[68] The Committee on the Rights of the Child has played an important role in nudging states to ensure that every stateless child born on their territory is able to acquire a nationality automatically. See Gerard-René de Groot, 'Children, their Right to a Nationality and Child Statelessness' in Alice Edwards and Laura van Waas, *Nationality and Statelessness under International Law* (CUP 2014) 144; Inge Sturkenboom and Laura van Waas, 'How Real is the Risk of a "Stateless Generation" in Europe?: Reflections on How to Fulfil the Right to a Nationality for Children Born to Refugee and Migrant Parents in the European Union' (14 October 2016).

[69] See e.g., *1961 Convention* (n 51) arts 5–9; *Convention on the Rights of Persons with Disabilities* (n 53) art 18; *American Convention* (n 36) art 20(3); *ECN* (n 7) art 4c; *ASEAN Human Rights Declaration* (n 60) art 18; *Commonwealth Convention on Human Rights* (n 61) art 24(2); *Arab Charter 2004* (n 62) art 29.

[70] van Waas, *Nationality Matters* (n 3) 103. See also HRC Res 32/5 (n 55).

[71] See e.g., *Genovese v Malta* (2014) 58 EHRR 25 (hereafter *Genovese v Malta*); *Mennesson v France*, Application No 65192/11 (26 June 2014) (hereafter *Mennesson v France*); *Labassee v France*, Application No 65941/11 (26 June 2014) (hereafter *Labassee v France*).

[72] See e.g., *Modise v Botswana* (n 3).

Article that deals specifically with the right to nationality',[73] the *UDHR* is 'recognised as forming part of Customary International Law'.[74] Accordingly, 'the power to deprive a person of his or her nationality' must be exercised in accordance with Article 15(2) *UDHR*.[75]

Finally, regarding the specific context of state succession, the International Law Commission ('ILC') *Draft Articles on Nationality of Natural Persons in relation to the Succession of States* (soft law) also contains important provisions.[76]

Taking into account Article 15 *UDHR* and other human rights treaties, the Human Rights Council has repeatedly described the right to a nationality as a fundamental human right.[77] The right is 'intimately linked' to the principle of non-discrimination, the duty not to render anyone stateless, and the right to identity.[78] The UN Secretary General in his 2009 report on human rights and arbitrary deprivation of nationality stressed that 'the evolution of international human rights has fundamentally changed the traditional approach based on the preponderance of the interests of States over the interests of individuals'.[79] It further stated that,

[t]he right to a nationality implies the right of each individual to acquire, change and retain a nationality. The right to retain a nationality corresponds to the prohibition of arbitrary deprivation of nationality ... an explicit and general prohibition of arbitrary deprivation of nationality can be found in numerous international instruments.[80]

The UN General Assembly too recognizes the fundamental nature of the prohibition of arbitrary deprivation of nationality.[81]

---

[73] African Court on Human and Peoples' Rights, *Anudo Ochieng Anudo v United Republic of Tanzania*, Application No 012/2015 (22 March 2018) [76].

[74] ibid, [76].   [75] ibid, [78].

[76] International Law Commission (ILC), *Draft Articles on Nationality of Natural Persons in relation to the Succession of States with Commentaries* (1999). These include the right to the nationality of at least one of the states concerned (art 1); prevention of statelessness (art 4); a presumption of nationality based on habitual residence (art 5); respect for the will of the persons concerned (art 11); the right to a nationality based on *jus soli* for children born after the succession of states (art 13); non-discrimination (art 15); and the prohibition of arbitrary deprivation of nationality (in terms of denial of acquisition and withdrawal decisions concerning) (art 16).

[77] HRC Res 7/10 (27 March 2008) UN Doc A/HRC/RES/7/10; HRC Res 10/13 (26 March 2009) UN Doc A/HRC/RES/10/13 (hereafter HRC Res 10/13); HRC Res 13/2 (14 April 2010) UN Doc A/HRC/RES/13/2 (hereafter HRC Res 13/2); HRC Res 20/4 (16 July 2012) UN Doc A/HRC/RES/20/4 (hereafter HRC Res 20/4); HRC Res 20/5 (16 July 2012) UN Doc A/HRC/RES/20/5 (hereafter HRC Res 20/5); HRC Res 26/14 (11 July 2014) UN Doc A/HRC/RES/26/14; HRC Res 32/5 (n 55); HRC Res 32/7 (18 July 2016) UN Doc A/HRC/RES/32/7.

[78] HRC Res 32/5 (n 55).

[79] UN HRC, 'Human Rights and Arbitrary Deprivation of Nationality: Report of the Secretary-General' (14 December 2009) UN Doc A/HRC/13/34, para 20.

[80] ibid, para 21. See also UN HRC, 'Human Rights and Arbitrary Deprivation of Nationality: Report of the Secretary-General' (19 December 2011) UN Doc A/HRC/19/43 (on the impact of arbitrary deprivation of nationality on the enjoyment of human rights) (hereafter UN HRC, 'Human Rights and Arbitrary Deprivation of Nationality 2011'); UN HRC, 'Human Rights and Arbitrary Deprivation of Nationality: Report of the Secretary-General' (19 December 2013) UN Doc A/HRC/25/28, paras 7–22 (on the grounds and conditions to be met for deprivation to be lawful) (hereafter UN HRC, 'Human Rights and Arbitrary Deprivation of Nationality 2013').

[81] UNGA Res 50/152 (9 February 1996) UN Doc A/RES/50/152, para 16.

2.3 The right to a nationality: jurisprudence

A growing body of international jurisprudence, which reveals instances of intrusions by international law into states' exclusive domain of competence, unthinkable prior to 1948, points to two significant constraints on states' discretion in matters relating to nationality: the prohibition of arbitrary deprivation of nationality and the duty to prevent statelessness. These constraints largely derive from the treaty obligations outlined in Part 2.2, and in some specific respects embody general principles of international law, custom, or *jus cogens*.[82]

The principle of non-discrimination is the backbone of these constraints. Non-discrimination also provides a critical link to the definition of a refugee because it 'goes to the very foundation of the refugee law regime', in particular to the concept of persecution in Article 1A(2) of the *Convention relating to the Status of Refugees* ('*Refugee Convention*').[83] Indeed, it is generally accepted that persecution consists of serious human rights violations, severe discrimination, or the cumulative effect of various measures not in themselves amounting to persecution, focussing for instance on the adverse impact of discrimination on a person's life. Hence, the discussion below provides crucial context for the remainder of the book.

2.3.1 Non-discrimination, equality, and arbitrary deprivation of nationality

The principle of non-discrimination is closely intertwined with the principle of equality;[84] both are fundamental elements of international human rights law and are key in combatting gender inequality and racial intolerance in matters concerning nationality. For instance, Article 9 *CEDAW* refers specifically to non-discrimination in relation to acquisition, change, or retention of nationality, statelessness, and conferral of nationality to children,[85] although we note that as of today, at least twenty states have attached reservations to this provision.[86] Another instance is Article 5 of the *International Convention in the Elimination of All Forms of Racial Discrimination*

---

[82] In particular the prohibition on racial discrimination that is now recognized as a *jus cogens* norm: ACERWC, 'Decision No 002: *Institute for Human Rights and Development in Africa and the Open Society Justice Initiative (On Behalf of Children of Nubian Descent in Kenya) v Kenya*' (22 March 2011) Comm No 002/Com/002/2009, para 57 (hereafter *Children of Nubian Descent v Kenya*) [56].

[83] Rebecca Dowd, 'Dissecting Discrimination in Refugee Law: An Analysis of its Meaning and its Cumulative Effect' (2011) 23 IJRL 28, 31.

[84] See e.g., *UDHR* (n 33) preamble, arts 1, 7; *International Covenant on Civil and Political Rights* (adopted 16 December 1966, entered into force 23 March 1976) preamble, arts 3, 26 (hereafter *ICCPR*); *International Covenant on Economic, Social and Cultural Rights* (adopted 16 December 1966, entered into force 3 January 1976) 993 UNTS 3, Preamble, art 3 (hereafter *ICESCR*); *Protocol No 12 to the Convention for the Protection of Human Rights and Fundamental Freedoms* (entered into force 1 April 2005) ETS 177, Preamble, art 1 (hereafter *Protocol No 12 to the ECHR*). See also *Case of the Yean and Bosico Children* (n 3) [141].

[85] *CEDAW* (n 52) art 9. See Alice Edwards, 'Displacement, Statelessness and Questions of Gender Equality under the Convention on the Elimination of All Forms of Discrimination Against Women' (Background Paper, UNHCR Legal and Protection Policy Research Series, April 2009).

[86] See UN CEDAW, 'Declarations, Reservations, Objections and Notifications of Withdrawal of Reservations relating to the Convention on the Elimination of All Forms of Discrimination against Women' (10 April 2006) UN Doc CEDAW/SP/2006/2.

('*ICERD*'), which prohibits discrimination on ground of race, colour, or national or ethnic origin, in the enjoyment of the right to nationality.[87] This provision applies to all forms of deprivation of nationality, i.e. denial of access to and withdrawal of citizenship.[88] The tension between state sovereignty and individual rights in developing such norms is reflected in Article 1(3) of the *ICERD*, which provides that, 'Nothing in this Convention may be interpreted as affecting in any way the legal provisions of States Parties concerning nationality, citizenship or naturalization, provided that such provisions do not discriminate against any particular nationality.' However we note that the Committee on the Elimination of Racial Discrimination ('CERD') has stated in its General Recommendation 30 that states must '[r]ecognize that deprivation of citizenship on the basis of race, colour, descent, or national or ethnic origin is a breach of States Parties' obligations to ensure non-discriminatory enjoyment of the right to nationality'.[89] Further, Spiro notes that CERD has 'more aggressively scrutinized state conduct in the area in recent years',[90] and that the evolution of CERD's views, coupled with parallel developments in international law, 'points to a growing antidiscrimination metric for practices relating to the acquisition of citizenship'.[91] He cites as evidence of this change the fact that the 1997 *ECN* prohibits discrimination in nationality rules on the basis of race. This in turn reflects the earlier *1961 Convention*'s Article 9, which prohibits a state from depriving 'any person or group of persons of their nationality on racial, ethnic, religious or political grounds'.[92]

The principles of equality and non-discrimination are enshrined in all core human rights treaties.[93] Some provisions, such as Article 14 *ECHR*, prohibit 'discrimination on any ground such as sex, race, colour, language, religion, political or other opinion, national or social origin, association with a national minority, property, birth or other status', but only in the enjoyment of the rights and freedoms *set forth in the Convention*. However, Article 26 *ICCPR*, Article 24 of the *American Convention*, and Article 1 *Protocol No 12 to the ECHR*,[94] guarantee the principle

---

[87] *International Convention on the Elimination of All Forms of Racial Discrimination* (opened for signature 7 March 1966, entered into force 4 January 1969) 660 UNTS 195, art 5 (hereafter *ICERD*) — protection against discrimination on ground of race, colour, or national or ethnic origin, in the enjoyment of the right to nationality, freedom of movement, and the right to leave and return to one's country.

[88] UN Committee on the Elimination of Racial Discrimination ('CERD'), 'General Recommendation 30: Discrimination against Non-Citizens' (23 February–12 March 2004) UN Doc CERD/C/64/Misc.11/rev.3, paras 13–15 (hereafter CERD General Recommendation 30). The Committee further recommended state parties adopt measures to reduce statelessness, in particular among children: at para 16.

[89] ibid, para 14.   [90] Spiro, 'A New International Law of Citizenship' (n 16) 722.

[91] ibid.   [92] *1961 Convention* (n 51) art 9.

[93] See e.g., *ICCPR* (n 84) art 26; *ICESCR* (n 84) art 2(2); *ICERD* (n 87) art 1(4); *CEDAW* (n 52) arts 1, 4(1); *Framework Convention for the Protection of National Minorities* (adopted 10 November 1994, entered into force 1 February 1998) art 4(3). Note that this is not an exhaustive list of instruments embodying a clause of non-discrimination.

[94] *Protocol No 12 to the ECHR* (n 84) was adopted with the aim of strengthening the prohibition against racial discrimination. It contains a general clause against discrimination by any public authorities on the grounds of race, colour, language, religion, or national or ethnic origin, in the enjoyment of any rights *set forth by law*. Such prohibition no doubt applies to nationality laws: Council of Europe, 'Explanatory Report to the Protocol No 12 to the Convention for the Protection of Human Rights and

of non-discrimination as a self-standing provision in that they guarantee the equal recognition, enjoyment, and exercise of other human rights. In such a case, the non-discrimination/equality guarantee may be invoked regardless of the nature of the right affected. Hence, even where the substantive right may not otherwise be protected in the relevant treaty, for example where economic, social, or cultural rights are engaged, the discriminatory basis makes such matters also a violation of civil and political rights.

The principle of equality requires that equal situations be treated equally and unequal situations differently. Failure to do so will amount to discrimination, unless an objective and reasonable justification exists.[95]

Further elements that set protection against discrimination apart in each of the main human rights treaties are the grounds upon which discrimination is prohibited (e.g. race, colour, descent, or national or ethnic origin in the *ICERD* but race, colour, sex, language, religion, political or other opinion, national or social origin, property, birth, or other status in the *ICCPR*) and the context (e.g. acquisition of nationality at birth, naturalization, or withdrawal).[96] Hence, Laura van Waas warns that however tempted one might be to conclude that 'the right to a nationality and the prohibition of discrimination work in conjunction to forbid distinctions on any of the grounds listed in all domestic rules and practice on the attribution of nationality', the reality is more complex.[97] This points to the need for precision in identifying the relevant norm or guarantee being invoked in a particular case. In other words, not every distinction in nationality laws will constitute a violation of international law; one must be clear that the distinction implicates a protected ground and that it in fact amounts to discrimination.

These guarantees, set out in both universal and regional instruments, have been embraced by international courts and adjudicators of human rights such that there is an emerging jurisprudence exploring the interaction between human rights norms and state discretion in matters of nationality. This jurisprudence highlights the importance of provisions on equality and non-discrimination in the context of nationality (particularly in matters concerning naturalization and arbitrary deprivation).

2.3.1.1 Discrimination in the context of naturalization

Article 26 of the *ICCPR* (the equality and non-discrimination provision) has been applied by the UN Human Rights Committee to strengthen the enjoyment of the

---

Fundamental Freedoms' (Rome 4 November 2000) para 22 (hereafter Council of Europe Committee of Ministers Recommendation (2000)). It entered into force in 2005 and has been ratified by twenty states (out of forty-seven members of the Council of Europe): Council of Europe, 'Chart of Signatures and Ratifications of Treaty 177' (*Council of Europe*, 21 January 2019) <http://www.coe.int/en/web/conventions/search-on-treaties/-/conventions/treaty/177/signatures?p_auth=0Kq9rtcm> accessed 22 January 2019.

[95] For instance, in its case law under *ECHR* art 14, the European Court of Human Rights has made reference to the 'principle of equality of treatment' (*Belgian Linguistic Case (No 2)* (1968) 1 EHRR 252 [10]), and to 'the equality of the sexes' (*Abdulaziz, Cabales and Balkandali v United Kingdom* (1985) 7 EHRR 471 [78]).

[96] van Waas, *Nationality Matters* (n 3) 103–14.   [97] ibid, 105.

right to citizenship through naturalization. In *Q v Denmark*, the Human Rights Committee recalled:

neither the Covenant nor international law in general spells out specific criteria for the granting of citizenship through naturalization and that States are free to decide on such criteria. However, when adopting and implementing legislation, States parties' authorities must respect the applicants' rights enshrined in article 26. The Committee recalls in this respect that article 26 requires reasonable and objective justification and a legitimate aim for distinctions that relate to an individual's characteristics enumerated in article 26, including 'other status' such as disability.[98]

Hence, if a state required the same level of language proficiency when applying for naturalization from a person with mental and learning difficulties (namely, severe psychosis and various physical disorders) as from anyone else, without any justification as to why this disability does not form the basis for a language exception provided for in the law relating to citizenship, this would constitute a violation of Article 26. That said, in other situations of naturalization, not involving a disability, language can be viewed as a legitimate requirement for eligibility to nationality, 'fall[ing] within the margin of appreciation reserved to the state',[99] thereby confirming that 'naturalization remains more robustly within the discretion of states'.[100]

Discrimination is also a major element of the prohibition of arbitrary deprivation of nationality. Case law on this issue can be found in the Americas, Africa, and Europe.

2.3.1.2 Arbitrary deprivation of nationality

The Inter-American Court of Human Rights, in the *Case of Ivcher-Bronstein v Peru*, held that arbitrary deprivation (withdrawal) of nationality constituted a violation of Article 20 of the *American Convention* (right to nationality) because the annulment of Mr Bronstein's nationality was not consensual and the procedure used to annul the nationality did not comply with provisions of domestic law; therefore it was arbitrary.[101] The Court found the state of Peru to have failed in its general obligation to respect the rights and freedoms recognized in the *American Convention*, as well as in its duty 'to organize the public authorities in order to ensure to all persons subject to its jurisdiction the free and full exercise of human rights'.[102] Peru's international responsibility was therefore engaged under international human rights law. As a result, Mr Bronstein's nationality was restored, and reparation and payment of compensation granted.

---

[98] UN Human Rights Committee, 'Communication No 2001/2010: *Q v Denmark*' (19 May 2015) UN Doc CCPR/C/113/D/2001/2010, para 7.3.

[99] *Constitution of Costa Rica Case* (n 35) para 63.

[100] Edwards, 'The Meaning of Nationality' (n 13) 18.

[101] *Case of Ivcher-Bronstein v Peru* (Merits, Reparations and Costs) Inter-American Court of Human Rights Series C No 74 (6 February 2001) [93] (hereafter *Bronstein v Peru*). For a full discussion of the Inter-American Court of Human Right's ('IACtHR') jurisprudence on nationality, see Marie-Bénédicte Dembour, *When Humans Become Migrants: Study of the European Court of Human Rights with an Inter-American Counterpoint* (OUP 2015) 130–54, 282–351.

[102] *Bronstein v Peru* (n 101) [168].

Four years later, in the *Case of the Yean and Bosico Children v Dominican Republic*, the Inter-American Court of Human Rights ruled that the prohibition on racial discrimination and the principle of equality before the law apply to access to nationality. It held:

> The determination of who has a right to be a national continues to fall within a State's domestic jurisdiction. However, its discretional authority in this regard is gradually being restricted with the evolution of international law, in order to ensure a better protection of the individual in the face of arbitrary acts of States. Thus, at the current stage of the development of international human rights law, this authority of the States is limited, on the one hand, by their obligation to provide individuals with the equal and effective protection of the law and, on the other hand, by their obligation to prevent, avoid and reduce statelessness.
>
> The Court considers that the peremptory legal principle of the equal and effective protection of the law and non-discrimination determines that, when regulating mechanisms for granting nationality, States must abstain from producing regulations that are discriminatory or have discriminatory effects on certain groups of population when exercising their rights.[103]

The Court further held that 'the obligation to respect and ensure the principle of the right to equal protection and non-discrimination is irrespective of a person's migratory status in a State', hence this principle applies to everyone 'without any discrimination based on regular or irregular residence, nationality, race, gender or any other cause'.[104] Indeed, 'The migratory status of a person cannot be a condition for the State to grant nationality.'[105] It is worth noting here that the Court seems to have introduced a new ground for non-discrimination in the context of nationality, namely migratory status.[106]

The Court ruled that the Dominican Republic's discriminatory application of its domestic laws and regulations (including its Constitution) on citizenship and birth registration made children of Haitian descent stateless and denied them their right to nationality for discriminatory reasons; 'the State failed to grant nationality to the children, which constituted an arbitrary deprivation of nationality'.[107] It follows from this case that discrimination in the access to nationality can constitute arbitrary deprivation of nationality under international human rights law.

Unfortunately, this judgment had the opposite effect to that intended and, on 23 September 2013, the Constitutional Tribunal ruled that anyone born and granted citizenship at birth, whose parents' migration status could not be proved, must have their nationality withdrawn. Further, this had retrospective effect back to 1929.[108]

---

[103] *Case of the Yean and Bosico Children* (n 3) [140]–[141].   [104] ibid, 155.

[105] ibid, 156.

[106] See also CMW and CRC Joint General Comment No 4, 23 (2017) (n 57) para 25; CMW and CRC Joint General Comment No 3, 22 (2017) (n 57).

[107] *Case of the Yean and Bosico Children* (n 3) [174]. See also *Gelman v Uruguay* (Merits and Reparations) Inter-American Court of Human Rights Series C No 221 (24 February 2011) [121], where the Inter-American Court of Human Rights considered the case of a child who had been kidnapped from her Argentinian parents and transferred to another family of Uruguayan citizenship resulting in the loss of her true identity. The Court recalled that a child is entitled to special protection under the *American Convention* as interpreted in harmony with provisions in the UN *CRC*.

[108] Liliana Gamboa and Julia Harrington Reddy, 'Judicial Denationalisation of Dominicans of Haitian Descent' (2014) (46) Forced Migration Review 52.

One year later, in the *Case of Expelled Dominicans and Haitians v Dominican Republic*,[109] the Inter-American Court of Human Rights ruled again that: 'The criteria used by the TC [Constitutional Tribunal] is discriminatory and contrary to the principle of equality before the law, since it ignores the characteristics of the person born in the DR [Dominican Republic] and focuses on the lack of documentation of their parents, without justifying this distinction.'[110]

One of the leading cases on nationality in Africa is *Modise v Botswana*.[111] In this case, the African Commission on Human and Peoples' Rights held the right to human dignity and recognition of his or her legal status, protected in Article 5 of the *African Charter*, to include the right to a nationality and protection against arbitrary deprivation of nationality.[112] It also found the denial of the right to citizenship by birth to be in violation of Article 3(2) of the *Charter*, namely, the right to equal protection of the law.[113] The Commission further found the repetitive expulsion from one state without the right to enter another state, caused by the Government of Botswana's failure to recognize the applicant's nationality, to constitute inhuman or degrading treatment under Article 5 of the *African Charter*, and to violate his rights to family life, freedom of movement, to leave and to return to his own country, property, and equal access to the public service of his country under the same *Charter*.[114]

In *Malawi African Association v Mauritania*,[115] a case concerning systematic violations of human rights, ethnic discrimination, arbitrary deprivation of nationality, and forced expulsion to Senegal and Mali, the African Commission on Human and Peoples' Rights held the eviction of Black Mauritanians from their houses and the deprivation of their Mauritanian citizenship to constitute a violation of their right to freedom of movement and residence within their own state, i.e. Mauritania.[116]

In *Children of Nubian Descent in Kenya v Kenya*, ACERWC held the practice of making children wait until they turn eighteen years of age to apply to acquire a nationality to be racially and ethnically discriminatory, as well as disproportionate and unnecessary to the protection of the state interest. It held:

The African Committee is not convinced, especially in relation to a practice that has led children to be stateless for such a long period of time, that the current discriminatory treatment of the Government of Kenya in relation to children of Nubian descent is 'strictly proportional

---

[109] *Case of Expelled Dominicans and Haitians v Dominican Republic* (Preliminary Objections, Merits, Reparations and Costs) Inter-American Court of Human Rights Series C No 282 (28 August 2014).

[110] Francisco Quintana, 'Inter-American Court Condemns Unprecedented Situation of Statelessness in the Dominican Republic' (*European Network on Statelessness*, 27 October 2014) <https://www.statelessness.eu/blog/inter-american-court-condemns-unprecedented-situation-statelessness-dominican-republic> accessed 12 November 2018 (citations omitted). ibid, [317].

[111] *Modise v Botswana* (n 3).

[112] ibid, [89]. See also African Commission on Human and Peoples' Rights, '234: Resolution on the Right to Nationality' (23 April 2013).

[113] *Modise v Botswana* (n 3) [89].   [114] ibid, 92–97.

[115] African Commission on Human and Peoples' Rights, 'Communication Nos 54/91, 61/91, 98/93, 164/97, 196/97, 210/98: *Malawi Africa Association v Mauritania*' (11 May 2000).

[116] ibid, [126]. *African (Banjul) Charter on Human and Peoples' Rights* (adopted 27 June 1981, entered into force 21 October 1986) 21 ILM 58, art 12(1) (hereafter *African Charter*) provides: 'Every individual shall have the right to freedom of movement and residence within the borders of the State provided he abides by the law.'

with' and equally importantly 'absolutely necessary' for the legitimate state interest to be obtained. The Committee is of the view that measures should be taken to facilitate procedures for the acquisition of a nationality for children who would otherwise be stateless, and not the other way round. As a result of all the above, the African Committee finds a violation of Article 3 of the African Children's Charter.[117]

The Committee of Experts further took 'the view that there is a strong and direct link between birth registration and nationality. This link is further reinforced by the fact that both rights are protected in the same Article under the African Children's Charter (as well as the UN Convention on the Rights of the Child).'[118]

According to settled case law of the ECtHR on Article 14 *ECHR*, discrimination means treating differently persons in similar situations, without an objective and reasonable justification. 'No objective and reasonable justification' means that the distinction at hand does not pursue a 'legitimate aim' or that there is not a 'reasonable relationship of proportionality between the means employed and the aim sought to be realised'.[119] However, as previously mentioned in this section, Article 14 *ECHR* only prohibits discrimination in '[t]he enjoyment of the rights and freedoms *set forth in the Convention*', and the right to a nationality is nowhere to be found in the *ECHR*.

Genovese v Malta constitutes a breakthrough in this legal quandary with the Strasbourg Court recognizing nationality as an inherent part of a person's social identity, protected as such an element of private life (Article 8 *ECHR*).[120] The Court further held Maltese citizenship law to be discriminatory and a serious violation of human rights (Article 14 in conjunction with Article 8) because it denied Maltese citizenship to an illegitimate child in cases where the illegitimate offspring was born to a non-Maltese mother and a Maltese father. This judgment therefore illustrates a clear departure from some of the earlier decisions where the (then) European Commission of Human Rights generally rejected such applications on the ground that Article 14 *ECHR* only prohibits discrimination with respect to the enjoyment of a right protected in the *Convention*, and that 'the right to acquire a particular nationality is neither covered by, nor sufficiently related to, this or any other provision of the Convention'.[121] The Court's new approach was confirmed in *Mennesson v France* and *Labassee v France*, two cases which also involved children's

---

[117] *Children of Nubian Descent v Kenya* (n 82) [57]. See also ACERWC, 'General Comment on Article 6 of the African Charter on the Rights and Welfare of the Child' (16 April 2014) ACERWC/GC/02.

[118] *Children of Nubian Descent v Kenya* (n 82) [42]. For a successful application of this ruling by a domestic court, see Supreme Court of Appeal of South Africa, *Minister of Home Affairs v DGLR*, Appeal Case No 1051/2015 (6 September 2016), confirming High Court of Pretoria, South Africa, *DGLR v Minister of Home Affairs*, Case No 38429/13 (3 July 2014)—where the Supreme Court ordered the government of South Africa to register an eight-year-old girl as South African by birth; the government had argued that although her parents were Cuban, she had no right to Cuban citizenship.

[119] *DH v Czech Republic* (2008) 47 EHRR 3, [175], [196].

[120] *Genovese v Malta* (n 71).

[121] See *Family K and W v Netherlands*, Application No 11278/84 (1 July 1985) 220 on the admissibility of the application.

right to a nationality.[122] The Court held that by refusing to register, in France, the birth certificates of children born in the United States from surrogacy arrangements (and whose biological fathers were French), the French authorities had weakened the children's identity within French society, and undermined their claim to French nationality. It therefore found a violation of Article 8 *ECHR* (private life).

However, in a completely different context, namely fraud, the Court has been willing to provide states with a broader margin of appreciation. In *Ramadan v Malta*, the Court considered the decision of the Maltese authorities to deprive the applicant of his Maltese citizenship (because of alleged fraud through marriage) not to be arbitrary, despite the risk of statelessness and the fact that he was a fully integrated member of the Maltese community with three children of Maltese citizenship.[123] Recently also, the Strasbourg Court rejected the application of Articles 10 and 11 (freedom of expression and assembly) to an applicant who had been denied nationality through naturalization based on his lack of loyalty to the state.[124] The Court explained 'that a "right to nationality" similar to that in art.15 of the Universal Declaration of Human Rights, or a right to acquire or retain a particular nationality, is not guaranteed by the Convention or its Protocols', although an arbitrary denial of nationality might exceptionally raise an issue under Article 8 if such a refusal has an impact on the individual's private life.[125] According to the Court, 'neither the Convention nor international law in general provides for the right to acquire a specific nationality':[126]

The issue whether or not the applicant has an arguable right to acquire citizenship of a state must in principle be resolved by reference to the domestic law of that state. Similarly, the question whether a person was denied a state's citizenship arbitrarily in a manner that might raise an issue under the Convention is to be determined with reference to the terms of the domestic law.[127]

Thus, the overall interaction of the ECtHR with the right to a nationality remains limited (a state of exception), which is disappointing considering the 'intimate link' between the right to identity (Article 8 *ECHR*) and the right of nationality, as reiterated by the Human Rights Council in Resolution 32/5.[128]

Another point worthy of note is the absence of consideration of deprivation of nationality (resulting in statelessness) in terms of treatment contrary to Article 3 *ECHR* in the Strasbourg case law. Indeed, we could not find any cases where arbitrary deprivation of nationality per se or statelessness had been argued (by an applicant) before the ECtHR in direct relation to a violation of Article 3 *ECHR*

---

[122] *Mennesson v France* (n 71); *Labassee v France* (n 71). See also *Foulon and Bouvet v France*, Application Nos 9063/14, 10410/14 (21 July 2016).
[123] *Ramadan v Malta* (2017) 65 EHRR 32. These findings are strongly rejected by Judges Pinto de Albuquerque and Zupančič in their dissenting opinions. See also Marie-Bénédicte Dembour, 'Ramadan v Malta: When Will the Strasbourg Court Understand that Nationality is a Core Human Rights Issue?' (*Strasbourg Observers*, 22 July 2016) <https://strasbourgobservers.com/2016/07/22/ramadan-v-malta-when-will-the-strasbourg-court-understand-that-nationality-is-a-core-human-rights-issue/> accessed 12 November 2018.
[124] *Petropavlovskis v Latvia* (2017) 65 EHRR 7.   [125] ibid, [73].   [126] ibid, [83].
[127] ibid, [84].   [128] HRC Res 32/5 (n 55) para 11.

(prohibition against torture, inhuman, or degrading treatment or punishment).[129] A possible explanation may be that it is very difficult to argue a tangible detriment under Article 3 *ECHR* where the threshold is higher than under Article 8 *ECHR*. However, related acts (such as arbitrary detention or the risk of expulsion) that could be connected to statelessness have been held to constitute treatment contrary to Article 3 *ECHR* by the ECtHR.[130] The same may be said of the jurisprudence in other regions, as evidenced in the case of *Modise v Botswana* decided by the African Commission on Human and Peoples' Rights discussed at 2.3.1.2.

This analysis reveals that the right to nationality has come to be understood as a core human rights issue. This is acknowledged in the case law of the Inter-American Court of Human Rights, the African Commission on Human and Peoples' Rights, the ACERWC, and the ECtHR. The overall picture is that the broad perspective of 'arbitrary deprivation' of nationality (i.e. arbitrary denial *and* withdrawal of nationality) is prohibited under international human rights law, based on the right to equal protection of the law, the right to non-discrimination, the right to a nationality, the right to human dignity, and the right to private life (legal identity). However, so far there has been a lack of arguments before, and therefore decisions by, courts acknowledging arbitrary deprivation as inhuman and degrading treatment or punishment, even when it leads to statelessness.

2.3.1.3 Discrimination and the duty to prevent statelessness

As leading researchers on statelessness have argued, '[m]ost stateless people are the victims of ineffective governance, political restructuring or discrimination by the states in which they live' and 'elements of discrimination and inequality are common to all forms of statelessness'.[131] The linkage between statelessness and discrimination

---

[129] Some interesting arguments were nevertheless made *by the applicant* in a decision from the old European Commission of Human Rights (*Harabi v Netherlands*, Application No 10798/84 (5 March 1986)), where the applicant submitted that his situation as a stateless person should have a bearing on the application of art 3 *ECHR*. The Commission accepted that 'the repeated expulsion of an individual, whose identity was impossible to establish, to a country where his admission is not guaranteed, may raise an issue under Article 3 (Art. 3) of the Convention'—it referred in particular to its decision in *Giama v Belgium*, Application No 7612/76 (17 July 1980), where the difficulty arising from seeking to expel an applicant without any papers to a country where he may be refused entry, was found to be admissible (at [31]) but was not dealt with any further because a settlement was reached. However, the Commission found the applicant (Mr Harabi) responsible for his predicament since he could have applied for Algerian nationality and been admitted there. It therefore rejected the application as manifestly ill-founded on all accounts (*ECHR* arts 3 and art 5(1)f).

[130] For instance, in *Kim v Russia*, Application No 44260/13 (17 July 2014) (hereafter *Kim v Russia*) the European Court of Human Rights found a violation of art 3 *ECHR* based on the conditions of Mr Kim (a person who had become stateless following the dissolution of the USSR) pending his (impossible-to-enforce) expulsion to a state that did not recognize him as one of its nationals, namely Uzbekistan, and which therefore refused to accept him on its territory. In *Daoudi v France*, Application No 19576/08 (3 December 2009), the European Court of Human Rights found that the deportation of the applicant to Algeria on grounds of national security (he was alleged to have been involved with a radical Islamic group) would constitute a violation of art 3 *ECHR*, but the revocation of his French nationality was not mentioned by the Court.

[131] Brad K Blitz and Maureen Lynch (eds), *Statelessness and Citizenship: A Comparative Study on the Benefits of Nationality* (Edward Elgar 2011) 4–5.

is indeed very strong.[132] To be a stateless person is to be 'a person who is not considered as a national by any State under the operation of its law';[133] this definition has acquired the status of customary international law.[134] As indicated in the sections above, the duty imposed on states to prevent, avoid, and reduce statelessness is established in a number of treaties, including the *1930 Hague Convention* and Protocol, the *1961 Convention*, and the *Convention on the Rights of the Child*. Numerous regional treaty provisions, interpreted by human rights courts, also enshrine an obligation on states to grant nationality if the person would otherwise be stateless. Indeed, the right to a nationality (including the right not to be arbitrarily deprived of one's nationality) is closely connected to the duty to prevent statelessness.

The links between arbitrary deprivation of nationality and statelessness have long been recognized by the Human Rights Council.[135] In its latest Resolution 32/5, the Human Rights Council acknowledged that 'incidents of discriminatory deprivation of nationality . . . have been a source of widespread suffering and statelessness in the past'. It also recalled that 'arbitrarily depriving a person of his or her nationality may lead to statelessness', and in this regard it expressed concern at 'various forms of discrimination against stateless persons that may violate obligations of States under international human rights law'.[136]

Statelessness often occurs as a result of direct discrimination touching on the right to a nationality itself (i.e. a person is treated less favourably and is denied access to nationality or deprived of her nationality because of her political opinions, race, ethnicity, or gender). Direct discrimination plays an important role in many causes of statelessness, such as the existence of discriminatory laws (e.g. laws preventing women from conferring their nationality onto their children), state succession, with persons belonging to ethnic minorities often becoming stateless (e.g. Eritreans in Ethiopia or Russians in Latvia), or racial discrimination (e.g. Rohingya in Myanmar).[137] The Human Rights Council has repeatedly acknowledged that 'the arbitrary deprivation of nationality disproportionately affects persons belonging to minorities'.[138]

---

[132] Amal de Chickera and Joanna Whiteman, 'Discrimination and the Human Security of Stateless People' (2014) 46 Forced Migration Review 56 (hereafter Chickera and Whiteman, 'Discrimination and the Human Security of Stateless People'). See also Amal de Chickera and Joanna Whiteman, 'Addressing Statelessness through the Rights to Equality and Non-Discrimination' in Laura van Waas and Melanie J Khanna (eds), *Solving Statelessness* (Wolf Legal Publishers 2016) 99.

[133] *Convention relating to the Status of Stateless Persons* (adopted 28 September 1954, entered into force 6 June 1960) 360 UTNS 117, art 1 (hereafter *1954 Convention*).

[134] UNGA, 'Report of the International Law Commission: Fifty-Eighth Session' UN GAOR 61st Session Supp No 10 UN Doc A/61/10 (Draft Articles on Diplomatic Protection with Commentaries) (2006) chIV(E)(1) (hereafter ILC Draft Articles on Diplomatic Protection).

[135] HRC Res 32/5 (n 55) Preamble. See also e.g., HRC Res 10/13 (n 77); HRC Res 13/2 (n 77); HRC Res 20/5 (n 77).

[136] HRC Res 32/5 (n 55) Preamble.

[137] Inter-Parliamentary Union and UNHCR, *Nationality and Statelessness: A Handbook for Parliamentarians No 22* (2014)) 30. See also Chickera and Whiteman, 'Discrimination and the Human Security of Stateless People' (n 132).

[138] HRC Res 32/5 (n 55) Preamble. See also e.g., HRC Res 10/13 (n 77); HRC Res 13/2 (n 77).

Once stateless, a person is particularly vulnerable to both direct and indirect discrimination touching on the effects of a lack of nationality (i.e. she is put at a disadvantage by a particular practice or provision which cannot be objectively justified or is disproportionate). For instance, the UN Human Rights Council considers that 'all persons, particularly women and children, without nationality or without birth registration are vulnerable to trafficking in persons and other abuses and violations of their human rights'.[139] In its Resolution 32/5, the Human Rights Council also emphasized that 'the statelessness of a person resulting from the arbitrary deprivation of his or her nationality cannot be invoked by States as a justification for the denial of other human rights'[140] and questioned whether deprivation of nationality can ever be proportionate to the interest to be protected 'in the light of the severe impact of statelessness, and to consider alternative measures that could be adopted'.[141]

In sum, the right to a nationality is a fundamental human right. Although its regulation remains largely an internal matter for states (there is still no universally guaranteed right to a nationality for everyone, except for children), international human rights law has evolved to impose significant constraints on states' discretion in this domain, namely, the right of non-discrimination, the prohibition against arbitrary deprivation of nationality, and the duty to prevent statelessness, which are all embodied in treaty law and soft law. Given the prevalence of discrimination as an ongoing and endemic cause of arbitrary deprivation of nationality and statelessness, the principle of non-discrimination is a vital safeguard; the role of international courts and adjudicators of human rights has been instrumental and there is now an emerging jurisprudence safeguarding the protection of the right to a nationality as an individual right against state discretion. The duty to prevent statelessness, which sits alongside the prohibition against arbitrary deprivation of nationality, has helped to give it further content.

This provides a vital foundation for refugee decision-makers when presented with cases in which applicants submit that deprivation of nationality and/or statelessness constitutes persecution. In our view, refugee decision-makers have a responsibility to ensure that their decisions are not mired in outdated assumptions about absolute sovereignty, and instead reflect the significant constraints now imposed on states in nationality matters by virtue of international human rights law.

2.3.1.4 Lawful withdrawal of nationality (and guarantees against statelessness)

Notwithstanding the progressive developments outlined in 2.3.1.3, there exist limited circumstances in which a state can lawfully deprive its nationals of nationality. It is important to outline briefly what these circumstances are because where they are present, this may argue against a successful claim on refugee (or complementary) protection grounds.

International law envisages that exceptionally states may lawfully withdraw nationality in certain circumstances, if the act pursues a legitimate aim and complies

---

[139] HRC Res 20/4 (n 77) Preamble.   [140] HRC Res 32/5 (n 55) para 3.
[141] ibid, para 16.

with the principle of proportionality, and the person concerned does not become stateless following loss of his or her nationality.[142]

Indeed, withdrawal of nationality on the ground of disloyalty and imposed by an individual decision has long been lawful. In his 1952 report on 'Nationality, Including Statelessness', Manley Hudson, Special Rapporteur observed that:

the tendency to provide for denationalization on the ground of disloyalty is increasing; a number of recently enacted nationality laws provide for this possibility. Disloyalty is considered to consist in evasion of military service, illegal emigration, refusal to return on request of the authorities, hostile association, desertion from the armed forces, committing of treason or of other activities prejudicial to the interests of the State.[143]

Article 7(1) of the 1997 *ECN* lists the following grounds for the lawful withdrawal of nationality *so long as it does not lead to statelessness*:

a. voluntary acquisition of another nationality;

b. ...

c. voluntary service in a foreign military force;

d. conduct seriously prejudicial to the vital interests of the State Party;[144]

e. lack of a genuine link between the State Party and a national habitually residing abroad;

f. where ... preconditions ... are no longer fulfilled;

g. adoption of a child if the child acquires or possesses the foreign nationality of one or both of the adopting parents.

Article 8(1) of the *ECN* further guarantees individuals the right to renounce a nationality provided they do not thereby become stateless.

Only most exceptionally can a state lawfully deprive a national of its nationality even where such an act would result in statelessness. Both the *1961 Convention* and the 1997 *ECN* allow for such possibility in very specific circumstances. Article 8(2) (b) of the *1961 Convention* contemplates deprivation of nationality obtained by misrepresentation or fraud even where it would lead to the person being stateless.[145] Further grounds of deprivation of nationality (even where it would lead to statelessness) are provided in Article 8(3) 'if at the time of signature, ratification or accession' the country in question made a reservation specifying its intention to retain the right

---

[142] *1961 Convention* (n 51) art 8(1); *ECN* (n 7) arts 4(b), 7(1), 7(3). See also ILC, 'Draft Articles on Nationality of Natural Persons in relation to the Succession of States with Commentaries' (1999) art 25.

[143] Manley O Hudson, 'Report on Nationality, Including Statelessness' (12 February 1952) UN Doc A/CN.4/50, 18.

[144] Council of Europe, 'Explanatory Report to the European Convention on Nationality' (Strasbourg 6 November 1997) (hereafter Explanatory Report to the ECN) explains that '[s]uch conduct notably includes treason and other activities directed against the vital interests of the State concerned (for example work for a foreign secret service) but would not include criminal offences of a general nature, however serious they might be'.

[145] Other permissible grounds are provided in art 8(2)(a).

to deprive individuals of their nationality that existed in its national law at that time, for example conduct seriously prejudicial to the vital interests of the state.[146]

Article 7(1)(b), read together with Article 7(3) of the 1997 *ECN*,[147] similarly allows deprivation of nationality, even if resulting in statelessness, if nationality has been obtained by means of fraudulent conduct, false information, or concealment of any relevant fact attributable to the applicant, under the theory of abuse of rights; these exceptions are to be interpreted restrictively.[148] In such cases, under the *ECN*, 'States are free either to revoke the nationality (loss) or to consider that the person never acquired their nationality (void ab initio)',[149] and practice varies in each contracting state. For instance, the United Kingdom considers British citizenship acquired fraudulently by impersonation (i.e., false representations about one's identity) as 'null' or void *ab initio*, and no right of appeal is provided in such cases, although judicial review might be allowed. However, where the fraud concerns other matters, nationality is said to be 'lost' and a (non-suspensive) right of appeal exists.[150]

It may be noted that in the EU, withdrawal of the nationality of one of the EU Member States on ground of deception, where the person would become stateless as a result and therefore lose EU citizenship, is a matter for EU law (Article 20 *Treaty on the Functioning of the European Union*) and must comply with the requirements of proportionality, namely, be justified by reasons of public interest and be proportionate to the aim pursued, having regard to the consequences that such act may have on her or his family, and the rights inherent in EU citizenship.[151]

The past decade has seen a renewed interest in legislative provisions allowing for deprivation of nationality in the context of so-called 'home-grown' terrorists on the ground of conduct seriously prejudicial to the vital interests of the state. As mentioned above, this possibility is contemplated in both the 1997 *ECN* and the *1961 Convention*, although the 1997 *ECN* does not tolerate statelessness resulting from such deprivation. Legislation allowing or strengthening governments' power to revoke the citizenship of suspected 'foreign fighters' has been introduced

---

[146] On the UK's declaration under art 8(3), see Guy S Goodwin-Gill, 'Mr Al-Jedda, Deprivation of Citizenship, and International Law' (Seminar, Middlesex University, 14 February 2014) 4. The points made in that paper were further developed in Guy S Goodwin-Gill, 'Deprivation of Citizenship Resulting in Statelessness and its Implications in International Law' (Opinion Piece, 12 March 2014); Guy S Goodwin-Gill, 'Deprivation of Citizenship Resulting in Statelessness and its Implications in International Law: Further Comments' (6 April 2014); Guy S Goodwin-Gill, 'Deprivation of Citizenship Resulting in Statelessness and its Implications in International Law: More Authority (If It Were Needed . . .)' (5 May 2014).

[147] *ECN* (n 59).

[148] See e.g., Case C-135/08 *Rottmann v Bayern* [2010] ECR I–1449 (hereafter *Rottmann v Bayern*): it is not contrary to EU law for a Member State to withdraw from a citizen of the Union the nationality of that Member State acquired by naturalization when the nationality was obtained by deception, on condition that the decision to withdraw complies with the principle of proportionality.

[149] Explanatory Report to the ECN (n 144) art 7(1)(b).

[150] For a critique of this distinction, see Adrian Berry, 'Who Are You? Fraud, Impersonation and Loss of Nationality Without Procedural Protection' (*European Network on Statelessness*, 25 June 2014) <http://www.statelessness.eu/blog/who-are-you-fraud-impersonation-and-loss-nationality-without-procedural-protection> accessed 12 November 2018.

[151] *Rottmann v Bayern* (n 148).

in a number of countries, for example Australia, Israel, the United Kingdom, and Belgium. However, it has been resisted in some other countries (e.g. France), and reversed in others (e.g. Canada), suggesting that the trend is not linear.[152] These issues are considered in the context of the examination of Persecution (Chapter 5) and Exclusion (Chapter 6).

Part 3: Nationality and the Enjoyment of Human Rights in International Law

This Part of the chapter now turns to consider the significance of having a nationality, in particular by examining the evolution of the concept in international law that enjoyment of certain rights is conditional on possessing a nationality. This is an important question for refugee lawyers because, as will be explored in Chapter 4, not having a nationality is not in and of itself sufficient to qualify for refugee protection. One has to establish a well-founded fear of being persecuted for reasons of race, religion, nationality, membership of a particular social group, or political opinion, and an inability to return to one's country of former habitual residence. While Part 2 provides important context to a refugee claim anchored in a denial or withdrawal of nationality, this Part provides the necessary background to assess a claim based on a denial of other human rights. As will be established, the advent of international human rights law means that international law no longer conditions access to rights on nationality; in other words, even those without a nationality are entitled to the enjoyment of human rights within their country of former habitual residence. As such, a violation of those rights may also be central to a claim of persecution.

3.1 The traditional function of nationality

Traditionally, the two principal 'rights' attached to nationality were the state's duty of (re)-admission of its nationals, and the right of states to exercise diplomatic protection. These are well-established attributes of nationality. In addition, nationals could exercise political rights.

3.1.1 *State's duty of (re)-admission of its nationals*

During the sixteenth and seventeenth centuries, scholars such as Francisco de Vitoria and Hugo Grotius asserted a right to travel (e.g. to practice trade), grounded in natural law or derived from natural law, as part of a broader right to communication between peoples, provided no harm was done to 'the natives'.[153] Both conceived the right to travel in terms of departure and admission whereby the right to leave one's

---

[152] To read more on this, see Michelle Foster and Hélène Lambert, 'Statelessness as a Human Rights Issue: A Concept Whose Time Has Come' (2016) 28 IJRL 564, 581–83 (hereafter Foster and Lambert, 'Statelessness as a Human Rights Issue').
[153] Chetail, 'The Transnational Movement of Persons' (n 19) 11.

own country and the right to admission into another country exist 'in one single continuum' (i.e. a general principle of free movement).[154] In the seventeenth century, Samuel Pufendorf, whilst still recognizing the right of every man to migrate at his pleasure, saw the right to leave as a free-standing right, separate from the general principle of free movement; admission, on the other hand, fell into the domain of sovereignty.[155] This 'normative disjuncture' soon became conventional wisdom, and was embraced, for instance, by Emer de Vattel in the eighteenth century.[156]

In the nineteenth and early part of the twentieth centuries, the practice of states as 'civilized nations' (*'droit positif interne'* which continued to be based primarily on liberal values) regarded both nationals of a state (namely, subjects or citizens) and aliens within a state (i.e. *étrangers*) to be members of that state based on their relationship with that state; the key difference was that nationals alone had an unconditional right to enter the territory of the state of their nationality, whereas aliens did not.[157]

The 1930 Hague Conference on the codification of the rules of international law on nationality in particular considered the issue of nationals who are abroad at the moment their nationality is withdrawn, observing that unless they have acquired the nationality of another state, they will be stateless. According to the doctrine of the 1920s and 1930s, frustration of the right of the state of sojourn to expel these persons as a result of the state of (former) nationality refusing to receive them would constitute a 'clear case of abuse of rights', whether or not a third state is willing to receive the expelled persons.[158] However, following sharp divide amongst states, the Final Act of the Hague Conference only agreed to recommend that in such instances of statelessness, states 'examine whether it would be desirable that . . . the State whose nationality he last possessed should be bound to admit him to its territory, at the request of the country where he is'.[159] Expulsion and refusal to re-admit one's nationals are ongoing challenges, including recent attempts by some states to expel or refuse readmission to their own nationals after stripping them of their nationality,[160]

---

[154] ibid.

[155] ibid. See also Satvinder Singh Juss, *International Migration and Global Justice* (Ashgate 2006).

[156] Chetail, 'The Transnational Movement of Persons' (n 19) 11–12.

[157] Ernst Isay, 'De la nationalité' in *Recueil des cours*, vol 5 (Académie de Droit International 1924) 429, 448 (hereafter Isay, 'De la nationalité').

[158] Lawrence Preuss, 'International Law and Deprivation of Nationality' (1935) 23 GeoLJ 250, 269. The 'denationalization' (and resulting statelessness) of persons who remain in their own country would *at the time* have no consequences in *public* international law but it would in *private* international law: at 270.

[159] ibid, 271–72.

[160] For instance, in *Pham v Secretary of State for the Home Department* [2015] UKSC 19, the UK Supreme Court ('UKSC') considered whether a British naturalized citizen from Vietnam (Mr Pham), who took no steps to renounce his Vietnamese citizenship acquired at birth, could lawfully be deprived of his British citizenship under s 40(2) of the *British Nationality Act 1981* on ground of suspicion of involvement in terrorist activities. The difficulty arose from the fact that the Vietnamese government had subsequently made clear that it would no longer regard him as a national of Vietnam, hence the Home Secretary's decision would render him stateless (which would be contrary to s 40(4) of the *British Nationality Act 1981*). The UKSC (in agreement with the UK Court of Appeal) held unanimously that art 1(1) of the *1954 Convention*, which defines a stateless person as 'a person who is not considered as a national by any State under the operation of its law', is concerned with the law, and not with a government's position that may render the appellant stateless as a matter of fact. Since Mr Pham was still

with the primary difference that the duty to prevent statelessness has gained considerable force in international law since 1930.[161] The key point is that traditionally the right to be admitted to a state was confined to nationals, and hence represented one of the most important attributes or benefits of possessing a nationality.

3.1.2 Diplomatic protection

The general rule on diplomatic protection was first laid out in the *Panevezys-Saldutiskis Railway Case* in 1939.[162] The Permanent Court of International Justice held:

> In taking up the case of one of its nationals, by resorting to diplomatic action or international judicial proceedings on his behalf, a State is in reality asserting its own right, the right to ensure in the person of its nationals respect for the rules of international law.... it is the bond of nationality between the State and the individual which alone confers upon the State the right of diplomatic protection, and it is as a part of the function of diplomatic protection that the right to take up a claim and to ensure respect for the rules of international law must be envisaged.[163]

As this quote indicates, although the exercise of diplomatic protection may in practice benefit an individual, it is not conceived of as an individual right but rather a right on the part of the state to exercise its discretion. In 1955, the International Court of Justice issued a landmark judgment on the issue of nationality in *Nottebohm*.[164] The case concerned a claim by Liechtenstein against Guatemala for the expulsion and seizure of property of Mr Nottebohm in 1943. Nottebohm was born in Germany in 1881 and had German nationality until his naturalization by Liechtenstein. In 1905, he transferred his residence and business to Guatemala, remaining there until 1943 without ever applying for Guatemalan citizenship. During those years, he occasionally travelled to Germany and a few times to Liechtenstein on holiday. In 1939, a month after the outbreak of the war, as he was visiting Liechtenstein, he applied for naturalization, thereby forfeiting his German nationality. In 1943, he was arrested in Guatemala, deported, and interned in the United States as an enemy alien (having been a German citizen). During his internment, the Guatemalan government instituted legal proceedings against Nottebohm to expropriate his substantial property in Guatemala (worth several million dollars) without compensation. After his release from internment, Nottebohm was refused entry into Guatemala and established his residence in Liechtenstein in 1946. Guatemala argued that Liechtenstein's claim for restitution of property and compensation on Nottebohm's behalf was inadmissible on the ground that Liechtenstein could not extend diplomatic protection to Nottebohm in a claim against Guatemala. The Court upheld

---

technically a national of Vietnam under the law of that country at the time of the order of deprivation of British citizenship, the Court took the view that the Home Secretary could not be held responsible for Mr Pham's statelessness; rather, it was the responsibility of the Vietnamese government.

[161] See discussion above at 2.3.1.4 on lawful deprivation of nationality.

[162] *Panevezys-Saldutiskis Railway Case* (Judgments, Orders and Advisory Opinions) 1939 PCIJ Rep Series A/B No 76.

[163] ibid, 16.   [164] *Nottebohm Case* (n 6).

Guatemala's objection, and declared that his naturalization by Liechtenstein could not be accorded international recognition. Hence Liechtenstein was precluded from extending its diplomatic protection to Nottebohm vis-à-vis Guatemala. It held:

> To exercise protection, to apply to the Court, is to place oneself on the plane of international law. It is international law which determines whether a State is entitled to exercise protection and to seise the Court. The naturalization of Nottebohm was an act performed by Liechtenstein in the exercise of its domestic jurisdiction. The question to be decided is whether that act has the international effect under consideration.[165]
>
> ...
>
> Conferred by a State, it only entitles that State to exercise protection vis-à-vis another State, if it constitutes a translation into juridical terms of the individual's connection with the State which has made him its national.[166]

Accordingly, diplomatic protection is firmly established as a right of states—not of an individual—determined by international law.[167] A state's assertion that a person possesses its nationality (in accordance with its own laws) is not conclusive evidence of that fact for the purpose of exercising diplomatic protection. It does nevertheless create a strong presumption, rebuttable in the absence of a meaningful social content, i.e. the genuine link approach.[168]

---

[165] ibid, 20–21.   [166] ibid, 23.

[167] The position of the International Law Commission is that states will use birth, descent, and naturalization as 'the connecting factors for the conferment of nationality', a state is not required 'to prove an effective or genuine link between itself and its national ... as an additional factor for the exercise of diplomatic protection': ILC Draft Articles on Diplomatic Protection (n 134) art 4 commentary, 32–33. The ILC took the view that the findings in *Nottebohm* should be limited to the facts of the case, and did not aim to create a general rule applicable to all states: at 33. See also Alice Sironi, 'Nationality of Individuals in Public International Law—A Functional Approach' in Alessandra Annoni and Serena Forlati (eds), *The Changing Role of Nationality in International Law* (Routledge 2013) 54 (hereafter Sironi, 'Nationality of Individuals in Public International Law').

[168] Jennings and Watts (eds), *Oppenheim's International Law* (n 5) 854–56. Note also contemporary examples of national legislation that reject the formal (legal) approach to nationality in favour of the sociological membership to a community (e.g., Israel, Greece, and the United Arab Emirates): de Castro, 'La nationalité' (n 15) 565–67. It may be noted that the decision in *Nottebohm*, to prioritize Mr Nottebohm's social and economic links with Guatemala over his juridical links with Liechtenstein on the international plane, has been strongly criticized for a number of reasons. First, it has been criticized for failing to protect the interest of individuals who do not possess sufficient ties with their state of nationality, for instance if they have lived abroad for a long period of time. This is recognized as a common feature 'in today's world of economic globalization and migration': ILC Draft Articles on Diplomatic Protection (n 134) art 4 commentary, 33. See also Sironi, 'Nationality of Individuals in Public International Law' (n 167) 58. Secondly, it has been criticized for undermining states' right to exercise diplomatic protection in respect of their nationals and for extending this right to third states: through an extension of the 'effective nationality' principle to cases of single nationality where there is no conflict and no choice: Hans Goldschmidt, 'Recent Applications of Domestic Nationality Laws by International Tribunals' (1959) 28 Fordham LRev 689 (hereafter Goldschmidt, 'Recent Applications of Domestic Nationality Laws'). Finally, it has been criticized for weakening the legal concept of nationality and states' own nationality laws in favour of a sociological approach to nationality. For the suggestion of an open and flexible approach more in tune with contemporary nationality's diverse functions, see Robert D Sloane, 'Breaking the Genuine Link: The Contemporary International Legal Regulation of Nationality' (2009) 50 Harv Int'l LJ 1; Carol A Batchelor, 'Statelessness and the Problem of Resolving Nationality Status' (1998) 10 IJRL 156. *Nottebohm* was further rejected in the *Flegenheimer* decision, albeit not necessarily for the correct reason: To read more on this point, see Goldschmidt, 'Recent Applications of Domestic Nationality Laws'.

The possession of a nationality has traditionally been fundamental to the enjoyment of diplomatic protection and thus one of the core benefits of nationality. However, there exists one exception, in soft law, to the general rule that a state might exercise diplomatic protection on behalf of its nationals only. The ILC Draft Articles on Diplomatic Protection (Article 8(2)) explicitly provides that in the case of refugees (including stateless refugees), the state that may exercise diplomatic protection shall be the state of the refugee's new lawful and habitual residence (and not the state of nationality).[169] Described as '[o]ne of the most revolutionary provisions of the ILC Draft Articles on Diplomatic Protection', this provision acknowledges the particular vulnerability of refugees against their state of nationality (or in the case of stateless refugees against their country of former habitual residence) and emphasizes their need for protection, in this case diplomatic protection.[170] Thus, the context in which a state may exercise diplomatic protection includes cases involving non-nationals. However, state discretion in this area remains strong and not all states have implemented these provisions.[171]

3.1.3 Political rights

Pre-1930s, in Europe and the Americas (the then 'civilized nations'), aliens or *étrangers* were generally recognized as legal subjects for the exercise of essential civil, socio-economic, and cultural rights, bearing in mind that these '*droits internationaux de l'homme*' were rather limited at the time and only started to be actionable internationally by individuals after the Second World War. The only exception to aliens or *étrangers* being able to exercise rights as legal subjects concerned political rights, which were reserved to nationals.[172] It is noteworthy that at the time (pre-1930s), the concept of *étranger* did not include the *heimatlos* or *apatrides* (stateless) who were considered on a par with cases of dual or multiple nationality as a 'danger' for the individual and the state,[173] and were denied all possibility to acquire the necessary documents indispensable for accessing basic civil rights, unlike aliens or *étrangers*.[174]

---

[169] ILC Draft Articles on Diplomatic Protection (n 134) art 8 commentary, paras 47–51. A similar provision exists for stateless persons who are not also refugees (art 8(1)); they can seek protection from their state of habitual and lawful residence on the ground that no issue of being 'unable or unwilling' to avail themselves of the protection of their own state arises. The terms 'lawful and habitual residence' are based on the 1997 *ECN* art 6(4)(g), where they are used in connection with the acquisition of nationality.

[170] Annemarieke Vermeer-Künzli, 'Diplomatic Protection and Consular Assistance of Migrants' in Vincent Chetail and Céline Bauloz (eds), *Research Handbook on International Law and Migration* (Edward Elgar 2014) 265, 272–73. The law on state responsibility *erga omnes* or on the nationality of claims may nonetheless apply in such a situation.

[171] For instance, in the UK, '[t]he protection of stateless persons and refugees is not a matter which Her Majesty's Government regard as falling within the scope of the concept of diplomatic protection as that is understood in current international law', although representations may be made very exceptionally and considerations of *non-refoulement* would need to be considered. See Mark Symes and Peter Jorro, *Asylum Law and Practice* (2nd edn, Bloomsbury Professional 2010) 320.

[172] A Verdross, 'Les règles internationales concernant le traitement des étrangers' in *Recueil des cours*, vol 37 (Académie de Droit International 1931) 339. Ernst Isay, for instance, notes that to let an alien go destitute and starve hungry would be contrary to *jus gentium*: Isay, 'De la nationalité' (n 157) 452.

[173] Isay, 'De la nationalité' (n 157) 438.

[174] Vichniac, 'Le statut international des apatrides' (n 23) 216.

In sum, the 'traditional' position in international law was that nationality was pivotal in a state's rights and obligations in respect of the exercise of diplomatic protection, the duty to re-admit their nationals from abroad, and the extension of political rights. International law was, however, largely silent on the treatment of those resident *within* a state's territory; meaning that those without nationality were entirely subject to the discretion of the state in which they resided in relation to fundamental civil, political, social, and economic rights. It in this regard that the post-Second World War era has witnessed fundamental change, to which we now turn.

3.2 Nationality and the enjoyment of human rights in the post-Second World War era

In addition to imposing constraints on state discretion in matters relating to acquisition and retention of nationality, considered in Part 2, international human rights law requires that everyone, regardless of their nationality or lack of, enjoy certain rights within a country. Of course, in practice many states do not accord equal rights to all those within its territory or jurisdiction, with lack of citizenship often being a marked distinction. Indeed, in some cases it is precisely this deprivation of rights for reasons of nationality (or non-nationality) that is the basis of refugee claims brought by stateless persons, as will be explored in Chapter 5. An understanding of the international human rights framework and its application to stateless persons is hence crucial to a principled application of the *Refugee Convention* to stateless persons.

3.2.1 *The right to return*

One of the most important—if not *the* most important—benefit of nationality is the right to return to one's country of nationality.[175] It is hence noteworthy that Article 12(4) of the *ICCPR* enshrines the right of everyone not to be 'arbitrarily deprived of the right to enter his own country'.

The Human Rights Committee has read this provision to include 'the right to return after having left one's own country' as well as the right 'to come to the country for the first time if he or she was born outside the country' (e.g. the person's country is the person's state of nationality).[176] It also held the right to return to be 'of the utmost importance for refugees seeking voluntary repatriation'.[177]

In addition, the UN Human Rights Committee has played a key role in consolidating protection of the right to return and the right to be admitted to one's own

---

[175] *UDHR* (n 33) art 13: '(1) Everyone has the right to freedom of movement and residence within the borders of each state. (2) Everyone has the right to leave any country, including his own, and to return to his country.' The *New York Declaration for Refugees and Migrants* reaffirms the commitment of the community of states to this right: UNGA Res 71/1 (3 October 2016) UN Doc A/RES/71/1, para 42, annex I para 11(a) (hereafter *New York Declaration*).
[176] UN Human Rights Committee, 'CCPR General Comment No 27: Article 12 (Freedom of Movement)' (2 November 1999) UN Doc CCPR/C/21/Rev.1/Add.9, para 19 (hereafter UN Human Rights Committee General Comment No 27).
[177] ibid. See also *New York Declaration* (n 175) para 75.

country. In its General Comment on Article 12 *ICCPR* (freedom of movement), the Human Rights Committee explained that 'the right to enter his own country' is there to protect everyone against forced exile or from being denied return, and that importantly:

The scope of 'his own country' ... is not limited to nationality in a formal sense, that is, nationality acquired at birth or by conferral; it embraces, at the very least, an individual who, because of his or her special ties to or claims in relation to a given country, cannot be considered to be a mere alien. This would be the case, for example, of nationals of a country who have there been stripped of their nationality in violation of international law, and of individuals whose country of nationality has been incorporated in or transferred to another national entity, whose nationality is being denied them. The language of article 12, paragraph 4, moreover, permits a broader interpretation that might embrace other categories of long-term residents, including but not limited to stateless persons ... In no case may a person be arbitrarily deprived of the right to enter his or her own country.[178]

The Human Rights Committee applied this reasoning to a case involving a national who wished to resist removal to his country of nationality due to his stronger ties to 'his own country', where he had lived for most of his life but did not possess nationality. In a departure from the majority views in *Stewart v Canada*,[179] the Human Rights Committee, in *Nystrom v Australia*,[180] took the view that the deportation of a Swedish national by Australia to Sweden was arbitrary based on two elements. The first element was that there are factors 'other than nationality which may establish close and enduring connections between a person and a country, connections *which may be stronger than those of nationality*';[181] hence, in this case, his 'own country' within the meaning of Article 12(4) *ICCPR* was Australia 'in the light of the strong ties connecting him to Australia, the presence of his family in Australia, the language he speaks, the duration of his stay in the country and the lack of any other ties than nationality with Sweden'.[182] The second element was 'that there are few, if any, circumstances in which deprivation of the right to enter one's own country could be reasonable',[183] thereby equating the right to enter one's own country to the right of a national to enter her country of nationality. It may be noted that the Committee's disregard for any link to nationality in favour of long-term residence and social ties

---

[178] UN Human Rights Committee General Comment No 27 (n 176) paras 20–21.

[179] UN Human Rights Committee, 'Communication No 538/1993: *Stewart v Canada*' (16 December 1996) UN Doc CCPR/C/58/D/538/1993, para 12.5: when 'the country of immigration facilitates acquiring its nationality, and the immigrant refrains from doing so, either by choice or by committing acts that will disqualify him from acquiring that nationality, the country of immigration does not become "his own country" within the meaning of article 12, paragraph 4, of the Covenant'. For an application of *Stewart*, see UN Human Rights Committee, 'Communication No 675/1995: *Toala v New Zealand*' (22 November 2000) UN Doc CCPR/C/70/D/675/1995.

[180] UN Human Rights Committee, 'Communication No 1557/2007: *Nystrom v Australia*' (1 September 2011) UN Doc CCPR/C/102/D/1557/2007, (hereafter *Nystrom v Australia*).

[181] ibid, para 7.4 (emphasis added).   [182] ibid, para 7.5.

[183] ibid, paras 7.5, 7.6. See also UN Human Rights Committee, 'Communication No 1959/2010: *Warsame v Canada*' (1 September 2011) UN Doc CCPR/C/102/D/1959/2010, paras 8.4–8.6 (hereafter *Warsame v Canada*).

was criticized by a minority of Committee members because it risks extending 'a kind of *de facto* second nationality to vast numbers of resident non-nationals'.[184]

Notwithstanding the dissenting view, this decision is to be applauded for its recognition that where there is a strong and effective connection between a non-national and a state, often particularly pronounced in the case of a stateless person born and habitually resident in that state, it is not open to the state to disregard this fundamental right to enter one's own country merely on the basis of domestic citizenship laws.[185]

Analogous reasoning can be found in the ECtHR's approach to assessing the legality of deportation of long-term residents in light of the right to private life, which is increasingly understood as encompassing 'the totality of social ties between settled migrants and the community in which they are living'.[186]

Further, the unique status and hence corresponding duty of states in relation to stateless persons has been increasingly recognized by the ECtHR. For example, in *Kim v Russia*, the Court held that in cases where expulsion is not possible because the country of birth and previous residence fails to recognize him as one of its nationals and refuses to admit him, detention for the purpose of deportation under Article 5(1)(f) is unlawful. In such cases, the expelling state (which is also the new country of residence) must take all necessary steps to ensure that the state of reception will issue the travel document; these steps must be taken without delay. The Court took special notice of 'the applicant's particularly vulnerable situation' as a stateless person, including his inability to benefit from consular assistance and advice, his lack of family connections, and financial resources.[187] The Court further noted, in the context of remedial measures (Article 46 *ECHR*), that the applicants' status as a stateless person put him at risk of being re-arrested and put in detention; hence, the Russian Government must take the necessary preventive measures to avoid this from happening.[188]

---

[184] Individual Opinion of Human Rights Committee members Gerald, Neuman and Iwasawa (dissenting), and Rodley (Sir), Keller and O'Flaherty (dissenting) in *Nystrom v Australia* (n 180) [3.5], also referred to in *Warsame v Canada* (n 183).

[185] This is not necessarily the view of the community of states (the *New York Declaration* (n 175) para 42 refers to states' obligation to re-admit 'their returning nationals': at annex I para 11(b)). See also European Commission, 'Communication from the Commission to the European Parliament, the European Council, the Council and the European Investment Bank on Establishing a New Partnership Framework with Third Countries under the European Agenda on Migration' (Strasbourg, 7 June 2016) COM (2016) 385 final. However, in the context of international cooperation and partnership framework of readmission agreements, the preferred terminology seems to be whether persons who are not permitted to stay 'can return ... to their countries of origin or nationality': *New York Declaration* (n 175) para 58.

[186] *Maslov v Austria* (2008) 47 EHRR 20, cited by Foster and Lambert, 'Statelessness as a Human Rights Issue' (n 152) 13. See also Council of Europe Committee of Ministers Recommendation (2000) (n 94) 15 concerning the security of long-term migrants.

[187] *Kim v Russia* (n 130) [54].

[188] ibid, [73]–[74]. See also *Hoti v Croatia*, Application No 63311/14 (26 April 2018) (hereafter *Hoti v Croatia*), where the European Court of Human Rights recognized the special situation of the applicant as a 'stateless migrant'.

This suggests that international law's capacity to demand recognition of at least certain rights accrued on a basis other than nationality in appropriate cases may yet be further developed.

3.2.2 *The enjoyment of human rights in one's country of habitual residence*

Human rights instruments by nature guarantee rights *regardless of citizenship*. Human Rights Committee General Comment No 31, for instance, reminds us that pursuant to Article 2(1) *ICCPR*:

the enjoyment of Covenant [ICCPR] rights is not limited to citizens of States Parties but must also be available to all individuals, regardless of nationality or *statelessness*, such as asylum seekers, refugees, migrant workers and other persons, who may find themselves in the territory or subject to the jurisdiction of the State Party.[189]

As originally stated by the Human Rights Committee in its General Comment No 15, 'the general rule is that each one of the rights in the Covenant [ICCPR] must be guaranteed without discrimination between citizens and aliens'.[190]

Indeed, all core international human rights treaties prohibit discrimination on the ground of nationality.[191] In particular, the *International Covenant on Economic, Social and Cultural Rights* ('*ICESCR*') which, together with the *ICCPR* comprises the so-called 'International Bill of Rights', provides that states must 'undertake to guarantee that the rights enunciated in the present Covenant will be exercised without discrimination of any kind as to race, colour, sex, language, religion, political or other opinion, national or social origin, property, birth or other status'.[192] The Economic Committee has reiterated that, '[t]he Covenant rights apply to everyone including non-nationals, such as refugees, asylum-seekers, stateless persons, migrant workers and victims of international trafficking, regardless of legal status and documentation'.[193]

In other words, a state may not deprive those stateless persons within its territory or jurisdiction of basic human rights on the basis of their citizenship alone, unless the distinction can be justified in accordance with international law. The default position is that a distinction must be justified as seeking to achieve a legitimate end by invoking appropriate and justified means.

---

[189] UN Human Rights Committee, 'General Comment No 31: The Nature of the General Legal Obligation Imposed on States Parties to the Covenant' (26 May 2004) UN Doc CCPR/C/21/Rev.1/Add. 13, para 10 (emphasis added).

[190] UN Human Rights Committee, 'General Comment No 15: The Position of Aliens under the Covenant' (11 April 1986) para 2 (hereafter UN Human Rights Committee General Comment No 15).

[191] In addition, the International Court of Justice has recognized that there exist certain obligations that states owe 'the international community as a whole' because all states have a legal interest in their protection (obligations *erga omnes*), independently from issues of nationality; this is the case in particular of the norms against slavery and racial discrimination: *Barcelona Traction, Light and Power Company, Limited (Belgium v Spain)* (Second Phase) [1970] ICJ Rep 3, 32 [33]–[34].

[192] *ICESCR* (n 84) art 2(2).

[193] UN Economic and Social Council, 'General Comment 20: Non-Discrimination in Economic, Social and Cultural Rights (2 July 2009) UN Doc E/C.12/GC/20, para 30 (hereafter UN Economic and Social Council General Comment 20).

The jurisprudence emanating from international human rights bodies suggests that distinctions based on citizenship will be closely scrutinized. For example, in *Gratzinger v Czech Republic*,[194] the UN Human Rights Committee held that the application of national legislation, which lays down a citizenship requirement for the restitution of confiscated property, where the state is basically responsible for the loss of citizenship, violates the applicants' rights under Article 26 of the *ICCPR*. In particular, it recalled its views in a similar case:

the authors in that case and many others in analogous situations had left Czechoslovakia because of their political opinions and had sought refuge from political persecution in other countries, where they eventually established permanent residence and obtained a new citizenship. Taking into account that the State party itself is responsible for the author's … departure, it would be incompatible with the Covenant to require the author … to obtain Czech citizenship as a prerequisite for the restitution of [his] property or, alternatively, for the payment of appropriate compensation.[195]

Jurisprudence from regional bodies suggests a willingness to intervene to protect the rights of stateless persons where appropriate. For example, in *Kuric v Slovenia*,[196] a case regarding the stripping of permanent residence from a population, some of whom had previously already been made stateless following state succession, the ECtHR found a violation of Article 8 *ECHR* on the ground that the applicants had been denied the possibility of preserving their legal status as permanent residents in Slovenia (they had been 'erased'). In particular, the Court found the interference (namely, the legislative measure) to lack the necessary standards of foreseeability and accessibility for it to be 'in accordance with the law'.[197] The Court then observed that the 'erasure' resulted in 'a number of adverse consequences, such as the destruction of identity documents, loss of job opportunities, loss of health insurance, the impossibility of renewing identity documents or driving licences, and difficulties in regulating pension rights'.[198]

It concluded:

the regularisation of the residence status of former SFRY citizens was a necessary step which the State should have taken in order to ensure that failure to obtain Slovenian citizenship would not disproportionately affect the art.8 rights of the 'erased'. The absence of such regulation and the prolonged impossibility of obtaining valid residence permits have upset the fair balance which should have been struck between the legitimate aim of the protection of national security and effective respect for the applicants' right to private or family life or both.[199]

Hence, Article 8 *ECHR* had been violated.[200]

---

[194] UN Human Rights Committee, 'Communication No 1463/2006: *Gratzinger v Czech Republic*' (25 October 2007) UN Doc CCPR/C/91/D/1463/200 (hereafter *Gratzinger v Czech Republic*).
[195] ibid, para 7.4, quoting UN Human Rights Committee, 'Communication No 586/1994: *Adam v Czech Republic*' (23 July 1996) UN Doc CCPR/C/57/D/586/1994, para 12.6.
[196] *Kuric v Slovenia* (2013) 56 EHRR 20 (hereafter *Kuric v Slovenia*).   [197] ibid, [346].
[198] ibid, [356]. See also *Kim v Russia* (n 130) [73].   [199] *Kuric v Slovenia* (n 196) [359].
[200] But see *Abuhmaid v Ukraine*, Application No 31183/13 (12 January 2017) for a failed attempt to see the status of Mr Abuhmaid (of Palestinian origin) as a long-term resident migrant regularized under arts 8 and 13 *ECHR*.

In *Andrejeva v Latvia*, the ECtHR held Latvia responsible, under Article 14 *ECHR* (non-discrimination) taken in conjunction with Article 1 of *Protocol No 1*, for a stateless person who was a 'permanently resident non-citizen' of Latvia, 'the only state with which she has any stable legal ties and thus the only state which, objectively, can assume responsibility for her in terms of social security'.[201] Hence a host state may no longer rely exclusively on the link of nationality to fulfil its *socio-economic* obligations; lack of nationality itself is not a legitimate ground for treating permanently resident non-citizens and citizens differently when it comes to pension entitlements. It may be worthwhile pointing out here that the 'permanently resident non-citizens' in this case are a specific category under Latvian law and are in fact stateless for the purposes of international law; their statelessness thus appears to have been central to the court's reasoning.[202] Similarly in *Hoti v Croatia*, the applicant had been unable to regularize his residence status permanently.[203] The Court concluded that Croatia's failure to regularize Mr Hoti's residence status in Croatia, despite having lived there for forty years as a 'stateless migrant', amounted to a violation of Article 8 *ECHR* (private life). Again, the Court's reasoning appears to have hinged on the applicant's statelessness and explicit reference was made to the 1954 *Convention relating to the Status of Stateless Persons*.

3.2.3 Exceptions to the principle of equality between nationals and non-nationals in international human rights treaties

Notwithstanding the default position of equality between citizens and non-citizens resident in a state, there exist exceptions to the rule that everyone (i.e. nationals and non-nationals) enjoys the same rights; as exceptions, these provisions should be interpreted restrictively. Thus, Article 25 *ICCPR* is expressly applicable only to citizens (i.e. rights to conduct public affairs, to vote, and to equal access to public service),[204] while Article 13 *ICCPR* applies only to aliens (i.e. procedural safeguards against arbitrary expulsions of aliens lawfully in the territory of a state, except when 'compelling reasons of nationality security' so require).[205]

In terms of social and economic rights, the text of the *ICESCR* underlines the importance of non-discrimination on specific grounds, including, most relevantly, birth and other status. The Committee on Economic, Social and Cultural Rights has explained, in relation to the explicitly protected ground 'birth', that '[d]istinctions must therefore not be made against those who are ... born of stateless parents'.[206] In

---

[201] *Andrejeva v Latvia* (2010) 51 EHRR 28 [88]. See also *Zeibek v Greece*, Application No 46368/06 (9 July 2009).
[202] We are grateful to Laura van Waas for this point. [203] *Hoti v Croatia* (n 188).
[204] No distinctions are permitted between citizens; distinctions between persons entitled to citizenship by birth or by naturalization 'may raise questions of compatibility with article 25': UN Human Rights Committee, 'General Comment No 25: Article 25 (Participation in Public Affairs and the Right to Vote) The Right to Participate in Public Affairs, Voting Rights and the Right of Equal Access to Public Service' (12 July 1996) UN Doc CCPR/C/57/D/586/1994 para 3. See also CERD General Recommendation 30 (n 88) para 3.
[205] No discrimination may be made between different categories of aliens in the application of art 13: UN Human Rights Committee General Comment No 15 (n 190) paras 2, 9, 10.
[206] UN Economic and Social Council General Comment 20 (n 193) para 26.

relation to 'other status', the Committee makes clear that this includes nationality and that,

[t]he ground of nationality should not bar access to Covenant rights, e.g., all children within a State, including those with an undocumented status, have a right to receive education and access to adequate food and affordable health care. The Covenant rights apply to everyone including non-nationals, such as refugees, asylum-seekers, stateless persons, migrant workers and victims of international trafficking, regardless of legal status and documentation.[207]

There is, however, one exception in Article 2(3) *ICESCR*, which states: 'Developing countries, with due regard to human rights and their national economy, may determine to what extent they would guarantee the economic rights recognized in the present Covenant to non-nationals.'

While there is little guidance available from the Economic Committee, basic principles of interpretation must be borne in mind in relation to this provision. The overarching principle is that this represents an exception to the general rule of non-discrimination and should hence be read narrowly. In addition, it is noteworthy that the text is inherently limited: it applies only to developing countries and to economic rights. Further and importantly, it requires a nuanced assessment, not blanket prohibition or deprivation, in requiring such states to consider, 'with due regard to human rights and their national economy', 'to what extent' they would guarantee such rights to non-nationals.[208]

Where there is ambiguity in a treaty's meaning, as in this case, reference to the *travaux* may illuminate.[209] Manisuli Ssenyonjo observes that Article 2(3) was proposed by Indonesia's delegate to the drafting committee 'in order to protect the rights of the nationals of former colonies, which had recently gained independence from colonial domination, against powerful economic groups of non-nationals who control important sectors of the economy'.[210] The purpose, in his view, could be said to 'end the domination of certain economic groups of non-nationals during colonial and post-colonial times'.[211] This is also supported by the consensus of leading scholars as embodied in the *Limburg Principles*.[212]

In short, therefore, great caution should be exercised before assuming that a state is justified in any discrimination against non-nationals based on Article 2(3) of the *ICECSR*, an issue to which we will return in Chapter 5.

A similar issue is raised by Article 1(2) of the *ICERD*, which contemplates the possibility of differentiating between citizens and non-citizens.[213] The Committee

[207] ibid, para 30. See also CERD General Recommendation 30 (n 88).

[208] James Hathaway and Michelle Foster, *The Law of Refugee Status* (2nd edn, CUP 2014) 234–35.

[209] See *Vienna Convention on the Law of Treaties* (adopted 22 May 1969, entered into force 27 January 1980) 1155 UTNS 331, art 32.

[210] Manisuli Ssenyonjo, *Economic, Social and Cultural Rights in International Law* (Hart 2016) 147.

[211] ibid.

[212] UN Commission on Human Rights, 'Note Verbale dated 5 December 1986 from the Permanent Mission of the Netherlands to the United Nations Office at Geneva Addressed to the Centre for Human Rights' (8 January 1987) UN Doc E/CN.4/1987/17, para 43 ('Limburg Principles').

[213] *ICERD* (n 87) art 1(2): 'This Convention shall not apply to distinctions, exclusions, restrictions or preferences made by a State Party to this Convention between citizens and non-citizens.'

on the Elimination of Racial Discrimination, however, recommends that state parties to the *Convention, as appropriate to their circumstances*, adopt measures relating to the full enjoyment of rights in the areas of education, housing, employment, and health, on an equal basis between citizens and non-citizens.[214]

Part 4: Conclusion

Nationality is the legal bond between a person and a state; it is what links individuals with international law. This legal bond also creates certain obligations on states vis-à-vis other states, including the obligation to (re-)admit one of its nationals from abroad. This bond continues to be determined by nationality laws. However, the content and operation of these laws has changed considerably under the influence of international human rights law, and with it the role of nationality in the protection and enjoyment of human rights.

As stated by the UN Secretary-General in his Report of 2009:

> the evolution of international human rights has fundamentally changed the traditional approach based on the preponderance of the interests of States over the interests of individuals.... the right of States to decide who their nationals are is not absolute and that, in particular, States must comply with their human rights obligations concerning the granting of nationality. This approach has been further evidenced in the practice of regional human rights courts.[215]

This chapter has examined how nationality has expanded from being a state's right to being also an individual right. The international human rights legal framework regulating nationality has been instrumental in this regard. Indeed, it has resulted in ever more constraints on states in matters relating to nationality. In particular, the prohibition on non-discrimination has had a major impact on the development and strengthening of the prohibition on arbitrary deprivation of nationality. The contribution of regional human rights courts and soft law in this matter has also been discussed. These developments have been very significant; however, international law still falls short of recognizing statelessness itself, or indeed arbitrary deprivation of nationality as constituting inhuman or degrading treatment or punishment. Rather the *expulsion* of a stateless person, or the repetitive expulsion from one state without the right to enter another state, caused by the failure to recognize an individual's nationality, may constitute inhuman or degrading treatment.

This chapter has also examined the expansion of human rights law to extend protection to all those within the territory or jurisdiction of a state, regardless of citizenship. While it is still the case that nationality is 'amongst the most important rights a state can assign to individuals',[216] human rights law encapsulates a broader vision of social, economic, and cultural inclusion that is not conditioned on citizenship.[217]

---

[214] CERD General Recommendation 30 (n 88) paras 29–38.
[215] HRC, 'Human Rights and Arbitrary Deprivation of Nationality' (n 2) para 20 (citations omitted).
[216] ILA, 'Final Report on Women's Equality' (n 39) 10.
[217] Kesby, *The Right to Have Rights* (n 15) 85–90.

These developments are important in the context of this book because our thesis is that international refugee law ought to be interpreted in a manner that is consistent with broader (relevant) developments in international law, especially human rights law. This chapter explained how the right to a nationality has come to be recognized as a human right essential to a person's integrity and inherent human dignity. Hence, restrictions on that right may in some circumstances constitute persecution or serious harm for the purpose of refugee law. Similarly given that human rights law extends the 'right to enjoy rights' to those without a nationality, a restriction on such rights may also constitute persecution in refugee law.

It has been observed that 'an injustice often involves two components—an injury and a continued withholding of what it is that the victim of the injustice has a right to'.[218] In that case, persons deprived of their nationality suffer a great injustice: the act of deprivation of nationality (injury) and the continued withholding from the enjoyment of the rights associated with nationality.[219] It is to this injustice that Chapters 4 and 5 now turn.

---

[218] Jeremy Waldron, 'Supersession and Sovereignty' (Julius Stone Address, University of Sydney, 3 August 2006) n 44.

[219] UN HRC, 'Human Rights and Arbitrary Deprivation of Nationality' (n 80) para 4 (citations omitted): 'Any interference with the enjoyment of nationality has a significant impact on the enjoyment of rights. Therefore, loss or deprivation of nationality must meet certain conditions in order to comply with international law, in particular the prohibition of arbitrary deprivation of nationality.' A detailed report of the impact of deprivation of nationality on the enjoyment of human rights appears in UN HRC, 'Human Rights and Arbitrary Deprivation of Nationality 2011' (n 80).

4

Access to the Refugee Convention
for Stateless Persons

The *Convention relating to the Status of Refugees* ('*Refugee Convention*') provides an exhaustive definition of those entitled to its rights and benefits,[1] and hence this definitional hurdle regulates the extent to which stateless persons may be protected as refugees at international law. Article 1A(2) states that a refugee is a person who,

> ... owing to well-founded fear of being persecuted for reasons of race, religion, nationality, membership of a particular social group or political opinion, is outside the country of his nationality and is unable or, owing to such fear, is unwilling to avail himself of the protection of that country; or who, not having a nationality and being outside the country of his former habitual residence as a result of such events, is unable or, owing to such fear, is unwilling to return to it.[2]

As this makes clear, a person does not need to possess a nationality in order to benefit from refugee protection. However, it does not follow that assessing the claim of a stateless person pursuant to the *Refugee Convention* is a straightforward exercise. Rather, as Maryellen Fullerton has observed, there can be 'complex legal and factual issues involved when stateless individuals file claims of protection under the aegis of refugee law'.[3]

In this chapter, we consider the preliminary issues involved in assessing refugee claims by de jure stateless persons. In Chapter 5, we then turn to the 'heart' of the refugee definition, namely the requirement to establish a risk of being persecuted for a *Convention* reason. In Chapter 6, we turn to the potential grounds on which a stateless person may be excluded or otherwise denied protection.

This chapter begins in Part 1 by reviewing two scholarly debates relating to the capacity of a stateless person to claim refugee status. One issue concerns whether a stateless person is required to establish well-founded fear, or whether an alternative and more straightforward test is appropriate, while the second conversely involves

---

[1] We describe it as exhaustive because of the mandatory language used, and the fact that any wider humanitarian discretion finds its place not in the *Convention* itself but in the Final Act of the Conference of Plenipotentiaries.

[2] *Convention relating to the Status of Refugees* (adopted 28 July 1951, entered into force 22 April 1954) 189 UNTS 137 (hereafter *Refugee Convention*) (emphasis added).

[3] Maryellen Fullerton, 'Without Protection: Refugees and Statelessness, A Commentary and Challenge' (Brooklyn Law School Legal Series Research Paper 351, 2013) 29 <https://papers.ssrn.com/abstract_id=2307531> accessed 13 November 2018.

International Refugee Law and the Protection of Stateless Persons. Michelle Foster and Hélène Lambert. © Michelle Foster and Hélène Lambert 2019. Published 2019 by Oxford University Press.

the question whether a stateless person can ever meet the criteria for refugee status where he or she is unable to return to their country of former habitual residence. Part 2 of the chapter turns to the meaning of 'not having a nationality' and considers the under-explored question of the relationship of this phrase in the refugee definition to the definition of stateless person in the *Convention relating to the Status of Stateless Persons* (*'1954 Convention'*), as well as examining the fraught question of inchoate nationality. Part 3 examines the meaning of 'country of former habitual residence'—a central concept for stateless refugee applicants.

Part 1: Can a Stateless Person Claim Refugee Status by Virtue of Statelessness?

1.1 The 'semicolon'

The *Refugee Convention* distinguishes, as set out in the definition at the start of the chapter, between those with a nationality and those without a nationality by means of a semicolon that separates the respective clauses in the definition. This grammatical feature has given rise to much debate: does the semicolon indicate that an entirely new clause was intended such that the requirements set for stateless persons to claim refugee status are entirely independent of the factors required for those with a nationality? It has been argued that the semicolon does indeed operate in this way and that since there is no mention of 'well-founded fear of being persecuted for reasons of race, religion, nationality, membership of a particular social group' in the second clause, all that is required to establish refugee status for a person 'without a nationality' is that he or she is 'outside the country of his former habitual residence' and unable to return to it. In other words, on this reading, a stateless person who is unable to return to her country of former habitual residence is a refugee.

This position has been argued for decades, with the leading refugee law scholar of his generation, Atle Grahl-Madsen, submitting that it is unnecessary to show a well-founded fear of being persecuted; the stateless person 'need only substantiate that he is unable to return to the country in question, in order to win recognition as a refugee'.[4] This position was also put persuasively and in depth by another leading scholar, Guy Goodwin-Gill, in a report prepared on behalf of the appellant in the case of *Revenko v Secretary of State for the Home Department* before the English Court of Appeal. In his report, Goodwin-Gill sought to argue that the phrase 'owing to a well-founded fear of being persecuted' in the first part of Article 1A(2) applies only to persons with a nationality, and does not modify what comes after the semicolon.[5] He did so based on an historical reading of Article 1A(2), in particular relying on the

---

[4] Atle Grahl-Madsen, *The Status of Refugees in International Law*, vol 1 (A W Sijthoff 1966) 261 (hereafter Grahl-Madsen, *The Status of Refugees in International Law*).
[5] Guy S Goodwin-Gill, '*Revenko v Secretary of State for the Home Department*: Report on Behalf of the Appellant' (UK Court of Appeal Civil Division, 23 July 2000) (hereafter Goodwin-Gill, '*Revenko*: Report on Behalf of the Appellant').

fact that the instruments that predated the *Refugee Convention* emphasized a lack of state protection as the hallmark of refugee status.[6] Hence, in his view:

> with respect to stateless persons, the central question is whether they enjoy the *protection* of a State. The (factual) inability to return where they once lived may confirm or establish that they do not enjoy such protection and that, without more, they are therefore refugees within the meaning of the Convention.[7]

Despite modern judicial consensus that all applicants, regardless of nationality, must establish a well-founded fear of being persecuted, other scholars have recently sought to revive the bifurcated view. For example, Heather Alexander and Jonathan Simon argue that persons who lack a nationality and are unable to return do not need to show in addition that they have a well-founded fear of persecution; unable to return is 'a legal term of art that signals irreparable, fundamental inability, rather than mere difficulty or complication with the paperwork'.[8] Hence, a person's inability to return is illustrative of 'a dire enough lack of fundamental protection as to merit inclusion in the 1951 Convention',[9] which may or may not include a well-founded fear of persecution.

In resolving this interpretive dilemma, we recall the *Vienna Convention on the Law of Treaties* ('*VCLT*'s) insistence that we must interpret a treaty in light of its 'ordinary meaning' read in context and in light of object and purpose, and to consider the *travaux* where ambiguity exists. Beginning with ordinary meaning, we observe that there are two qualifying phrases in the second clause: a person without a nationality must be outside his country *as a result of such events*, and, if unwillingness to return rather than inability is relied upon, this unwillingness must be *owing to such fear*. The events referred to are the 'events occurring before 1 January 1951' and the fear is clearly the 'well-founded fear of being persecuted for reasons of race, religion, nationality, membership of a particular social group or political opinion'.

In his report, Goodwin-Gill considered not only the pre-*Refugee Convention* instruments for protecting refugees, but also the drafting history of the *Refugee Convention*, and in particular the United Kingdom's proposal to insert 'as a result of such events' into the definition.[10] He concluded that the 'limited purpose of the amendment was thus to ensure that those with and those without a nationality were treated equally by reference to *causal events*, namely, "events occurring before 1 January 1951"'.[11] In his view, the removal of the phrase 'as a result of such events' by the *1967 Protocol relating to the Status of Refugees* ('*1967 Protocol*') would 'appear to place the stateless claimant to refugee status in a preferential position, so far as he or

---

6 See also Chapter 2 of this book.
7 Goodwin-Gill, '*Revenko*: Report on Behalf of the Appellant' (n 5) para 50 (emphasis in original).
8 Heather Alexander and Jonathan Simon, '"Unable to Return" in the 1951 Refugee Convention: Stateless Refugees and Climate Change' (2014) 26 Fla J Int'l L 531, 533 (hereafter Alexander and Simon, 'Unable to Return').
9 ibid, 560.
10 Goodwin-Gill, '*Revenko*: Report on Behalf of the Appellant' (n 5) paras 29–30.
11 ibid, para 31 (emphasis in original). This is also the argument of Alexander and Simon in 'Unable to Return' (n 8) 543.

she is no longer required to link inability to return to particular events, and also not required to show that a well-founded fear of persecution is the reason for being out-side the country of former habitual residence'.[12] This differential treatment would be justified in his view because of 'the stateless person's *a priori* unprotected status'.[13]

A second argument put by Goodwin Gill concerned the interaction between the *1954 Convention* and the 1951 *Refugee Convention*. In particular, he argued that the *1954 Convention*[14] 'covers only the situation of stateless persons admitted to residence or otherwise lawfully within State territory'.[15] With its 'focus on improving the legal situation of such persons, it does *not* deal with the stateless person whose lack of protection is manifest in an inability to return to some other country'.[16] This appears to rest on the argument that the *Refugee Convention* deals with refugees and stateless persons outside their country, while the *1954 Convention* responds to the predicament of those who are lawfully admitted or residing in a country. Yet this is difficult to reconcile with the text of the *1954 Convention*. The definition of a 'state-less person' for the purposes of the *1954 Convention* contains no such qualification, and the rights regime suggests otherwise in that while some rights are conditioned on lawful stay, others are not. For example, Article 27 provides that the 'Contracting States shall issue identity papers to any stateless person in their territory who does not possess a valid travel document.'

As already explained in Chapter 2, the drafters clearly envisioned that stateless persons could qualify as refugees; there was no suggestion that they would be excluded altogether. However, a thorough reading of the drafting history of the Conference of Plenipotentiaries suggests that there was in fact concern to ensure symmetry be-tween refugees with a nationality and those without a nationality in terms of the definition. The British proposal referred to by Goodwin-Gill was accepted at the Thirty-Fourth Meeting of the Conference of Plenipotentiaries,[17] but the issue had been raised by the UK representative two weeks earlier during the Twenty-Third Meeting. In speaking to an earlier proposal to amend Article 1A(2), Mr Hoare (the delegate for the United Kingdom) explained that the purpose of his amendment 'was consequently to link stateless persons to those who were governed by the *twin conditions of a date and a well-founded fear of persecution* as the motives for their departure'.[18] He further explained that his 'sole concern was to make sure *that the same criteria* were applied to persons having nationality and to stateless persons'.[19]

[12] Goodwin-Gill, '*Revenko*: Report on Behalf of the Appellant' (n 5) 10–11.
[13] Goodwin-Gill, '*Revenko*: Report on Behalf of the Appellant' (n 5) para 51.
[14] *Convention relating to the Status of Stateless Persons* (adopted 28 September 1954, entered into force 6 June 1960) 360 UNTS 117 (hereafter *1954 Convention*).
[15] Goodwin-Gill, '*Revenko*: Report on Behalf of the Appellant' (n 5) para 27.
[16] ibid (emphasis in original).
[17] Conference of Plenipotentiaries on the Status of Refugees and Stateless Persons, 'Summary Record of the Thirty-Fourth Meeting' (30 November 1951) UN Doc A/CONF.2/34, 12 (hereafter COP, 'Summary Record of 34th Meeting').
[18] Conference of Plenipotentiaries on the Status of Refugees and Stateless Persons, 'Summary Record of the Twenty-Third Meeting' (26 November 1951) UN Doc A/CONF.2/SR.23 8 (UK) (emphasis added) (hereafter COP, 'Summary Record 23rd Meeting').
[19] ibid, 10 (emphasis added).

When the matter returned to the agenda during the Thirty-Fourth Meeting, the UK representative, again observed that '[h]e could not imagine that those who had drafted the compromise text in question [the definition] had intended to make any difference between persons having a nationality and stateless persons' for the purpose of eligibility for refugee status.[20] He therefore proposed the addition of the phrase 'as a result of such events' into the text of the definition in order to rectify any discrepancy that still existed. This was supported by the Belgian representative, who 'agreed that it could not have been the intention of the drafters to make such a discrimination',[21] and the proposal was adopted by the Conference by seventeen votes to none, with three abstentions.[22]

This specific discussion, spanning several meetings of the Conference of Plenipotentiaries, supports the notion that the drafters indeed intended symmetry between stateless persons and those with a nationality in establishing qualification for refugee status. In addition, the explicit decision *not* to adopt the Draft Protocol relating to the Status of Stateless Persons ('Draft Protocol on Stateless Persons'), as discussed in depth in Chapter 2, further confirms that they did not intend for the *Refugee Convention* to support de jure stateless persons on the basis of their mere statelessness and inability to return alone. Of course, as will be explored further in Chapter 5, a denial of entry may well amount to persecution in a particular case; the point here is simply that mere inability to return was not, in itself, intended to operate as the entirety of the criterion for refugee status in the case of stateless persons.

It is relevant to note that the drafters of the *1954 Convention*, whose views arguably represent contemporaneous understanding of the relationship between statelessness and the *Refugee Convention*, assumed that stateless persons *who also qualified as refugees* would be protected by the *Refugee Convention*, but that an independent treaty was needed for those who could not establish the core attributes of refugeehood.[23] As the Preamble of the *1954 Convention* states, '... only those stateless persons who are also refugees are covered by the Convention relating to the Status of Refugees of 28 July 1951, and ... there are many stateless persons who are not covered by that Convention.'[24]

Finally, while it is true that the effect of the removal of the temporally limiting phrase '[a]s a result of events occurring before 1 January 1951' by the *1967 Protocol* renders the reference to *such events* irrelevant for both refugees with and without a nationality, there is no evidence in the background material that stateless refugees were considered at all in this context.[25] Rather, the debate surrounding the formulation of the *Protocol* was minimal and focused on the removal of the temporal limit 'which would make the 1951 Convention universally applicable to refugees and would secure for new groups of refugees the same status as that enjoyed by those

---

[20] COP, 'Summary Record of 34th Meeting' (n 17) 12 (UK).   [21] ibid (Belgium).
[22] ibid.   [23] See Chapter 2, Part 4.   [24] *1954 Convention* (n 14) Preamble para 3.
[25] *Protocol relating to the Status of Refugees* (adopted 31 January 1967, entered into force 4 October 1967) 606 UNTS 267, art 1(2) (hereafter *1967 Protocol*). See also *Revenko v Secretary of State for the Home Department* [2000] EWCA Civ 500; [2000] 3 WLR 1519 [61] (hereafter *Revenko*).

already covered by the 1951 Convention'.[26] There is nothing to suggest that the removal of the temporal limit was intended to liberate stateless refugees from the core definitional requirements to establish entitlement to refugee status.

These arguments have been considered and accepted by senior courts globally such that while some earlier judgments were willing to countenance a distinct and less onerous test for stateless persons to satisfy the refugee definition,[27] senior courts have now uniformly rejected the argument that the hurdle for stateless persons to establish refugee status is any lower than that for those with a nationality. Authority can be found in Australia,[28] New Zealand,[29] Canada,[30] the US,[31] the United Kingdom,[32] France,[33] Germany,[34] Ireland,[35] and in the EU Directive. If uncertainty remained in Europe, this was removed by Article 2(d) of the Qualification Directive which defines a refugee as:

[26] See Terje Einarsen, 'Drafting History of the 1951 Convention and the 1967 Protocol' in Andreas Zimmermann (ed), *The 1951 Convention Relating to the Status of Refugees and its 1967 Protocol* (OUP 2011) 37, 71–72 (hereafter Zimmermann, *The 1951 Convention*).

[27] See e.g., the Australian case of *Savvin v Minister for Immigration & Multicultural Affairs* (1999) 166 ALR 348 (hereafter *Savvin 1*), Dowsett J, noting that his view was in conflict with that taken by other single judges of the Federal Court, e.g. in *Rishmawi v Minister for Immigration & Multicultural Affairs* (1997) 77 FCR 421 (hereafter *Rishmawi*) and *Husein Ali Haris v Minister for Immigration and Multicultural Affairs* [1998] FCA 78 (12 February 1998). However, the single judge decision in *Savvin 1* was overturned by the Full Federal Court—see reference to earlier decisions in *Revenko* (n 25) [29]–[31].

[28] *Rishmawi* (n 27) 372–3; *Diatlov v Minister for Immigration and Multicultural Affairs* (1999) 167 ALR 313, 320–1 (Sackville J); *Minister for Immigration and Multicultural Affairs v Savvin* (2000) 171 ALR 483 (hereafter *Savvin 2*).

[29] For a very early decision, see *Refugee Appeal No 1/92 Re SA* [1992] NZRSAA 5 (30 April 1992) (hereafter *Refugee Appeal No 1/92*): 'there is no correlation, either positive or negative, between refugeehood and statelessness ... Statelessness is not the essential quality of a refugee.' The issue was thoroughly and categorically dealt with in *Refugee Appeal No 72635* [2002] NZRSAA 344 (6 September 2002) [65]–[68] (hereafter *Refugee Appeal No 72635*) [67]: 'The Authority has never accepted the proposition that statelessness equals refugee status.'

[30] In *Thabet v Canada (Minister of Citizenship and Immigration)* [1998] 4 FC 21 (11 May 1998) (hereafter *Thabet*), the Federal Court of Appeal of Canada considered that the essential question to ask comes down to 'why the applicant is being denied entry to a country of former habitual residence'.

[31] As stated by the US Court of Appeals for the Seventh Circuit, the fact that a person is stateless alone 'is not a ground for asylum': *Fedosseeva v Gonzales*, 492 F 3d 840, 845 (7th Cir, 2007) (hereafter *Fedosseeva*), citing *Zahren v Gonazales*, 487 F 3d 1039, 1040 [3] (7th Cir, 2007). See also *Ahmed v Ashcroft*, 341 F 3d 214, 218 (3rd Cir, 2003).

[32] See *Adan v Secretary of State for the Home Department* [1999] 1 AC 293, 304; *Revenko* (n 25).

[33] Cour nationale du droit d'asile ('CNDA') [French National Court of Asylum], decision no°10018108, 16 November 2011 (hereafter Decision no°10018108); CNDA, decision no°09002572 C+, 23 December 2010 reported in 2010 Rec Lebon 33 (hereafter Decision no°09002572 C+).

[34] See e.g., Bundesverwaltungsgerichts [German Federal Administrative Court], 10 C 50.07, 26 February 2009 (hereafter 10 C 50.07).

[35] *AAAAD v Refugee Appeals Tribunal and the Minister for Justice, Equality and Law Reform* [2009] IEHC 326 (17 July 2009) (hereafter *AAAAD*) (authorizing leave to bring judicial review to an applicant outside Kuwait). In *AAAAD*, the Irish High Court considered both the purposive approach adopted by Pill LJ in *Revenko* and the literal approach adopted by Katz J in *Savvin 2* and held both to be appropriate since both approaches led to the same conclusion: a stateless person who is unable to return to the country of her former habitual residence is not, by reason of those facts alone, a refugee within the meaning of art 1A(2); she also needs to show a present, well-founded fear of persecution on a *Refugee Convention* ground.

a third-country national who, owing to a well-founded fear of being persecuted for reasons of race, religion, nationality, political opinion or membership of a particular social group, is outside the country of nationality and is unable or, owing to such fear, is unwilling to avail himself or herself of the protection of that country, or a stateless person, who, being outside of the country of former habitual residence *for the same reasons as mentioned above*, is unable or, owing to such fear, unwilling to return to it.[36]

Key arguments adopted by courts have focused on the literal text, the historical background, and the object and purpose of the *Refugee Convention*.

Turning first to the literal or textual arguments, the most thorough reasoning is found in the decision of Justice Katz in the Full Federal Court of Australia in *Minister for Immigration and Multicultural Affairs v Savvin* ('*Savvin 2*'). In a judgment that has found favour with courts in other jurisdictions,[37] Katz J noted that historically there had existed 'a hesitant attitude on the part of the judiciary to the use of punctuation marks as a constructional aid',[38] including in both domestic and international courts. However, in his view, this hesitance was 'on the wane'.[39] Applying 'accepted grammatical principles', Katz J accordingly found that 'the semicolon does not do the work of dividing the definition into two independent parts'.[40] Rather, he held that because the semicolon in this case is preceded by 'or', it has the effect 'merely of a comma',[41] and hence the definition of refugee is 'one complete clause'. Katz J concluded that the formulation of the second part of the clause, namely, '*or who, not having a nationality and being outside the country of his former habitual residence*',

avoids the necessity, in what is already a very long clause, to repeat, so far as a stateless person is concerned, the phrase, '*Owing to well-founded fear of being persecuted for reasons of race, religion, nationality, membership of a particular social group or political opinion*', which opens the clause. That opening phrase is instead taken to be impliedly applicable to a stateless person simply by reason of the form of words used in relation to such a person in the later part of the clause.[42]

Second, courts have been persuaded by arguments predicated on the historical material, including the fact that the Conference of Plenipotentiaries deferred consideration of a convention or protocol on statelessness,[43] and that various drafts throughout the process of formulating the *Refugee Convention* indicated that for both stateless persons and refugees the criteria would be cumulative, requiring 'a well-founded fear of persecution for a specified reason as a condition of refugee status'.[44]

A third argument is based on the contextual relevance of the *1954 Convention*. In *Diatlov*, Sackville J of the Federal Court of Australia, considered the *1954 Convention*

---

[36] Directive 2011/95/EU of the European Parliament and of the Council of 13 December 2011 on standards for the qualification of third-country nationals or stateless persons as beneficiaries of international protection, for a uniform status for refugees or for persons eligible for subsidiary protection, and for the content of the protection granted (recast) [2011] OJ L 337/9, 13 (emphasis added) (hereafter Qualification Directive 2011/95/EU).

[37] See in particular the very thorough review and adoption of Katz J's approach by the Irish High Court in *AAAAD* (n 35).

[38] *Savvin 2* (n 28) [76].   [39] ibid, [80].   [40] ibid, [82].   [41] ibid, [84].

[42] ibid, [85].   [43] *Revenko* (n 25) [64].   [44] *Savvin 2* (n 28) [22] (Drummond J).

part of the context of construing the meaning of the 1951 *Refugee Convention* and its *1967 Protocol* and drew the following conclusion:

to construe the *Refugees Convention,* as amended by the 1967 *Protocol,* as protecting a stateless person who is outside the country of his or her former habitual residence and unable to return, regardless of whether the person's inability to return is associated with a fear of persecution for a *Refugees Convention* reason ... would be to render superfluous much of the *Stateless Persons Convention.*[45]

His Honour also observed that the existence of the *1954 Convention* provided an effective response to the concern expressed by the first-instance judge in *Savvin v Minister for Immigration & Multicultural Affairs* ('*Savvin 1*'), who thought that the imposition of a well-founded fear requirement for stateless persons would leave them unprotected at international law.[46]

Finally, some judges have found extrinsic materials, such as the United Nations High Commissioner for Refugees ('UNHCR') Handbook and Guidelines on Procedures and Criteria for Determining Refugee Status (UNHCR 'Handbook'), persuasive,[47] while others have relied on judgments from other jurisdictions as is typical of the increasing 'cross-fertilisation' of international refugee law that has marked the past few decades.[48]

For these reasons, courts are now clear that 'not all stateless persons are refugees'[49] because Article 1A(2) sets 'a single test for refugee status',[50] namely the need to show a well-founded fear of being persecuted. As Goodwin-Gill and Jane McAdam acknowledge in the third edition of Goodwin-Gill's classic treatise, the 'view now generally accepted, and which makes sense in pursuit of a "single test" for refugee status is that':

no substantial difference is intended between stateless and other refugees, and that the Convention aims to provide protection to a person, whether outside their country of nationality, or, not having a nationality and outside their country of former habitual residence, who has a well-founded fear of being persecuted on Convention grounds.[51]

---

[45] *Diatlov v Minister for Immigration and Multicultural Affairs* [1999] FCA 468 (25 October 1999) [29] (hereafter *Diatlov*).

[46] ibid, [30], citing Dowsett J in *Savvin 1* (n 27).

[47] See United Nations High Commissioner for Refugees (UNHCR), 'Handbook and Guidelines on Procedures and Criteria for Determining Refugee Status' (Geneva December 2011) UN Doc HCR/1P/4/ENG/REV. 3, paras 101–05 (hereafter UNHCR, 'Handbook').

[48] Hélène Lambert, 'Transnational Judicial Dialogue, Harmonization and the Common European Asylum System' (2009) 58 ICLQ 519; Guy S Goodwin-Gill and Hélène Lambert (eds), *The Limits of Transnational Law: Refugee Law, Policy Harmonization and Judicial Dialogue in the European Union* (CUP 2010).

[49] *Revenko* (n 25) [44], citing UNHCR, 'Handbook' (n 47) para 102.

[50] *Revenko* (n 25) [67] (Pill LJ). According to Pill LJ, 'the phrase "wellfounded fear of persecution" is the key phrase in the definition of Article 1A(2)': at [65]. See also *Refugee Appeal No 72635* (n 29) [68]: 'there is but a single test for refugee status'.

[51] Guy Goodwin-Gill and Jane McAdam, *The Refugee in International Law* (3rd edn, OUP 2007) 69–70 (hereafter Goodwin-Gill and McAdam, *The Refugee in International Law*). See also Guy S Goodwin-Gill, *The Refugee in International Law* (2nd edn, OUP 1996) 19–20; James Hathaway and Michelle Foster, *The Law of Refugee Status* (2nd edn, CUP 2014) (hereafter Hathaway and Foster, *The Law of Refugee Status 2*).

1.2 Inability to return as exclusion from refugee status?

A second preliminary question is the converse of that addressed in Part 1.1, namely whether an inability to return can, in the case of a stateless person, exclude the possibility of protection under the *Refugee Convention*. This question has been contested for decades. It appears to have its origins in the view of James Hathaway who, in the first edition of *The Law of Refugee Status*, argued that:

> where the stateless refugee claimant has no right to return to her country of first persecution or to any other state, *she cannot qualify as a refugee because she is not at risk of return to persecution*. Assessment of the claimant's fear of returning to the country of first persecution is a nonsensical exercise, as she could not be sent back there in any event.[52]

In such cases, it was said that protection should be provided not under the auspices of the *Refugee Convention* but under the *1954 Convention*.[53] This position was grounded in a purposive approach to the interpretation of 'country of his former habitual residence' which was said to require an 'identification of one or more countries to which [the refugee] is readmissible',[54] and in a purposive approach to the regime as a whole. On the latter point, Hathaway explained:

> Since refugee law is essentially a means of preventing the sending back of an individual to a state in which a risk of persecution exists, the proper point of reference is the country to which the claimant would normally be expected to return if not admitted to the asylum state.[55]

There are several fundamental problems with this approach.

First, this interpretation is not anchored in the text of the refugee definition which, as stated above, provides in relation to stateless persons, that a refugee is a person who, 'not having a nationality and being outside the country of his former habitual residence as a result of such events, is unable or, owing to such fear, is unwilling to return to it'.[56]

The definition focuses attention on whether a stateless person is *unable or unwilling* to return to a country of former habitual residence due to a well-founded fear of being persecuted there. The fact that return is not a presently viable or immediate option does not bear on whether the person has a well-founded fear of being persecuted in that country. Indeed, as the New Zealand Tribunal has observed, the very *text* of the refugee definition contemplates that a stateless applicant may be *unable to return* to his or her country of nationality; hence to deny refugee status on this basis 'would appear to be at odds with the wording of Article 1A(2) and the underlying objectives and purpose of the Convention'.[57] Further, the invocation of the word

---

[52] James Hathaway, *The Law of Refugee Status* (Butterworths 1991) 62 (emphasis added) (hereafter Hathaway, *The Law of Refugee Status*).

[53] ibid.   [54] ibid, 62.   [55] ibid.   [56] *Refugee Convention* (n 2) art 1A(2).

[57] *Refugee Appeal No 74880* [2005] NZRSAA 294 (29 Sept 2005) [70] (hereafter *Refugee Appeal No 74880*); *Refugee Appeal Nos 73861, 73862* [2005] NZRSAA 228 (30 June 2005) [78] (hereafter *Refugee Appeal Nos 73861, 73862*).

'former' in relation to country of habitual residence suggests that the connection with that country may not necessarily be a continuing one.[58]

Second, this position contradicts the clear intention on the part of the drafters, as set out in depth in Chapter 2, namely, that stateless persons who have a well-founded fear of being persecuted should be protected as refugees. The inclusion of the word 'unable' reflects the well-recognized phenomenon that, as explained in the UNHCR Handbook, 'once a stateless person has abandoned the country of his former habitual residence for the reasons indicated in the definition, he is usually unable to return'.[59] Of course the same predicament may confront a refugee with a nationality as recognized by the Ad Hoc Committee, which 'agreed that for the purposes of this sub-paragraph and sub-paragraph A-2(c) and therefore for the draft convention as a whole, 'unable' refers primarily to stateless refugees, but includes also refugees possessing a nationality who are refused passports or other protection by their government.[60]

In other words, a person's entitlement to refugee status—whether stateless or not—was never intended to be negated by a legal or factual inability to return to his or her country of origin at a particular point in time. On the contrary, the drafters were aware of the invocation of denationalization as a tool of persecution in the decades that preceded the *Refugee Convention*'s drafting.[61] As observed by the Canadian Federal Court, a state 'could strip a person of his right to return to that country', as a 'final act of persecution'.[62] To deny refugee status where the claimant did not have a legal right to return 'would allow the persecuting state control over the claimant's recourse to the [Refugee] Convention and effectively undermine its humanitarian purpose'.[63] Hence, to carve out an exception for those stateless persons who have no legally enforceable right to return to their country of origin or former residence would significantly undermine the objective and clear intentions of the drafters.

Third, this position arguably confuses the definition and the rights regime provided by the *Refugee Convention*. If a person is unable to return to the country in which they fear persecution, then he or she is not in need of one of the rights set by the *Convention*, namely protection against *refoulement*, at that particular time. However, the *Refugee Convention* provides a secure legal status and a range of rights beyond non-return, and there is no reason to deny stateless persons access to the full range of rights to which they are entitled simply because they do not need to rely on one of those rights at the time of refugee status determination. To use a different example, the fact that a refugee does not need immediately to rely on employment

---

[58] As later acknowledged in the revised edition of Hathaway and Foster, *The Law of Refugee Status 2* (n 51) 70

[59] See UNHCR, 'Handbook' (n 47) para 101.

[60] As cited by Federal Court of Australia in *Rishmawi* (n 27).

[61] See Chapter 2. See also *Refugee Appeal Nos 73861, 73862* (n 57) [76], where the NZ Refugee Status Appeals Authority ('RSAA') made a similar point.

[62] *Maarouf v Canada (Minister of Employment and Immigration)* [1994] 1 FC 723; (1993) 23 Imm LR (2d) 163, 173–74 (hereafter *Maarouf*).

[63] ibid.

rights set by the *Refugee Convention* because he or she is a child attending elementary school does not detract in any way from his or her qualification for refugee status.

Fourth, there is a pragmatic problem with this approach in that it assumes that the lack of a legal right to return guarantees that a person will not in fact be returned. Yet as the New Zealand Refugee Status Appeals Authority ('NZ RSAA') correctly observed, 'because it may also be possible in practice to remove persons to a state which they are not legally entitled to enter, legal returnability cannot be considered a *sine qua non* for the recognition of the refugee status of a stateless person'.[64] However even where the test has been confined to one of factual inability, decision-makers have acknowledged the practical 'difficulties inherent in the "returnability as a matter of fact test"'.[65]

Notwithstanding the above arguments, the view that ability to return is determinative in the case of stateless applicants initially led some courts to interpret incorrectly Article 1A(2) in a number of cases involving stateless persons and hence to reject their claims for refugee status.[66] For instance, in a case dealing with Bedoon in Kuwait, the NZ RSAA held that where a Bidoon is not returnable, he cannot in consequence be considered as at real risk of persecution under the *Refugee Convention*.[67]

This view has, however, been strongly criticized by other scholars,[68] and despite some limited judicial acceptance has not generally been followed in the case law. Indeed, jurisprudence in Australia,[69] Canada,[70] New

---

[64] *Refugee Appeal No 72635* (n 29) [133]. However, it should be noted that this case retained the requirement that factual inability to return is necessary: at [134], [144], [149].

[65] *Refugee Appeal No 74880* (n 57) [61]–[64].

[66] *Refugee Appeal No 75093* [2005] NZRSAA 136 (23 May 2005) (hereafter *Refugee Appeal No 75093*); *Refugee Appeal No 73512* [2003] NZRSAA 7 (13 January 2003) (hereafter *Refugee Appeal No 73512*); *Refugee Appeal No 74308* [2002] NZRSAA 401 (18 October 2002) (hereafter *Refugee Appeal No 74308*); *Refugee Appeal No 72635* (n 29); *Refugee Appeal No 73873* [2006] NZRSAA 77 (28 April 2006) (hereafter *Refugee Appeal No 73873*). See also Guy S Goodwin-Gill's paper, 'Stateless Persons and Protection under the 1951 Convention or Refugees, Beware of Academic Error!' (Colloque portant sur 'Les récents developpements en droit de l'immigration', Barreau de Québec, 22 January 1993) (hereafter Goodwin-Gill, 'Stateless Persons and Protection under the 1951 Convention'), in which he outlines a number of Canadian tribunal decisions which initially adopted this approach. For a comprehensive summary of early Canadian board decisions that rejected refugee claims, especially from Palestinian stateless applicants, on the 'non-returnability' point, see Ardi Imseis, 'Statelessness and Convention Refugee Determination: An Examination of the Palestinian Experience at the Immigration and Refugee Board of Canada' (1997) 31 UBC Law Rev 317, 329–31.

[67] NZ RSAA: *Refugee Appeal No 72635* (n 29) [149], and in Australia, *Refugee Review Tribunal Appeal 0808284* [2009] RRTA 454 (21 May 2009). See also in New Zealand, *Refugee Appeal No 74308* (n 66) [43]; *Refugee Appeal No 75093* (n 66) [39]–[43]; *Refugee Appeal 73873* (n 66) [54].

[68] Goodwin-Gill, 'Stateless Persons and Protection under the 1951 Convention' (n 66). See also Goodwin Gill and McAdam, *The Refugee in International Law* (n 51). Grahl-Madsen also took the view that the right to return was not a barrier to protection for stateless persons: see Grahl-Madsen, *The Status of Refugees in International Law* (n 4) 261.

[69] *Taiem v Minister for Immigration and Multicultural Affairs* (2002) 186 ALR 361 [14] (hereafter *Taiem*); *Rishmawi* (n 27); *SZIPL v Minister for Immigration* [2007] FMCA 643 (17 May 2007) [4] (hereafter *SZIPL*); *MZZQN v Minister for Immigration* [2014] FCCA 2886 (10 December 2014) [15]. Indeed in Australia, s 5(1) of the *Migration Act 1958* (Cth) was amended from 16 December 2014 to provide that 'receiving country', in relation to a non-citizen, means: '(b) if the non-citizen has no country of nationality—a country of his or her former habitual residence, *regardless of whether it would be possible to return the non-citizen to the country*:' (emphasis added).

[70] See *Maarouf* (n 62); *Abdel-Khalik v Canada (Minister of Employment and Immigration)* [1994] FCJ No 111; *Bohaisy v Canada (Minister of Employment and Immigration)* 1994 CarswellNat 645; *Zdanov*

Zealand,[71] the United States,[72] and the United Kingdom[73] is emphatic that an ability to return is not a prerequisite for stateless persons to establish refugee status. While New Zealand decision-makers initially adopted the view that legal returnability was a prerequisite for stateless applicants, that position has now been rejected in more recent jurisprudence.[74] Where there is a question about returnability, decision-makers across all jurisdictions simply assess the claim on the hypothesis that return is possible, with the assessment focusing on the likely fate of the applicant should return be effected.[75] The position that returnability is determinative has now been revised by James Hathaway and Michelle Foster in the second edition of the *The Law of*

---

v Canada (Minister of Employment and Immigration) [1994] FCJ No 1090; *Shaat v Canada (Minister of Employment and Immigration)* [1994] FCJ No 1149; *Desai v Canada (Minister of Citizenship and Immigration)* [1994] FCJ No 2032; *Thabet* (n 30).

[71] See below at n 74.

[72] *Ouda v Immigration and Naturalization Service*, 324 F 3d 445, 450–2 (6th Cir, 2003) (hereafter *Ouda*).

[73] See *BA v Secretary of State for the Home Department* [2004] UKIAT 00256 (hereafter *BA*), citing *Saad, Diriye and Osorio v Secretary of State for the Home Department* [2001] EWCA Civ 2008; [2002] INLR 34, where the UK Court of Appeal held that even if there are practical obstacles, an appeal on asylum grounds requires substantive consideration on the hypothetical basis of whether—if returned—an appellant would face a real risk of persecution; this position further holds true because 'the duty of confidentiality owed by the Secretary of State to the asylum claimant prevents approaches to the country of origin prior to the final determination of whether a claimant is a refugee': *BA* at [47], see also at [60]. See also *OH v Secretary of State for the Home Department* [2004] UKIAT 00254. It may be noted that this later, and correct approach is in stark contrast with the approach at the European Court of Human Rights in human rights cases (as opposed to *Refugee Convention* cases): if the threat of expulsion or deportation is not imminent, then there can be no violation of the *Convention: Vijayanathan v France* (1993) 15 EHRR 62—discussed in *BA* at [48]. In the UK, see also *MA (Ethiopia) v Secretary of State for the Home Department* [2009] EWCA Civ 289, [2010] INLR 1 [43] (hereafter *MA*).

[74] In *Refugee Appeal Nos 73861, 73862* (n 57) the NZ RSAA criticized the earlier decisions of the authority, particularly that in *Refugee Appeal No 72635* (n 29), finding that the 'non-returnability' approach is 'difficult to reconcile with the actual wording of Article 1A(2); ... misconstrues the requirements of a well-founded fear; ... is not supported by the case law; ... has the result of undermining an internationally uniform outcome ... [and] is still problematic in respect of Article 33(1)': at [68]. In *Refugee Appeal No 74880* (n 57), the Authority observed that the 'concerns expressed in *Refugee Appeals Nos 73861 and 73862* (30 June 2005) as to the "returnabilty as a matter of fact" question are ones which are respectfully shared': at [72]. In *Refugee Appeal No 75694* [2006] NZRSAA 97 (24 May 2006) (hereafter *Refugee Appeal No 75694*) the Authority concluded: 'For the sake of certainty we note that in making this finding we accept that all stateless persons who have a well-founded fear of being persecuted in their country of former habitual residence for a Convention reason are entitled to the protection of the Refugee Convention: *Refugee Appeal Nos 73861–2* (30 June 2005). This is regardless of whether or not they are returnable as a matter of fact to their country of former habitual residence': at [45]. See also *Refugee Appeal No 74467* [2004] NZRSAA 283 (1 September 2004) (hereafter *Refugee Appeal No 74467*). However, we observe that factual inability to return has not yet been emphatically rejected in New Zealand. While some New Zealand decisions clearly state that returnability is irrelevant (e.g. *Refugee Appeal No 73861* and *Refugee Appeal No 75694*), other cases appear to assume it is still an issue. For instance, in *Refugee Appeal No 76506* [2010] NZRSAA 90 (29 July 2010) [69], [76], although *Refugee Appeal No 74880* is cited in relation to problems with the factual returnability approach, it still frames returnability as a question that needs to be addressed: at [70].

[75] See UK cases: *BA* (n 73) [46]: 'the appeals of the two Bedoon appellants on asylum grounds nevertheless require substantive consideration on the hypothetical basis of whether—if returned—an appellant would face a real risk of persecution'. See also *YL v Secretary of State for the Home Department* [2003] UKIAT 00016 [62] (hereafter *YL*); *SZTEO v Minister for Immigration* [2015] FCCA 2228 (21 August 2015) [10]; *SZSPX v Minister for Immigration* [2013] FCCA 1715 (25 October 2013) [42], [69]–[70] (Barnes J).

Refugee Status,[76] in which it is acknowledged that 'no one factor should be treated as essential' and hence the returnability criterion 'should be understood as relevant to, rather than determinative of, the existence of a country of former habitual residence'.[77]

Accordingly, a right of return is not required in order for a stateless person to qualify for refugee status pursuant to Article 1A(2).[78] While, as discussed below, the question of returnability may be relevant to other aspects of the definition, it is not in itself determinative of capacity to satisfy the refugee definition in the case of a stateless applicant.

Part 2: When is an Individual with or without a Nationality?

Having determined that a stateless applicant may qualify for refugee status so long as the core definitional requirements are met, namely well-founded fear of being persecuted for a *Refugee Convention* reason, we now turn to the question of what it means to 'not hav[e] a nationality' and how that should be determined.

It is worth observing at the outset that the term 'nationality' is used a number of times in the *Refugee Convention* in various contexts. It is invoked in Article 1 as a ground for persecution, a point of reference for establishing a country of origin, a ground of cessation of refugee status, and a ground of exclusion from refugee status. Articles 8 and 17 of the *Refugee Convention* also make references to nationals and nationality in the context of exceptional measures (Article 8) and wage-earning employment (Article 17), and Article 34 requires states to facilitate the naturalization and assimilation of refugees into their new community. Even in the context of Article 1A(2) it is recognized that while country of nationality denotes country of citizenship, the *Convention* ground 'nationality' has a wider meaning.

It is important that this question be answered at the outset of a refugee status determination procedure,[79] because it may have significant bearing on the claim in terms of identifying the 'country of reference', the nature of the harm feared, and even the *Convention* grounds.[80]

---

[76] Hathaway and Foster, *The Law of Refugee Status 2* (n 51) 69, noting that the original position is 'not correct': at n 321.

[77] ibid, 70.   [78] ibid, 69.

[79] See e.g., *Smith v Secretary of State for the Home Department (Liberia)* [2000] UKIAT 00TH02130 (hereafter *Smith*); CNDA, decision nos°12008037, 12008038, 6 July 2012.

[80] See e.g., the decision of the UK Asylum and Immigration Tribunal in *KA v Secretary of State for the Home Department* [2008] UKAIT 00042 [6] (hereafter *KA*): 'It follows that his nationality has to be determined as part of the process of determining his status as a refugee or otherwise. If he has no nationality, his status has to be determined by his country of former habitual residence.' Similarly, the Australian Federal Magistrate's Court acknowledged 'in order to properly determine whether or not an applicant is truly a refugee a Tribunal must first examine the existence or otherwise of his or her nationality. Only when it is satisfied on the basis of the law of the country of claimed nationality that an applicant is stateless should it apply the test based upon that person's country of habitual residence': *SZIPL* (n 69) [12].

Yet despite the importance of this issue, there is very little analysis or guidance in appellate jurisprudence or in the leading textbooks[81] on the question of how a decision-maker should determine 'not having a nationality' for the purposes of refugee law.[82] Of course, in by far the majority of cases there is no question the applicant is a national of a particular country and hence there are no complicated issues arising in relation to nationality. However where nationality is uncertain and/ or the applicant claims to be stateless, decision-makers must determine whether the applicant does or does not have a 'country of nationality' and if not what is the country of 'former habitual residence'.[83] There is guidance, particularly from the UNHCR, as to the relationship between the 1951 *Refugee Convention* and *1954 Convention*; specifically that refugee status should be assessed prior to a formal determination of statelessness.[84] However, there does not appear to be any guidance on how 'not having a nationality' is to be determined for the purposes of refugee law or the extent to which cross-fertilization between the regimes may benefit refugee status determination.[85]

---

[81] None of the leading textbooks appear to discuss this precise question. There is discussion about issues such as inchoate or dual nationality, but not the precise issue as to how we understand statelessness in this context. However, it appears to be assumed that 'not having a nationality' means stateless: see e.g., Zimmermann, *The 1951 Convention* (n 26) 462. Eric Fripp argues that the definition of statelessness in art 1(1) of the *1954 Convention*, with its reference to 'by operation of its laws' provides a more extensive meaning of 'nationality' than traditionally understood ('under its law', *Convention on Certain Questions relating to the Conflict of Nationality Laws* (opened for signature 12 April 1930, entered into force 1 July 1937) 179 UNTS 89, art 1 (hereafter *1930 Hague Convention*)). Eric Fripp, *Nationality and Statelessness in the International Law of Refugee Status* (Hart 2016) 43 [1.82] (hereafter Fripp, *Nationality and Statelessness*). Hence, he appears to argue that not having a nationality in the refugee definition should be interpreted by reference to the *1930 Hague Convention*: see at 235.

[82] The UNHCR 'Handbook' (n 47) states straightforwardly that '[t]his phrase, which relates to stateless refugees, is parallel to the preceding phrase, which concerns refugees who have a nationality': at para 101. Even Fripp only dedicates half a page to it, see *Nationality and Statelessness* (n 81) 235.

[83] In France, the Cour Nationale du Droit d'Asile (which is a specialized court) is competent in most cases to decide whether a person is eligible to claim the nationality of his or her country of habitual residence, in accordance with the law applicable in that country: see Conseil d'État [French Administrative Court] ('CE'), decision nos°362703, 362704, 362705, 18 June 2014. See also Marie-Christine de Montecler, 'Office de la CNDA pour determiner la nationalité d'un demandeur d'asile' (2014) (20) AJDA 1128. However, should nationality be seriously disputed, the CNDA must refer the issue to the Ordinary Court (Jurisdiction Civile de Droit Commun) by application of art 29 of the *Civil Code*, and wait for a decision before being able to proceed with the case: CE, decision no°344265, 26 May 2014; CE, decision no°357433, 26 May 2014. See C Viel, 'Détermination de la nationalité du demandeur d'asile: le Conseil d'Etat encadre l'office de la CNDA' (2004) (235) Dictionnaire permanent—Droit des étrangers 10, 11.

[84] UNHCR, 'Handbook on Protection of Stateless Persons' (Geneva 2014) paras 78–81 (hereafter UNHCR, 'Handbook on Stateless Persons'): a combined procedure, or if separate and running in parallel, then the asylum process should ideally take place first where findings of fact there might assist statelessness determination: at para 80. Switzerland provides such an example of practice where refugee status determination precedes or is simultaneous to stateless person status determination: Bundesverwaltungsgericht [German Federal Administrative Court], *A v Bundesamt für Migration*, C-1873/2013, 9 May 2014 (hereafter *A v BFM*).

[85] In practice in some stateless status determination procedures such as that in the UK, there is yet no cross-fertilization between asylum procedure and statelessness procedure, and it is unlikely this will change any time soon. But this is a new system—having been introduced in April 2013. But see as an example of cross-fertilization: *A v BFM* (n 84); Karen Hamann, 'Statelessness Determination: The Swiss Experience' (February 2017) 54 FMR 96.

There are two issues in this context: (1) the correct interpretation of 'not having a nationality' and its relationship to the definition of statelessness in the *1954 Convention*; and (2) the evidentiary challenge of satisfying the legal test.

2.1 The legal test

As explained in Chapter 2, the drafting history is clear that the refugee definition was intended to apply both to refugees with a nationality and those without a nationality, that is, those who were stateless. However, there is little guidance as to precisely how 'not having a nationality' was intended to be understood.

The Ad Hoc Committee's Draft Protocol on Stateless Persons that accompanied early drafts of the *Refugee Convention* did not attempt to define 'stateless person', but referred simply to 'stateless persons to whom the Convention ... [did] not apply'.[86] As Nehemiah Robinson observed at the time, the Draft Protocol referred simply to ' "stateless persons" as if this term had an established meaning'.[87]

Throughout the meetings of the Conference of Plenipotentiaries on the Status of Refugees and Stateless Persons, which adopted the final text of the 1951 *Refugee Convention*, delegates referred interchangeably to 'persons without nationality' and 'stateless persons'.[88] In some suggested amendments the phrase 'person who has no nationality' was invoked;[89] however, nothing appeared to turn on the form of words and there does not appear to have been any debate or discussion on the precise form of words used. The clear implication from the debates is that those 'not having a nationality' were stateless, and none of the representatives identified the need to define the concept in any further detail.

The later Draft Protocol on Stateless Persons proposed by the United Nations Secretariat, which formed the basis of discussion for the Conference that adopted the *1954 Convention*, defined 'stateless person' in Article 1 as 'a person who is not considered as a national by any State under the operation of its law'.[90] This in turn had drawn on the approach of Manley O Hudson, the International Law Commission's ('ILC') Special Rapporteur on Nationality, including Statelessness, in his first report. Hudson's focus in fact was on the distinction between de jure and de facto stateless persons and in that context he had observed that the Secretariat's

---

[86] UNGA 'Draft Protocol relating to the Status of Stateless Persons. Draft Final Clauses (Prepared by the Secretariat on the Request of the President of the Conference)' (19 July 1951) (hereafter Draft Protocol on Stateless Persons).

[87] Nehemiah Robinson, *Convention relating to the Status of Stateless Persons: Its History and Interpretation, A Commentary* (UNHCR 1997) (hereafter Robinson, *Statelessness Convention, A Commentary*).

[88] See e.g., COP, 'Summary Record 23rd Meeting' (n 18) 8 (UK). See also 'refugees who possessed a nationality and for those who were stateless': at 9 (Israel); 'different conditions were required of persons possessing a nationality and of stateless persons respectively': at 9–10 (UK).

[89] See e.g., Israel's amendment to art 1: UNGA, 'Draft Convention relating to the Status of Refugees: Amendment to Article 1/Israel' (17 July 1951) UN Doc A/CONF.2/82/Rev.1; and the United Kingdom's amendment: UNGA, 'Draft Convention relating to the Status of Refugees: Amendment to Article 1 / United Kingdom' (3 July 1951) UN Doc A/CONF.2/27.

[90] Guy S Goodwin-Gill, 'Convention relating to the Status of Stateless Persons' (UN Audiovisual Library of International Law 2010) 4.

'Study of Statelessness' had described the former as 'persons who are not nationals of any State'.[91] He concluded that stateless persons 'in the legal sense of the term' are 'persons who are not considered as nationals by any State according to its law'.[92] The Conference on Stateless Persons adopted that interpretation, with the only meaningful debate focusing once again on the issue of de jure vs de facto stateless persons.[93] The definition of de jure stateless persons per se was not at issue.

The history of the two conventions was clearly intertwined. Indeed, Robinson observed at the time that, 'the two conventions are not consecutive but parallel instruments'.[94] While stateless persons who feared persecution would be protected as refugees, other stateless persons needed to turn to the *1954 Convention*. These were not, however, designed to be mutually exclusive categories since stateless refugees could theoretically enjoy protection under both regimes. It is reasonable then to conclude that the notion of stateless person was intended to be understood in the same way in both treaties, notwithstanding a difference in language. In other words, 'not having a nationality' means 'not considered as a national by any State'.[95] There is no logical reason, nor any that can be found in the drafting history, to suggest that these were intended to have different meanings at international law. Indeed, we could argue that the *context* of the *Refugee Convention*—for the purpose of Article 31 of the *VCLT*—includes the proximate debate and formulation of a regime to protect stateless persons. This same context suggests that even if the 'ordinary meaning' of 'not having a nationality' is not statelessness, it is certainly 'a special meaning'. Article 31(4) of the *VCLT* provides that,[96] '[a] special meaning shall be given to a term if it is established that the parties so intended', which can apply where the terms of a treaty 'have a technical or "special meaning" due to the particular field the treaty covers'.[97] In such a case, 'the particular meaning may already appear from the context and object and purpose of the treaty, it is essentially the ordinary meaning in the particular context'.[98] The background and context to the drafting[99] and adoption of both conventions strongly suggests that the special meaning of 'not having a nationality' was statelessness,[100] and the contemporaneous formulation of a clear

[91] International Law Commission ('ILC'), 'Report on Nationality, Including Statelessness by Mr. Manley O. Hudson, Special Rapporteur' (21 February 1952) UN Doc A/CN.4/50, 17 (hereafter 'Report on Nationality, Including Statelessness by Mr Manley O. Hudson'.
[92] ibid (emphasis omitted).   [93] As explained in Chapter 2, Part 4.
[94] Robinson, *Statelessness Convention, A Commentary* (n 87) pt 2 art 1.
[95] In adopting this view, the NZ RSAA has emphasized that the *1951 Refugee Convention* and *1954 Convention* were 'in a sense, drafted side by side': *Refugee Appeal No 72635* (n 29) [92].
[96] *Vienna Convention on the Law of Treaties* (opened for signature 23 May 1969, entered into force 27 January 1980) 1155 UNTS 331, art 31(4) (hereafter *VCLT*).
[97] Oliver Dörr, 'Article 31: General Rule of Interpretation' in Oliver Dörr and Kirsten Schmalenbach (eds), *Vienna Convention on the Law of Treaties: A Commentary* (Springer-Verlag Berlin 2012) 521, 568 (hereafter Dörr, 'Article 31').
[98] ibid.
[99] As Julian Davis Mortenson observes, establishing a 'special meaning' pursuant to art 31(4) 'often requires reference to travaux': 'The *Travaux* of *Travaux*: Is the Vienna Convention Hostile to Drafting History?' (2013) 107 AJIL 780, 787.
[100] Oliver Dörr explains that in art 31(4) the notion of 'special meaning' refers to two different kinds of cases, the first of which is relevant in the present context. He explains that 'it may be that the terms of a treaty have a technical or "special meaning" due to the particular field the treaty covers': Dörr, 'Article 31' (n 97) 568.

definition of statelessness within a legal framework is hence critical to interpreting that phrase in the refugee definition.

An alternative argument in support of the notion that 'not having a nationality' should be interpreted in line with the *1954 Convention* is that the *VCLT* requires an interpreter to take into account, '[a]ny relevant rules of international law applicable in the relations between the parties'.[101] This includes customary international law,[102] and it is noteworthy that both the ILC and the UNHCR regard the definition of 'stateless person' in the *1954 Convention* as representing customary international law.[103]

Turning to a consideration of judicial approaches to this question, while decision-makers unanimously accept that 'not having a nationality' refers to statelessness,[104] there is a surprising lack of clarity and precision in identifying the relevant test for assessing whether a refugee applicant is stateless.

One approach is to adopt the 1954 definition in a straightforward manner. In New Zealand, for example, the tribunal has long taken the view that the natural and obvious source of the concept of 'stateless' is Article 1 of the *1954 Convention*. As early as 1992, the tribunal decided that '[w]hile New Zealand is not a party to the 1954 Convention Relating to the Status of Stateless Persons we neverthe-less intend to adopt this definition for the purpose of the present case'.[105] The reference to lack of state ratification serves to emphasize that in adverting to the 1954 definition a refugee decision-maker is not thereby purporting to exercise jurisdiction pursuant to the 1954 treaty, but rather drawing on the definition of 'stateless person' in that treaty as a source for the meaning of that term at inter-national law.[106] This has been the consistent approach in New Zealand, with the RSAA's successor—the Immigration and Protection Tribunal—adopting the same approach.[107] Reference to the *1954 Convention* is also found in Ireland[108] and

---

[101] *VCLT* (n 96) art 31(3)(c).   [102] Dörr, 'Article 31' (n 97) 562.

[103] UNGA, 'Report of the International Law Commission: Fifty-Eighth Session' UN GAOR 61st Session Supp No 10 UN Doc A/61/10 (Draft Articles on Diplomatic Protection with Commentaries) (2006) chI(E)(2) (hereafter UNGA, 'Report of the International Law Commission: Fifty-Eighth Session'): 'Paragraph 1 deals with the diplomatic protection of stateless persons. It gives no definition of stateless persons. Such a definition is, however, to be found in the Convention Relating to the Status of Stateless Persons of 1954 which defines a stateless person "as a person who is not considered as a na-tional by any State under the operation of its law". This definition can no doubt be considered as having acquired a customary nature': at 48 (citations omitted).

[104] Indeed, the Qualification Directive adopts the phrase 'stateless person' rather than person 'not having a nationality': see Qualification Directive 2011/95/EU (n 36) arts 2(d), 2(n).

[105] *Refugee Appeal No 1/92* (n 29). See also *Refugee Appeal No 72635* (n 29) [78].

[106] See Michelle Foster, *International Refugee Law and Socio-Economic Rights: Refuge from Deprivation* (CUP 2007) ch 2, in which this approach to treaty interpretation is discussed in depth.

[107] See e.g., *BG (Fiji)* [2012] NZIPT 800091 (20 January 2012) [78] (hereafter *BG (Fiji)*): 'The most widely accepted definition of statelessness is that contained in Article 1 of the Convention Relating to the Status of Stateless Persons 1954 which provides that a stateless person means a person who is not considered as a national by any State under the operation of its law.'

[108] In Ireland, the High Court has acknowledged that the term 'stateless' is 'given a definition in Article 1 of the *UN Convention relating to the Status of Stateless Persons* of 1954 (to which the State is a party)' but ultimately it defers to the notion that 'whether the applicants are in their particular personal circumstances "stateless" is first and foremost a matter of policy for the respondent Minister': *Spila v Minister for Justice, Equality & Law Reform* [2012] IEHC 336 (31 July 2012) [16].

Canada,[109] although it is not always as systematically applied in the jurisprudence. It is occasionally found, but is far less common, in other jurisdictions.[110]

A second approach is to effectively adopt the test in the *1954 Convention* without necessarily referring to it explicitly. For example, in Australia, the relevant ministerial guidelines for decision-makers assessing protection claims provides that for the purposes of the *Refugee Convention*, statelessness is 'established where no country recognises the person as holding citizenship'.[111] In other jurisdictions, a central focus of inquiry on the domestic citizenship laws of the country in question suggests an understanding of the definition of statelessness at international law.[112]

However, a far more common approach is to not identify the legal test/principle at all and rather move directly to the evidential question of whether the applicant is stateless. For example, in one appellate decision the Federal Court of Australia noted (without criticism) that the decision-maker below had 'not specified the necessary criteria to demonstrate statelessness or the fact that the appellant was undocumented, but has identified a number of topics from the material which are capable of informing the answer to that issue'.[113] While it is rare to find such an explicit articulation of the subjective approach at the appellate level, the approach itself is commonly implemented.[114] Indeed, by far the majority of decisions simply assess as a matter of fact whether a person is stateless without reference to a legal framework. The difficulty with this approach is that it can result in a subjective and in some cases irrelevant list of factors invoked in assessing whether a person is stateless. For example, in another Australian decision, the reviewer had regard to whether the applicant's experience in his home country suggested he was stateless, a question that turned on the reviewer's assessment of credibility, rather than the question of the applicant's legal status.[115]

---

[109] In Canada, reference to the *1954 Convention* is found in the Immigration and Refugee Board of Canada, 'Interpretation of the Convention Refugee Definition in the Case Law' (December 2010) Legal References, ch 2 para 2.2 <http://www.irb-cisr.gc.ca/Eng/BoaCom/references/LegJur/Pages/RefDef02.aspx> accessed 14 November 2018 where it is stated that 'A stateless person is someone who is not recognized by any country as a citizen', citing a 1994 decision that in turn cited the *1954 Convention*.

[110] See e.g., *Federovski, Re Judicial Review* [2007] NIQB 119, [13]. The recently formulated UNHCR Guidelines, 'Representing Stateless Persons before U.S. Immigration Authorities' (August 2017)) (hereafter UNHCR, 'Guidelines on Representing Stateless Persons') clearly make the link between the 1954 definition and the *Refugee Convention*: at 3–13.

[111] Department of Immigration and Border Protection (Cth), *Procedures Advice Manual 3: Refugee and Humanitarian—Protection Visas—All Applications—Common Processing Guidelines*, 16 February 2016, [78].

[112] *Tretsetsang v Canada (Citizenship and Immigration)* [2015] 4 FCR 521, 2015 FC 455 (hereafter *Tretsetsang*).

[113] *DZACV v Minister for Immigration and Citizenship* [2012] FCA 1443 (17 December 2012) [24]. Yet in other cases the Court has found that the Tribunal was in error for not determining nationality in accordance with the law of the relevant country as required by the *Migration Act 1958* (Cth), where it is stated at s 36: '(6) For the purposes of subsection (3), the question of whether a non-citizen is a national of a particular country must be determined solely by reference to the law of that country.' See e.g., *SZIPL* (n 69) [5].

[114] See e.g., *Queen on the Application of (ZA) (Kuwait) v Secretary of State for the Home Department* [2011] EWCA Civ 1082, [6]–[8].

[115] *SZQOX v Minister for Immigration* [2012] FMCA 566 (29 June 2012) [10].

Adoption of the legal test of whether an applicant is 'considered a national by any State' by contrast would focus the assessment on the legal question at issue. It must be emphasized that the focus in refugee law is of course on whether the applicant is unable to return due to persecution, whereas an assessment under the *1954 Convention* is purely a question of de jure statelessness. For this reason, it is not suggested that in order to assess refugee status, a stateless applicant must be assessed through a formal statelessness status determination procedure. On the contrary, the UNHCR cautions that refugee status should be considered prior to a formal statelessness determination precisely because to contact home authorities to ascertain nationality may put an applicant for refugee status at risk.[116] As was well elucidated by the UK Tribunal, in asylum cases there may be 'valid reasons for a claimant not approaching his or her embassy or consulate—or the authorities of the country direct—about an application for citizenship or residence' because in some cases 'such an approach could place the claimant or the claimant's family at risk'.[117] However, an understanding of the legal framework for determining statelessness would provide clarity and structure around the assessment, and also make clear three important principles: (1) that the burden of proof is shared; (2) that the question is confined to whether the applicant has a nationality, not whether the nationality is 'effective'; and (3) that assessing nationality is neither a historical nor a predictive exercise. While Part 2.2 below examines the last two principles, Part 2.3 deals with the burden of proof.

2.2 Establishing statelessness in refugee status determination

Assessing whether an applicant for refugee status can be said to 'not hav[e] a nationality' requires, like its counterpart in the *1954 Convention*, 'proof of a negative'.[118] However it is vital to observe that the lack of nationality 'does not need to be established in relation to every State in the world'.[119] Rather, an assessment of potential nationality is only required in relation to states with which a person has 'a relevant

---

[116] A good example of implementation in practice is the UK: 'Applications for leave on the basis of statelessness will not be accepted for consideration until any asylum claim has been finally determined or withdrawn'; UK Home Office, 'Asylum Policy Instruction: Statelessness and Applications for Leave to Remain' (18 February 2016) s 3.1 (hereafter UK Home Office, 'Asylum Policy Instruction'). Thus, the Immigration Law Practitioners' Association ('ILPA') recommends that in most cases it may be best to put a claim for statelessness 'after the asylum claim has been finally determined' because refugee status is preferable to leave to remain as a stateless person. Hence, once refugee status is granted, 'there will be little point in pursuing a statelessness application': Judith Carter and Sarah Woodhouse, 'Statelessness and Applications for Leave to Remain: A Best Practice Guide' (ILPA, 3 November 2016) 48 (hereafter Carter and Woodhouse, 'A Best Practice Guide'). However, in countries where recognition as a stateless person gives the applicant a more favourable legal position (e.g. Switzerland), it may be necessary to examine their position under the *1954 Convention* prior (or simultaneously) to applying the *Refugee Convention*; or if refugee status has already been granted, it is good practice to allow for stateless person status to be granted as well, in addition to refugee status, as held by the Swiss Federal Administrative Court in *A v BFM* (n 84) [9]–[10]. The Federal Court further considers that recognized refugees cannot be required to travel to their country of habitual residence and to ask citizenship there because by doing so their refugee status could be withdrawn in accordance with art 1C of the *Refugee Convention*.

[117] *YL* (n 75) [46].   [118] UNHCR, 'Handbook on Stateless Persons' (n 84) para 88.

[119] ibid, para 92.

link', which is generally constituted by 'birth on the territory, descent, marriage, adoption or habitual residence'.[120] As the UNHCR observes, in some cases this may limit the scope of inquiry to only one state.[121] This principle has been accepted in both statelessness determination procedures and for the purposes of assessing nationality in refugee law.[122]

The question of whether a person can be said to 'not hav[e] a nationality' is examined, as is the parallel 'not considered a national ... under the operation of its law', first and foremost 'in accordance with the municipal laws of the State concerned'.[123] In other words, circumstantial evidence such as the place of birth, and personal history such as schooling and employment, 'might all be relevant considerations in determining citizenship, subject to the relevant terms of the municipal law', but the key consideration must be 'the municipal law or any applicable legislative or quasi-legislative process'.[124] This can be a challenge in countries that do not define statelessness in their domestic laws.[125] In some jurisdictions it is recognized that where the operation of a foreign country's nationality law is complex it may be appropriate to obtain expert evidence in order to assist in the refugee status determination procedure.[126]

Further, it is important to note that the notion of 'law' should be understood broadly to encompass 'not just legislation, but also ministerial decrees, regulations, orders, [and] judicial case law'.[127] In other words, while an analysis focused solely on the nationality laws in a person's country of origin may suggest that an individual is a national of that country, the 'written law' may be 'substantially

[120] ibid, paras 18, 92. This is also supported by the Commentary to the Text of the 1954 Convention: 'it certainly was not the intention of the conference to require a formal proof from states with which the person had no intimate relationship': Nehemiah Robinson, 'Convention relating to the Status of Stateless Persons: It's History and Interpretation: A Commentary' (World Jewish Congress, Institute of Jewish Affairs, 1955) para 4.
[121] UNHCR, 'Handbook on Stateless Persons' (n 84) para 18.
[122] *Queen on the application of Hermon Tewolde v Immigration Appeal Tribunal* [2004] EWHC 162 (Admin), [19] (hereafter *Tewolde*), referring to *R v Secretary of State for Home Department, ex parte Bradshaw* [1994] Imm AR 359 (hereafter *Bradshaw*). See also *Refugee Appeal No 74236* [2005] NZRSAA 351 (2 December 2005) (hereafter *Refugee Appeal No 74236*), in which the RSAA assessed the applicant's nationality only against Palestine (given his family's origin) and Lebanon (where the applicant was born and had always lived): at [44]–[46].
[123] *WZAQH v Minister for Immigration* [2013] FCCA 182 (9 May 2013) [21] (hereafter *WZAQH*). The question of whether a person is a national of any particular state is a matter of law for that state': *ST v Secretary of State for the Home Department* [2011] UKUT 00252 (IAC) [74] (hereafter *ST*), referring to *KK v Secretary of State for the Home Department* [2011] UKUT 92 (IAC) (hereafter *KK*). See also *Darji v Secretary of State for the Home Department* [2004] EWCA Civ 1419. In *Lhazom v Canada (Citizenship and Immigration)*, 2015 FC 886 (hereafter *Lhazom*), the Canadian Federal Court noted that determining citizenship 'involves the interpretation of foreign law, which is a question of fact': at [7].
[124] *WZAQH* (n 123) [27], [29], emphasizing that these other factors (i.e. family, schooling, and employment history) do not 'preclude the necessity to have regard to the most relevant consideration, namely the municipal law or any applicable legislative or quasi-legislative process': at [29].
[125] For instance, in the US, see David C Baluarte, 'Life after Limbo: Stateless Persons in the United States and the Role of International Protection in Achieving a Legal Solution' (2015) 29 Geo Immigr L J 351, 360.
[126] *Koe v Minister for Immigration and Multicultural Affairs* (1997) 74 FCR 508, 515.
[127] UNHCR, 'Handbook on Stateless Persons' (n 84) para 22.

modified when it comes to its implementation in practice'.[128] For example, while the Constitution of the Dominican Republic entrenches the concept of *jus soli*—nationality by birth—it contains exceptions for 'the legitimate children of foreign residents in the country as diplomatic representatives or individuals in transit in the country'.[129] On its face one would assume that a person born to parents who had lived '20, 30, and even 40 years in the Dominican Republic'[130] could not be considered 'in transit' and hence the logical conclusion would be that such persons were citizens of the Dominican Republic pursuant to a constitutional right. However, in practice, since the early 1990s, children of Haitian immigrants born in the Dominican Republic have been denied citizenship—first due to the refusal of the Civil Registry officials to register the birth of such children,[131] and later by virtue of a ruling by the Constitutional Court that defined, 'retroactively, the criteria for acquiring citizenship by application of the principle of *jus soli* by giving a new interpretation to the concept of foreigners in transit, equating this concept with that of a foreigner in an irregular migratory situation'.[132] This underlines the need to assess both the law *and implementation of the law* of the relevant state in order accurately to determine whether a person has a nationality or whether the person is indeed stateless.[133]

This important point is exemplified in the refugee context in a decision of an Australian tribunal that overturned the first-instance finding that the applicant was not stateless because amendments to the *Bangladesh Citizenship Act* in 2008 ensured that a child born to a Bangladeshi citizen mother 'becomes a Bangladeshi citizen by descent'.[134] On review, the Tribunal examined also the *implementation* of the law, and relied on evidence that despite these amendments there remained 'a practical difficulty of proof of birth in Bangladesh' and specifically 'non-registration of the birth of children to a refugee parent in Bangladesh',[135] which was the predicament of the applicant. Hence, the relevant laws did not *in practice* 'confer citizenship on stateless Rohingya'.[136] A similar

---

[128] ibid, para 24. See also UNHCR, 'Guidelines on Representing Stateless Persons' (n 110) 7. A particularly good example of this is the issue of South Korean citizenship for North Koreans. As Seunghwan Kim has argued, South Korean citizenship is 'purely theoretical', and is not granted in practice: see Seunghwan Kim, 'Lack of State Protection or Fear of Persecution? Determining the Refugee Status of North Koreans in Canada' (2016) 28 IJRL 85, 90. In addition to the case law discussed in that article, we also note interesting French case law on this point: see CNDA, decision no°09020156, 17 March 2011.

[129] Inter-American Commission on Human Rights ('IACHR'), 'Situation of Human Rights in the Dominican Republic' (31 December 2015) OEA/Ser.L/V/II Doc 45/15, [83] <http://www.oas.org/en/iachr/reports/pdfs/DominicanRepublic-2015.pdf> accessed 14 November 2018 (hereafter IACHR, 'Situation of Human Rights').

[130] ibid, [83].   [131] ibid, [1].

[132] ibid, [2]. See full report for more recent developments that have attempted to ameliorate the position for many of those that were deprived of citizenship through these measures. See also the decision of the Constitutional Court: República Dominicana Tribunal Constitucional [Domican Republic Constitutional Court], Sentencia TC/0168/13, 23 September 2013.

[133] See, to the contrary, *Pham v Secretary of State for the Home Department* [2015] UKSC 19.

[134] *1606601* (Refugee) [2016] AATA 4488 (14 September 2016) at [45] (hereafter *1606601*).

[135] ibid, [49].   [136] ibid, [50].

approach has been adopted by the Canadian Federal Court,[137] and the New Zealand Tribunal.[138]

However, it is important to clarify that this emphasis on law and its implementation is not the same question as whether the nationality is *effective*[139] or whether the person is *de facto* stateless. It has on occasion been argued that the key question in this context is *effectiveness* of nationality, such that where a nationality 'gives no substantive rights to the person acquiring it' it 'ought not to be considered as nationality for the purposes of refugee status determination'.[140] However, we agree with the British tribunal's rejection of this argument on the basis that it 'appears . . . to insert a quite unnecessary construct into the clear provisions of the Refugee Convention'.[141] In particular, the notion of de facto statelessness is not a term of international law,[142] having been explicitly excluded from the definition of the *1954 Convention*. Of course, the circumstances said to illustrate ineffectiveness of nationality or to amount to de facto statelessness may indicate that a person has a well-founded fear of being persecuted, which is the central issue in refugee status determination. Such matters should be assessed by reference to the core requirements of the refugee definition rather than by extraneous concepts that reduce rather than enhance clarity due to their potentially varied meanings and interpretation.

In terms of establishing whether a person has a particular nationality, both evidence concerning the laws and their implementation in the identified county of reference, as well as evidence relating to the individual's personal circumstances, may be relevant.[143] As the UNHCR explains, the applicant's personal history can assist to identify which states need to be assessed in examining an applicant's potential nationality.[144] This may include testimony from the applicant, identity documents,

---

[137] In *Lhazom* (n 123) the Court overturned the decision below because the Tribunal had assumed that a decision of the Supreme Court of India meant that the applicant was entitled to citizenship by birth, yet 'the Indian government does not appear to recognize that right': at [20]. See also *X (Re)*, 2015 CarswellNat 3329, which cited with approval an earlier Refugee Appeal Division decision that had observed that while the Appellant 'may, on paper, have been entitled to citizenship at birth, such entitlement is meaningless if not recognized by the authorities who bestow the benefits and privileges of citizenship': at [37].

[138] In *Refugee Appeal No 73873* (n 66) the Authority considered initially the Egyptian Citizenship Code which appeared to suggest that on the face of this provision, the applicant 'may be entitled to Egyptian citizenship': at [39]. However, country information indicated that the 'Code does not apply in any way to Palestinians in Egypt': at [40]. The Authority accepted that the applicant was 'not entitled to Egyptian citizenship. Such doubt as there is, should be resolved in favour of the appellant': at [42].

[139] We note that Hathaway and Foster invoke the concept of 'effectiveness' but explain that it refers to situations where the 'putative state of citizenship "does not accept that [its nationality] laws apply in the way [assumed]" ': *The Law of Refugee Status 2* (n 51) 57. This is in substance the same point that is being made here, namely that one must consider the implementation of the law as well as its theoretical status.

[140] *KA* (n 80) [7], in which the Tribunal was paraphrasing the argument put by Mr Fripp for the applicant in that case. But see Fripp, *Nationality and Statelessness* (n 81) 170–72.

[141] *KA* (n 80) [7]. For a similar decision, see *BG (Fiji)* (n 107), where the NZ Immigration and Protection Tribunal correctly found that 'discrimination in the enjoyment of rights between groups of citizens does not of itself render members of the disadvantaged group stateless under international law': at [78].

[142] As the UNHCR observes in its 'Handbook on Stateless Persons' (n 84), 'the term de facto statelessness is not defined in any international instrument and there is no treaty regime specific to this category of persons': [7].

[143] ibid, para 83.　　　　[144] ibid, para 84.

travel documents, marriage and school certificates, and other documents pertaining to countries of residence.[145] Possession of a passport creates a prima facie presumption;[146] the claim that a passport was issued merely for travelling purposes as a matter of convenience needs to be substantiated in order to rebut the presumption of nationality.[147] However, where a passport or travel documents were obtained illegally or by reference to 'illegitimate papers',[148] it cannot be concluded that the individual is a national of that country.[149] The steps taken by a government to facilitate or make it more difficult for an applicant to prove their nationality are further relevant considerations.[150] For example, in a decision concerning the application for refugee status of a man born in the Ukraine who claimed to be stateless, the New Zealand Tribunal found that while on its face the Ukrainian citizenship law appeared to stipulate that persons in the situation of the applicant were citizens, in fact, 'it is far from clear that the granting of Ukrainian citizenship is a mere formality so as to in fact make any notional right he may have to Ukrainian citizenship one which is readily realisable ... In the circumstances, the appellant must be given the benefit of the doubt as to this issue.'[151]

2.3 Burden and standard of proof

It is sometimes assumed that the burden of proof in establishing nationality in refugee status determination is on the applicant, albeit that this can shift.[152] For

---

[145] ibid. For a full list, see paras 84–86. See also Mark Symes and Peter Jorro, *Asylum Law and Practice* (Bloomsbury 2003) 327 (hereafter Symes and Jorro, *Asylum Law and Practice*); Hathaway and Foster, *The Law of Refugee Status 2* (n 51) 54.

[146] See *AZK15 v Minister for Immigration* [2015] FCCA 2303 (25 August 2015). In *Mathews v Canada (Minister of Citizenship and Immigration)* [2003] FCJ No 1777, the Federal Court of Canada held that '[a] holder of a particular country's passport is presumed to be a citizen of that country. Unless contested, a passport is evidence of nationality.' See also decision of the French authority at Conseil d'État [French Administrative Court], decision no°190036, 20 March 2000.

[147] UNHCR, 'Handbook' (n 47) para 93. See also UNHCR, 'Handbook on Stateless Persons' (n 84) para 95. See also *Asad v Ashcroft*, 135 Fed Appx 839 (6th Cir, 2005) [14]–[15]. See *NBKE v Minister for Immigration & Citizenship* [2007] FCA 126 (15 February 2007), where the applicant argued that the passport was obtained fraudulently. In *Mijatovic v Canada (Minister of Citizenship and Immigration)* [2006] FCJ No 860 (QL), the Federal Court of Canada stated, '[t]he Board is entitled to assume that a refugee claimant is a citizen of a country whose passport he or she holds. This presumption, however, can be rebutted. If there is evidence to indicate that a refugee claimant is not in fact a national of the country which issued the passport, the Board must consider the implications of such evidence. In *Radic*, Justice William P McKeown noted that the Board is expected to be aware of concepts such as the use of passports of convenience': at [26].

[148] In *1114181* [2013] RRTA 2 (4 January 2013) (hereafter *1114181*) the Australian Refugee Review Tribunal ('RRT') considered the applicant's Iraqi passport and accepted that it was not validly issued and she was not a national of Iraq (or Iran or Kuwait) and was therefore stateless: at [64].

[149] *Refugee Appeal No 74308* (n 66) [44].

[150] Symes and Jorro, *Asylum Law and Practice* (n 145) 327, citing *MA (Disputed Nationality) Ethiopia* [2008] UKAIT 00032. See also UNHCR, 'Handbook on Stateless Persons' (n 84) paras 37, 38. See also *Refugee Appeal No 74236* (n 122), in which the RSAA referred to country information that revealed the relevant authority did not recognize citizenship in cases such as the applicant's, nor did the government of Lebanon, again relying on country information: see at [45]–[46].

[151] *Refugee Appeal No 73575* [2004] NZRSAA 215 (30 June 2004) [41] (hereafter *Refugee Appeal No 73575*).

[152] *Smith* (n 79); *BA* (n 73) [26].

example, British decision-makers have characterized the question as being whether the appellant has been able to 'discharge the burden of proof upon her',[153] on the basis that 'the burden of proof rests on an appellant to prove his nationality or lack of it'.[154] Further, there is sometimes said to be a distinction between situations where nationality (or indeed statelessness) is doubtful[155] and those where it is disputed.[156] For instance, in the United Kingdom, it is said that the burden of proof is on the applicant in cases of doubtful nationality, but it is on the Home Office in cases of disputed nationality.[157]

However, neither of these approaches is defendable at international law. The distinction between doubtful and disputed nationality is not a legally meaningful one in either the context of the *Refugee Convention* or the *1954 Convention*, and the notion that the burden is on the applicant is inconsistent with principle.

The problems with imposing the burden on the applicant are well exemplified in the British jurisprudence, where the 'Bradshaw principle' holds that 'before a person could be regarded as stateless, she should make an application for citizenship of the countries with which she was most closely connected'.[158] This is clearly grounded in the notion that the burden of proof rests on the applicant, viz, '[b]earing in mind that the burden of proof rests on the claimant, it is always relevant to enquire in such cases whether a person has taken steps to apply for the nationality of the country in question or, if they have taken steps, whether they have been successful or unsuccessful'.[159] However, it is also sometimes expressed in a way that invokes an 'exhaustion of domestic remedies' concept, as indicated in its description as follows: 'before an applicant for asylum can claim the protection of a surrogate state, he or she must first take all steps to secure protection from the home state'.[160] Or, as stated in another case, the applicant 'is obliged to extinguish the eligibility [for citizenship of a country with which he/she has a close connection] before claiming statelessness'.[161] In some cases, this *evidentiary* principle is elided with the *substantive* question of whether an applicant can be denied refugee status because she has an inchoate nationality.[162] Although these are related, they are conceptually different issues, the latter of which is explored below in Part 2.6.1.

---

[153] *HS v Secretary of State for the Home Department* [2004] UKIAT 00090 [68].

[154] *BA* (n 73) [26].

[155] For instance, where the authorities of the new country do not accept the applicant's claimed nationality but acknowledge that there is no other country where the applicant could be removed to.

[156] This is where the nationality/statelessness claimed by the applicant is disputed by the authorities of the new country, who believe that the applicant is a national/or a former habitual resident of a different country to which he could be removed.

[157] UK Home Office, 'Nationality: Doubtful, Disputed and Other Cases' (Home Office, 2 October 2017) 14.

[158] As cited in *Queen on the application of Nhamo v Secretary of State for the Home Department* [2012] EWHC 422 (Admin), 2012 WL 382718 [52] (hereafter *Nhamo*).

[159] *YL* (n 75) as cited in *Tewolde* (n 122) [19]. See also *B (Lebanon) v Secretary of State for the Home Department* [2003] UKIAT 00104 [14]; *YL* [44].

[160] *Nhamo* (n 158) [52].   [161] *Tewolde* (n 122) [20].

[162] This appears to rest on the distinction between, on the one hand, a legal nationality (i.e. nationality by operation of law) that simply needs to be acknowledged in documentary form, and, on the other, the question whether an applicant could apply for citizenship, the latter of which is discussed in Part 2.6.1.

Application of the evidentiary principle that an applicant must furnish evidence of failed or rejected attempts to obtain citizenship may impose a requirement to apply for citizenship of more than one country, since 'any country with which he has a close connection' must be approached.[163] One exception is where there are 'serious obstacles' to a person availing themselves of an opportunity to acquire nationality,[164] or where an approach to authorities 'could place the claimant or the claimant's family at risk'.[165]

In practice, however, this doctrine can create insurmountable obstacles to a refugee claim,[166] and in any event is inconsistent with principle on two grounds. The first is that it engages in a retrospective examination of what the applicant should have done, which is inconsistent with the forward-looking apprehension of risk inherent in refugee status assessment,[167] and the second is that it relies on an adversarial model in which the burden of proof is imposed on the applicant alone.

As to the burden of proof, the UNHCR explained the true position decades ago in a classic statement concerning the refugee status determination process in which the 'benefit-of-the-doubt' principle, which predates the *Refugee Convention* as a refugee law concept,[168] was expounded:

It is a general legal principle that the burden of proof lies on the person submitting a claim. Often, however, an applicant may not be able to support his statements by documentary or other proof, and cases in which an applicant can provide evidence of all his statements will be the exception rather than the rule. In most cases a person fleeing from persecution will have arrived with the barest necessities and very frequently even without personal documents. Thus, while the burden of proof in principle rests on the applicant, the duty to ascertain and evaluate all the relevant facts is shared between the applicant and the examiner. Indeed, in some cases, it may be for the examiner to use all the means at his disposal to produce the necessary evidence in support of the application. Even such independent research may not, however, always be successful and there may also be statements that are not susceptible of

---

[163] *Tewolde* (n 122) [19]. See also *Tikhonov v Secretary of State for the Home Department* [1998] UKIAT G0052, [1998] INLR 737, in which the Tribunal relied on *Bradshaw* (n 122) and the notion that the onus is on the applicant. The Tribunal in this case denied refugee status on the grounds that 'the evidence disclosed no attempt by him to apply for citizenship in Lithuania, Moldova or Russia': 744–45.

[164] *BA* (n 73) [26].   [165] *YL* (n 75) [46]. See also *MA* (n 73) [79].

[166] The decision of the UK Tribunal in *Secretary of State for the Home Department v KF* [2005] UKIAT 00109, [2006] INLR 42 (hereafter *KF*) provides insight into the nature of the onus. Here, the Tribunal overturned the adjudicator's finding that the applicant was stateless on the basis that the applicant had not undertaken sufficient action to determine nationality, stating: 'But to fail to assert the relevant nationality and the basis for it, to fail to seek the right documents, or to follow up a refusal with letters, or to seek further assistance, legal or NGO, in pursuing the claim or to produce to the asserted country of nationality those documents which are obtainable is to fall well below the minimum necessary for any claim of statelessness': at [20]. For similar sentiment, see *Tretsetsang* (n 112) [31]: 'There is nothing unreasonable about expecting the applicant to take legal action if his state of nationality attempts to deny his rights.'

[167] A good example of this is where refugee claims have been rejected due to the applicant failing to 'demonstrate any diligent efforts to secure documents': *X (Re)*, 2010 CarswellNat 2654 [17].

[168] Louise W Holborn observed that one of the 'underlying principles of interpretation' adopted by the International Refugee Organization was that the 'applicant was given the benefit of the doubt': Louise W Holborn, *The International Refugee Organization: A Specialized Agency of the United Nations, Its History and Work, 1946–1952* (OUP 1956) 207.

proof. In such cases, if the applicant's account appears credible, he should, unless there are good reasons to the contrary, be given the benefit of the doubt.[169]

The challenges adverted to in this passage have particular resonance for stateless persons since the very nature of statelessness means that applicants 'are often unable to substantiate the claim [that they are stateless] with much, if any, documentary evidence'.[170] This is due to the fact that stateless persons are often deprived of documentation including birth registration, identity, and other documents.[171] As Lord Justice Sedley observed, '[t]o prove that one is an undocumented bedoon paradoxically requires documents'.[172] For this reason, the UNHCR Handbook on Protection of Stateless Persons recognizes that in the case of statelessness determination, 'the burden of proof is in principle shared, in that both the applicant and examiner must cooperate to obtain evidence and to establish the facts. The procedure is a collaborative one.'[173] Or in the words of the Canadian Federal Court, '[b]oth parties therefore have a role to play [in establishing identity]'.[174] The UNHCR further recommends that '[s]tatelessness determination authorities need to take [inability to obtain documentary evidence] into account, where appropriate giving sympathetic consideration to testimonial explanations regarding the absence of certain kinds of evidence'.[175]

While this guidance was developed for the specific context of a formal stateless determination procedure, it is relevant and persuasive in the refugee context where the applicant claims to be stateless. This is not only due to practical and logistical challenges, but the 'fundamental point of principle'[176] that states parties have a legal duty to implement the *Refugee Convention* in good faith, which means facilitating the identification of those entitled to protection,[177] not introducing procedural barriers that in practice represent substantial obstacles to delivering protection obligations. In this regard it is instructive to observe that the 'Bradshaw principle', prevalent in the British jurisprudence, stems from *obiter* comments in a decision

---

[169] UNHCR, 'Handbook' (n 47) para 196.

[170] UNHCR, 'Handbook on Stateless Persons' (n 84) para 90.

[171] This was recognized in *Minister of Public Safety and Emergency Preparedness v Rooney*, 2016 FC 1097 [46]–[47] (hereafter *Rooney*).

[172] *SA (Kuwait) v Secretary of State for the Home Department* [2009] EWCA Civ 1157 [2], cited with approval in *A-S v SSHD* [2011] EWHC 564 (Admin) [3].

[173] UNHCR, 'Handbook on Stateless Persons' (n 84) para 89. See also Laura van Waas, *Nationality Matters: Statelessness under International Law* (Intersentia 2008) at 402–07, 430–32 (hereafter van Waas, *Nationality Matters*).

[174] *Rooney* (n 171) [43].

[175] UNHCR, 'Handbook on Stateless Persons' (n 84) para 90. A good example of this in practice is provided in the decision of the New Zealand RSAA in *Refugee Appeal No 75093* (n 66), where the Authority accepted that in light of the applicant's personal history, it was 'unlikely that [his] birth was registered' in Iraq and thus 'it is probable he cannot establish' Iraqi nationality: see [33]–[35].

[176] Hathaway and Foster, *The Law of Refugee Status 2* (n 51) 119. Katia Bianchini observes that in a 2015 judgment the Italian Cassation Court stated, in relation to assessing statelessness pursuant to the *1954 Convention*, that the burden of proof for the stateless applicant has to be reduced '*as the matter concerns fundamental human rights*': Katia Bianchini, *Protecting Stateless Persons: The Implementation of the Convention relating to the Status of Stateless Persons Across EU States* (Brill Nijhoff 2018) 165, citing Corte Cass 3 April 2015 n 4262, (emphasis in original).

[177] It is this principle that is paramount, not the need to deter 'bogus claimants': see *YL* (n 75) [44].

that did not concern an application for protection under the *Refugee Convention*.[178] The appropriateness of applying this principle in the protective framework of the *Refugee Convention* may thus be ripe for reconsideration.[179]

The sole focus on conclusive documentary evidence above is inconsistent with two lines of reasoning that have developed in cases involving refugee claims by stateless individuals. First, while many decision-makers will instinctively seek to obtain and rely predominantly, if not solely, on documentary evidence to establish nationality, the correct position is elucidated by the US Court of Appeals for the Second Circuit, namely, that 'there is no requirement that this showing [nationality or lack of nationality] be made through non-testimonial evidence'.[180] As the Court observed, the ordinary principle applies, namely, that 'credible testimony' alone may found a claim.[181] Further, the Court emphasized that the fact that the decision-maker below considered that the applicant had 'failed to establish his nationality' did not 'obviate the need to resolve conclusively [his] country of nationality and citizenship'.[182] This principle is also well exemplified in a recent Australian tribunal decision in which '[d]espite evidence suggesting that the applicant's children are Iranian citizens',[183] from which the government had inferred Iranian citizenship of the parents, the Tribunal relied substantially on the applicant's credible oral testimony in support of the finding that 'he is a stateless person'.[184] This reasoning also resonates with that of courts considering cognate issues. For example, in a recent judgment of the European Court of Human Rights (ECtHR), which concerned the question whether the insecurity of residence status in Croatia for a stateless man violated Article 8 of the *European Convention on Human Rights*, the Court found that

[178] In *Bradshaw* (n 122), the Outer House of the Court of Session considered whether the Secretary of State had been correct to conclude that the petitioner was an illegal entrant. While the Court considered the definition of statelessness under the *1954 Convention*, there was no reference to authority; rather, the judge adopted a personal view ('it seems to me that': at 366) that was in any event *obiter* given that 'I am not prepared to reach an opinion without either hearing oral evidence or receiving affidavits from those authoritatively qualified to advise me on the nationality laws of the Russian Federation and the Ukraine': at 366.

[179] We note that in *YL* (n 75) the Asylum and Immigration Tribunal ('IAT') stated that the Bradshaw principle was 'all the more necessary in the case of someone claiming to be a refugee under the Refugee Convention': at [44]. This was because to 'leave it as an optional matter would also make it possible for bogus claimants to benefit from international protection even though in law they had nationality of a country where they would not be at risk of persecution': at [44].

[180] *Urgen v Holder* 768 F 3d 269 (2nd Cir, 2014) 273 (hereafter *Urgen*). See in Australia, *SZOXM v Minister for Immigration* [2011] FMCA 564 (22 July 2011) [20].

[181] *Urgen* (n 180); see also Hathaway and Foster, *The Law of Refugee Status 2* (n 51) 136–37.

[182] *Urgen* (n 180) 273.

[183] *1707843 (Refugee)* [2018] AATA 1004 (7 March 2018) [95]. We note that this decision concerned the correctness of a visa cancellation. The applicant had been found to be a refugee but the Department later sought to cancel the protection visa on the basis that the applicant had falsely claimed he was stateless when he was (allegedly) a citizen of Iran: see at [1]–[3].

[184] ibid, [95]. This may be contrasted with a similar cancellation decision in which the cancellation was upheld on the basis of a document issued by the UNHCR which noted the applicant's nationality as Iraqi rather than stateless, yet it is questionable in light of the fact that there was no evidence as to how the UNHCR determined citizenship in that case: *1708563* [2017] AATA 2223 (23 August 2017) [18]–[19].

'there are no reasons to doubt the applicant's arguments that he was advised by the Albanian authorities that he was not an Albanian national'.[185]

The second is the principle that should the nationality of an applicant prove to be indeterminable, the decision-maker should extend 'the benefit of the doubt' to the applicant.[186] As the NZ RSAA explained:

> it would be best in keeping with the [Refugee] Convention, as well as with the humanitarian spirit underlying the instrument, to give the applicant the benefit of the doubt. This will mean in some cases considering him a national of his country of origin ... but should it, for some reason, be more favourable for a person of indeterminable national status to be considered a stateless person, he should be considered as such.[187]

That case involved a stateless Palestinian who had lived in Morocco for a number of years and had stayed for short periods in a number of EU countries. The Tribunal first ascertained that the applicant was not under the protection of the UN Relief and Works Agency and hence Article 1D did not apply;[188] his claim for refugee status should be considered within the ambit of Article 1A(2). The Tribunal, applying this principle to the facts of the case, concluded that to consider him stateless

> is the most favourable view of the facts for the simple reason that if the appellant is in fact a Jordanian national, he is not in fear of the Jordanian authorities and his claim to refugee status would be defeated for that reason alone. If, on the other hand, we attribute for these purposes Israeli citizenship to the appellant, that likewise would be to his disadvantage because he would then stand in a wholly different position to those Palestinians living in the Occupied Territories ... Although their political and economic position has not escaped

---

[185] *Hoti v Croatia*, Application No 63311/14 (26 April 2018) [110].

[186] 'Where his nationality cannot be clearly established, his refugee status should be determined in a similar manner to that of a stateless person, i.e. instead of the country of his nationality, the country of his former habitual residence will have to be taken into account': UNHCR, 'Handbook' (n 47) para 89. See *1317610* [2014] RRTA 472 (28 May 2014) (hereafter *1317610*), where the RRT gave the applicant 'the benefit of the doubt' and accepted 'he is not a citizen of Iraq and that he unlawfully obtained an Iraqi passport. The Tribunal accordingly finds that the applicant is stateless': at [49]. The 'benefit-of-the-doubt' principle has been applied in general in refugee claims by stateless applicants in New Zealand, see *Refugee Appeal No 74467* (n 74) [40]. It may be that an applicant claims to hold a particular nationality and to fear being persecuted if returned to the country of nationality yet doubts exist as to the validity of the nationality claim. In that context, courts have also insisted on a shared burden and application of the benefit of the doubt principle. For instance, in a case concerning a Somali applicant who had lived for several years in a Kenyan refugee camp, the Belgian authorities relied on some inconsistencies in his testimony to doubt the veracity of his claimed nationality. They therefore assessed the application solely in relation to the country of 'former habitual residence', namely Kenya. On review, the Council for Alien Law Litigation annulled the decision on the grounds that it had failed to investigate thoroughly all the relevant elements presented by the applicant to establish whether or not he was of Somalian nationality, including contacting the refugee camp in which he lived for many years: Conseil du Contentieux des Etrangers ('CCE') [Belgian Council for Alien Law Litigation], *X v le Commissaire général aux réfugiés et aux apatrides*, arrêt no°87989, 21 September 2012 [6.3.3].

[187] *Refugee Appeal No 1/92* (n 29), as cited in *Refugee Appeal No 73873* (n 66) [60]. See also *Refugee Appeal No 73575* (n 151) [33]. See also *Refugee Appeal No 75093* (n 66), in which the NZ Tribunal found that, 'while the appellant may be a national of Iraq, it is probable that he cannot establish this'; hence 'the appellant cannot return to Iraq': at [35]. The Tribunal concluded he was therefore 'a de facto stateless person', citing *Refugee Appeal No 72635* (n 29) [80], [108]–[110], at [36], and has no country of nationality. See also *Refugee Appeal No 73873* (n 66) [42].

[188] See Chapter 6 for further discussion of Article 1D.

criticism, it could at least be argued that Palestinians of Israeli citizenship are better off than those Palestinians living in the Occupied Territories.[189]

He was therefore treated as a stateless person; his statelessness arises from the fact that there is no Palestinian state and he does not enjoy Israeli or Jordanian citizenship. Other examples in which this principle has been invoked include the possession of a passport which the applicant claims to have obtained through bribery or otherwise illegally.[190]

The key question after all is not solely whether the applicant is stateless but whether he or she has a well-founded fear in either the country of nationality or his or her country of former habitual residence. An excessive focus on establishing *conclusively* whether a person is stateless detracts from this core focus and may result in a rejection of refugee status even when a person has a well-founded fear in relation to a country to which he or she could be returned.[191]

Finally, the standard of proof remains that relevant to all aspects of the inclusive clause of the refugee definition, namely 'real chance'. This is clear and well established in relation to the *Refugee Convention*. In addition, in relation to determining whether a person is stateless for the purposes of the *1954 Convention*, the UNHCR advises states 'to adopt the same standard of proof as that required in refugee status determination',[192] thus emphasizing again the shared protective objective underlying both regimes. The well-established 'real chance' test applies to all aspects of the refugee status determination process, and there is no justification for adopting a different standard of proof in relation to other aspects of the inclusion clause in relation to stateless persons. Accordingly, the idiosyncratic Canadian position that in order to be found a *Refugee Convention* refugee 'a stateless person must show that, on a balance of probabilities he or she would suffer persecution in any country of former habitual residence'[193] is incorrect.[194]

In the final two sections in this Part we consider two issues that have sometimes raised complex issues for decision-makers in relation to identifying whether an applicant for refugee status should be considered to have a nationality.

2.4 Nationality conferred without consent

As explained in Chapter 3, there is still no duty on states to confer nationality,[195] except perhaps where the state is a party to the 1961 *Convention on the Reduction of*

---

[189] *Refugee Appeal No 1/92* (n 29).   [190] See e.g., *1317610* (n 186) [49].

[191] This was recognized in one (relatively rare) UK decision. In *Smith* (n 79), the Tribunal found that even where a positive finding of nationality cannot be made, the task of the decision-maker is not concluded because the decision-maker must 'go on and assess the appellant's claim by reference to his claimed country of persecution': at [55].

[192] UNHCR, 'Handbook on Statelessness Persons' (n 84) para 91.

[193] *Chehade v Minister of Citizenship and Immigration* 2017 FC 282 [28] (hereafter *Chehade*), citing *Thabet* (n 30) [30]. See also *Minister of Citizenship v Alsha'bi* 2015 FC 1381 [74].

[194] This position appears to be inconsistent with the standard of proof adopted in refugee cases in general in Canada: see *Adjei v Minister of Employment and Immigration*, RSC 1976, C 52 (27 January 1989).

[195] NZ RSAA in *Refugee Appeal No 72635* (n 29), cited in Symes and Jorro, *Asylum Law and Practice* (n 145) 312.

Statelessness. However, what of the situation where a state imposes a nationality on a person without the individual's consent? If statelessness represents 'a human rights deficit', is nationality, *any nationality*, better than statelessness?[196] If an applicant for refugee status disputes the nationality, does this mean the impugned country of nationality is not considered the country of reference in the refugee determination?

The British Digest of International Law states:

There is today a strong current of international legal thinking to the effect that, apart from the case of concessions of territory or in very special circumstances, international recognition need not be accorded to the nationality of a State conferred on the recipient *not at his request or without his consent*, unless, by both parentage and permanent domicile, he has a genuine connexion with that State.[197]

It follows that assigning nationality to a person against her will would most likely contravene international law, unless she has a real connexion with that state (e.g. birth or descent, possibly also long-term residence).[198] Today, this rule may also extend to the context of state succession. The ILC Draft Articles on Nationality of Natural Persons in relation to the Succession of States with Commentaries expressly provides that 'in matters concerning nationality, due account should be taken both of the legitimate interests of States and those of individuals'.[199] Furthermore, Article 8(2) provides:

A successor State shall not attribute its nationality to persons concerned who have their habitual residence in another State against the will of the persons concerned unless they would otherwise become stateless.

This provision therefore restricts the power of a successor state to attribute its nationality to persons concerned not residing in its territory and having the nationality of another state, except on a consensual basis. However, the exception in relation to persons who would otherwise be stateless is important and suggests that imposing nationality in such a situation would not violate international law. Article 11 of the

[196] Audrey Macklin, 'Sticky Citizenship' in Rhoda E Howard-Hassmann and Margaret Walton-Roberts (eds), *The Human Right to Citizenship: A Slippery Concept* (University of Pennsylvania Press 2015) 231 (hereafter Macklin, 'Sticky Citizenship').

[197] *British Digest of International Law Part VI: The Individual in International Law*, vol 5 (Stevens & Sons 1965) 25 (emphasis added), citing Paul Weis, *Nationality and Statelessness in International Law* (Steven & Sons 1956) 110–13; John Mervyn Jones, *British Nationality Law and Practice* (Clarendon Press 1947) 15; Gerald Fitzmaurice, 'The General Principles of International Law Considered from the Standpoint of the Rule of Law' in *Recueil des Cours*, vol 92 (Académie de Droit International 1957) 198–201, cited in D J Harris, *Cases and Materials on International Law* (5th edn, Sweet & Maxwell 1998) 587.

[198] For instance, the UN Committee on the Elimination of Racial Discrimination ('CERD'), 'General Recommendation 30: Discrimination against Non-Citizens' (23 February–12 March 2004) UN Doc CERD/C/64/Misc.11/rev.3 recommends that states party, '[r]egularize the status of former citizens of predecessor States who now reside within the jurisdiction of the State Party'.

[199] ILC, *Draft Articles on Nationality of Natural Persons in relation to the Succession of States with Commentaries* (ILC 1999) (hereafter ILC, *Draft Articles*) Preamble. We note that the Council of Europe *Convention on the Avoidance of Statelessness* mirrors the provisions in the *Draft Articles on Nationality of Natural Persons in relation to the Succession of States: Council of Europe Convention on the Avoidance of Statelessness in Relation to State Succession* (opened for signature 19 May 2006, entered into force 1 May 2009) CETS 200, art 5.

ILC Draft Articles on Nationality of Natural Persons in Relation to the Succession of States with commentaries deals specifically with the issue of 'respect for the will of persons concerned' whenever those persons are qualified to acquire the nationality of two or more states concerned.[200] In any such cases, 'Each State concerned shall grant a right to opt for its nationality to persons concerned who have appropriate connection with that State if those persons would otherwise become stateless as a result of the succession of States.'[201]

The commentary to this provision explains that, 'The function which international law attributes to the will of individuals in matters of and loss of nationality in cases of succession of States is, however, among the issues on which doctrinal views considerably diverge.'[202]

In the view of the ILC, whilst the individual's will is a paramount consideration, this does not mean that every acquisition of nationality upon a succession of states must have a consensual basis.[203] Finally, it may also be noted that the ILC's Draft Articles on Diplomatic Protection with Commentaries provides, by reference to the *Namibia* case, that if 'a person acquires a nationality involuntarily in a manner inconsistent with international law, as where a woman automatically acquires the nationality of her husband on marriage, that person should in principle be allowed to be protected diplomatically by her or his former State of nationality'.[204]

As this indicates, there remains disagreement about the ramifications of an imposition of nationality without consent, at least in the context of dual nationality.[205] In the context of persons who would otherwise be stateless, however, the position is more settled, namely, that conferral of nationality is not unlawful.

In truth, a dispute about whether a nationality was conferred legally or with consent has rarely arisen in the context of refugee status determination. To the extent that courts have considered the legality of state action in relation to nationality, it has more commonly arisen where there is a failure to accord, or explicit deprivation of, nationality, an issue to which we return in depth in Chapter 5 in the context of deprivation of nationality as persecution.

2.5 Illegality in withholding or deprivation of citizenship

The converse of the imposition of nationality without consent is its withdrawal or deprivation. As explored in Chapter 3, the classic position that states retain absolute discretion in decisions concerning nationality has been significantly tempered by

[200] See generally van Waas, *Nationality Matters* (n 173) 140 and Ineta Ziemele, 'State Succession and Issues of Nationality and Statelessness' in Alice Edwards and Laura van Waas (eds), *Nationality and Statelessness under International Law* (CUP 2014) 217, 230.

[201] ILC, *Draft Articles* (n 199) art 11(2).

[202] According to the ILC, several commentators have stressed the importance of the right of option in this respect but whilst most of them are satisfied to deduce this right from a treaty, others consider that the right of option exists independently as an attribute of the principle of self-determination: ibid.

[203] ibid, art 11 commentary.

[204] UNGA 'Report of the International Law Commission: Fifty-Eighth Session' (n 103) 34–35.

[205] For a comprehensive discussion, see Paul Weis, *Nationality and Statelessness in International Law* (2nd edn, Sijthoff & Noordhoff 1979) 110–13.

international law, especially human rights constraints, meaning that some instances of withdrawal or deprivation constitute a violation of international law. A question thus arises as to how an asylum state should view such unlawful acts from the perspective of identifying the country of reference in refugee law.

In the context of the *1954 Convention*, the UNHCR's position is that while the contravention of international obligations 'must not be condoned', it is 'generally irrelevant for the purposes of Article 1(1) [of the *1954 Stateless Convention*]'.[206] As explained in the UNHCR Handbook on Protection of Stateless Persons, '[t]he alternative would mean that an individual who has been stripped of his or her nationality in a manner inconsistent with international law would nevertheless be considered a "national" for the purposes of Article 1(1); a situation at variance with the object and purpose of the 1954 Convention'.[207] In other words, since the relevant question in the context of the *1954 Convention* is whether an individual has or does not have a nationality for the purpose of determining entitlement to specified rights, to adopt the legal fiction that a person stripped of nationality remains a national due to illegality would eviscerate an individual's entitlement to protection under that regime.

While that appears to be uncontroversial in relation to the *1954 Stateless Convention*, a question has been raised as to whether the same analysis is appropriate in the context of the *Refugee Convention*. Eric Fripp argues that where a state has deprived an individual of nationality in violation of international law, the state should at least in some cases nonetheless continue to be considered the 'country of nationality' for the purposes of assessing entitlement to refugee status. He suggests that such an interpretation can be justified either based 'directly on international law principles relating to recognition' or 'a parallel interpretive policy or practice'.[208]

In terms of the interpretative policy or practice, Fripp argues that there is 'learning which points to a legitimate practice of interpretation, or judicial practice, which ignores the effect of deprivation of nationality where this is connected to the reasons for asylum being sought'.[209] In support he relies heavily on the classic refugee law scholar Grahl-Madsen, however that authority was confined to the situation where a refugee is denationalized *after* leaving their country of nationality.[210] Since determination of refugee status is declaratory, a person who has become a refugee by virtue of being outside their country of nationality on a relevant ground, will not be affected in 'his claim to refugee status if he subsequently loses his nationality'.[211] Grahl-Madsen observed that Zink's contention that the phrase, 'the country of his nationality' should be understood in the sense 'the country whose nationality he possesses, or whose nationality he has lost in connexion with leaving the country' was 'not devoid of virtue'.[212] Indeed, in Grahl-Madsen's view, 'one is in good company

[206] UNHCR, 'Handbook on Stateless Persons' (n 84) para 56.   [207] ibid.
[208] Fripp, *Nationality and Statelessness* (n 81) 215.   [209] ibid, 211.
[210] See Grahl-Madsen, *The Status of Refugees in International Law* (n 4) 159—he only explicitly adopts Zink's views in relation to *sur place* claims.
[211] ibid, 157. Fripp doesn't seem to distinguish between those denationalized while still in the country, those denationalized on exit, and those denationalized only after they had left. See also Zimmermann, *The 1951 Convention* (n 26) 443, para 588.
[212] Grahl-Madsen, *The Status of Refugees in International Law* (n 4) 159, citing Zink.

if one refuses to give effect to measures of denationalization against persons still residing in their home country'.[213] However he continued as follows:[214]

However, if the country of a person's (lost) nationality may also be construed as the country of his former habitual residence, it will, in normal cases, hardly be worth the effort to try to determine which of the two concepts should be applied. In some cases it may actually be advantageous for a denationalised person to be placed on an equal footing with other stateless persons.[215]

Not only is there little authority in refugee law scholarship for Fripp's view or any jurisprudential support for the invocation of non-recognition in this context,[216] it is difficult to reconcile with the plain text of the refugee definition, particularly when regard is had to the drafting history. In a provisional draft by the Ad Hoc Committee on Statelessness and Related Problems, the definition of the term 'refugee' included, '[a]ny person who (i) is and remains outside the countries of his nationality, *former nationality* or former habitual residence owing to persecution'.[217] However, one week later, the Ad Hoc Committee adopted a definition that omitted reference to 'former nationality', with only 'country of his nationality' and 'country of former habitual residence' remaining.[218] The reason for this change in terminology is

---

[213] Grahl-Madsen, *The Status of Refugees in International Law* (n 4).

[214] This section was not cited by Fripp, *Nationality and Statelessness* (n 81).

[215] Grahl-Madsen, *The Status of Refugees in International Law* (n 4) 159 (the latter comment about advantages likely relates to his view that for a stateless person, non-return is sufficient to justify refugee status).

[216] Fripp acknowledges that '[n]on-recognition principles have not been expressly invoked in the jurisprudence concerning denationalization (and ensuing denial of relevant rights) as persecution': Eric Fripp, 'Deprivation of Nationality, "the Country of His Nationality" in Article 1A(2) of the Refugee Convention, and Non-Recognition in International Law' (2016) 28 IJRL 453, 475 (hereafter Fripp, 'Deprivation of Nationality'). Indeed, in *ST* (n 123) the Upper Tribunal of the Immigration and Asylum Chamber noted, in relation to refusal of the right to return, that 'it matters not whether a person who has been arbitrarily deprived of their nationality is, as a result, regarded as stateless or as a person who, in terms of international law, still possesses that nationality, albeit that the rights associated with it cannot in practice be exercised': at [87].

[217] Ad Hoc Committee on Refugees and Stateless Persons, 'Provisional Draft of Parts of the Definition Article of the Preliminary Draft Convention relating to the Status of Refugees, Prepared by the Working Group on This Article' (23 January 1950) UN Doc E/AC.32/L.6, art I (2) (emphasis added) (hereafter 23 January Provisional Draft). A Belgian proposal was in similar terms in extending the definition to anyone who: (a) was a victim of the Nazi regime in Germany or in a territory allegedly annexed by Germany, or of a regime which fought on the German side in the Second World War or of a regime set up in a German-occupied country which helped Germany in its fight against the United Nations; or was, or has, or was a justifiable fear of becoming, a victim of the Falangist regime in Spain; (b) for any of these reasons is outside the country of which he is, or formerly was, a national or, if he has no nationality, outside the country where he used previously to reside; and (c) is unable or unwilling, for the same reasons, to claim the protection of the country of which he is a national: Ad Hoc Committee on Refugees and Stateless Persons, 'Belgium: Proposal for Article I paragraph A. 2 of Document E/AC.32/L.6/Rev.1' (31 January 1950) UN Doc E/AC.32/L.18.

[218] Ad Hoc Committee on Statelessness and Related Problems, 'Decisions of the Committee on Statelessness and Related Problems Taken at the Meetings of 31 January 1950' (31 January 1950) UN Doc E/AC.32/L.20 (hereafter Ad Hoc Committee, 'Decisions of the Committee Meeting 31 January 1950'); Ad Hoc Committee on Statelessness and Related Problems, 'Draft Convention relating to the Status of Refugees, Decisions of the Working Group Taken on 9 February 1950' (9 February 1950) UN Doc E/AC.32/L.32, 2.

not clear,[219] although it is notable that the Director General of the International Refugee Organization ('IRO') sent a cable to the Committee in the interim arguing that 'the inclusion of all three qualifications (nationality, former nationality, former habitual residence) may give rise to misunderstandings'.[220] As was pointed out by the observer of the IRO, the term 'former nationality' 'does not necessarily mean the nationality of the country from which the refugee has been displaced'.[221] The following day the Committee adopted a version of the definition that omitted 'former nationality'. This issue was not further discussed; thus, the proposed draft convention submitted at the conclusion of the Ad Hoc Committee's deliberations omitted the reference to 'former nationality'.[222] It does not appear to have been revived throughout the subsequent deliberations of the Ad Hoc Committee on Refugees and Stateless Persons, nor the Conference of Plenipotentiaries.

In light of this history it is difficult to justify reading the term 'country of former nationality' back into the definition. Nor is it straightforward: given the lack of clarity in relation to the application of the international law principle of non-recognition in this context,[223] the most that can be said is that '*in certain circumstances* the action of a State as regards nationality does not command recognition by another State or international body in the application of article 1A(2)'.[224] However this interpretation does not promote consistency in decision-making given the lack of clarity as to precisely when the non-recognition principle can or should be adopted.[225] Nor,

[219] There does not appear to be discussion of this precise point in the summary records of the Ad Hoc Committee's meetings.

[220] Ad Hoc Committee on Statelessness and Related Problems, 'Memorandum from the Secretariat of the International Refugee Organization' (30 January 1950) UN Doc E/AC.32/L.16, 3 (hereafter Ad Hoc Committee, 'Memorandum from the Secretariat of the IRO'). The *Constitution of the International Refugee Organization and Interim Measures to Be Taken in respect of Refugees and Displaced Persons* (opened for signature 15 December 1946, entered into force 20 August 1948) 18 UNTS 3 (hereafter *IRO Constitution*) also did not include express reference to country of former nationality. Instead, it provides that the term 'refugee', 'applies to a person who has left, or who is outside of, his country of nationality or of former habitual residence, and who, whether or not he had retained his nationality' belongs to various categories. We thank Guy Goodwin-Gill for pointing this out and for helpful feedback on this section.

[221] Ad Hoc Committee, 'Memorandum from the Secretariat of the IRO' (n 220) 3. It was clear that these comments were directed to the 23 January Provisional Draft: see page 2 para 1: 'The contents of the cable are based on definitions drafted by the working group on 20 January which have since been superseded by those in the draft of 23 January (E/AC/32/L.6).'

[222] UN Economic and Social Council, 'Report of the Ad Hoc Committee on Statelessness and Related Problems' (17 February 1950) UN Docs E/1618, E/AC.32/5, 12 (hereafter UNESC, 'Report of the Ad Hoc Committee').

[223] Fripp's argument rests on the principle of non-recognition in international law, but this is not a principle strictly relevant to the present context. As James Crawford explains, '[t]he typical act of recognition has two legal functions. First, the determination of statehood, a question of law: such individual determination may have evidential value. Secondly, a condition of the establishment of formal relations, including diplomatic relations and the conclusion of bilateral treaties: it is this second function which has been described by some as "constitutive", but it is not a condition of statehood': James Crawford, *Brownlie's Principles of Public International Law* (8th edn, OUP 2012) 147, 155–65 (hereafter Crawford, *Brownlie's Principles of Public International Law*).

[224] Fripp, *Nationality and Statelessness* (n 81) 217 (emphasis added). In the International Journal of Refugee Law article, he states that '[i]t is possible to imagine conjectural cases in which principle might not favour non-recognition'; thus '[i]nevitably, analysis of cases will be fact sensitive': Fripp, 'Deprivation of Nationality' (n 216) 474.

[225] Fripp states that the effect of non-recognition is that the interpretation of the term 'the country of his nationality . . . may well include a State that has denationalized its former citizen': 'Deprivation of

in our view, is it necessary to adopt this strained and complicated interpretation in order adequately to accommodate the protection needs of those who have been de-nationalized by their country of origin.

The core concern animating Fripp's proposed approach is that the state that has deprived the individual of nationality should remain a country of reference for the purposes of assessing refugee status. Fripp argues that the country that has denationalized the applicant should remain the 'country of nationality' for the purposes of refugee law because to do otherwise 'adds a potential denial of international protection to the arbitrary removal of that individual's nationality and intuitively seems wrong'.[226] The implication appears to be that if the country of origin does not remain the country of nationality, then refugee status may be denied.[227]

However, in our view the *Refugee Convention* itself provides a far more straight-forward and far less complicated method of achieving this outcome.[228] As explained above, where a person does 'not hav[e] a nationality' then the reference state is the country of former habitual residence. Indeed, in by far the majority of cases involving denationalization, decision-makers simply adopt this approach, that is, to consider the state of origin (in relation to which the legality of denationalization is contested) as the country of former habitual residence.[229] This is also the approach

Nationality' (n 216) 475. However, his proposed interpretation is never stated in a way that is definitive or straightforward to apply. In his book he concludes, '[o]verall, the best approach seems to be that in certain circumstances the action of a State as regards nationality does not command recognition by another State or international body in the application of article 1A(2) CSR51': Fripp, *Nationality and Statelessness* (n 81) 216–17.

[226] Fripp, *Nationality and Statelessness* (n 81) 211.

[227] This is made explicit in Fripp, 'Deprivation of Nationality' (n 216), where he argues that, in relation to art 1A(2) of the *Refugee Convention*, 'recognition of statelessness following denationalization would lead to the State responsible ceasing to provide the point of reference for status determination': 472.

[228] The lack of certainty seems to be reflected in Fripp's equivocal language: 'In the current state of development of international law, therefore, the effect of non-recognition is that the interpretation of the term "the country of his nationality" in article 1A(2) should in many cases in which denationalisation is potentially relevant to asylum include the State which has denationalized its former citizen in a manner contrary to established international law principles, because the community of States engaged in the CSR51 [Refugee Convention] regime, and/or the individual State considering whether a claimant's situation engages that regime, will not give effect to that change for the purpose of identifying the reference State under article 1A(2) CSR51 and then determining whether a well-founded fear of persecution for a relevant reason exists in relation to that State. This is wholly consistent with the ordinary meaning of "country of nationality" in article 1A(2) CSR51 once account is given to the international law context': ibid at 214–15.

[229] Indeed, this seems to be what the UK courts have done—even according to Fripp: see *Nationality and Statelessness* (n 81) 208. In *EB (Ethiopia) v Secretary of State for the Home Department* [2007] EWCA Civ 809, [2008] 3 WLR 1188, the court cited a letter of 17 July 2000 to the US Immigration and Naturalisation Service from a senior official of UNHCR stating '[i]f, as a result of the deprivation of nationality, these persons become stateless, they would be entitled to recognition as refugees ... as Ethiopia would be their country of former habitual residence': at [31]. An analysis of the key cases involving deprivation of citizenship as persecution across a range of jurisdictions reveals that decision-makers routinely assess the country of (former) nationality straightforwardly as the country of former habitual residence: see *Refugee Appeal No 75694* (n 74) [36]; *Refugee Appeal No 76077* [2009] NZRSAA 37 (19 May 2009) [2] (hereafter *Refugee Appeal No 76077*). In the US, see *Haile v Gonzales*, 421 F 3d 493 (7th Cir, 2005) (hereafter *Haile*). In France, see CNDA, decision no°12013646 C, 26 June 2013; CNDA, decision no°09019611, 14 February 2011.

of leading modern refugee law scholars.[230] The isolated instances in which this approach has not been implemented straightforwardly are anomalous, and are based on an incorrect assumption that there can only be one country of former habitual residence.[231]

By contrast, in the jurisdictions that correctly recognize that there can be more than one country of former habitual residence, decision-makers have had no difficulty in assessing the refugee claim in relation to the state that denationalized the applicant as the country of former habitual residence, notwithstanding subsequent residence in an intermediary, or even several intermediary, states.[232] This will be explored further in Part 2.6.

In sum, any illegality on the part of the state in withdrawing or refusing nationality will, of course, be extremely pertinent to the question whether a person is at risk of persecution in that state, or whether she is unable or unwilling to seek the protection of that state, but in our view it does not bear on the question of the state of reference.

2.6 The individual's role in nationality acquisition and retention

In this final section we consider the role of the individual in the acquisition of citizenship. We first consider whether an applicant can be refused refugee status because he or she could—and therefore should—acquire a nationality to which they may be

---

[230] Goodwin-Gill and McAdam state, after discussing cases where refugees leaving their country are stripped of their citizenship, '[r]efugee status in such cases might appear determinable in the light of the situation prevailing in the country of origin as the "country of former habitual residence" ': *The Refugee in International Law* (n 51) 68. Even where deprivation of nationality is illegal under international law, 'such acts are not opposable'. Accordingly, 'the country where the applicant is seeking refuge must disregard the illegality of such acts and must, therefore, consider the person as not having acquired, or lost respectively, the nationality of the country concerned': Zimmermann, *The 1951 Convention* (n 26) 443. We note that Fripp criticises this approach although also acknowledges that their approach is 'well founded': *Nationality and Statelessness* (n 81) 216. In our view, notions of opposability or non-recognition are not relevant in the refugee context.

[231] This indeed appears to be Fripp's assumption as well, where he states, 'But, an individual treated as stateless by reason of deprivation of nationality by State X, who is found to have established habitual residence in State Y before seeking asylum elsewhere, would be assessed by reference to State Y': Fripp, 'Deprivation of Nationality' (n 216) 478. In Germany, the position is particularly anomalous as the relevant legislation 'focuses on the country where the foreigner, as a stateless person, last "had" his habitual residence': 10 C 50.07 (n 34) [30]; see also at [36]. This is the decision discussed by Fripp at length that is said to indicate the need for the non-recognition approach. Similarly, the other decision discussed by Fripp, from the High Court of Ireland, is respectfully incorrect in failing to identify Bhutan—the country of original nationality (subsequently revoked as a tool of persecution)—as a country of former habitual residence in accordance with the principles outlined below in Part 4: see *D T v Refugee Appeals Tribunal* [2012] IEHC 562. The facts set out at para 2 make it abundantly clear that Bhutan satisfied the definition of country of former habitual residence.

[232] See above, n 229. The better approach is exemplified in the French decision, CNDA, decision no° 09019611 R, 14 February 2011, where Myanmar was properly focused upon as the country of former habitual residence notwithstanding the fact that he was a resident of Bangladesh. We note that Fripp's analysis is confined to denationalization and hence would not provide guidance in the case of a stateless applicant who was arguably denied nationality contrary to international law (e.g. on the basis of discrimination).

entitled, and then finally consider the position of an applicant who has voluntarily renounced his or her citizenship.

2.6.1 Inchoate nationality

The first question to consider is whether an applicant can be understood to 'not have[a] a nationality' where there is a state in relation to which he or she could apply for, and would likely be granted, citizenship. In this situation it has been argued that where nationality is inchoate such that it can be activated by the straightforward action of an applicant, refugee status should be refused so long as there is no well-founded fear of persecution in the country of inchoate nationality.[233] While reson-ating with the evidentiary issues discussed above, this issue goes beyond a matter of discharging a burden to establish statelessness. It raises the substantive question whether an applicant can be effectively *excluded* from refugee status on the basis that while he or she technically does not have a nationality at the time of refugee status determination, such nationality could be acquired in the future.

An analysis of the case law across a range of jurisdictions reveals varied applications of this principle. The most closely circumscribed application is where nationality is said to be truly inchoate in that access is a 'mere formality'[234] and where there is 'no discretion' to refuse citizenship on the part of the relevant state.[235] In some jurisdic-tions, while inchoate nationality is recognized as a basis for refusing refugee status, it is applied carefully with due regard to the reality that '[a]cquisition of nationality is not necessarily straightforward, and accordingly the [decision-maker] must be satis-fied that the [relevant person] is able to obtain the nationality of another country as a matter of "mere formality" '.[236] Hence where naturalization 'entails the exercise of Presidential discretion' in the relevant state, acquisition of nationality by such means has been correctly understood not to constitute a 'mere formality'.[237] Similarly, in considering the requirement for an applicant for Eritrean citizenship to provide three witnesses holding Eritrean passports to testify in favour of the application,

---

[233] See e.g., Hathaway and Foster, *The Law of Refugee Status 2* (n 51) 57–59. Other refugee law com-mentators either do not address this issue explicitly (e.g. Goodwin-Gill and Zimmermann) or take a different approach; see e.g., Grahl-Madsen, *The Status of Refugees in International Law* (n 4) [70]. For a thorough consideration of the relevant case law and an argument against inchoate nationality, see Fripp, *Nationality and Statelessness* (n 81) 172–98.

[234] See *Bouianova v Canada* [1993] FCJ No 576 [8] (hereafter *Bouianova*). In a number of decisions concerning applications for refugee status from the former USSR, the French Cour Nationale du Droit d'Asile rejected their claim of 'not having a nationality' on the ground that the Russian citizenship law of 1991 recognizes all permanent residents of Russia to be *automatically* citizens of Russia, so long as they have not expressly declared that they do not wish to become Russian citizens within one year of the citizenship law entering into force (in 1992): Decision no°10018108 (n 33).

[235] Hathaway and Foster, *The Law of Refugee Status 2* (n 51) 59. This seems to be the approach of the French authorities: see Decision no°10018108 (n 33); Decision no°09002572 C+ (n 33). See also *KK* (n 123) [81]–[83]; *Secretary of State for the Home Department v SP (North Korea)* [2012] EWCA Civ 114; *GP v Secretary of State for the Home Department* [2014] UKUT 391 (IAC).

[236] *Refugee Appeal No 76077* (n 229) [116]. See also *Refugee Appeal No 75694* (n 74), finding that the grant of Ethiopian nationality 'would not be automatic', and hence the applicant could not be con-sidered to have nationality there: at [31]–[32]; *Refugee Appeal No 73575* (n 151) [32], [41].

[237] *Refugee Appeal No 76077* (n 229) [118].

the New Zealand Tribunal rightly considered that since the appellant did not know three appropriately documented Eritreans, the grant of such citizenship involved more than a 'mere formality'.[238]

However, not all applications of the principle have been so narrowly tailored. On the contrary, some courts have extended application of the principle to cases where it is 'relatively simple' to secure a citizenship,[239] where it is 'within the control of the applicant to acquire the citizenship',[240] or where 'it is reasonably likely that the [relevant] authorities would accept ... that he is a citizen'.[241] These tests raise concerns because they suggest a lower degree of certainty in relation to the likelihood that the applicant will in fact be granted nationality in a particular country. For example, the summary dismissal of a refugee claim by a stateless applicant on the basis that he could, on return to Jordan, 'challenge the decision that he lost his Jordanian citizenship',[242] without any meaningful analysis of the chance of success of such a challenge, highlights the degree to which these tests have departed from a 'mere formality' approach. Likewise, a decision by a British tribunal to reject a refugee claim on the basis that the applicant should first apply for Eritrean citizenship, notwithstanding his lack of the requisite witnesses referred to above,[243] and a Canadian decision that found that the requirements of a waiting period and an initial transitional status constituted a 'simple procedure', even while acknowledging that 'a certain waiting period may be considered by some as more than a simple procedure'[244] raise serious concerns.

Indeed, the EU Qualification Directive provides that an assessment of refugee status should take into account simply 'whether the applicant could reasonably be expected to avail himself or herself of the protection of another country *where he or she could assert citizenship*'.[245] This test transforms the focus from the likely grant of nationality to whether the applicant could merely 'assert citizenship', with no corresponding reference to the likelihood of such assertion being accepted by a particular state.[246]

---

[238] *Refugee Appeal No 75694* (n 74).

[239] See Hathaway and Foster, *The Law of Refugee Status 2* (n 51) 59–61; *X (Re)*, 2013 CarswellNat 6584 [31] (hereafter *X (Re)* 2013).

[240] *Petrov v Canada (Citizenship and Immigration)*, 2014 FC 658 [18]. Decision no°10018108 (n 33); Decision no°09002572 C+ (n 33). See also *Reza v Canada (Citizenship and Immigration)*, 2009 FC 606 [22]–[23].

[241] *Secretary of State for the Home Department v AS* [2002] UKIAT 05943 [9].

[242] *Yah Abedalaziz v Canada (Citizenship and Immigration)*, 2011 FC 1066 [52].

[243] *KF* (n 166) [34].   [244] *X (Re)* 2013 (n 239) [31].

[245] Qualification Directive 2011/95/EU (n 36) art 4(3)(e) (emphasis added).

[246] As such it has been criticized as being inconsistent with the *Refugee Convention*. For instance, the UNHCR states that art 4(3)(e) 'should not be incorporated into national legislation and practice if full compatibility with Article 1 of the 1951 Convention is to be ensured': UNHCR, 'Annotated Comments on the EC Council Directive 2004/83/EC of 29 April 2004 on Minimum Standards for the Qualification and Status of Third Country Nationals or Stateless Persons as Refugees or as Persons Who Otherwise Need International Protection and the Content of the Protection Granted' (30 September 2004) OJ L 304/12, 15 (hereafter UNHCR, 'Annotated Comments on the EC Council Directive 2004/83/EC'). See also Gregor Noll, 'Evidentiary Assessment in Refugee Status Determination and the EU Qualification Directive' (2006) 12 EPL 295, 308, observing that the UNHCR's view 'is formally correct and must be endorsed'. See also *KK* (n 123) [41] in which the Tribunal noted (in *obiter*) that in giving evidence in that case, 'Professor Goodwin-Gill ... suggests that Article 4(3)(e) should therefore be read

This inability to contain the inchoate nationality principle to one that is narrowly tailored and controlled suggests a pragmatic reason for rejecting the principle outright. In other words, even if a narrow application could be justified, the above analysis suggests that it is too easily open to distortion, misapplication, and erroneous analysis to warrant a place in refugee law. In our view, however, there are also fundamental matters of principle for rejecting all forms of the inchoate nationality principle regardless of how narrowly or broadly framed.[247]

First, considering the ordinary meaning of the text of the definition we observe that Article 1A (2) invokes the term 'the country of *his nationality*'.[248] This clear and unambiguous language on its face dictates that for a state to constitute a country of reference, the person *is*—not 'may' or 'likely' or even 'probably to become'—a national of that country.[249] Refugee status determination is widely accepted to be declaratory—not constitutive—and hence where the factual prerequisites are established, it is not open to a decision-maker to reject a claim unless there is an explicit exclusion or limitation in the text of the *Convention*. To thus reject a claim based on a hypothetical step that may or could be taken in the future is inconsistent with the declaratory nature of refugee status determination.

This conclusion is further supported by a contextual reading of the 1951 *Refugee Convention* in the form of other related provisions. Article 1A(2) explicitly envisages that a person may be required to seek protection in a second country of nationality, but again the language is clear: 'the term "the country of his nationality" shall mean each of the countries *of which he is a national*'.[250] In terms of cessation of refugee status, Article 1C is clear that when assessing whether the *Convention* shall cease to apply on the basis of an alternative nationality, only voluntarily reacquisition of his nationality, or the acquisition of a new nationality, is relevant. Article 1C does not refer to potential or possible acquisition. Where the *Convention* does envisage something less than nationality as a basis for exclusion, it requires recognition 'by the competent authorities of the country in which he has taken residence as having the rights and obligations which are attached to the possession of the nationality of that country'.[251] This requires a qualitative and substantive analysis of the rights and obligations enjoyed by a de facto citizen, which is a distinctly different question from whether an individual may have some abstract right to a nationality in a country

---

as though the words "of which he is a citizen" appeared, instead of "where he could assert citizenship". Nothing in the present appeal turns on this issue, although we note that Article 4 is primarily concerned with the grant of international protection within the European Union, under the Directive, which may not be exactly congruent with the recognition of refugee status under the Convention': at [41].

[247] For a thoughtful discussion of the issues of principle, see Macklin, 'Sticky Citizenship' (n 196) 223.

[248] *Refugee Convention* (n 2) art 1A(2) (emphasis added).

[249] Hathaway and Foster acknowledge that as 'a matter of strict literal construction, this is undoubtedly correct': *The Law of Refugee Status 2* (n 51) 58. In an interesting Canadian Federal Court decision, in which the applicants argued that they may ultimately lose their Israeli citizenship because they had made false declarations as to their religion in order to obtain the Israeli citizenship, the Court found that they 'are still citizens of Israel, against which they have expressed no grievance': *Drozdov v Canada* [1995] FCJ No 20.

[250] *Refugee Convention* (n 2) art 1A(2) (emphasis added).   [251] ibid, art 1E.

which he or she may never even have visited, let alone taken up residence. This wider context of the *Refugee Convention* hence strongly supports the interpretation evident in the ordinary meaning of the term 'country of his nationality'. Indeed, the UNHCR, in considering the issue of inchoate nationality in light of the text of the *Convention*, is emphatic that 'there is no margin beyond these provisions'.[252] The principle of good faith, together with the object and purpose of the *Refugee Convention*, similarly support this approach given that the protective objective of the *Convention* would be substantially undermined by excluding applicants based on prospective nationality when we consider that granting of nationality still today remains highly discretionary and arbitrary practices are persistent.[253]

Second, this approach is strongly supported by reference to Article 1(1) of the *1954 Convention* which, as explained above, is highly relevant to the interpretation of 'not having a nationality' in Article 1A(2) of the *Refugee Convention*. The language of the *1954 Convention* similarly suggests an inquiry into the present status ('who is not considered a national'), a position made clear in the UNHCR's explanation that an individual's nationality is to be assessed at the time of determination and is 'neither a historic nor a predictive exercise',[254] a position that has been affirmed in domestic implementation.[255]

Third, this position is consistent with general principles of international nationality law according to which no state can require another state to grant or impose nationality on a person.[256] Such principles are required to be taken into account by the rules of treaty interpretation, given that they represent 'relevant rules of international law applicable in the relations between the parties'.[257]

---

[252] UNHCR, 'Annotated Comments on the EC Council Directive 2004/83/EC' (n 246) 15. See also Hemme Battjes, *European Asylum Law and International Law* (Brill 2006) 266; UNHCR, 'Handbook' (n 47) para 87.

[253] In *SZPZI v Minister for Immigration* [2011] FMCA 530 (22 July 2011) the Federal Magistrates Court of Australia observed that once the decision-maker had 'accepted that the applicant is a stateless person, his opinions on the applicant's preference for seeking protection in Australia rather than seeking the nationality of Iran or Iraq had no relevance to an assessment of Australia's protection obligations': at [9].

[254] UNHCR, 'Handbook' (n 47) para 50.

[255] For the UK, this means that the determination of statelessness is 'not a historic or predictive exercise': UK Home Office, 'Asylum Policy Instruction' (n 116) s 4.4; UNHCR, 'Handbook on Stateless Persons' (n 84) para 50. ILPA thus argues that '[t]he Home Office should not ... refuse to recognise a person as stateless because it believes that they might be able to acquire a nationality, or acquire documents to establish their nationality, in the future': Carter and Woodhouse, 'A Best Practice Guide' (n 116) 21.

[256] As James Crawford explains: 'The whole pattern of rules and the practice of states is based on the circumstance that states set the conditions under which nationality is acquired and lost': *Brownlie's Principles of Public International Law* (n 223) 523. Or as ILC Special Rapporteur Manley Hudson put it, '[i]n principle, questions of nationality fall within the domestic jurisdiction of each state': 'Report on Nationality, Including Statelessness by Mr Manley O. Hudson' (n 91) at 509. We note that Hathaway and Foster reject this argument as 'misplaced deference', 'since the impact of treating the state as a country of reference is in no sense to compel that government to grant its citizenship': *The Law of Refugee Status 2* (n 51) 63. However, we maintain that it is inconsistent with this principle.

[257] The *VCLT* (n 96) provides that in interpreting a treaty, '[t]here shall be taken into account, together with the context ... any relevant rules of international law applicable in the relations between the parties': art 31(3)(c). We also note that in *Katkova v Canada (Minister of Citizenship & Immigration)* [1997] FCJ No 549 the Canadian Federal Court overturned the Immigration and Refugee Board ('IRB') decision which rejected a refugee claim by a Russian Jew on the basis that Israel's law of return

Finally, this position is further consistent with the following two general principles of international law: a state's duty to 'prevent[] arbitrary deprivation of nationality' and a state's duty to 'eliminat[e] provisions that permit the renunciation of a nationality without the prior possession or acquisition of another nationality'.[258] To suggest that international protection should be denied because nationality can/may be acquired in future would undermine the application of these principles.

In sum, in our view there is no basis on which to allow for inchoate nationality, and case law to this effect should be revisited.[259]

2.6.2 *Voluntary renunciation of nationality*

The final issue in this Part is whether there is any basis for rejecting a refugee claim by a stateless person who is stateless by virtue of his or her voluntary renunciation of citizenship. While this issue does not appear to have arisen with any frequency in refugee law adjudication,[260] it is possible that recent developments in a number of Western democracies that have introduced or enhanced 'renunciation by conduct' provisions in domestic citizenship laws, designed to respond to 'home grown terrorists and foreign fighters', could raise this issue,[261] although this will be explored later in relation to deprivation of nationality as persecution (Chapter 5) and Article 1F (Chapter 6).

In short, we argue that the position in refugee law in this regard, leaving aside issues that may invoke Article 1F, is that adopted in relation to Article 1 of the *1954 Convention*, namely, that voluntary renunciation is not a permitted ground for exclusion by the treaty.[262] Recalling that the question is simply whether a person is, at the time of determination, a national of a particular country, there is no basis on

---

guaranteed (virtually) automatic citizenship. The Federal Court relied on the *Nottebohm* decision for the argument that nationality requires 'a genuine and effective link between the person and the state', yet in this case the claimant had no connection with Israel. See also *Solodjankin v Canada (Minister of Citizenship & Immigration)* [1995] FCJ No 155, rejecting the IRB decision that the applicants were not stateless because they were Russian citizens by birth right. The Court found they had to 'apply' to have their citizenship returned.

[258] UNGA Res 50/152 (9 February 1966) UN Doc A/RES/50/152, para 16.

[259] Our view is that the alternative argument put forward in Hathaway and Foster, *The Law of Refugee Status 2* (n 51) needs to be revised.

[260] We note that the issue of whether statelessness is 'voluntary' or 'optional' has sometimes arisen in refugee law in the context of inchoate nationality; in other words, not so much in the context of renunciation but whether the applicant should be required to apply for a nationality. For instance, in *Bouianova* (n 234), the Federal Court of Canada found that as the applicant's application for citizenship of Russia would be a 'mere formality', he or she should apply and therefore seek protection in Russia. In support, the Court observed that 'statelessness is not one that is optional for an applicant': at [12]. However, that decision seemed to overlook the fact that being stateless did not constitute prima facie entitlement to refugee status. There are isolated cases involving renunciation (e.g. *Refugee Appeal No 76187* [2008] NZRSAA 53 (18 June 2008) (hereafter *Refugee Appeal No 76187*)); however, they have correctly been assessed on the basis of whether the applicant has a well-founded fear of persecution in their country of former habitual residence.

[261] In this context there would be a question whether renunciation was indeed voluntary given that while the relevant conduct may have been voluntary, the conduct is unlikely to be undertaken with the intention of renouncing citizenship.

[262] UNHCR, 'Handbook' (n 47) para 51.

which to undertake a further analysis of the reasons for that position in relation to identifying the country of reference. Of course, as in the situation described above in relation to illegality, the broader context may be highly relevant to assessing well-founded fear of being persecuted. Our point is simply that the applicant's conduct in relation to the acquisition or renunciation of nationality cannot constitute a ground for prima facie or summary exclusion from refugee status unless a specific provision in the *Convention*—such as Article 1E or 1F—is invoked in a particular case. Where a person has renounced his or her citizenship, then that country remains a country of reference by virtue of former habitual residence.[263] Rather than become distracted by issues of renunciation, the analysis should focus squarely on whether there is a well-founded fear of being persecuted in the country of former habitual residence which, of course, remains the central issue in any refugee claim.

Having thus resolved many of the preliminary issues in relation to identifying a stateless applicant, we now turn to consider the meaning of country of 'former habitual residence', which is a critical term for such applicants.

Part 3: Country of Former Habitual Residence

Once it has been determined that an applicant is without a nationality,[264] the country of 'former habitual residence' must be examined as the country of reference for assessing whether the applicant has a well-founded fear of persecution.[265]

A *country* of nationality must be a recognized state capable of conferring citizenship.[266] The meaning of one's country of nationality has been found to be the state because only a state recognized by the international community can grant nationality, hence only states possessing such powers can qualify as a country of nationality.[267]

However, there is a question whether 'country of former habitual residence' could legitimately be interpreted as permitting consideration of a region, area or territory that would not be understood as a state, as the point of reference for assessing

---

[263] This was applied straightforwardly by the New Zealand RSAA in *Refugee Appeal No 76187* (n 260) in a case where the appellant had renounced his US citizenship. The authority simply assessed his claim against the United States as the country of former habitual residence, and found that the United States was able and willing to protect him: see at [35].

[264] In the case of an applicant with a nationality, the fear of persecution must be assessed by reference to that country, and not that of his or her country of last habitual residence if different from the country of nationality: Czech Republic Supreme Administrative Court, *VS v Ministry of Interior*, 25 November 2011, 6 Azs 29/2010-85.

[265] France: CE, decision no°255687, 18 January 2006; CE, decision no°330338, 15 December 2010; CE, decision no°335236, 30 March 2011; CE, decision no°336441, 11 May 2011; CNDA, decision no°12017790 C, 19 February 2013; CE decision nos°363069, 363070, 363071, 5 February 2014. Belgium: Conseil du Contentieux des Etrangers, arrêt no°61 832, 19 May 2011.

[266] See Mary Crock and Laurie Berg, *Immigration Refugees and Forced Migration: Law, Policy and Practice in Australia* (The Federation Press 2011) ch 13, n 11 (hereafter Crock and Berg, *Immigration Refugees*), citing *Koe v MIEA* (1997) 78 FCR 289 (hereafter *Koe*).

[267] *VD v Secretary of State for the Home Department* [2001] UKIAT 00002, cited in Symes and Jorro, *Asylum Law and Practice* (n 145) 311–12. See also UNHCR, 'Handbook on Stateless Persons' (n 84) paras 16–21.

refugee status in the case of a stateless person. There is authority that supports such an approach. It has been held that it is sufficient if 'the territory has the attributes of a state, such as defined borders, systems of law and a permanent identifiable community'.[268] Thus, in the case of a stateless person who had lived all of his life in a refugee camp (e.g. situated in Algeria but entirely under the administrative, police, judicial, military, and political control of Sahrawi Arab Democratic Republic), the French courts considered that he had become an 'habitual resident' of the authority that controls the camp (in that case, the partially recognized Sahrawi Arab Democratic Republic).[269] Similarly, in the context of a refugee claim by a stateless Palestinian from the West bank, the Australian tribunal found that while 'Palestine is not a State capable of granting nationality',[270] the phrase 'country of former habitual residence' 'is used to denote a country which need not have this capability'.[271]

The Australian Federal Court has taken the view that:

The objective of the Convention is to provide a practical humanitarian solution to the problems of refugees. It should be interpreted with this objective in mind. Individuals should not be denied the protection of the Convention by an unnecessarily narrow reading of the definition of 'refugee'. It is not appropriate to conclude that an applicant has no recourse under the Convention simply because his or her 'country' of former habitual residence happens to be a colony or other entity that is not an independent sovereign state.[272]

While it may be thought difficult to justify two different interpretations of the same word—country—in the same paragraph, there is a very strong purposive argument that indeed this should be accepted in light of the factual reality that many stateless persons are stateless precisely because they live in an area controlled by an entity that does not have state recognition, and hence is unable to grant nationality. This is further supported by the text of the refugee definition which, in relation to stateless persons, speaks not of 'protection' of the 'country of former habitual residence' but merely an inability or unwillingness 'to return to it', suggesting that a country of former habitual residence need not have the attributes of a state.

On balance, taking into account the protective object and purpose of the *Convention*, the better view is that country of former habitual residence need not denote a state recognized as such in international law.[273]

[268] Crock and Berg, *Immigration Refugees* (n 266) ch 13, n 12, citing *Koe* (n 266) 298–99. We note that in *SZUNZ v Minister for Immigration and Border Protection* [2015] FCAFC 32 (13 March 2015) (hereafter *SZUNZ*) the Full Federal Court queried whether 'Western Sahara' could be considered a country; however, this is not authoritative on this point given the vagueness of the evidence and the lack of focused attention to this issue in the judgment.
[269] CNDA, decision no°11026661, 13 February 2012.
[270] *1504584 (Refugee)* [2017] AATA 650 (4 April 2017) [26].
[271] ibid, [27] citing *Koe* (n 266) 298. See also *V00/11398* [2001] RRTA 419 (2 May 2001). The same reasoning was invoked in France, where asylum seekers' habitual residence was assessed as the Palestinian Authority in Gaza as that Authority continues to exercise control (and full powers) over that territory, even if its power does not include the granting of nationality: CE, decision nos°363181, 363182, 5 November 2014.
[272] *Koe v Minister for Immigration & Ethnic Affairs* [1997] FCA 912 (8 September 1997) (Tamberlin J).
[273] For the opposite view, see Symes and Jorro, *Asylum Law and Practice* (n 145) 321; *BZAAH v Minister for Immigration and Citizenship* [2013] FCAFC 72 (12 July 2013) [25].

3.1 How do we determine whether a country is one of former habitual residence?

The Ad Hoc Committee on Statelessness and Related Problems incorporated the phrase 'country of former habitual residence' into its earliest drafts of the refugee definition, yet due to its non-controversial nature it was not the subject of any debate in full committee.[274] Early drafts did not, however, link the concept specifically to stateless persons, but rather adopted a similar approach to the IRO *Constitution* which had defined a refugee (inter alia) as 'a person who has left, or who is outside of, his country of nationality or of former habitual residence'.[275] The advice received from the Director General of the IRO, discussed above in Part 2.5, included the opinion that the *Refugee Convention* should be amended to conform to the interpretation adopted by the IRO, namely, that '[t]he notion "former habitual residence" has been interpreted by the IRO to apply only to stateless persons'.[276] Accordingly, the Ad Hoc Committee thereafter linked the concept of 'former habitual residence' only to those without a nationality.[277]

In terms of the meaning of 'former habitual residence', the Ad Hoc Committee observed in its final report simply that 'the country of former habitual residence' was intended, 'for the purposes of this convention' to mean 'the country in which he had resided and where he had suffered or fears he would suffer persecution if he returned'.[278] There does not appear to have been further discussion about the meaning or interpretation of the phrase in the second session of the Ad Hoc Committee or the Conference of Plenipotentiaries.

There was, however, debate within the Ad Hoc Committee concerning the difference between the concepts of domicile and residence. Although this related to the proposed article concerning the personal status of a refugee, which eventually became Article 12 in the *Refugee Convention*, it nonetheless provides insight into the drafters' understanding that there was a meaningful distinction between domicile, on the one hand, and residence, on the other. Article 12(1) provides that the personal status of a refugee 'shall be governed by the law of the country of his domicile, or, if he has no domicile, by the law of the country of his residence'.[279] Debates concerning earlier versions of this Article indicated that the drafters understood that domicile indicates a stronger connection with a country than residence.[280] For

---

[274] Ad Hoc Committee on Statelessness and Related Problems, 'Comments of the Committee on the Draft Convention' (10 February 1950) UN Doc E/AC.32/L.32/Add 1. See Goodwin Gill and McAdam, *The Refugee in International Law* (n 51) 526.

[275] *IRO Constitution* (n 220) 18 Annex I, pt 1, s A(1). The draft of 23 January 1950 by the Working Group provided that the definition included, '[a]ny person who (i) is and remains outside the countries of his nationality, former nationality or former habitual residence owing to persecution, or well founded fear of persecution': 23 January Provisional Draft (n 217), art 1(A)(2).

[276] Ad Hoc Committee, 'Memorandum from the Secretariat of the IRO' (n 220) 3 [4].

[277] Ad Hoc Committee, 'Decisions of the Committee Meeting 31 January 1950' (n 218) arts 1(A)(1)–(2).

[278] UNESC, 'Report of the Ad Hoc Committee' (n 222) 39. See also UNHCR, 'Handbook' (n 47) para 103, where this definition is adopted.

[279] *Refugee Convention* (n 2) art 12(1).

[280] See also Goodwin-Gill and McAdam, *The Refugee in International Law* (n 51) 526–27.

example, it was noted that '[d]omicile presupposed that a person was normally living and working in a country and had the intention to remain there',[281] that 'it was often easier to establish residence than domicile',[282] and that domicile was 'the country in which the refugee had established his permanent residence' and would not apply to a refugee 'only staying in the country for a short time and who intended to settle in another country'.[283] Although not specifically adverted to in the debates, this reference to 'intention' in the context of domicile reflects a longstanding interpretation of the concept of domicile.[284] As explained by Grahl-Madsen, there is 'no need to prove any *animus manendi*, because "habitual residence" does not mean domicile, but merely residence of some standing or duration'.[285] The drafting history thus appears to support Grahl-Madsen's view that in order for a country to qualify as a country of former habitual residence 'the person concerned must have resided in that country',[286] but in general 'a liberal interpretation' is appropriate such that it 'cannot be required that he shall have stayed there for any specific period of time, but he should be able to show that he has made it his abode or the centre of his interests'.[287] Jurisprudence also consistently supports the view that 'habitual residence' 'does not mean domicile, but merely residence of some standing and duration'.[288]

While as explained above, the question whether an applicant has no nationality is determined by reference to the domestic law of the relevant state with which the applicant has a connection, it is clear that 'former habitual residence' is a factual, not legal assessment.[289] As the Full Federal Court of Australia has explained, 'it may not

---

[281] Ad Hoc Committee on Statelessness and Related Problems, 'First Session: Summary Record of the Eighth Meeting Held at Lake Success, New York, on Monday, 23 January 1950, at 3 p.m' (30 January 1950) UN Doc E/AC.32/SR.8, 3 [4] (Mr Cha (China)).

[282] ibid, 5 [14] (Mr Giraud (Secretariat)).

[283] Ad Hoc Committee on Statelessness and Related Problems, 'First Session: Summary Record of the Ninth Meeting Held at Lake Success, New York, on Tuesday, 24 January 1950, at 11 a.m' (3 February 1950) UN Doc E/AC.32/SR.9, 2 [2] (Sir Leslie Brass (UK)).

[284] See Hathaway and Foster, *The Law of Refugee Status 2* (n 51) 67, citing the *Hague Convention on Civil Procedure* (adopted 14 November 1896, entered into force 27 April 1899) 88 British & Foreign State Papers 555, and the common law notion of domicile.

[285] Grahl-Madsen, *The Status of Refugees in International Law* (n 4) 160. This is also the view of Robinson in *Statelessness Convention, A Commentary* (n 87) 90, and Hathaway and Foster in *The Law of Refugee Status 2* (n 51).

[286] Grahl-Madsen, *The Status of Refugees in International Law* (n 4) 160.

[287] ibid, 160. This has been adopted in NZ: see *Refugee Appeal No 72635* (n 29) [113]–[116].

[288] NZ RSAA, *Refugee Appeal No 72635* (n 29) [113], observing that '[t]here appears to be a consensus' on this point. See also UNHCR, 'Guidelines on Representing Stateless Persons' (n 110) 14, citing Board of Immigration Appeals' approach. See *Paripovic v Gonzales* 418 F 3d 240 (3rd Cir, 2005) 244 (hereafter *Paripovic*), citing and endorsing legislation that defined 'residence' as a 'place of general abode; the place of general abode of a person means his principal, actual dwelling place in fact, without regard to intent'.

[289] See NZ *Refugee Appeal No 72635* (n 29) [116]. In Canada, see *Kadoura v Canada (Minister of Citizenship and Immigration)* [2003] FCJ No 1328 [14] (hereafter *Kadoura*), citing *Kruchkov v Canada (Solicitor General)* [1994] FCJ No 1264. See also *Chehade* (n 193) [21]. There appears to be conflicting approaches on the question of whether within a domestic judicial review setting the determination of country of former habitual residence is one of fact or law (for the purposes of determining amenability to judicial review). In the US, it has been held that it is a matter of fact (see *Al Najjar v Ashcroft* 257 F 3d 1261 (11th Cir, 2001) [72] (hereafter *Al Najjar*)), but at other times it has been said to be 'a question of law', although even in the latter case it was said, 'because the meaning of that phrase is ambiguous, we

be readily assumed that the laws of individual countries deal with "habitual" residency as a legal concept'.[290] Rather, the High Court of Australia has observed that the concept of 'habitual residence',

involves a 'broad factual inquiry', factors relevant to which include 'the actual and intended length of stay in a state, the purpose of the stay, the strength of ties to the state and to any other state (both in the past and currently), [and] the degree of assimilation into the state'.[291]

In terms of length of residence, the New Zealand Tribunal has helpfully observed that 'residence of some standing or duration' does not require a minimum[292] or fixed period, but that the individual 'has in fact taken up residence and lived in the country for a period which showed that the residence had become, and was likely to continue to be, habitual'.[293]

While decision-makers assess in an individual case 'the length and character of the time a refugee spent in a country',[294] the notion of 'habitual residence' generally implies some period of *residence* and degree of establishment. Combined with the fact that 'habitual' could be understood as 'usual',[295] it seems clear that generally a brief stay or visit will not suffice. Accordingly, the US Court of Appeals for the Sixth Circuit sensibly endorsed the Board of Immigration Appeals' decision that Lebanon was not a country of former habitual residence merely because Lebanon had issued a travel document valid for five years, given that the applicant had visited Lebanon for only one month several years before claiming asylum in the United States.[296] It follows that a right to reside without actual residence is unlikely to be sufficient either.[297]

However, there is limited authority for the proposition that in very particular circumstances a state may be properly understood as constituting a country of 'former habitual residence' where it can be said that such country is 'the centre of [a person's]

---

must defer to the Board so long as its "answer is based on a permissible construction of the statute" ': *El Assadi v Holder*, 418 Fed Appx 484 (6th Cir, 2011) 485 (hereafter *El Assadi*).

[290]   *SZUNZ* (n 268) [29] (Buchanan J).

[291]   *Tahiri v Minister for Immigration and Citizenship* [2012] HCA 61 (13 December 2012) [16] (per French CJ, Bell and Gageler JJ), citing its earlier decision in *LK v Director-General, Department of Community Services* [2009] HCA 9 (11 March 2009). *Tahiri* concerned the phrase 'usually resident' in the *Migration Act* 1958 (Cth) while the latter case concerned the phrase 'habitual residence' in the context of the *Convention on the Civil Aspects of International Child Abduction* (concluded 25 October 1980, entered into force 1 December 1983) 1343 UNTS 89, art 31. *Tahiri* was cited by the Full Federal Court in *SZUNZ* (n 268).

[292]   In Canada, it has also been emphasized that it does not require 'a minimum period of residence': see *Kadoura* (n 289) [14], citing *Maarouf* (n 62) 939.

[293]   *Refugee Appeal No 72635* (n 29) [116].

[294]   See *YL* (n 75) [17]; *El Assadi* (n 289) 2. For a detailed analysis of what 'country of former habitual residence' means in the doctrine, see *Refugee Appeal No 1/92* (n 29).

[295]   *Paripovic* (n 288), citing *Chen v Mayflower Transit Inc* (2004) 315 F Supp 2d 886, 911 n 22.

[296]   *El Assadi* (n 289) 485–86.

[297]   See *Kadoura* (n 289), where the Court upheld the decision below that Lebanon was not a country of former habitual residence because '[e]ven if he has a right to reside in Lebanon, he has never actually resided there': at [15].

interests', although that person has not in fact resided there.[298] While this is difficult to reconcile with the ordinary meaning of 'residence', there is a convincing purposive argument that where an applicant has a right to return and reside in a state, the risk of being persecuted must be assessed in relation to that state in order to avoid a violation of the principle of *non-refoulement*. This is particularly the case in relation to stateless children born abroad who may be returned to their parents' country of former habitual residence even though they have never resided there. In such a context the Australian courts have accepted that where a child is born in Australia and 'had no nationality or country of former habitual residence, it was appropriate, sensible, practical and fair'[299] to consider his or her claims against the country to which she may be returned, typically the parents' country of former habitual residence or nationality.

The fact that habitual residence in the relevant state was some time in the past does not preclude that state from constituting a reference country for the purposes of assessing a stateless applicant's claim to refugee status. This has been accepted in a variety of cases but is particularly important where the applicant or their family were denationalized and expelled from their country of origin,[300] or otherwise expelled from their country of origin as a form of persecution.[301]

In terms of the degree of establishment required, in the US context it has been emphasized that the test for 'habitual residence' is less onerous than that required to establish 'firm resettlement' such that the fact that a person habitually resided in a country does not mean that he or she was 'firmly resettled there'.[302] The 'firmly resettled' principle in US asylum law is related to Article 1E of the *Refugee Convention*, which excludes a refugee where he or she enjoys de facto citizenship in another state. However, establishing habitual residence is qualitatively different from attaining a status that is akin to citizenship. For this reason, the notion that the phrase 'former habitual residence' seeks to 'establish a relationship to a state which is broadly comparable to that between a citizen and his or her country of nationality', needs to be treated with caution.[303]

---

[298] We note that there are some limited tribunal decisions that have found a country to constitute one of former habitual residence even where the applicant had never lived there: see *GRF(Re)*, Nos AAO-01454, AAO-01462, AAO-01463 [2001] CRDD No 88 (12 July 2001) 16 (hereafter *GRF(Re)*).

[299] *1617142* (Refugee) [2017] AATA 990 (7 June 2017) [56]. See also *SZEOH v Minister for Immigration* [2005] FMCA 1178 (26 August 2005) [9].

[300] See the cases cited at n 229 regarding denationalization and country of former habitual residence.

[301] For instance, in *Refugee Appeal No 73512* (n 66), the New Zealand RSAA found that Uganda was a country of former habitual residence where 'the appellant and his family were relocated from Uganda by the UNHCR at the time of expulsion of Asians in the early 1970's by then President Idi Amin': at [42].

[302] See UNHCR, 'Guidelines on Representing Stateless Persons' (n 110) 14 n 57, citing the Asylum Officer Basic Training Course, 'Lesson: Definition of Refugee; Definition of Persecution; Eligibility Based on Past Persecution' (6 March 2009).

[303] *Maarouf* (n 62). Although the Federal Court of Canada did not attribute this statement to Hathaway, it is certainly similar to *The Law of Refugee Status* (n 52), which stated, 'the stateless person must stand in a relationship to a state which is broadly comparable to the relationship between a citizen and her country of nationality': at 61. See also Hathaway and Foster, *The Law of Refugee Status 2* (n 51) 67.

The final issue that has arisen is whether it is necessary for a stateless applicant to establish that he or she had *legally* resided in the country of former habitual residence in order for that country to constitute a country of reference for refugee law. There is little authority on this specific point, but it overwhelmingly suggests that legality is not required.[304] As the German Federal Administrative Court has emphasized, 'habitual residence ... does not presuppose that the stateless person's residency must be lawful'.[305] Rather, 'it is sufficient if the stateless person actually focused his life in that country, and therefore did not merely remain there transiently, while the competent authorities initiated no measures to end his residency'.[306] Similarly, the Full Federal Court of Australia has emphasized that '[r]esidence may be habitual even if unlawful'.[307] This approach is also consistent with well-established principles including that analysis of former habitual residence is a factual analysis that focuses not on the laws of the relevant country but on the history and experience of the applicant, and that there is no requirement that the applicant have a legal right to return in order for a country to be considered one of former habitual residence.[308]

Canadian decision-makers have repeatedly emphasized that the interpretation of the phrase 'country of former habitual residence' should not be 'so unduly restrictive as to pre-empt providing shelter to a stateless person who has demonstrated a well-founded fear of persecution on any of the grounds listed in the *Convention*'.[309] Rephrased as the benefit-of-the-doubt principle, this is an important point to bear in mind when assessing the complex histories frequently presented by stateless persons whose lived experiences will, by definition, often be insecure, transient, non-linear, and complicated.

3.2 Multiple countries of former habitual residence?

In many cases a stateless person will have resided in more than one country prior to seeking asylum. The question thus arises as to whether it is possible for an applicant to be understood as having more than one 'country of habitual residence' for the purposes of the *Refugee Convention*.

The UNHCR Handbook observes that, '[a] stateless person may have more than one country of former habitual residence, and he may have a fear of persecution in

---

[304] Hathaway and Foster cite one Austrian Board decision that found illegal presence did not suffice: see *The Law of Refugee Status 2* (n 51) 68 n 315. On the other hand, in several cases decision-makers have straightforwardly found a country to be one of former habitual residence even though the applicant did not stay there legally: see (in addition to those cited in the following footnotes) *Elastal v Canada (Minister of Citizenship and Immigration)* [1999] FCJ No 328, [2], [7], [18]. We note that there was no discussion of the legality issue in this case.

[305] 10 C 50.07 (n 34) [31].   [306] ibid, [31].

[307] *SZUNZ* (n 268) [107], where Wigney J cited the primary judge's reasoning, and noted that 'both the appellant and the respondent [the Minister] embraced the primary judge's construction of the definition': at [108].

[308] See above Part 1.2.

[309] *Kadoura* (n 289) [14], citing *Maarouf* (n 62) 739. This statement from *Maarouf* is often repeated by the Immigration and Refugee Board, see e.g., *GRF(Re)* (n 298) 5; *X(Re)*, 2016 CarswellNat 10720 [16] (hereafter *X(Re)* 2016).

relation to more than one of them'.[310] Similarly, it is widely accepted that an applicant may have more than one country of former habitual residence for the purposes of refugee law. Jurisprudence in leading common law jurisdictions in which this issue has been considered adopts a similar view, including in Australia,[311] Canada,[312] and New Zealand.[313] Similarly, the key textbooks endorse this view.[314]

However in two jurisdictions—the United States and Germany—domestic legislation has been introduced which imposes a more stringent requirement than that set by the *Refugee Convention*. In the United States, a stateless applicant must establish their refugee claim in relation to their country of '*last* habitual residence'.[315] For example, the US statute states that a refugee includes a 'person having no nationality, [who] is outside any country in which such person last habitually resided'.[316] Although this is sometimes interpreted flexibly such that a country of birth constituted the reference country notwithstanding subsequent residence elsewhere,[317] the legislative provision remains a significant constraint on the ability to fully assess asylum claims brought by stateless persons. And although the Qualification Directive simply replicates the language of the *Refugee Convention* by stating, 'being outside of the country of former habitual residence',[318] in Germany the statute requires reference to the last country of former habitual residence.[319]

There are several fundamental problems with this approach. First, it introduces limiting words into the *Convention* that are simply not present. The refugee definition refers to '*former* habitual residence', but does not specify whether the relevant country must be the most recent, the first,[320] or any other particular country of former habitual residence in order to constitute a reference country for the purpose of assessing well-founded fear. This is not permissible under the rules of treaty interpretation, which require an interpretation based on ordinary meaning—not ordinary meaning of the *Convention* language as adjusted by domestic statute—and in light of context, object, and purpose. Given the protective object and purpose of the

---

[310] UNHCR, 'Handbook' (n 47) [104].

[311] See *Al-Anezi v Minister for Immigration and Multicultural Affairs* (1999) 92 FCR 283 (hereafter *Al-Anezi*); *Taiem* (n 69); *SZUNZ* (n 268).

[312] *Thabet* (n 30); *Rahman v Minister of Citizenship and Immigration*, 2016 FC 1355 [14].

[313] *Refugee Appeal No 72635* (n 29) [117]–[118]; *Refugee Appeal Nos 73861, 73862* (n 57) [69].

[314] See e.g., Zimmermann, *The 1951 Convention* (n 26) at 462. See Hathaway and Foster, *The Law of Refugee Status 2* (n 51) 72–74.

[315] 8 USC § 1101(a)(42)(A)(2012), as cited in UNHCR, 'Guidelines on Representing Stateless Persons' (n 110) 13 (emphasis added).

[316] 8 USC § 1101(a)(42)(A), 1158(b) (1), as cited in *Fedosseeva* (n 31).

[317] See *Ouda* (n 72); *Haile* (n 229).

[318] Qualification Directive 2011/95/EU (n 36) art 2(d). At art 2(n) it states, 'country of origin' means 'the country or countries of nationality or, for stateless persons, of former habitual residence'. This could be read as allowing for multiple countries of former habitual residence.

[319] In Germany, the position is particularly anomalous as the relevant legislation (s 3(1) of the *German Asylum Procedure Act*) 'focuses on the country where the foreigner, as a stateless person, last "had" his habitual residence': 10 C 50.07 (n 34) [30]. See also at [36].

[320] Grahl-Madsen took the view that country of former habitual residence should be interpreted to mean country of initial persecution: see *The Status of Refugees in International Law* (n 4) 162. However, as the Canadian Federal Court recognized in *Maarouf*, the Grahl-Madsen approach is 'unnecessarily restrictive': (n 62) at 10.

Convention, the introduction of additional text that has a limiting effect is difficult to justify. Indeed, there does not appear to be any attempt in these jurisdictions to explain the rationale for such an approach.[321]

Second, this approach raises a genuine risk of violation of Article 33 of the *Convention* if only the last country of former habitual residence is assessed as against the criteria for refugee status, even where it is clear that the applicant may be removed to a prior country of former habitual residence in which a claimed fear of persecution has not been assessed.[322]

In our view the correct interpretation of the *Convention* is that a person may have more than one country of former habitual residence for the purposes of assessing future risk. This does not, however, resolve the interpretive dilemma. Rather another question arises, namely whether it is necessary for the applicant to establish a well-founded fear of being persecuted in relation to *every* country of former habitual residence.

In some jurisdictions, decision-makers have referred to the explicit provision in relation to dual nationals as relevant to this issue, that is, the requirement that in the case

of a person who has more than one nationality, the term 'the country of his nationality' shall mean each of the countries of which he is a national, and a person shall not be deemed to be lacking the protection of the country of his nationality if, without any valid reason based on well-founded fear, he has not availed himself of the protection of one of the countries of which he is a national.[323]

It has been argued that the drafters intended that those with and without nationality should be treated identically, and hence it is appropriate to extrapolate from the explicit provision for dual nationals and impose the same requirement on those with more than one country of former habitual residence.[324] This approach has

---

[321] The issue does not seem to have been discussed in the case law in either the United States or Germany. In the only other jurisdiction of which we are aware that has adopted a single country of former habitual residence approach, the High Court of Ireland, it is not at all clear from the judgment that the Court was aware that an alternative approach was to consider both Nepal and Bhutan countries of former habitual residence: see *D T (No 2) v Refugee Appeal Tribunal*, 2012 IEHC 562. We note that leave was granted to appeal to the Supreme Court of Ireland in this case but the Supreme Court did not deal with this issue: see *D T v Minister for Justice and Law Reform* [2017] IESC 45.

[322] This is clearly the case in the US. For instance, in *Al Najjar* (n 289) the Court acknowledged that both United Arab Emirates and Saudi Arabia were 'appropriate countries of removal' for one of the appellants (Mazen), yet only the claim in relation to the UAE was assessed as that happened to be the 'last habitual residence' of the applicant. Indeed, the Court acknowledged that the 'statutory methodology for determining the potential country of deportation is different from that utilized to pinpoint the asylum testing country': *Al Najjar* (n 289) 1292. For another example, see *Paripovic* (n 288) 242, where the immigration judge had issued a deportation order 'designating Serbia as the primary deportation country and Croatia as the alternate', even though the statute only permits an assessment against one of these countries. This concern was identified decades ago by the Canadian Federal Court of Appeal in *Thabet* (n 30). As Linden J observed, the 'last country of former habitual residence' approach 'could create a situation where Canada is in contravention of article 33 of the Convention': at 9. However, we note that this risk remains in Canada: see *X(Re)* 2016 (n 309) [22].

[323] *Refugee Convention* (n 2) art 1(A)(2).

[324] See *Thabet* (n 30), where Linden J stated, '[s]tateless people should be treated as analogously as possible with those who have more than one nationality. There is a need to maintain symmetry between these two groups, where possible': at 12.

been most clearly articulated by the Canadian Federal Court of Appeal in *Thabet*, in which it was explained that, '[so] long as the claimant does not face persecution in a country of former habitual residence that will take him or her back, he or she cannot be determined to be a refugee'.[325] Although basing this reasoning on the notion that 'there is no obligation to a person if an alternate and viable haven is available elsewhere',[326] the content of such 'haven' is clearly confined to whether the individual 'would be safe from persecution'.[327] If the state in question will not permit re-entry, then nothing more is required in order to establish refugee status,[328] but if re-entry is available, that appears to be sufficient to negate the claim for refugee status.[329]

The difficulty with this argument is that while it is true that the drafters intended that only stateless persons who feared persecution could qualify for refugee status,[330] and in that sense did envisage symmetry between those with and without a nationality, there is no evidence that they intended identical treatment in every respect. Indeed, the fact that an explicit provision was introduced for dual nationals but not for non-nationals suggests precisely the opposite: that those without a nationality were not to be subject to the same requirement. There is no logical reason for assuming that the inclusion of a provision for dual nationals but not for stateless persons was an oversight.[331] Rather, there is a sensible reason to treat the two groups differently in this respect because there is a very significant qualitative difference between them. States have an obligation to allow their nationals to enter, and reside in their country of nationality, and to enjoy the full range of rights and entitlements available to all nationals within that state. By contrast, the fact that a stateless person has resided in a country of former habitual residence does not necessarily entitle the person to any of the same protections as nationals. Indeed, this is acknowledged in the very text of the *Refugee Convention*, in which in relation to nationals the question is whether the applicant is unable or unwilling 'to avail himself of the protection of that country', whereas for those without a nationality the question is simply whether the applicant is unable or unwilling 'as a result of such events', 'to return to it'.[332]

---

[325] ibid, [28]–[29]. This has been adopted in New Zealand; see *Refugee Appeal Nos 73861, 73862* (n 57) [69].

[326] *Thabet* (n 30).   [327] ibid.

[328] *Popov v Minister of Citizenship and Immigration*, 2009 FC 898 [42]–[44]. In *Thabet* (n 30), the Court observed that it 'is unlikely that many countries of former habitual residence will grant their former residents the right to return, but there may be lands that do normally accept back former habitual residents': 12.

[329] The reasoning in *Thabet* has also been adopted in New Zealand: see *Refugee Appeal No 72635* (n 29) [121] where, following a comprehensive review of the various approaches available, the Tribunal concluded, '[i]n short, the well-founded fear of being persecuted for a Convention reason must be established in relation to each and every country of former habitual residence before a State party to the Convention has obligations to the stateless person'.

[330] See above Part 1.

[331] See the discussion in the UN Economic and Social Council, 'Summary Record of the 160th Meeting' (2 August 1950) UN Doc E/AC.7/SR.160, 6–7 (hereafter UN Economic and Social Council, 'Summary Record of the 160th Meeting').

[332] *Refugee Convention* (n 2) art 1A(2).

This is widely understood to reflect the fact that only *nationals* are entitled to the protection referred to in the text.[333]

This qualitative difference also explains why the surrogacy principle—which has been engaged by some courts in this context—cannot justify the extension of the dual nationality provision to stateless persons, since that principle rests on the supposition that the *Refugee Convention* was designed to intervene following 'a breakdown of national protection',[334] that is, the protection states owe to their nationals. Hence caution should be exercised in introducing a restrictive interpretation that is not supported by the text of the *Convention* but only on 'the philosophy of refugee law in general'.[335]

It is only where the requirements of Article 1E have been met that the *Refugee Convention* explicitly allows for the exclusion of stateless refugees due to an alternative source of protection. Hence it is only where a stateless person 'is recognized by the competent authorities of the country in which he has taken residence as having the rights and obligations which are attached to the possession of the nationality of that country', that the 'Convention shall not apply'.[336] The circumstances in which a stateless person will have a status in any country that would meet the requirements of Article 1E will be rare.[337] This has been recognized at least implicitly by the French authorities in insisting that in the case of a Palestinian born in Egypt, temporary residence in Syria, Lebanon, Sudan, and Libya was irrelevant because in those other countries he 'lived irregularly and could not claim the protection of the authorities'.[338] Since he still had family in Egypt and 'maintains his centre of material and moral interest there' it was the only reference state in which a well-founded fear needed to be established.[339]

In sum, the position first outlined in the UNHCR Handbook is in our view the correct one, namely that 'the definition does not require that he satisfies the criteria in relation to all of them'.[340] Rather, so long as an applicant can establish a

---

[333] See the discussion in the UN Economic and Social Council, 'Summary Record of the 160th Meeting' (n 331), where Mr Henkin (United States) clarified that 'protection' was a term of art, and meant diplomatic protection, which could only be given by the country of nationality and not by the country of former habitual residence': 6.

[334] Hathaway, *The Law of Refugee Status 2* (n 51) 104. The surrogacy or *Ward* principle (referring to the Canadian Supreme Court's adoption of it in *Ward*) was explicitly relied upon in *Thabet* (n 30) (at [28]) and also in the NZ decision *Refugee Appeal No 72635* (n 29) [122], describing it as the notion that 'international refugee law was formulated to serve as a back-up to state protection': at [122].

[335] *Refugee Appeal 72635* (n 29) [122].   [336] *Refugee Convention* (n 2) art 1E.

[337] *Minister of Citizenship and Immigration v Alsha'bi*, 2015 FC 1381, stating, '[a] claimant who is acknowledged to be stateless does not have a country of nationality or status in any country that is substantially similar to nationality and, for that reason, would not fall within the application of the [art 1E] exclusion': at [66].

[338] CNDA, decision n° 11030207 C+, 22 May 2014 (translation by Rebecca Dowd).

[339] ibid.

[340] UNHCR, 'Handbook' (n 47) [104]. This has also been accepted in Australian jurisprudence. In *Al-Anezi* (n 311) [22], Lehane J held that: 'It would be surprising if a stateless person who, owing to a well-founded fear of persecution for a Convention reason, had left (was outside) a country of former habitual residence and was unable or, due to such a fear, unwilling to return to that country, ceased to be a refugee merely because of subsequent habitual residence in another country in which he or she had no fear of persecution.' See also *1114181* (n 148) [15]–[19].

well-founded fear of persecution in relation to at least one of his or her countries of former habitual residence, the only remaining question is whether he or she enjoys the status of a de facto citizen[341] such that exclusion pursuant to Article 1E is warranted. Cases that have concluded that stateless individuals can be returned to a country that offers nothing more than the ability to return are in our view ripe for reconsideration.

Part 4: Conclusion

In this chapter we have identified the key preliminary challenges faced by stateless applicants seeking recognition as a refugee within the *Refugee Convention*. While some of the initial uncertainty has been resolved, the analysis in later Parts of the chapter revealed that decision-makers continue to find elements of the refugee definition problematic when applied to stateless applicants. Yet a careful and considered analysis, taking into account relevant principles of international law, and the guidance of reasoned judicial authority, reveals that most of these perceived obstacles are surmountable. In Chapter 5, we turn to the question of the specific ways in which a stateless applicant may establish a fear of 'being persecuted' for *Convention* reasons.

---

[341] Mr van Heiven Goedhart observed in the debate in the Conference of Plenipotentiaries that Article 1E (then in the form of Article 1D) applied when 'a person had the status of de facto citizenship, that was to say, if he really had the rights and obligations of a citizen of a given country': COP, 'Summary Record 23rd Meeting' (n 18) 11.

5

Statelessness as Persecution

Examining the Causes and Consequences of Statelessness through the Lens of Refugee Law

In this chapter we turn our attention to the core of the refugee claim, namely the content of the concept of persecution. It is here that we seek to interrogate in depth the degree to which the *Convention relating to the Status of Refugees* ('*Refugee Convention*'), in accommodating and reflecting contemporary human rights norms, may provide a broader ambit of protection to stateless persons than may have been considered possible in the early decades of its operation. While refugee law jurisprudence examining this issue is 'in its early stages',[1] it is timely to explore the approaches adopted to date, with a view to developing a clearer framework for decision-makers grappling with these issues. As greater attention internationally is focused on the plight of the stateless, including those in transit and seeking protection elsewhere, the need for a thoughtful and informed framework in refugee law is becoming more acute.

In Parts 1, 2, and 3, we examine the extent to which denial or deprivation of nationality, and/or the denial of the right to return, may be considered a violation of human rights sufficient to constitute serious harm in refugee law.[2] In this regard, we seek to problematize the simplistic statement that being stateless is not sufficient to constitute refugee status by exploring whether, in cases where discrimination is at the heart of the predicament of a stateless person, refugee status may indeed be warranted. In Parts 4, 5, and 6, we explore the ramifications of statelessness, focusing particularly on the denial of social and economic rights, and consider in what circumstances such violations in relation to stateless persons will amount to persecution on the grounds of nationality. We do not consider separately the meaning of the term 'nationality' for the purposes of the *Refugee Convention* grounds, given that it is very well accepted that nationality includes its converse, namely not having

---

[1] Maryellen Fullerton, 'Comparative Perspectives on Statelessness and Persecution' (2015) 63 UKanLRev 863, 864. She goes on to explain that the limited case law leaves 'a multitude of issues yet to be addressed': at 899.

[2] This chapter, particularly in Parts 1 and 2, builds on a pilot study by Hélène Lambert, United Nations High Commissioner for Refugees ('UNHCR'), 'Refugee Status, Arbitrary Deprivation of Nationality, and Statelessness within the Context of Article 1A(2) of the 1951 Convention and its 1967 Protocol relating to the Status of Refugees' (UNHCR Legal and Protection Policy Research Series PPLA/2014/01, October 2014). See also Hélène Lambert, 'Comparative Perspectives on Arbitrary Deprivation of Nationality and Refugee Status' (2015) 64 ICLQ 1.

a nationality.[3] In addition, cases involving stateless applicants rarely turn on the nature of the *Convention* ground; rather it is often readily accepted that the ground nationality is apt, or in the alternative race, or membership of a particular social group.[4] However, the question of when a particular form of harm can be said to be 'for reasons of' a Convention ground is sometimes contentious and will be discussed below, particularly in relation to Parts 1–3.

In Chapter 4 it was established that statelessness per se does not give rise to refugee status. In other words, inability to return does not automatically confer refugee status on a stateless person. However, it does not therefore follow that the predicament of being stateless, or its consequences, cannot constitute persecution. In other words, challenging the notion that there is a 'sharp'[5] or 'clear distinction between stateless persons and refugees'[6] is at the heart of this chapter.

Our analysis of a wide range of jurisprudence suggests that decision-makers have, in many contexts, failed adequately to appreciate the significant overlap between statelessness and refugeehood, leading to an impoverished consideration of when denial of nationality, withdrawal of nationality, and/or denial of re-entry may amount to persecution. In part, this appears to be explicable on the basis of an inadequate understanding of the causes of statelessness—almost an assumption that it is accidental,[7] 'unfortunate',[8] unavoidable, or simply the result of a legitimate exercise of state sovereignty in relation to nationality laws. The fact that the formulation of nationality laws was traditionally an issue solely within the discretion of a sovereign state and that 'statelessness is often the result of the operation and conflict of nationality laws and does not necessarily signify persecution in terms of the Refugee Convention',[9] appear to have obfuscated the fact that statelessness can—in many situations—be understood as the result of persecutory acts. As the New Zealand Refugee Status Appeals Authority ('RSAA') has noted, while statelessness

---

[3] James C Hathaway and Michelle Foster, *The Law of Refugee Status* (2nd edn, CUP 2014) (hereafter Hathaway and Foster, *The Law of Refugee Status 2*), 397–99. Although see Australian Refugee Review Tribunal ('Australian Tribunal') decision *1114181* [2013] RRTA 2 (4 January 2013) (hereafter *1114181*).

[4] For instance, in *SZPZI v Minister for Immigration & Anor* [2011] FMCA 530 (22 July 2011) (hereafter *SZPZI*) the Federal Magistrates Court of Australia found that the tribunal had fallen into error in failing to consider whether the group 'undocumented residents' constituted a social group for the purposes of the *Refugee Convention*: at [50], [52]–[54]. In *1000094* [2010] RRTA 277 (16 April 2010) (hereafter *1000094*) the Australian Tribunal found the stateless applicant to fall within the particular social group 'Palestinian refugees in Lebanon': at [157]–[158].

[5] *Refugee Appeal No 72635* [2002] NZRSAA 344 (6 September 2002) [152] (hereafter *Refugee Appeal No 72635*): 'The Refugee Convention distinguishes sharply between stateless persons and refugees.'

[6] *Refugee Appeal No 73861* [2005] NZRSAA 228 (30 June 2005) [58] (hereafter *Refugee Appeal No 73861*).

[7] In *N99/31199* [2000] RRTA 1058 (20 November 2000) (hereafter *N99/31199*) the Australian Tribunal found that the deprivation of citizenship by the Kuwaiti government in relation to the Bidoon applicant 'would not be a result of persecution by the Kuwaiti State but because, through an accidental combination of missed opportunities, the applicant is stateless'.

[8] In *N99/31199*, the Australian Tribunal also referred to the applicant's predicament as resulting from 'an unfortunate combination of circumstances'.

[9] *Refugee Appeal Nos 73861, 73862* [2005] NZRSAA 228 (30 June 2005) [58] (hereafter *Refugee Appeal Nos 73861, 73862*).

'is sometimes simply the product of misfortune',[10] in other cases 'the stripping of nationality can be an act (often the final act) of persecution'.[11] Failure adequately to appreciate this in refugee law may simply be reflective of the wider international community's failure to prioritize statelessness as a human rights issue until recently;[12] indeed, our understanding of statelessness has developed very substantially in recent years and we can attribute significant gains in knowledge to the past decade alone. In this chapter, we seek to integrate these developments as appropriate into refugee law doctrine.

Part 1: Denial of Nationality as Persecution

This Part relates to persons who never had a nationality. Despite the right to a nationality being enshrined in several human rights treaties and recognized as 'amongst the most important rights a state can assign to individuals',[13] this is the category of case that has proven most challenging in the refugee context. That is, where a person claims that the failure of their country of origin to afford them nationality constitutes persecution, their claim most acutely challenges the notion that states are untrammelled in devising and applying their own nationality laws.

Not only has this issue challenged and troubled decision-makers, but key refugee law texts have failed comprehensively to grapple with the question of whether denial of nationality can constitute persecution,[14] meaning there is little by way of academic analysis to redress gaps in the jurisprudence.

Few cases have addressed this issue in isolation, but many of those applicants that have asserted that their statelessness emanates from a persecutory policy or treatment have been met with scepticism. A common thread running through these cases is conclusory reasoning in the form of the statement, '[r]efugee status is not accorded to persons merely because they are stateless'.[15]

An examination of the jurisprudence reveals three key challenges. First, many refugee law decision-makers appear unfamiliar with or unaware of the pertinent international law norms, and specifically the significant constraints imposed by

---

[10] *Refugee Appeal 74880* [2005] NZRSAA 294 (29 September 2005) [75] (hereafter *Refugee Appeal No 74880*).

[11] ibid.

[12] Michelle Foster and Hélène Lambert, 'Statelessness as a Human Rights Issue: A Concept Whose Time Has Come' (2016) 28 IJRL 564 (hereafter Foster and Lambert, 'Statelessness as a Human Rights Issue'); Rosemary Byrne, 'James C. Hathaway and Michelle Foster. The Law of Refugee Status' (2015) 26 EJIL 564.

[13] Committee on Feminism and International Law, 'Final Report on Women's Equality and Nationality' (International Law Association Conference, London, 2000) 10. See also Warren CJ, dissenting, in *Perez v Brownell* (1958) 356 US 44, 64 (hereafter *Perez v Brownell*) (nationality 'is nothing less than the right to have rights').

[14] See account by Eric Fripp, *Nationality and Statelessness in the International Law of Refugee Status* (Hart 2016) 313–16 (hereafter Fripp, *Nationality and Statelessness*). We acknowledge that the second edition of Hathaway and Foster, *The Law of Refugee Status* (n 3) discusses these issues in the context of freedom of movement, but we contend that there is a need to focus on deprivation itself as the issue.

[15] *N99/31199* (n 7); *Abauaelian v Gonzales*, 132 Fed Appx 121 (9th Cir, 2005).

human rights law on state discretion in relation to nationality laws. Second, many cases suggest a failure properly to *apply* modern human rights norms in practice. Third, even where a norm is properly identified and applied, there is a question as to whether denial of citizenship is sufficient on its own to constitute persecution.

Turning to the first issue, perhaps the clearest exemplification of the international law challenge is in *BA v Secretary of State for the Home Department*,[16] where the appellant had submitted to the UK Upper Tribunal (formerly the Asylum and Immigration Tribunal) that it 'should regard denial of nationality as in itself a persecutory act'.[17] The Tribunal did not accept this submission, holding that, 'It may be that the right to a nationality is an emerging norm, but it has plainly not yet become part of international law. Given this state of affairs, we cannot see that denial of nationality as such amounts to persecution.'[18]

This conclusion regarding the inadequacy of international law was drawn without explicit reference to any international legal instruments or scholarship. Tribunals in other jurisdictions have adopted a similar stance in concluding that, '[n]ot automatically obtaining the nationality of a country by being born on its soil is not, *in our opinion*, a breach of a fundamental right any more than not obtaining it by filiation';[19] it is 'a legal issue decided by individual countries and is not persecutory'.[20] In a New Zealand decision, the RSAA began its consideration of the international law issues with the statement that 'questions of nationality are principally within the jurisdiction of a state',[21] and that 'international law does not impose a duty on States to confer their nationality'.[22] This led to the conclusion that 'broadly speaking, statelessness is considered to be the result of the operation and conflict of nationality laws, not the result of persecution'.[23] And in Australia the Federal Court observed, in upholding the decision of the tribunal below, that '[t]o the extent that the nationality claims [the discriminatory denial of nationality] depend upon conventions other than the [Refugee] Convention, they were not within the range of matters required to be considered',[24] suggesting a wholesale misunderstanding of the relevant legal framework.

In our view, however, an analysis that rests on the notion that international law has not yet evolved to the point of recognizing a universal 'right to nationality' that can be invoked by any individual in relation to any particular country in every situation—a proposition with which we agree—does not dispose of the issue. Rather, all cases that have raised this issue in the refugee context have at their core an

---

[16] *BA v Secretary of State for the Home Department* [2004] UKIAT 00256 (hereafter *BA*).

[17] ibid, [62].

[18] ibid, [63]. We note that no authority was cited. The United Kingdom Asylum and Immigration Tribunal ('UK Tribunal') did, however, consider the applicants at risk of persecution in relation to the other rights that would be affected. See below at n 59.

[19] *X (Re)*, 2002 CanLII 52637 (CA IRB) 3 (emphasis added).   [20] ibid, 3.

[21] *Refugee Appeal No 72635* (n 5) [70], and that it 'is not necessary in the present context to determine what limits international law places on the right of States to regulate nationality': at [73].

[22] ibid, [83].   [23] ibid, [90].

[24] *SZTFX v Minister for Immigration and Border Protection* [2015] FCA 402 (30 April 2015) [47] (hereafter *SZTFX*).

allegation that the denial of nationality in relation to the applicant's group is linked to a protected status, usually race, but sometimes another ground such as gender.

It is in this context that it is vital for decision-makers to delve deeper into the evolving developments in international human rights law in relation to the right to nationality outlined in Chapter 3.

For example, Article 9(1) of the *Convention on the Elimination of Discrimination Against Women* ('*CEDAW*') obligates states party to 'grant women equal rights with men to *acquire*, change or retain their nationality'.[25] Notwithstanding this, gender discrimination in nationality laws remains prevalent globally, with a recent United Nations High Commissioner for Refugee's ('UNHCR') survey revealing that 'equality between men and women relating to conferral of nationality upon children has not yet been attained in 25 countries, and these countries are located in almost all parts of the world'.[26] In addition to the impact on women of such discrimination, 'gender inequality in nationality laws can create statelessness where children cannot acquire nationality from their fathers'.[27]

The *International Convention on the Elimination of All Forms of Racial Discrimination* ('*ICERD*') obligates states to 'prohibit and to eliminate racial discrimination in all its forms and to guarantee the right of everyone, without distinction as to race, colour, or national or ethnic origin, to equality before the law, notably in the enjoyment of the following rights', which includes '(iii) [t]he right to nationality'.[28] While Article 1(3) of the *ICERD* seeks to carve out an exception for nationality and citizenship laws, this is applicable only so long as '*such provisions do not discriminate against any particular nationality*'.[29] The Committee on the Elimination of all Forms of Racial Discrimination has further explained that in accordance with the *ICERD* states must, 'ensure that particular groups of non-citizens are not discriminated against with regard to access to citizenship or naturalization, and to pay due attention to possible barriers to naturalization that may exist for long-term or permanent residents'.[30]

Coupled with the well accepted *jus cogens* status of racial discrimination,[31] it is difficult to sustain the argument that citizenship laws that exclude a certain group

---

[25] *Convention on the Elimination of Discrimination Against Women* (opened for signature 1 March 1980, entered into force 3 September 1981) 1249 UNTS 13 (emphasis added).

[26] UNHCR, 'Background Note on Gender Equality, Nationality Laws and Statelessness 2018' (8 March 2018) 2 (hereafter UNHCR, 'Background Note on Gender Equality'). For a history of gendered exclusions from citizenship, see Leti Volpp, 'Feminist, Sexual and Queer Citizenship' in Ayelet Shachar, Rainer Bauböck, Irene Bloemraad, and Maarten Vink (eds), *The Oxford Handbook of Citizenship* (OUP 2017) 53.

[27] UNHCR, 'Background Note on Gender Equality' (n 26) 2.

[28] *International Convention on the Elimination of All Forms of Racial Discrimination* (adopted 21 December 1965, entered into force 4 January 1969) 660 UNTS 195, art 5(d)(iii).

[29] ibid (emphasis added). 'Nothing in this Convention may be interpreted as affecting in any way the legal provisions of States Parties concerning nationality, citizenship or naturalization, provided that such provisions do not discriminate against any particular nationality': art 1(3).

[30] UNHCR, 'CERD General Recommendation XXX on Discrimination against Non-Citizens' (1 October 2002) para 13.

[31] See UN General Assembly (UNGA), 'Report of the International Law Commission on the Work of its Fifty-Third Session' UN GAOR 53rd Session Supp No 10 UN Doc A/56/10 (Commentary to Draft Article 26 on Responsibility of States for Internationally Wrongful Acts) (2001) ch IV(E) (2) 85 para 5, in which the International Law Commission ('ILC'), in unequivocal terms, states that

based on race or ethnicity could be justified as within the sovereign discretion of the state.

In terms of grounds other than gender or race, the *International Covenant on Civil and Political Rights* ('*ICCPR*') contains a general equality clause which explicitly prohibits any discrimination on grounds such as 'race, colour, sex, language, religion, political or other opinion, national or social origin, property, birth or other status',[32] extending the prohibited grounds beyond those listed in *CEDAW* and the *ICERD*. Finally, Article 7(1) of the *Convention on the Rights of the Child* ('*CRC*') provides that, '[t]he child shall be registered immediately after birth and shall have the right from birth to a name, *the right to acquire a nationality*' which, when read with Article 2(1) *CRC*, also prohibits discrimination 'of any kind, irrespective of the child's or his or her parent's or legal guardian's race, colour, sex, language, religion, political or other opinion, national, ethnic or social origin, property, disability, birth or other status'.[33] Of course, not every distinction constitutes discrimination; hence not every distinction in domestic citizenship laws will contravene international norms. The point is rather that it cannot be assumed that states are unconstrained by international law in the formulation and application of their nationality laws.

The regional human rights treaties reveal a more complex picture. While there is an explicit 'right to a nationality' in the *American Convention on Human Rights*,[34] and a free-standing right to equality guarantee in the *African Charter on Human and Peoples' Rights*,[35] which would apply to the formulation and application of nationality laws, the *European Convention on Human Rights* ('*ECHR*') contains neither of these provisions. However, states parties to the *Refugee Convention* governed by the European Union Directive—which references the *ECHR* in interpreting 'being persecuted'—can and should nonetheless refer to wider international human rights norms in interpreting the notion of 'being persecuted'.[36]

In sum therefore, while it remains the case that it is difficult to point to an absolute right to a nationality in international law, where there is evidence of discrimination

---

those 'peremptory norms that are clearly accepted and recognized include the prohibitions of aggression, genocide, slavery, racial discrimination, crimes against humanity and torture, and the right to self-determination'.

[32] *International Covenant on Civil and Political Rights* (adopted 16 December 1966, entered into force 23 March 1976) 999 UNTS 171, art 26.

[33] *Convention on the Rights of the Child* (adopted 20 November 1989, entered into force 2 September 1990) 1577 UNTS 3, art 2(1) and 7(1) (emphasis added).

[34] *American Convention on Human Rights* (adopted 22 November 1969, entered into force 18 July 1978) 1144 UNTS 123, art 20(1). Article 20 also states: '2. Every person has the right to the nationality of the state in whose territory he was born if he does not have the right to any other nationality. 3. No one shall be arbitrarily deprived of his nationality or of the right to change it.'

[35] *African Charter on Human and Peoples' Rights* (adopted 27 June 1981, entered into force 21 October 1986) 1520 UNTS 217, art 3.

[36] Article 9 of the Qualification Directive mentions the European Convention but not in an exclusive manner: Directive 2011/95/EU of the European Parliament and of the Council of 13 December 2011 on standards for the qualification of third-country nationals or stateless persons as beneficiaries of international protection, for a uniform status for refugees or for persons eligible for subsidiary protection, and for the content of the protection granted (recast) [2011] OJ L 337/9, art 9(1)(a) (hereafter Qualification Directive 2011/95/EU). Further, the Directive is clear that is it 'based on the full and inclusive application of the Geneva Convention of 28 July 1951 relating to the Status of Refugees': at [3].

on a protected ground in formulating nationality laws, human rights obligations are engaged. In light of the well-entrenched refugee law doctrine that persecution is constituted by the sustained or systemic violation of human rights norms,[37] such norms must be considered in the context of refugee status determination where denial of nationality is relevant.

However, articulation of the clear norms that pertain to these cases does not respond to all the challenges raised because in many cases, decision-makers are willing to concede that, 'the denial of citizenship by reason of nationality, race, religion or membership of a particular social group may constitute persecution',[38] yet appear reluctant to closely examine the historical or socio-political background to a particular country's nationality laws. Further in some cases, decision-makers refer only to the domestic citizenship legislation in question, or the stated policy of the home country, without further examining whether this apparently neutral law or policy is in fact applied in a discriminatory fashion. Yet when we consider UNHCR's analysis that suggests more than 75 per cent of the world's known stateless populations belong to minority groups, we may immediately question the predominant approach in refugee law that appears to assume that failure to acquire nationality and persecution are mutually exclusive categories.

As the UNHCR observes, '[d]iscrimination on the basis of ethnicity, race, religion or language is a recurrent cause of statelessness globally'.[39] In some cases, discrimination against minorities in relation to the conferral of citizenship 'is prescribed by law',[40] for example, as is the case in Myanmar in which the Muslim Rohingya, 'the largest known stateless group in the world',[41] are excluded from a list of 'national ethnic groups' which automatically acquire citizenship at birth pursuant to the 1982 Citizenship Law.[42] More frequently, such discrimination 'is based on formal or informal policies and practices that affect certain groups disproportionately'.[43] Yet refugee decision-makers appear remarkably resistant to interrogating the purported neutrality of citizenship laws and policies of sovereign states.

Several prominent populations frequently come before decision-makers across the range of jurisdictions examined, and one particularly noteworthy group that provides an instructive case study on this point is the Bidoon from Kuwait; bidoon, meaning 'without nationality'.[44]

---

[37] Hathaway and Foster, *The Law of Refugee Status* 2 (n 3).

[38] *BZADW v Minister for Immigration and Border Protection* [2014] FCA 541 (26 May 2014) [21] (hereafter *BZADW*). See also *071626084* [2007] RRTA 304 (21 November 2007) 25 (hereafter *071626084*). This explains the divergence between the New Zealand Refugee Status Appeals Authority's ('RSAA') decision in *Refugee Appeal No 72645/01* [2001] NZRSAA 298 (24 September 2001) and *Refugee Appeal No 74467* [2004] NZRSAA 283 (1 September 2004) (hereafter *Refugee Appeal No 74467*) as discussed below. See at [100]: 'Our divergence is not one of principle so much as a different perspective on the historical/factual background.'

[39] UNHCR, ' "This Is Our Home" Stateless Minorities and Their Search for Citizenship' (November 2017) Preface (hereafter UNHCR, 'This Is Our Home').

[40] ibid.   [41] ibid, 6.

[42] ibid; *Burma Citizenship Law* (Myanmar) Pyithu Hluttaw Law No 4 of 1982, 15 October 1982 [Chairman of the Council of State (Burma) trans, *Working People's Daily*, 16 October 1982].

[43] UNHCR, 'This Is Our Home' (n 39) 1.

[44] See e.g., the explanation of the origin of the term set out in *BA* (n 16) [5].

In cases across several jurisdictions, despite evidence having been presented to the relevant authority suggesting that discrimination lies at the core of Kuwait's citizenship law and policy, decision-makers generally have taken a similar position to the NZ Tribunal in *Refugee Appeal No 72635*, in which it concluded:[45]

Our finding on the extensive evidence is that the appellant is stateless for one reason only, namely because Kuwaiti citizenship law is based on *jus sanguinis*. . . . The *jus sanguinis* model is common throughout the world, and the Middle-East in particular. . . . The difficulty faced by the appellant is that his status of 'stateless' under Kuwaiti law is the result of the operation of the *jus sanguinis* principle, not his race, nationality or membership of a particular social group.[46]

In a subsequent decision, the UK Tribunal similarly rejected the submission that the refusal of the Kuwaiti authorities to 'determine the nationality applications of the Bidoon is persecution',[47] on the basis that the Kuwaiti 'authorities' position is that significant numbers of the Bidoon in fact have nationalities of other countries, and that investigations are ongoing, albeit very slowly, to establish their backgrounds and to decide whether or not they are entitled to nationality'.[48] The UK Upper Tribunal relied on the fact that Kuwait had established a committee to review the status of the Bidoon as sufficient to reject the denial of citizenship as persecution argument, notwithstanding the Tribunal's concession that the Bidoon Committee's work was 'tortuous'. The fact that the Committee's work remained 'ongoing' was sufficient, regardless of the effectiveness of its work.[49] This was in spite of the evidence before the Tribunal that 'there was a gap between the law and its application in Kuwait',[50] that there was evidence of corruption in the work of the Kuwaiti committee,[51] and that there was no credible evidence that the majority of Bidoon were in fact nationals of other countries, as claimed by the Kuwaiti government.

A decision by the Canadian Tribunal shortly thereafter similarly concluded that the applicants' statelessness was not due to discrimination, citing UK Operational Guidance that repeated the Kuwaiti government's allegation that 'the vast majority of Bidoons were concealing their true identities and were not actually stateless'.[52] The Tribunal thus concluded that 'obtaining Kuwaiti citizenship depends on a person's ancestral ties to the country', essentially 'a law of general application',[53] and not on racial discrimination.[54]

The consistency of this resistance properly to question the formal policy of another state, particularly in the context of refugee law in which decision-makers frequently do precisely that in order to properly assess the cogency of a refugee claim, suggests something peculiar at play in these cases. In our view, this *sui generis* approach in denial of nationality as persecution cases is embodied in the conclusion

---

[45] *Refugee Appeal No 72635* (n 5).
[46] ibid, [182]–[183], as cited in *Refugee Appeal No 74467* (n 38) [84]. This was also applied so as to reject the application in a similar fact case in *Refugee Appeal No 74449* [2003] NZRSAA 332 (26 August 2003) [50] (hereafter *Refugee Appeal No 74449*).
[47] *NM v Secretary of State for the Home Department* [2013] UKUT 356(IAC) [96] (hereafter *NM*).
[48] ibid, [97].   [49] ibid.   [50] ibid, [8].   [51] ibid, [47].
[52] *X (Re)*, 2014 CarswellNat 5790, 5791 [20].   [53] ibid, [20], [26].   [54] ibid, [20].

of the Australian Refugee Review Tribunal ('RRT'), which found that, notwithstanding the evidence of discrimination before the Tribunal, 'the actions of the
Kuwaiti Government towards Bedoun are not persecutory *but a sovereign right of
a nation to determine its citizens*'.[55] It is this assumption of and deferral to absolute
sovereignty that underpins these analyses in both the particular context of Kuwait
and in others as well.[56]

By stark contrast to these decisions, a rare application of international legal
norms—albeit implicit rather than explicit—can be identified. In a lucid and in-
sightful decision from New Zealand also concerning the Bidoon from Kuwait,
Member Shaw questioned the neutrality of the Kuwaiti law. The judgment began
with the observation that Kuwait faced an 'extraordinary situation' in that by 1988
up to one-third of the population was 'stateless'—'a situation not encountered in
other Middle Eastern countries', which commonly employ the *jus sanguinis* principle as a basis of nationality law.[57] In the Member's view, '[c]learly something more
was operative in the creation of statelessness'.[58] Indeed, a thorough examination
of country information revealed that 'the statelessness of the bidoons is intimately
linked to the fact that discriminatory notions have informed both the content and
implementation of Kuwait's Citizenship Law'.[59] Such discrimination was identified as gender discrimination in that 'women's right to citizenship in Kuwait is
limited and contingent',[60] and discrimination based on race and nationality in that
in Kuwait 'citizenship has been used by the ruling elite "to organise and define the
internal power relationships"'.[61] Gender discrimination was also identified by the
Australian Tribunal in a decision concerning the refugee claim of a stateless woman
from Lebanon whose child would also be stateless by virtue of Lebanon's nationality
law that prevents Lebanese women from passing their nationality to their child.[62] In
rejecting the argument that these were laws 'of general application' which were 'appropriate to achieve a legitimate object' (the test adopted in Australian refugee law),

---

[55] *N99/31199* (n 7) (emphasis added). We note that this reluctance to see the discriminatory basis
of Kuwaiti citizenship law also appears to have been the approach taken by the Australian Tribunal and
upheld by the Federal Court in *BZADW* (n 38) [21].

[56] In particular, decision-makers often 'gloss over' the evidence of discrimination. See e.g., in relation
to the claim of a Palestinian stateless man from Lebanon, and his wife who based her claim on her marriage to a stateless person, where the Canadian Tribunal considered the gender discrimination central
to Lebanese citizenship laws which prevented her citizenship passing to her husband, but concluded
that that this was 'a law of general application': *GRF(Re)*, Nos AAO-01454, AAO-01462, AAO-01463
[2001] CRDD No 88 (12 July 2001) 11. See also *Fedosseeva v Gonzales*, 492 F 3d 840 (7th Cir, 2007),
in which the Seventh Circuit Court rejected the applicant's argument that Latvia's failure to accord her
citizenship due to her Russian ethnicity was discriminatory, on the basis of 'significant changes' that
had occurred in Latvia, including 'its admission to the European Union and NATO and an increase
in the number of Russian members of the Latvian parliament': at 848. However, as in the Bidoon case
described above, this appears to rely on *sui generis* developments at the expense of a close analysis of the
application of nationality laws in the particular case.

[57] *Refugee Appeal No 74467* (n 38) [87].		[58] ibid, [87].

[59] ibid, [88]. See also *BA* (n 16), in which the UK Tribunal acknowledged that 'in Kuwait the authorities, having acted to exclude most Bedoon from Kuwaiti nationality and from lawful residence status,
have then confined access to basic civil, political, social, economic and cultural rights to those having
either Kuwaiti nationality or (as lawful residents) foreign nationality': at [64].

[60] *Refugee Appeal No 74467* (n 38) [90].		[61] ibid, [94].

[62] *1617142 (Refugee)* [2017] AATA 990 (7 June 2017) [52] (hereafter *1617142*).

the Tribunal found that the relevant laws 'have a discriminatory character, which singles out women and their children for adverse treatment and disadvantage'[63] and 'that the use of highly discriminatory laws against Lebanese women and their children does not amount to an appropriate measure'.[64]

This reasoning represents a sophisticated analysis that rejects the sense of inevitability and helplessness surrounding the issue of statelessness—embodied in the earlier NZ RSAA's lament that 'statelessness is a phenomenon as old as the concept of nationality'[65]—by adopting a modern approach that recognizes the non-discrimination norms that pertain to and make unlawful many situations of statelessness.

The relevance and importance of the international human rights framework is underscored by the work of the international bodies charged with supervising the key international human rights regimes most relevant to refugee law determination. The conclusions of these committees have the potential to provide guidance to refugee decision-makers as to the degree to which individual states comply with their obligations—thus ensuring a dynamic and evolutionary approach to assessing 'being persecuted' in refugee law and an accurate understanding of the pertinent legal issues in the context of individual countries. For example, the Committee on the Elimination of Racial Discrimination, the international body charged with supervisory responsibility in relation to states parties to the *ICERD*, observed as recently as 2017 in relation to the situation of the Bidoon in Kuwait, that:

the Committee remains deeply concerned by the situation of Bidoon, many of whom have lived in Kuwait for generations but are deemed 'illegal residents' by the State party. It expresses serious concern at persistent reports that Bidoon do not enjoy equal access to social services, due process and legally valid civil documentation, including birth registration documents ... the Committee recommends that the State party: (a) Find a durable solution to the problems faced by Bidoon, including by considering naturalizing those who have lived in Kuwait for long periods and have a genuine and effective link to the State.[66]

As explained above, while there are many situations in which a more thorough examination of the evidence would likely suggest that persecution underpins failure to accord nationality, there are other situations that are more complex. Perhaps the most contentious relates to stateless Palestinians residing in countries such as Israel, the United Arab Emirates, or Lebanon, where decision-makers have stressed the right *of states* to grant nationality and have generally refused refugee status.[67] In a British decision this was justified on the basis that:

---

[63] ibid, [68].　[64] ibid, [69].

[65] *Refugee Appeal No 72635* (n 5) [183], citing Ad Hoc Committee on Refugees and Stateless Persons, 'A Study of Statelessness' (1949) E/1112.

[66] UN Committee on the Elimination of Racial Discrimination ('CERD'), 'Concluding Observations on the Combined Twenty-First to Twenty-Fourth Periodic Reports of Kuwait' (19 September 2017) UN Doc CERD/C/KWT/CO/21–24, paras 27–28.

[67] Another very prevalent case study is Palestinian applicants from various countries in the Middle East that apply *jus sanguinis* and hence do not grant citizenship to Palestinians. In these cases, decision-makers generally reject claims: see e.g., *Ahmed v Ashcroft*, 341 F 3d 214 (3rd Cir, 2003), applying *Faddoul v INS*, 37 F 3d 185 (5th Cir, 1994) (hereafter *Faddoul*) and *Najjar v Ashcroft*, 257 F 3d 1262 (11th Cir, 2001). See also *Elfarra v Ashcroft*, 88 Fed Appx 141 (8th Cir, 2004) (hereafter *Elfarra*).

there is no country which is excluding them from nationality to which they would be otherwise entitled. There is no state of Palestine to offer them citizenship and neither is there any international obligation on the State of Israel, who retain a large measure of control over the Occupied Territories, to offer them citizenship.[68]

Similarly, in *Refugee Appeal No 1/92 Re SA*, the appellant submitted to the NZ RSAA that the fear of persecution was based on (denial of) nationality and it referred to a passage from James Hathaway's *The Law of Refugee Status*: 'Persons who are denied full citizenship in their own state (such as Palestinians in Israel) could qualify as nationally defined refugees insofar as their inferior political status can be shown to put them at risk of persecution.'[69]

The Tribunal rejected the argument based on the information in its possession that it 'cannot accept that Israel denies Palestinians citizenship in "their own state", particularly when there is clear evidence that those Palestinians who remained in Israel after 1948 have been granted the status of Israel citizens'.[70]

As for the situation in Israel in more recent years, the Tribunal was convinced that the 'denial' of nationality was simply the product of:

(a) The fact that there is no sovereign Palestinian State

(b) The fact that Israel recognizes West Bank inhabitants as Jordanian citizens.[71]

The Tribunal therefore concluded, 'Palestinians are not denied full citizenship, but even if they are, such denial arises not from a denial by the Israel authorities, but rather as a result of the international law governing the administration of occupied territory by a military occupant and the absence of a Palestinian State.'[72]

However, in France, in a case concerning a Palestinian born in Egypt to an Egyptian mother and Palestinian father, and who lived in Egypt until he was thirty, the Cour Nationale du Droit d'Asile concluded that the absence of provisions on acquiring Egyptian nationality for persons of Palestinian origins in the Egyptian legislation, coupled with the grave consequences this had on the applicant for many years, meant that the applicant had a well-founded fear of being persecuted in Egypt for political and ethnic reasons.[73]

---

[68] *AB v Secretary of State for the Home Department* [2005] UKIAT 00046 (1 February 2005) [35] (hereafter *AB*). They were nevertheless granted leave to remain by the Secretary of State because there was no realistic prospect of return to any part of the Occupied Territories. See also *SHM v Refugee Appeals Tribunal* [2009] IEHC 128; *KK IH HE v Secretary of State for the Home Department* [2004] UKIAT 00293 (hereafter *KK*); *MM and FH v Secretary of State for the Home Department* [2008] UKAIT 00014 (hereafter *MM and FH*) reaffirming *KK*.
[69] *Refugee Appeal No 1/92 Re SA* [1992] NZRSAA 5 (30 April 1992) (hereafter *Refugee Appeal No 1/92*), citing JC Hathaway, *The Law of Refugee Status* (Butterworths 1991) 144.
[70] *Refugee Appeal No 1/92* (n 69).   [71] ibid.
[72] ibid. The NZ RSAA further explained that states may derogate from certain human rights (including the right to nationality) in situations of emergency provided the derogation measures respect the principles of proportionality, non-discrimination, and consistency, although this is questionable as a matter of international law and no clear authority supports this position. The Tribunal found the appellant's fear of persecution to be unfounded.
[73] Cour Nationale du Droit d'Asile [French National Court of Asylum] ('CNDA'), decision no°11030207 C+, 22 May 2014.

While this category of case is difficult, it is important for refugee decision-makers to take account of developments in international law. There is growing awareness of the right 'to one's own country' that although possibly not amounting to a right to nationality, suggests that states may not be untrammelled in their ability to deport and refuse re-entry, an issue that is explored in Part 3. In addition, even if the denial of nationality may be defended, the consequences particularly in relation to exclusion from economic life, may not be justified, a point we explore further in Part 5.

A third key issue identified in our analysis of cases concerning denial of nationality is whether, even if the denial is found to violate international human rights norms, the denial of nationality is alone capable of constituting persecution—particularly given the need for a forward-looking assessment—or must be supplemented by other consequential forms of rights violations in order to constitute persecution.

There is significant authority that suggests that 'the denial of citizenship by reason of nationality, race, religion or membership of a particular social group may constitute persecution'.[74] Bearing this in mind, courts in several jurisdictions have been willing to recognize that the denial of nationality *may* amount to persecution if it is on a *Refugee Convention* ground and its effects are particularly serious.[75]

However, in many cases the relevant decision-maker does not further analyse or apply this notion because he or she fails to find the requisite discrimination present.[76] In one decision, the notion that the denial of persecution could in and of itself amount to persecution was rejected on the (erroneous) basis that such denial did not engage international law.[77]

More commonly, however, there is a suggestion or hint that the denial of nationality, even if in violation of international law, is not sufficiently serious and must therefore be supplemented by other consequential human rights violations. In many other cases decision-makers simply examine all the aspects of the claim of

---

[74] *BZADW* (n 38) [21]. See also *JV (Tanzania) v Secretary of State for the Home Department* [2007] EWCA Civ 1532 [10] (hereafter *JV (Tanzania)*): a denial of citizenship 'may amount to persecution' if 'the denial is actuated for a Convention reason'.

[75] United Kingdom: *JV (Tanzania)* (n 74): a denial of citizenship may amount to persecution only if the denial is for a *Refugee Convention* reason; hence, in all such cases, a judge would be asking the key question: 'why did the Tanzanian authorities deny the appellant's claim to Tanzanian citizenship?'. If the answer to that question is that 'the appellant's claim was denied because of the authority's [erroneous] interpretation of the legislation and not for any other, certainly not for any capricious or discriminatory reason', then the 'case should be struck down as frankly perverse': at [10]. Germany: Oberverwaltungsgericht Sachsen-Anhalt [German High Administrative Court], 3 L 374/09, 25 May 2011 (translated summary from European Database of Asylum Law): the denial of nationality may only constitute political persecution if it is linked with characteristics relevant to asylum. The denial of nationality which merely represents an administrative sanction for a breach of duty that is incumbent on all citizens alike cannot be considered a persecution. France: CNDA, decision no°10015655 C, 5 January 2011 ((hereafter Decision no°10015655 C) (refugee status granted to a Rohingya from Myanmar (Burma) based on the legislation in force since 1982, which denies Rohingya of their citizenship rights, coupled with the ill-treatment of Rohingya (as an ethnic group) by the Burmese authorities); CNDA, decision no°640897/08021356, 14 December 2009 *Mlle H* (hereafter Decision no°640897/08021356) (refugee status granted based on the refusal of the Russian authorities to grant nationality to an (orphan) stateless person from North Korea because of her ethnicity, coupled with her ill-treatment for many years).

[76] *JV (Tanzania)* (n 74) [10].   [77] *BA* (n 16) [63].

persecution in one holistic assessment,[78] without parsing out the independent claim in relation to nationality. For example, in a claim involving a Rohingya man from Myanmar, the NZ RSAA explained, in finding that he qualified for refugee status that he:

is not recognised as a citizen of Myanmar and therefore is deprived of the rights enjoyed by citizens: the right to leave the country and to return, the right to register his marriage and his children's births, the right to travel within Myanmar, the right to establish his own business and his children's rights to tertiary education.[79]

The same approach has been adopted in a similar factual context in French jurisprudence.[80]

This compilation of all harms into one analysis means that decision-makers rarely pause to consider deeply the meaning of not having a nationality. Nor, in cases where it is implied or held that it is not sufficient, is there any detailed reasoning to explain *why* it is not sufficient to constitute persecution in its own right. This is particularly problematic in the context of claims by children.[81]

The question of the gravity of harm occasioned by the fact of not having a nationality appears to be more straightforward in cases involving active withdrawal of nationality, considered in Part 2. We acknowledge that it may be more difficult as a matter of law to establish that the *denial* as opposed to *withdrawal* of nationality violates human rights norms in a particular case;[82] however, once there is a violation, the gravity of not having a nationality should arguably be considered as equally serious. Hence the discussion below may well be relevant and instructive in the future consideration of this issue in the context of denial of nationality as well as active withdrawal.

Part 2: Withdrawal of Nationality as Persecution

This Part concerns stateless persons who had a nationality that was subsequently withdrawn by a state authority including by operation of the law. It excludes situations where an individual voluntarily requested the loss of nationality.

Two key issues arise in the context of considering refugee claims centred on withdrawal of nationality. The first question is whether the withdrawal of nationality is

[78] See for instance, *071626084* (n 38).
[79] *Refugee Appeal No 76254* [2008] NZRSAA 82 (16 September 2008) [34] (hereafter *Refugee Appeal No 76254*).
[80] See Decision no°10015655 C (n 75), finding that the applicant had a well-founded fear in Myanmar 'on the basis of his ethnicity owing to the personalized persecution he was victim to, as well as the law in force since 1982 which denies Rohingya of their citizenship rights and the treatment of Rohingya by the Burmese authorities'. See also Decision no°640897/08021356 (n 75).
[81] See Jason Pobjoy, *The Child in International Refugee Law* (CUP 2017) 101–57 (hereafter Pobjoy, *The Child in International Refugee Law*).
[82] As the US Court of Appeals for the Seventh Circuit noted in *Giday v Gonzales*, 434 F 3d 543 (7th Cir, 2006) (hereafter *Giday*), there is a 'distinction between denying citizenship to a non-citizen resident and stripping a person of citizenship already attained': at 554, citing *Haile v Gonzales*, 421 F 3d 493, 496 (hereafter *Haile v Gonzales*).

a violation of international law, and in particular human rights law, so as to engage a consideration of whether it amounts to 'being persecuted' for the purposes of refugee law. Second, if it is a violation of international human rights law, the question is whether it is sufficiently serious to constitute persecution.

In terms of the first issue, an analysis of jurisprudence across a wide range of jurisdictions reveals that very little controversy has arisen, presumably because the factual background in these cases immediately suggests an illegitimate exercise of state power. It appears to be appropriately accepted by decision-makers that where withdrawal of nationality is due to a protected ground, such as race, gender, ethnicity, or political opinion, it cannot be justified as a matter of international law. This is also reflected in the limited scholarship that has considered this issue.[83]

In US jurisprudence, for example, appellate courts have readily intervened to rectify misguided deferral to state sovereignty in the context of withdrawal of citizenship. In *Haile v Gonzales*,[84] the Immigration Judge ('IJ') had rejected the asylum claim in part on the principle 'that a country has the sovereign right to bestow or deny citizenship as it sees fit',[85] citing previous authority in support.[86] However, on appeal, the US Court of Appeals for the Seventh Circuit identified the issue as 'whether Ethiopia has the sovereign right to discriminate against ethnic Eritreans by *stripping* them of their citizenship',[87] concluding that the IJ's reasoning was 'problematic' because it 'fails to acknowledge the fundamental distinction between denying someone citizenship and divesting someone of citizenship'.[88] Indeed, the Court considered that there was no authority for the view that 'a government has the sovereign right to strip citizenship from a class of persons based on their ethnicity'.[89] Rather, 'It is arguable that such a program of denationalization and deportation is in fact a particularly acute form of persecution.... Historically, denationalization has been a precursor to even worse things—it was one of the first steps taken by the Nazi regime against the Jews.'[90]

The Seventh Circuit cited with approval the work of a human rights group that had expressed concern about the 'increasing use of denationalization as a political weapon' particularly given that 'the victims of this form of persecution are unable to challenge it as it occurs under the guise of states' sovereign rights'.[91]

---

[83] See e.g., Deborah E Anker, *Law of Asylum in the United States* (Thomson Reuters 2017) 356–57 (hereafter Anker, *Law of Asylum in the United States 2017*).

[84] *Haile v Gonzales* (n 82).   [85] ibid, 494.

[86] On appeal, the US Court of Appeals for the Seventh Circuit noted that the Immigration Judge had relied on a Fifth Circuit decision in *Faddoul* (n 67) and also *De Souza v INS*, 999 F 2d 1156 (7th Cir, 1993): see *Haile v Gonzales* (n 82) 496, but emphasized that those cases involved denial not deprivation of citizenship.

[87] *Haile v Gonzales* (n 82) 494 (emphasis in original).   [88] ibid, 496 (emphasis omitted).

[89] ibid.

[90] ibid. See also *Giday* (n 82) 554, in which the Seventh Circuit discussed *Haile v Gonzales* with approval. For academic literature on the persecutory nature of the Ethiopian Government's actions, see John Campbell, 'The Enduring Problem of Statelessness in the Horn of Africa: How Nation-States and Western Courts (Re)Define Nationality' (2011) 23 IJRL 656.

[91] *Haile v Gonzales* (n 82) 496, citing Open Society Justice Initiative, 'Statelessness, Discrimination and Denationalization: Emerging Problems Requiring Action' (29 April 2005). We note that in this case the Court remanded the case to be assessed according to the Court's reasoning; hence a final decision on the merits was not issued by the Seventh Circuit.

Similarly, the Court of Appeals for the Second Circuit intervened when the Board of Immigration Appeals ('BIA') failed to assess the argument that the loss of citizenship in that case was not simply an administrative oversight but rather a case of the 'Kazak government's use of the registration requirement as a pretext to denationalize non-ethnic Kazakhs'.[92]

The reason for this more straightforward acceptance in the cases of withdrawal as opposed to denial may simply be a matter of clearer evidence on point, since a withdrawal is, of course, more difficult to justify than a failure to provide nationality from the outset. As such, there is very little discussion about the international law framework in these cases; rather, the discussion moves quickly to whether the harm amounts to being persecuted for the purposes of refugee law.

Notwithstanding the straightforward nature of the cases to date on this question, it is conceivable that refugee decision-makers may be presented with more challenging scenarios from the perspective of international law in the future. In particular the recent uptake in denationalization as a method of responding to the 'war on terror' and 'foreign fighters',[93] could potentially give rise to refugee claims on the part of those who have been denationalized, particularly when we consider that deportation or banishment is a key motivation for these recent policies.[94] However, any such claim would require careful analysis. As Matthew Gibney explains, states 'have always possessed some grounds through which to take away citizenship, including fraud, disloyalty, acquisition of another citizenship, marriage to a foreigner, and threat to public order'.[95] Indeed, as we explained in Chapter 3, there are limited circumstances where deprivation of nationality is lawful at international law.[96] The *1961 Convention* outlines various circumstances in which a state may withdraw nationality, although most are 'conditional upon their possession or acquisition

---

[92] *Jourbina v Holder*, 532 Fed Appx 1 (2nd Cir, 2013) 2 (hereafter *Jourbina*). The case was on this basis (and others) remanded for reconsideration.

[93] There is now a considerable body of scholarship examining recent legislative changes: see e.g., Matthew Gibney, ' "A Very Transcendental Power": Denaturalisation and the Liberalisation of Citizenship in the United Kingdom' (2013) 61 Political Studies 637; Matthew Gibney, 'Should Citizenship Be Conditional? The Ethics of Denationalization' (2013) 75 Journal of Politics 646; Audrey Macklin, 'Citizenship Revocation, the Privilege to Have Rights and the Production of the Alien' (2014) 40 Queens LJ 1; Sandra Mantu, ' "Terrorist" Citizens and the Human Right to Nationality' (2018) 26 Journal of Contemporary European Studies 28; Sangeetha Pillai and George Williams, 'Twenty-First Century Banishment: Citizenship Stripping in Common Law Nations' (2017) 66 ICLQ 521; Rayner Thwaites 'The Security of Citizenship?: Finnis in the Context of the United Kingdom's Citizenship Stripping Provisions' in Fiona Jenkins, Mark Nolan, and Kim Rubenstein (eds), *Allegiance and Identity in a Globalised World* (CUP 2014) 243.

[94] Audrey Macklin, 'Introduction' in Audrey Macklin and Rainer Bauböck eds, *The Return of Banishment: Do the New Denationalisation Policies Weaken Citizenship* (EUI Working Papers 2015) 1. This also raises additional international law concerns, see Guy Goodwin-Gill, 'Deprivation of Citizenship Resulting in Statelessness and its Implications in International Law' (Opinion Piece, 12 March 2014); Guy Goodwin-Gill, 'Deprivation of Citizenship Resulting in Statelessness and its Implications in International Law: Further Comments' (6 April 2014) <https://www.law.oxoac.u/research-and-subject-groups/human-rights-law/publications?page=10> accessed 9 December 2018.

[95] Matthew J Gibney, 'Denationalization' in Ayelet Shachar, Rainer Bauböck, Irene Bloemraad, and Maarten Vink (eds), *The Oxford Handbook of Citizenship* (OUP 2017) 359. See further his discussion of denationalization's history at 364–67 (hereafter Gibney, 'Denationalization').

[96] See Chapter 3, Part 2.3.1.4.

of another nationality'.[97] As stated in Article 8(1) of the *1961 Convention*, '[a] Contracting State shall not deprive a person of his nationality if such deprivation would render him stateless'. Thus, where an individual has been denationalized under a security or public order measure, he or she is likely to retain an alternative nationality given that most relevant domestic legislation applies to dual nationals.[98] Refugee status would thus be denied unless the applicant could also establish a fear of being persecuted in the alternative country of nationality.

Where, however, denationalization results in statelessness, a careful assessment would need to be undertaken of the legitimacy of this measure given that it is only in exceptional circumstances that a State may legitimately denationalize so as to render an individual stateless.[99] Where the instance of denationalization could not be justified at international law, a finding of persecution may be appropriate. Further, such persecution may well be linked to a person's political opinion, race, or particular social group.[100]

In relation to the second key question, namely gravity of harm, while there is some mixed jurisprudence, the balance clearly favours the view that withdrawal of nationality may well constitute persecution in and of itself. However, as in the case of denial of nationality, many decision-makers do not assess the gravity of the denial of nationality separately from other forms of harm.[101] There are some cases in which withdrawal of nationality was found *not* to amount to persecution in and of itself. For example, in the case of a stateless Bidoon from Kuwait, the Federal Magistrates Court of Australia concluded that 'loss of nationality per se is not sufficient to satisfy the requirements arising from the Refugees Convention for protection' (as held in *Diatlov*), because 'persecutory behavior on the part of the Kuwaiti authorities' is also required.[102] Similarly, in a case involving a Faili Kurd born in Iran it was held by the Australian Federal Court that, 'discrimination does not, without more, amount to persecution. Specifically in the context of refusal of nationality, it is not that refusal which could be said to be persecutory but rather the conduct which might flow from it.[103]

---

[97] *Convention on the Reduction of Statelessness* (adopted 30 August 1961, entered into force 13 December 1975) 989 UNTS 175, arts 5, 6, 7(hereafter *1961 Convention*).

[98] However, we note that the decision of the UK Supreme Court in *Pham v Secretary of State for the Home Department* [2015] UKSC 19 reveals how illusory this protection may be if two countries effectively engage in a 'race to denationalize'. Lucia Zedner explains that although in the UK 'resort to citizenship deprivation and deportation by the UK government has increased very rapidly', the government is careful to point out that 'all were considered to have another alternative nationality': 'Citizenship Deprivation, Security and Human Rights' (2016) 18 EJML 222, 231.

[99] Foster and Lambert, 'Statelessness as a Human Rights Issue' (n 12) 582–83.

[100] See e.g., the argument put by Tufyal Choudhury in 'The Radicalisation of Citizenship Deprivation' (2017) 37 Critical Social Policy 225.

[101] See e.g., *VO3/16458* [2004] RRTA 592 (2 September 2004) 5 (hereafter *VO3/16458*).

[102] *DZABG v Minister for Immigration* [2012] FMCA 36 (25 January 2012) [133], [135] (hereafter *DZABG*). See also *MZXAN v Minister for Immigration* [2006] FMCA 847 (30 June 2006) (hereafter *MZXAN*), where the applicant was stateless and a former resident of Zambia and the Court referred to *Savvin v Minister for Immigration & Multicultural Affairs* (1999) 166 ALR 348. See also, in the United States, *Maksimova v Holder*, 361 Fed Appx 690 (6th Cir, 2010) [6]–[7] (hereafter *Maksimova*).

[103] *SZTFX* (n 24) [40].

In the UK, the Court of Appeal held persecution to be a matter of fact, not law.[104] Consequently, it is not possible 'to state as a universal proposition that deprivation of nationality must be equated with persecution'.[105] In the words of Stanley Burnton LJ:

the deprivation of a person's nationality can amount to persecution. It will do so if the consequences are sufficiently serious. And clearly, deprivation may be one aspect of ill treatment by the state that in its totality amounts to sufficiently serious ill treatment as to constitute persecution ... the question whether deprivation of nationality constitutes persecution, assuming the deprivation is for reasons referred to in Article 1A(2), will depend on the consequences of the deprivation for the person in question in the state in question.[106]

However, in the preponderance of cases, withdrawal of nationality leading to statelessness, on a ground protected by the *Refugee Convention*, is accepted to amount to persecution, in principle, without needing to show more in terms of additional harm. A number of these cases concern Ethiopians who have or are perceived to have Eritrean origins (through their mother or father) and who according to the Ethiopia–Eritrea Claims Commission, based on the 2003 Proclamation of Ethiopian Nationality, are no longer considered by Ethiopia to be Ethiopian nationals after they were forced to flee during the war.

In *EB (Ethiopia) v Secretary of State for the Home Department*, the UK Court of Appeal recognized that persons without nationality are entitled to refugee status if they can show that they have been stripped of their nationality on discriminatory grounds (i.e. linked to a *Refugee Convention* reason).[107] For the UK Court of Appeal, the reasons behind the decision of the state authorities to deprive a national of their nationality is crucial to a finding of persecution. Both Longmore LJ and Jacob LJ accepted that EB had been deprived of her citizenship by reason of her father's Eritrean origins (i.e. race) and was therefore unable to exercise her citizen's individual rights (i.e. to leave freely and to re-enter freely one's country, and the right to vote). She was entitled to refugee status; as a matter of law no further ill-treatment was required.[108]

The Gauteng High Court of Pretoria (Republic of South Africa) similarly acknowledged that the applicant, 'as a "dual national", i.e. an Ethiopian who is perceived to have Eritrean origins (through her mother), who left Ethiopia for another country, is no longer determined by Ethiopia to be an Ethiopian national. This constitutes an arbitrary deprivation of her nationality, and renders her stateless.'[109]

---

[104] *MA (Ethiopia) v Secretary of State for the Home Department* [2009] EWCA Civ 289, [2010] INLR 1 [59] (hereafter *MA (Ethiopia)*).

[105] ibid, [59].   [106] ibid, [66].

[107] *EB (Ethiopia) v Secretary of State for the Home Department* [2007] EWCA Civ 809, [2008] 3 WLR 1188 (hereafter *EB*).

[108] ibid—holding *MA (Ethiopia)* (n 104) to have been decided wrongly. See Shauna Gillan, 'Refugee Convention: Whether Deprivation of Citizenship Amounts to Persecution' (2007) 21 JIANL 347. For an application of *EB* by the UK Upper Tribunal, see *ST v Secretary of State for the Home Department CG* [2011] UKUT 00252 (IAC) (hereafter *ST*): 'removal of the ID card was itself ill-treatment that was capable of amounting to persecution. As a matter of law, no further ill-treatment needed to be found': at [76].

[109] *M v Minister of Home Affairs* (6871/2013) [2014] ZAGPPHC 649 (22 August 2014) [154]. The Court was here quoting from the applicant's arguments; however, the court agreed with the applicant's submissions later in the judgment: see at [159].

In the court's view, the applicant would fear persecution by reason of her race and/or tribe and/or membership of a particular social group if she were to be returned to either Ethiopia or Eritrea; she therefore qualifies for refugee status.[110]

In the United States, courts have long acknowledged nationality as a 'man's basic right, for it is nothing less than the right to have rights'.[111] In *Haile v Holder*, a case involving an Ethiopian citizen of Eritrean ethnicity threatened with 'denationalization' and expulsion to Eritrea who fled to the United States and claimed asylum, the US Court of Appeals for the Seventh Circuit rejected the 'denationalization plus' position of the Board, considering instead that the stripping of one's nationality because of a *Refugee Convention* ground, *even without more*, constituted persecution.[112] The Court considered that, just like the Nazi treatment of Jews, 'his denationalization was persecution and created a presumption that he has a well-founded fear of being persecuted'.[113]

In a number of US cases, withdrawal of nationality was discussed but not decided, as the cases were referred back to the lower court, whose responsibility it is to determine the meaning of the term of 'persecution'. Thus, the US Court of Appeals have remanded to the Board of Immigration Appeals a number of cases where the BIA had failed to consider whether the revocation of citizenship that led to the petitioner being stateless had been ethnically motivated and therefore constituted persecution (past and/or future).[114] In *Stserba v Holder*, for instance, the Court held that '[a]lthough not every revocation of citizenship is persecution, ethnically targeted denationalization of people who do not have dual citizenship may be persecution'.[115] It further held: 'In recognition of each state's sovereign right, denying citizenship to a noncitizen applicant is not necessarily persecution. There is, however, a "fundamental distinction between *denying* someone citizenship and *divesting* someone of citizenship".'[116]

The Court considered denationalization resulting in statelessness to be an 'extreme sanction' and further held: 'a person who is made stateless due to his or

---

[110] ibid, [159].

[111] *Perez v Brownell* (n 13) (Earl Warren dissenting). See also *Trop v Dulles*, 356 US 86 (1958) (hereafter *Trop*), where the US Supreme Court described deprivation of nationality as 'the total destruction of the individual's status in organized society' and found it to be a cruel and unusual punishment: at [101]–[102]. See also Maryellen Fullerton, 'The Intersection of Statelessness and Refugee Protection in US Asylum Policy' (2014) 2 JMHS 144.

[112] *Haile v Holder*, 591 F 3d 572 (7th Cir, 2010) (hereafter *Haile v Holder*). In *Stserba v Holder*, 646 F 3d 964 (6th Cir, 2011) (hereafter *Stserba*), the US Court of Appeals Sixth Circuit held that stripping a person of nationality on a protected ground, rendering them stateless, *could* amount to persecution.

[113] *Haile v Holder* (n 112) 756. The petition for review was granted and the case was returned to the Board for determination consistent with the opinion of the Court of Appeal. In a number of cases, courts of appeal have not found it necessary finally to resolve the issue, but have accepted in principle that denationalization can amount to persecution. See e.g., *Mengstu v Holder*, 560 F 3d 1055 (9th Cir, 2009) 1058; *Gebkirstos v Gonzales*, 177 Fed Appx 584 (9th Cir, 2006) 585 (hereafter *Gebkirstos*).

[114] *Jourbina* (n 92); *Stserba* (n 112); *Gebkirstos* (n 113); *Giday* (n 82); *Haile v Gonzales* (n 82).

[115] *Stserba* (n 112) 973.

[116] ibid (emphasis in original). Denaturalization proceedings impose a 'rigorous burden of proof' on the government..

her membership in a protected group may have demonstrated persecution, even
without proving that he or she has suffered collateral damage from the act of
denationalization'.[117]

In both *Gebkirstos v Gonzales* and *Giday v Gonzales*, the Courts stated that 'a
program of denationalization and deportation would indeed seem to constitute persecution' and remanded to the BIA for reconsideration.[118]

Other cases where withdrawal of nationality leading to statelessness, on a
ground protected by the *Refugee Convention*, was found to amount to persecution,
without needing to show more in terms of additional harm, can be found in France,
Germany, and New Zealand. For instance, the French Cour Nationale du Droit
d'Asile ('CNDA') considered that a person's statelessness constitutes persecution,
where statelessness is the concrete legal consequence of a decision taken by the national authorities to deprive an applicant of his nationality and the act was undertaken on the basis of one of the grounds protected in the *Refugee Convention*.[119] The
German courts too have held deprivation of nationality to constitute a severe violation of human rights amounting to persecution, if based on a *Convention* ground.[120]
The Federal Administrative Court recalled its previous case law that withdrawal of
citizenship may constitute persecution relevant to asylum because persecution is
more than just interference with life, limb, and liberty.[121] However, such an act is
not persecution if it merely represents an administrative sanction for a breach of
duty that applies to all citizens alike.[122] Finally, in New Zealand, the RSAA has long
acknowledged that statelessness can arise from nationality being withdrawn for discriminatory reasons,[123] such as for reason of (lack of) nationality and membership
of the social group of Bidoons.[124]

In *Refugee Appeal No 76077*, the NZ RSAA explained: 'while it is one thing for a
state to withhold nationality, it is quite a different matter when a state, having conferred nationality upon a person, then withdraws it by what in the case of the wife
might be characterised, ... as a "wilful act of neglect, discrimination or violation"'.[125]

The NZ RSAA then held nationality to be 'a matter of "profound significance"'[126]
and with important and specific consequences, which it explained is the reason why

---

[117] *Stserba* (n 112) 974 (emphasis omitted).   [118] *Gebkirstos* (n 113) 2; *Giday* (n 82) 554.
[119] CNDA, decision no°09002572 C+, 23 December 2010—the case failed because the applicant
did not demonstrate that he was not entitled to claim Mauritanian citizenship pursuant to the law or by
virtue of the fact that his mother is a recognized Mauritanian citizen. In two other cases, the deprivation
of Rohingyas' nationality in Myanmar was taken into account as one factor amounting to persecution,
alongside the denial of civil, political, economic, social, and cultural rights in the form of restrictions,
prohibitions, and discrimination: CNDA, decision no°12013646 C, 26 June 2013 (hereafter Decision
no°12013646 C); CNDA, decision no° 09019611, 14 February 2011.
[120] Bundesverwaltungsgerichts [German Federal Administrative Court], 10 C 50.07, 26 February
2009 (hereafter 10 C 50.07)—this judgment confirms the approach of the High Administrative Court
of Mecklenburg-Vorpommern.
[121] ibid, [17]–[18].   [122] ibid, [24].
[123] *Refugee Appeal No 76077* [2009] NZRSAA 37 (19 May 2009) [112] (hereafter *Refugee Appeal No
76077*)—referring to *Refugee Appeal No 72635* (n 5) [80].
[124] *Refugee Appeal No 74467* (n 38) [94]; *Refugee Appeal No 76506* [2010] NZRSAA 90 (29 July
2010) (hereafter *Refugee Appeal No 76506*).
[125] *Refugee Appeal No 76077* (n 123) [103]—referring to *Refugee Appeal No 72635* (n 5) [81].
[126] *Refugee Appeal No 76077* (n 123) [105].

the state of Israel took the trouble to remove her nationality arbitrarily.[127] It concluded that 'the arbitrary revocation of the wife's citizenship was for reason of her Christianity and specifically because she is a Messianic Jew', and that 'the serious harm to which she would continue to be exposed if she were to be returned to Israel is . . . for a convention ground, namely religion'.[128]

The reference to citizenship, or its withdrawal, being of 'profound significance' is worth reflecting on, as few cases have examined in depth why (or why not) deprivation of citizenship is in and of itself sufficiently significant to meet the persecution threshold. In one of the few exceptions to this phenomenon, in *Stserba v Holder*, referred to earlier in this section, the US Court of Appeals for the Sixth Circuit reflected on why revoking citizenship on account of ethnicity 'may be persecution',[129] observing that '[r]egardless of the practical ramifications that befall a denationalized person, the inherent qualities of denationalisation are troubling'.[130] Drawing on US constitutional jurisprudence that has considered revocation of citizenship as cruel and unusual punishment in contravention of the Eighth Amendment, the Court cited the US Supreme Court's view that the essence of denationalization is 'the total destruction of the individual's status in organized society'; it is 'a form of punishment more primitive than torture'.[131]

The German Federal Administrative Court has emphasized the fact that deprivation of citizenship 'deprives the individual in question of his or her fundamental status as a citizen';[132] it 'excludes him or her from the state's system of protection and peace'.[133]

In a case concerning racial discrimination with respect to the conferral of nationality in the Dominican Republic, the Inter-American Court of Human Rights observed that it 'considers that the failure to recognize juridical personality harms human dignity, because it denies absolutely an individual's condition of being a subject of rights and renders him vulnerable to non-observance of his rights by the State or other individuals'.[134]

Such judicial reflection is consistent with the empirical research that has been undertaken and highlighted in recent years, as the international community has focused more intently on understanding the urgency of the need to address the plight of stateless persons. Gibney explains that by 'taking away an individual's citizenship, the state inflicts a kind of civic death upon one of its members'.[135] Indeed, the evidence of those who are stateless suggests 'daily indignities and suffering',[136] and 'the devastating psychological toll of statelessness',[137] and suggests a strong desire to belong that has independent meaning and force from the consequential harm

---

[127] ibid, [106].   [128] ibid, [112].   [129] *Stserba* (n 112).   [130] ibid, 974.
[131] ibid, citing *Trop* (n 111) 101–02.   [132] 10 C 50.07 (n 120) [19].
[133] ibid, [19].
[134] *Case of the Yean and Bosico Children v Dominican Republic* (Preliminary Objections, Merits, Reparations and Costs) Inter-American Court of Human Rights Series C No 130 (8 September 2005).
[135] Gibney, 'Denationalization' (n 95) 359.
[136] UNHCR, 'This Is Our Home' (n 39) 1.
[137] UNHCR, 'I Am Here, I Belong: The Urgent Need to End Childhood Statelessness' (November 2015) 1 (hereafter UNHCR, 'I Am Here, I Belong').

caused by not having a nationality. Conversely, research carried out in relation to formerly stateless persons who have ultimately acquired citizenship has elicited evidence that interviewees were now 'treated as a human being', felt like 'I exist', and that their group could 'recover their pride and self-respect'.[138] This insight is not new: Hannah Arendt wrote not only of the 'right to have rights'[139] but also argued that 'the loss of a polity itself expels him [man] from humanity'.[140] Hence to cursorily dismiss the 'enormity' and 'horrible punishment'[141] that denationalization represents does not adequately account for and properly evaluate the weight of this human rights violation.

This is even more so when we consider that it is well-accepted refugee law doctrine that harm need not be physical; indeed, psychological harm may constitute persecution.[142] Recognition of the ongoing serious harm caused by denationalization itself also obviates any concern that denationalization is relevant only to past persecution. As the German Federal Administrative Court has acknowledged, deprivation of citizenship 'causes ongoing, significant harm to the individual concerned'.[143] In a similar vein, the NZ RSAA observed that, '[t]he serious harm ... is not confined to the moment when her citizenship was lost. The impact of that action endures.'[144]

We now turn to an examination of the refusal of the right to re-enter one's country of former habitual residence as a separate element of persecution. Indeed, as observed by Stanley-Burton LJ, '[d]eprivation of nationality may lead to inability to return to one's country of nationality, but they are not identical'.[145]

Part 3: Refusal to Re-Enter as Persecution

The question whether denial of re-entry can amount to persecution in the case of a stateless applicant for refugee status has been the subject of considerable discussion and jurisprudential analysis in recent years, yet there remains confusion in understanding the relevant human rights framework that underpins such cases. Moreover, scholarly analysis is very limited,[146] albeit that recent work has acknowledged that 'arbitrary exclusion of habitually resident stateless persons appears an area to which international refugee law may have greater relevance than has been acknowledged hitherto'.[147] In this Part we examine the extent of such relevance.

---

[138] Brad K Blitz and Maureen Lynch (eds), *Statelessness and Citizenship: A Comparative Study on the Benefits of Nationality* (Edward Elgar 2011) 200.

[139] Hannah Arendt, *The Origins of Totalitarianism* (Harcourt 1951) 177.   [140] ibid, 297.

[141] See Brett Stark and Jodi Ziesemer, 'The Right to Have Rights: Loss of Citizenship, Asylum, and Constitutional Principles' (2016) 30 GeoImmigLJ 429, 446, citing the US Supreme Court in *Kennedy v Mendoza-Martinez*, 372 US 144 (1963) 573.

[142] On this point, see reference to mental or psychological harm in UNHCR, 'Representing Stateless Persons before U.S. Immigration Authorities' (August 2017) 15 (hereafter UNHCR, 'Guidelines on Representing Stateless Persons').

[143] 10 C 50.07 (n 120) [22].   [144] *Refugee Appeal No 76077* (n 123) [111].

[145] *MA (Ethiopia)* (n 104) [73].

[146] Deborah Anker is an exception in that she refers briefly to the issue, in *Law of Asylum in the United States 2017* (n 83) 356.

[147] Fripp, *Nationality and Statelessness* (n 14) 321.

In Chapter 4 we explained that an inability to return does not, in the case of a stateless person, exclude the possibility of protection under the *Refugee Convention*. On the other hand, mere inability to return is not, in itself, intended to operate as the entirety of the criterion for refugee status in the case of stateless persons. In this Part, we explore a distinct issue, namely whether denial of entry to a stateless person (by the country of former habitual residence) may amount to persecution in a particular case.

Senior courts and tribunals in Australia, New Zealand, the US, the UK, Canada, Ireland, Germany, Austria, France, and Belgium have all decided cases on whether denial of the right to return (re-enter) constitutes persecution. Our analysis of this wide range of cases suggests that in many respects the above issues have been conflated. In particular, a finding that the presence of the semi-colon in Article 1A(2) does not mean that an inability to return *automatically* translates into qualification for refugee status[148] has often been extrapolated into a conclusion that inability to return *cannot* amount to persecution.[149] Yet as the Federal Court of Canada has recognized, 'denial of a right to return may in itself constitute an act of persecution'.[150]

It is important to note at the outset that we are here not concerned with cases in which the applicant *could have applied* for the necessary travel document/s to allow him or her re-entry into the country of his or her habitual residence but failed to do so for no good reason (namely a reason not relevant to the *Refugee Convention*).[151] In other words, we are not here concerned with a practical obstacle that can be removed. Rather, our focus is where the state of origin/former habitual residence has or will refuse entry.

At its heart, the confusion surrounding these issues in the refugee law context is grounded in the assumption that while citizens have a right to enter and return to their country of nationality, non-citizens have no such right.

This is highlighted in UK jurisprudence where, for example in *Lazarevic v Secretary of State for the Home Department*, it was acknowledged that if a state 'arbitrarily excludes one of its citizens, thereby cutting him off from enjoyment of all

---

[148] See Chapter 4, Part 1.1 'The "semicolon" '.

[149] See e.g., *MZXAN* (n 102) [25]–[32]; *DZABG* (n 102) [136]–[137].

[150] *Maarouf v Canada (Minister of Employment and Immigration)* [1994] 1 FC 723 (13 December 1993) (hereafter *Maarouf*). See also *Kadoura v Canada (Minister of Citizenship and Immigration)* [2003] FCJ No 1328 (10 September 2003) [14] (hereafter *Kadoura*).

[151] Thus, *MA (Ethiopia)* (n 104) establishes that a person seeking to rely upon the denial of a right of return must take 'all reasonably practicable steps to seek to obtain the requisite documents' to facilitate his or her return: at [50]. See e.g., *Kelzani v Secretary of State for the Home Department* [1978] Imm AR 193 and *YL v Secretary of State for the Home Department* [2003] UKIAT 00016 (hereafter *YL*). In *Chief Executive of the Department of Labour v Yadegary* [2008] NZCA 295 (13 August 2008), the applicant, a national from Iran, had intentionally destroyed his Iranian passport and declined to apply for a replacement on the ground of fear of persecution. His application for refugee status was refused. Since no agreement existed between New Zealand and Iran whereby he could be removed without his consent, he couldn't be returned to Iran, at least not until a diplomatic solution had been reached. The Court considered that in these circumstances a lengthy detention was unlawful. See also in France CNDA, decision n°08017005, 23 December 2009. See in Canada *Salah v Canada (Minister of Citizenship and Immigration)* [2005] FC 944 (6 July 2005) [7]–[8].

these benefits and rights enjoyed by citizens and duties owed by a State to its citizens, there is in my view no difficulty in accepting that such conduct can amount to persecution'.[152]

However, seldom are the courts ready to accept 'a true analogy between a state's denial of entry to one of its own citizens and denial of entry to a stateless person (who, unlike a citizen, has no right of entry into the country)'.[153] This is said to be on the basis that, in the words of the UK Court of Appeal,

[t]he denial does not interfere with a stateless person's right in the way that it does with the rights of a national. There is a fundamental distinction between nationals and stateless persons in that respect. It is one thing to protect a stateless person from persecutory return to the country of his former habitual residence (as the Refugee Convention does), but it would be quite another thing to characterise a denial of re-entry as persecutory. The lot of a stateless person is an unhappy one, but to deny him a right that he has never enjoyed is not, in itself, persecution. Stateless persons are themselves the subject of an international treaty, namely the Convention relating to the Status of Stateless Persons (1954).[154]

The problem is that this view is simply not accurate as a matter of international law. It is widely understood that *citizens* (including naturalized citizens) have the right to enter and return to their country of nationality.[155] Accordingly courts have recognized that either a direct or indirect refusal, for example in the form of the discriminatory removal of identification documents, can constitute persecution within the meaning of the 1951 *Refugee Convention* if 'done as it was with the motive of making it difficult for EB in future to prove her Ethiopian nationality' and if done by the authorities.[156] This is because the ability 'freely to leave and freely to re-enter one's country' is considered a basic right.[157]

---

[152] *Lazarevic v Secretary of State for the Home Department* [1997] EWCA Civ 1007 (Hutchison LJ).

[153] As observed by Richards LJ, *obiter dicta*, in *AK v Secretary of State for the Home Department* [2006] EWCA Civ 1117 [47] (hereafter *AK*).

[154] *MA (Palestinian Territories) v Secretary of State for the Home Department* [2008] EWCA Civ 304 [26] (Maurice Kay LJ) (hereafter *MA (Palestinian Territories)*). This had also been the conclusion in the decision below: *MA v Secretary of State for the Home Department* [2007] UKAIT 00017 [122] (hereafter *MA*). We note that in *MT (Palestinian Territories) v Secretary of State for the Home Department* [2008] EWCA Civ 1149, the UK Court of Appeal could 'see the force' of the appellant's argument that his denial of re-entry to the West Bank was because he was a stateless Palestinian Arab, which constituted persecution; however, the Court felt bound by the decision in *MA*: see at [46]–[47], and at [58], where the Court recognized that '[r]efusal of re-entry to a stateless person to the country of his former habitual residence is a subject that raises difficult issues of law'. See also *SH (Palestinian Territories) v Secretary of State for the Home Department* [2008] EWCA Civ 1150 [31]. See further *HS v Secretary of State for the Home Department* [2011] UKUT 124 (IAC) [185] (hereafter *HS*), finding that the Tribunal was bound by the previous UK authority in relation to this point.

[155] *Abdelrazik v Canada (Minister of Foreign Affairs & International Trade)* 2009 FC 580 (4 June 2009). In *Abdelrazik*, Zinn J held that the Canadian Government breached the applicant's right to enter Canada (protected under s 6(1) of the *Canadian Charter of Rights and Freedoms*) as a recognized refugee and naturalized Canadian citizen, and urged Canada to issue him with an emergency passport in order that he may return to and enter Canada, and to arrange transportation for him from Khartoum to Montreal within 30 days.

[156] *EB* (n 107) [63].

[157] ibid, [67]. See also, *ST* (n 108), applying *EB*. In *MA (Ethiopia)* (n 104), Stanley Burnton LJ agreed that 'if the appellant were able to establish that she has been arbitrarily refused the right to return to Ethiopia for a Convention reason, that would in my view amount to persecution' because 'the right

Yet it is not the case that no parallel right exists in relation to non-citizens. Rather, Article 12(4) of the *ICCPR* is the key to a principled resolution of these issues because it explicitly extends the right to enter (and remain) to one's *own country*, which is not restricted to one's country of citizenship: 'No one shall be arbitrarily deprived of the right to enter his own country.' This guarantee—in the very widely ratified *ICCPR*—is perhaps the single most important provision touching on the refugee status of stateless persons and yet is rarely engaged or analysed in the refugee case law.[158]

In its General Comment No 27, the UN Human Rights Committee held exile from one's own country to be prohibited by Article 12(4):

The right of a person to enter his or her own country recognizes the special relationship of a person to that country. The right has various facets. It implies the right to remain in one's own country. It includes not only the right to return after having left one's own country; it may also entitle a person to come to the country for the first time if he or she was born outside the country (for example, if that country is the person's State of nationality). The right to return is of the utmost importance for refugees seeking voluntary repatriation. It also implies prohibition of enforced population transfers or mass expulsions to other countries.[159]

Most importantly, 'his own country' in the context of Article 12(4) *ICCPR* allows for a relevant link *not* dependent upon the possession of nationality or citizenship:

The scope of 'his own country' is broader than the concept 'country of his nationality'. It is not limited to nationality in a formal sense, that is, nationality acquired at birth or by conferral; it embraces, at the very least, an individual who, because of his or her special ties to or claims in relation to a given country, cannot be considered to be a mere alien. This would be the case, for example, of nationals of a country who have there been stripped of their nationality in violation of international law, and of individuals whose country of nationality has been incorporated in or transferred to another national entity, whose nationality is being denied them. The language of article 12, paragraph 4, moreover, permits a broader interpretation that might embrace other categories of long-term residents, including but not limited to stateless persons arbitrarily deprived of the right to acquire the nationality of the country of such residence. Since other factors may in certain circumstances result in the establishment of close and enduring connections between a person and a country, States parties should include in their reports information on the rights of permanent residents to return to their country of residence.[160]

---

to live in the home country and all that goes with that', is one of the most fundamental rights attached to nationality: at [60]. However, the case failed on the facts due to weak evidence.

[158] In *MA (Palestinian Territories)* (n 154) the Court of Appeal referred to art 12(4) but observed that '[a]s we have only had limited written submissions on this point, I am reluctant to say more about it in this judgment': at [28]. For a relatively rare example of reliance in refugee law on art 12, see *Refugee Appeal No 76254* (n 79) [35]–[38]. In Australia, the Tribunal recognized the significance of art 12(4) in the context of a Palestinian man from the Gaza Strip who would be denied re-entry by Israel on return to his country of former habitual residence, observing that 'If the Applicant was denied entry then this could constitute persecution': *V00/11398* [2001] RRTA 419 (2 May 2001) (hereafter *V00/11398*).

[159] UN Human Rights Committee, 'CCPR General Comment No 27: Article 12 (Freedom of Movement)' (2 November 1999) UN Doc CCPR/C/21/Rev.1/Add.9 , para 19.

[160] ibid, para 20.

Finally, the UN Human Rights Committee defined the concept of arbitrariness as follows:

In no case may a person be arbitrarily deprived of the right to enter his or her own country. The reference to the concept of arbitrariness in this context is intended to emphasize that it applies to all State action, legislative, administrative and judicial; it guarantees that even interference provided for by law should be in accordance with the provisions, aims and objectives of the Covenant and should be, in any event, reasonable in the particular circumstances. The Committee considers that there are few, if any, circumstances in which deprivation of the right to enter one's own country could be reasonable. A State party must not, by stripping a person of nationality or by expelling an individual to a third country, arbitrarily prevent this person from returning to his or her own country.[161]

Thus, the right to return (and remain) of certain non-nationals to their own country or permanent home is guaranteed under Article 12(4).[162] However, when:

the country of immigration facilitates acquiring its nationality, and the immigrant refrains from doing so, either by choice or by committing acts that will disqualify him from acquiring that nationality, the country of immigration does not become 'his own country' within the meaning of article 12, paragraph 4, of the Covenant.[163]

However although there are circumstances in which a state will not qualify as a person's 'own country' for the purposes of Article 12(4), once it does so there are no defences or exceptions that would justify the violation of Article 12(4).[164] This is because Article 12(3), which permits restrictions, applies only to Article 12(1) and (2), but not to Article 12(4).[165]

Hence the key questions in refugee law are whether (1) the attachment of the applicant to the country of former habitual residence is sufficient to have attained the status of 'own country'; and (2) whether the denial of the right to return is arbitrary.

Since the UN Human Rights Committee issued the General Comment referred to above in 1999, it has continued to elucidate the scope and meaning of Article 12(4) through jurisprudence and concluding observations in relation to individual states parties. Such guidance may be of particular pertinence to refugee decision-makers in understanding and identifying the factors relevant to an assessment of

---

[161] ibid, para 21.

[162] See also UN Human Rights Committee, 'Communication No. 538/1993: *Stewart v Canada*' (16 December 996) UN Doc CCPR/C/58/D/538/1993, paras 12.3, 12.4, 12.5.

[163] ibid, paras 12.5, 12.8. For an application of this view, see UN Human Rights Committee, 'Communication No 675/1995: *Taola v New Zealand*' (2 November 2000) UN Doc CCPR/C/70/D/675/1995, para 11.5.

[164] Of course, art 12 may be subject to a derogation in an emergency that threatens the life of the nation but in any event cannot discriminate—see art 4. This was emphasized in *V00/11398* (n 158), which highlighted the prohibition on derogation on discriminatory grounds.

[165] 'The above-mentioned rights shall not be subject to any restrictions except those which are provided by law, are necessary to protect national security, public order (ordre public), public health or morals or the rights and freedoms of others, and are consistent with the other rights recognized in the present Covenant': *International Covenant on Civil and Political Rights* (adopted 16 December 1966, entered into force 23 March 1976) 999 UNTS 171 (ICCPR) art 12(3). In the refugee context this was acknowledged in *Refugee Appeal No 76254* (n 79) [37].

'own country', as well as providing insight into the Committee's views in relation to particular populations.

One particularly noteworthy decision is *Nystrom v Australia*, in which the Human Rights Committee took the view that the deportation of a Swedish national by Australia to Sweden was arbitrary, based on the strong and special ties he had with that country: he had a family in Australia, he spoke English, and he had stayed in the country virtually all his life. In contrast, the only tie he had with Sweden was that of nationality. Thus, his 'own country' was Australia and not that of his nationality.[166]

The Committee explained that 'there are factors other than nationality which may establish close and enduring connections between a person and a country, connections which may be stronger than those of nationality'.[167] The Committee indicated that relevant factors include 'long standing residence, close personal and family ties and intentions to remain, as well as ...the absence of such ties elsewhere'.[168] This broader approach to interpreting Article 12(4) has been reiterated in subsequent decisions.[169]

While Stefan Lars Nystrom was not stateless, such a predicament would presumably have only served to strengthen his claim that Australia constituted his 'own country', given that the strong links to Australia would not in that case need to be balanced against the strength of connection to another country of nationality. Indeed, in the subsequent decision in *Warsame v Canada*, the fact that the applicant had no proof of any Somali citizenship such that he had a 'lack of any other ties than at best formal nationality with Somalia' was a persuasive factor in finding that Canada was his 'own country'.[170]

The relevant factors identified above—'close and enduring connections', 'long standing residence', and 'close personal and family ties'—are not trivial to satisfy. Yet given the fact that many of the world's stateless persons have lived all or virtually all of their lives in their country of birth, it is clear that Article 12(4) has significant relevance to the refugee status determination of many of those stateless persons who seek protection outside their country of former habitual residence.

Once it has been concluded in a particular case that a country of former habitual residence constitutes the applicant's 'own country', a refusal by that country of the right of the applicant to return is very likely to be arbitrary. This is because the Human Rights Committee has emphasized that there are 'few, if any, circumstances

---

[166] UN Human Rights Committee, 'Communication No 1557/2007: *Nystrom v Australia*' (1 September 2011) UN Doc CCPR/C/102/D/1557/2007, para 7.5 (hereafter *Nystrom*). The Human Rights Committee further held 'that there are few, if any, circumstances in which deprivation of the right to enter one's own country could be reasonable': at paras 7.5, 7.6. See also >UN Human Rights Committee, 'Communication No 1959/2010: *Warsame v Canada*' (1 September 2011) UN Doc CCPR/C/102/D/1959/2010, paras 8.4–8.6 (hereafter *Warsame*).

[167] *Nystrom* (n 166) para 7.4.   [168] ibid.

[169] See *Warsame* (n 166) as cited in Sarah Joseph and Melissa Castan, *The International Covenant on Civil and Political Rights: Cases, Materials, and Commentary* (3rd edn, OUP 2013) 415 (hereafter Joseph and Castan, *The International Covenant*). The fact that the UN Human Rights Committee has broadened the approach beyond the original General Comment 27 is clear from the views of the dissenting members in *Nystrom* and *Warsame*: at 415–16.

[170] *Warsame* (n 166) para 8.5.

in which deprivation of the right to enter one's own country could be reasonable'.[171] And where there is evidence of discrimination, as is the case in many refugee claims, the deprivation is clearly arbitrary.

The question whether this human rights violation is sufficiently serious to constitute persecution has been less controversial in the case-law. In *Vaca v Colombia*, the Human Rights Committee explained that the violation of a person's right to remain, return, and reside in her country under Article 12 *ICCPR* 'necessarily has a negative impact on [her] enjoyment of the other rights ensured under the Covenant'.[172]

Accordingly, denial of the right to return has been found to be capable of constituting persecution for the purposes of refugee law in various jurisdictions, either as a matter of principle,[173] or in fact in a particular case,[174] although in some cases this is one factor among a range of human rights violations that together constitute persecution.[175] Although rarely discussed in depth, it is manifest that denial of re-entry to the country in which one has established a home results in a range of consequential human rights violations that almost certainly constitute persecution. As emphasized by the Australian Tribunal in a case concerning a man of Nepali ethnicity who had been expelled from Bhutan—his country of former habitual residence—'the applicant's exclusion from the right to Bhutanese citizenship and the right to return to the country where his family had lived for generations, as well as all the

---

[171] ibid, para 8.6. This was also confirmed in UN Human Rights Committee, 'Communication No 859/1999: *Vaca v Colombia*' (15 April 2002) UN Doc CCPR/C/859/1999 (hereafter *Vaca*).

[172] *Vaca* (n 171) para 7.4.

[173] In Canada, it has been well accepted since *Thabet v Canada (Minister of Citizenship and Immigration)* [1998] 4 FC 21 (11 May 1998) that the denial of a right to return 'can in itself be an act of persecution': at [31]. Hence, the decision-maker is 'compelled to ask itself why the Applicant is being denied entry to a country of former habitual residence because the reason for the denial may, in certain circumstances, constitute an act of persecution by the state': at [32]. See also, 'being denied a right to return ... may in itself constitute an act of persecution by the state': *X (Re)*, 2000 CanLII 21408 (CA IRB) 4 (hereafter *X (Re)* 2000), citing *Maarouf* (n 150) 739–40, and other decisions (see n 8). See also *Kadoura* (n 150) [16]; *Rahman v Canada (Minister of Citizenship and Immigration)*, 2016 FC 1355 (8 December 2016) [23] (hereafter *Rahman*) and *Chehade v Canada (Minister of Citizenship and Immigration)* 2017 FC 282 (16 March 2017) [20].

[174] In *Ouda v Immigration and Naturalization Service*, 324 F 3d 445 (6th Cir, 2003) (hereafter *Ouda*), the US Court of Appeals for the Sixth Circuit observed, with approval (in relation to this asylum claim of Palestinians from Kuwait), that '[a]sylum applicants have argued that a country's refusal to accept them is further evidence of persecution': at 452, citing various decisions. The Court found in this case that '[t]he mere fact that the Oudas were ordered by the government to leave Kuwait because they were perceived enemies of their country is sufficient alone to establish past persecution': at 454. In *ST* (n 108), the UK Upper Tribunal found that although the question whether denial of a right to return constitutes persecution is an issue of fact, 'the denial of a right to return is very likely to constitute persecution, in very many cases': at [89]. We note that this was in the context of arbitrary deprivation of nationality. Similarly, in *MA (Ethiopia)* (n 104) the Court held that the arbitrary refusal of return 'would in my view amount to persecution': at [60]. This was also in the context of a deprivation of citizenship; however, the refusal was considered independently. Sometimes the claim is considered cumulatively; for instance, the Australian Tribunal explained in one case that, 'the Jordanian government's refusal to renew the applicant's passport is amongst a long list of discriminatory treatments it subjects Palestinian refugees to': *0805551* [2009] RRTA 24 (15 January 2009) [56]. In *Tesfamichael v Minister for Immigration and Multicultural Affairs* [1999] FCA 1661 (2 December 1999), the Australian Federal Court acknowledged that to 'expel a national from that person's country of nationality, perhaps leaving behind family and property, would fall within the category of harm sufficient to constitute persecution': at [54].

[175] *V00/11398* (n 158).

disadvantages that emanated from the depravation of these rights amount to persecution for the Convention reason of ethnicity'.[176]

In addition, such harm is clearly ongoing and forward-looking. As concluded by the NZ RSAA, in relation to stateless Palestinians who were unable to return to their country of former habitual residence, Saudi Arabia, the applicant's 'exclusion from Saudi Arabia, itself a form of persecution, is ongoing'.[177] Similarly, in relation to the claim of an ethnic Rohingyan man from Myanmar, the NZ RSAA had no difficulty in finding, by reference to Article 12(4) of the *ICCPR*, that the 'breach of these core human rights enshrined in Article 12 is sufficient on its own to constitute discrimination amounting to persecution'.[178]

In the United States, Deborah E Anker recounts that the issue was particularly acute in cases involving Palestinians during the Gulf War, an era that witnessed many Palestinians forcibly expelled and then denied re-entry to various countries of former habitual residence in the Middle East.[179] She cites the Immigration and Naturalization Service (INS) General Counsel's Memorandum, which stated that 'expulsion or denial of reentry qualifies a person as a refugee eligible for asylum if the expulsion violates basic human rights and therefore amounts to persecution'.[180]

In Ireland, although the High Court accepts that practical obstacles alone are not sufficient for a stateless person who is unable to return to his or her country of former habitual residence to be considered a refugee, it nevertheless granted leave to bring judicial review on the ground that the reason the applicant was outside Kuwait was because he had been refused entry for a *Refugee Convention* reason, and this refusal itself may amount to 'persecution'.[181]

---

[176] *071626084* (n 38).

[177] *Refugee Appeal Nos 73861, 73862* (n 9) [117] (Member Shaw), and at [128] (Member Millar): 'I find their exclusion from Saudi Arabia to be part of ongoing persecution and therefore their fear of persecution is well-founded.' See also at [125].

[178] *Refugee Appeal No 76254* (n 79) [38]. It went on to note that in the appellant's case there were also additional sources of discriminatory treatment that amounted to persecution: at [38].

[179] Deborah E Anker, *Law of Asylum in the United States* (Thomson Reuters 2013) 305 (hereafter Anker, *Law of Asylum*).

[180] ibid, 305–6, citing Memorandum from INS Office of the General Counsel, 'Legal Opinion: Your Memorandum of June 6, 1992: Palestine Applicants' to Margaret Ramos, Supervisory Asylum Officer, Houston Asylum Office (19 August 1992). She argues that 'expulsion of a noncitizen or non-national, under certain circumstances, also can amount to persecution': at 304. Indeed, the UN HRC has reflected on the plight of Palestinians, finding that in relation to Palestinians 'travelling in and between East Jerusalem, the Gaza Strip and the West Bank', Israel is urged to 'respect the right to freedom of movement provided for under article 12, including the right to return to one's country': UN Human Rights Committee, 'Concluding Observations of the Human Rights Committee: Israel' (18 August 1998) UN Doc CCPR/C/79/Add.93, para 22.

[181] *AAAAD v Refugee Appeals Tribunal* [2009] IEHC 326 (17 July 2009) [86]. A slightly different issue arose in Belgium, where the *Conseil du Contentieux des Etrangers* recognized the refugee status of a national from Uzbekistan on the ground that his presence in Belgium for more than eight years, and his claim that as a result he had lost his Uzbek nationality, and no longer had a valid passport or a residence in Uzbekistan, meant that he would not be able to re-enter Uzbekistan without the authorities knowing that he applied for asylum in Belgium ('illegal exit abroad'). He would therefore be at risk of persecution: Conseil du Contentieux des Etrangers ('CCE') [Belgian Aliens Litigation Council], *X v Commissaire général aux réfugiés et aux apatrides*, arrêt no°22144, 28 January 2009 (hereafter CCE, arrêt no°22144). But see *LM v Secretary of State for the Home Department* [2012] UKUT 00390 (IAC), which held that such return and the treatment feared does not usually constitute persecution unless the

The UNHCR has observed that where a stateless individual has been 'trafficked out of their country of habitual residence',

the lack of documentation coupled with lack of citizenship may render them unable to secure return to their country of habitual residence. While this alone does not make someone a refugee, the individual concerned may be eligible for refugee status where the refusal of the country of habitual residence to allow re-entry is related to a Convention ground and the inability to return to the country leads to serious harm or a serious violation, or violations, of human rights amounting to persecution.[182]

Notwithstanding the acceptance that a denial of the right to return may constitute persecution, some decision-makers have dismissed refugee claims in this context due to a failure to establish a nexus between the denial of re-entry and a *Refugee Convention* ground. However, sometimes this conclusion flows from an erroneous assumption that non-citizens—even those who have lived in a state since birth—have no rights in relation to return.[183] On such reasoning, 'any difficulty in re-entering would be as a result of laws of general application',[184] 'rather than any Convention ground'.[185]

On the other hand, in some cases the denial of re-entry has been linked to political opinion in the particular context of the applicant's predicament,[186] but in most cases race or ethnicity is said to account for the risk. For example, in the case of a Palestinian man denied re-entry to Gaza by the Israeli government, the Australian Tribunal observed that while it 'is an arguable point as to whether the identity of Palestinian is a political, racial or national identity', 'in common usage it now overlaps with all three of these and so satisfies the requirement for a Convention ground to be made out'.[187] However, an alternative ground may simply be nationality or

---

applicant has a particular profile or distinguishing features (refugee status) or if the applicant is likely to be detained on return (subsidiary protection status based on Article 3 *European Convention on Human Rights* ('*ECHR*')).

[182] UNHCR, 'Guidelines on International Protection: The Application of Article 1A(2) of the 1951 Convention and/or 1967 Protocol relating to the Status of Refugees to Victims of Trafficking and Persons at Risk of Being Trafficked' (7 April 2006) UN Doc HCR/GIP/06/07, para 44.

[183] See e.g., *SHM v Refugee Appeals Tribunal* [2009] IEHC 128 (12 March 2009), which concerned the refugee claim of a woman born in Libya to Palestinian parents and who had been raised in Libya but, having left to study, was prohibited from return. Despite acknowledging the strict inhibitions on freedom of movement imposed by the Libyan government on Palestinians, the High Court of Ireland observed that the Libyan government's policy 'may constitute discrimination or it may equally be consistent with the exercise of Libya's legitimate right to regulate immigration': at [56].

[184] *WZAPN v Minister for Immigration* [2013] FMCA 6 (31 January 2013) [60] (hereafter *WZAPN*). See also *X (Re)* 2000, (n 213) 8, and *X (Re)*, 2016 CanLii 105364 (CA IRB) [32]: 'the denial of the right to return under an immigration law of general application does not amount to persecution'.

[185] *WZAPN* (n 184) [60]. See also *BZADW* (n 38) [27], [32]..

[186] See NZ RSAA *Refugee Appeal Nos 73861, 73862* (n 9) [128]. See also Unabhängiger Bundesasylsenat [Austrian Independent Federal Asylum Senate], *DA v Federal Asylum Authority*, decision no°203.029/0-II/28/98, 10 November 1999 (on file with authors). In this case, the Court held that '[a] state's refusal to allow a citizen re-entry into his territory is a severe violation of the personal sphere amounting to a significant break of relations between the state and his citizen, leaving the latter in a hopeless situation'; and that 'this measure would be directly aimed at the applicant's attributed oppositional opinion and on her personal background as a woman of "western" upbringing'.

[187] *V00/11398* (n 158). See also *Rahman* (n 173) [30].

lack of nationality in such cases. In other words, if a person has a right to return to his or her *own country* and yet a state prohibits such return due to the applicant's statelessness, then the risk of harm can be attributed to (lack of) nationality. To so conclude does not mean that any person who is unable to return to a country of former habitual residence is automatically a refugee, since the test for establishing 'own country' is likely to require a higher threshold than habitual residence. However, it remains an issue that warrants much closer and more thoughtful consideration in the refugee context.

In sum, we agree with the conclusion of Michelle Foster and James Hathaway that a correct application of Article 12(4) to the refugee context has the potential to 'open the doors to refugee status for a significant subset of the stateless population'.[188]

Part 4: Denial of Civil and Political Rights as Persecution

This chapter has thus far considered the question whether the denial or withdrawal of nationality, or denial of the right to return, can constitute persecution for the purposes of the *Refugee Convention*. We now turn to consider the consequences of being stateless and begin with the denial of other civil and political rights. It is well documented that if returned to their country of origin or of former habitual residence, many stateless persons 'face almost insurmountable obstacles to securing access to their rights, including birth certificates and other identity documents, education, worker rights, health care, freedom from arbitrary detention, family unity, and freedom of movement'.[189] In the jurisprudence, violation of civil and political rights tantamount to persecution in relation to stateless persons typically involves physical injury, arrest, detention, and/or deportation/expulsion. In many cases, such violations occur in connection with denial or withdrawal of nationality, denial of the right to return, and/or denial of socio-economic rights as persecution. Hence, it is common to have one or more of these issues overlapping in the jurisprudence of national courts, and it is therefore sometimes difficult to assess the discrete issue of civil and political rights violations in a vacuum. However, we consider this issue discretely in this section in order to identify and analyse particular challenges that pertain to stateless persons when they raise these issues as part of a claim to refugee status.

Common types of treatment found to amount to persecution in the jurisprudence of domestic courts entail indignities and violence (e.g. harassment,[190] beating and extortion, torture, kidnapping, killing) and/or arbitrary arrest and detention,[191]

---

[188] Hathaway and Foster, *The Law of Refugee Status 2* (n 3) 251.

[189] UNHCR, 'Guidelines on Representing Stateless Persons' (n 142) 17.

[190] See e.g., the decision of the Australian Tribunal in *1113683* [2012] RRTA 611 (9 August 2012) [56] (hereafter *1113683*).

[191] See e.g., the decision of the Australian Tribunal in *1000094* (n 4) [155]–[156], and also in *1108899* [2012] RRTA 133 (7 March 2012) [57]–[58] (hereafter *1108899*). See also *Qassim v Minister of Immigration, Refugees, Citizenship Canada* (2018) FC 226 (28 February 2018) at [55]–[59].

either on their own[192] or taken cumulatively with, for instance, the requirement to carry an ID document (in the case of a stateless Faili Kurd in Iran[193]); the serious difficulties (high insecurity) associated with living in a refugee camp;[194] travel restrictions, including restrained possibilities to leave the country;[195] targeting by authorities based on national security concerns;[196] the loss of all one's belongings followed by expulsion;[197] being stateless and deported;[198] being stateless, dispossessed of property, and having housing destroyed.[199] It is noteworthy that the majority of cases involving stateless applicants where denial of civil and political rights is found to amount to persecution, and indeed many of those involving socioeconomic rights, concern Palestinians. Such cases may be complicated by the presence of Article 1D of the *Refugee Convention*, a potential ground of exclusion from *Convention* protection, but this is an issue that is explored in depth in Chapter 6. In

---

[192] In *Rahman* (n 173), the Federal Court found that the risk 'of arbitrary and indeterminate detention' could amount to persecution 'in itself': at [23]. In a 2015 Canadian decision, the Immigration and Refugee Board found that the stateless Palestinian was at risk of persecution in the form of severe violence if returned to Syria: *X (Re)*, 2015 CarswellNat 3687 [15]–[16] (hereafter *X (Re)* 2015). See also in Australia: *1317610* [2014] RRTA 472 (28 May 2014) (stateless Bidoon born in Kuwait). New Zealand: *Refugee Appeal No 73873* [2006] NZRSAA 77 (28 April 2006) (stateless Palestinian from Egypt); *Refugee Appeal No 74236* [2005] NZRSAA 351 (2 December 2005) (stateless Palestinian living in Lebanon); *Refugee Appeal No 76254* (n 79) (ethnic Rohingya from Myanmar). United States: *Marouf v Lynch*, 811 F 3d 174 (6th Cir, 2016) (stateless Christian Palestinians living in the West Bank—past persecution still presumed to exist). Canada: *X (Re)*, 2013 Can LII 99310 (CA IRB) (Sunni Muslim born in Lebanon as a Palestinian refugee); *Asali v Canada (Minister of Public Safety & Emergency Preparedness)*, 2007 FC 991 (1 October 2001) (Palestinian children living in the West Bank at risk of being shot and used as human shields). United Kingdom: *SA and IA v Secretary of State for the Home Department* [2009] UKAIT 00006 (hereafter *SA*); *NA v Secretary of State for the Home Department* [2008] UKAIT 00046 (hereafter *NA* 2008). France: CNDA, decision no°14014878, 9 November 2015 (Palestinian formerly residing in Syria). Belgium: CCE, arrêt no°22144 (n 181) (stateless person from Uzbekistan who would be arrested, interrogated, and possibly tortured if returned for having applied for asylum in Belgium).
[193] *SZPZI* (n 4).
[194] See e.g., Australia: *1108899* (n 191) (Palestinian refugee in Lebanon). Belgium: CCE, *Houssam v Commissaire général aux réfugiés et aux apatrides*, arrêt no°27366, 14 May 2009, and CCE, *X v Commissaire général aux réfugiés et aux apatrides*, arrêt no°26112, 21 April 2009 (both cases related to Palestinians in Lebanon). Hungary: Fővárosi Törvénytár [Hungarian Metropolitan Court], *HAI v Office of Immigration and Nationality (OIN)*, decision no 3.K. 30.602/2013/15, 29 August 2013 (stateless Palestinian living in a refugee camp in Lebanon). Canada: *X(Re)* 2015 (n 192) (stateless Palestinian in Syrian camp, at high risk of being killed due to his ethnicity).
[195] See Immigration and Refugee Board of Canada, Refugee Appeal Division, RAD File No MB6-00677 (27 October 2016) at [69].
[196] See e.g., *1113683* (n 190) (stateless Palestinian in Lebanon 'fitting' the profile of persons collaborating with an armed group); *Refugee Appeal No 75694* [2006] NZRSAA 97 (24 May 2006) (stateless person from Ethiopia identified for deportation).
[197] *071626084* (n 38) (stateless former resident of Bhutan identified for deportation).
[198] In *Refugee Appeal No 73861* (n 6) (stateless Palestinians born and living in Saudi Arabia), the Tribunal held: 'The appellant's predicament is not simply that inherent in the condition of being stateless. He has suffered past persecution. Following his arrest, he was denied a fair trial, arbitrarily detained, subjected to ill-treatment in the form of solitary confinement, beatings and sexual assaults and arbitrarily stripped of his right of residency and deported. His exclusion from Saudi Arabia, itself a form of persecution, is ongoing. His inability to return to Saudi Arabia arises directly from his persecution': at [117]—refer to Part 3 of this chapter.
[199] France: Decision no°10015655 C (n 75) (Rohingya from Myanmar detained for two years); Decision no°12013646 C (n 119) (Rohingya from Myanmar subject to abuses and numerous restrictions, prohibitions, and discriminations on the enjoyment of civil, political, and socio-economic rights). See also CNDA, decision no°09019611, 14 February 2011.

the remainder of this chapter we focus only on the question whether the feared harm amounts to persecution.

4.1 The role of nationality in the enjoyment of rights

In some instances, denial of a single civil and political right will be sufficient to trigger 'persecution'. For instance, in *Ouda v INS*, the US Court of Appeals for the Sixth Circuit held that '[t]he mere fact that the Oudas were ordered by the government to leave Kuwait because they were perceived enemies of their country is sufficient alone to establish past persecution'.[200] However, generally, more is needed.

In numerous cases, denial of civil and political rights has been found *not* to amount to persecution, based on what is arguably a narrow interpretation of which denials of rights rise to the level of persecution under the *Refugee Convention*. For instance, the Federal Court of Australia *rejected* the arguments put forward by the applicant that denial of the rights attached to nationality, such as the right to own a passport or personal ID card, the right to obtain a birth certificate (a violation of Article 8 *CRC*), the right to obtain a marriage certificate, the right to vote or participate in Iran's political processes (a violation of Article 21 *Universal Declaration of Human Rights* ('*UDHR*') and Article 23 *ICCPR*), the right to seek a legal remedy before the law (a violation of Article 10 *UDHR*), the right to freedom of movement and residence etc., fell within the scope of Article 1A(2) of the *Refugee Convention*.[201] The Court held:

> To the extent that the nationality claims depend upon conventions [i.e. human rights treaties] other than the [Refugee] Convention, they were not within the range of matters required to be considered by the Reviewer. The way in which the nationality claims would be viewed, therefore, would be confined only to the denial of those basic services and economic hardship that threatened a person's capacity to subsist.[202]

Although in part a reflection of the Australian legislative framework,[203] the judgment is concerning for its failure adequately to engage with the ramifications for the stateless individual of what essentially amounts to a denial of legal personhood.

In another case, also involving a stateless Faili Kurd from Iran, the FFCA did not accept that 'a restriction on movement was sufficiently serious to constitute persecution in a Convention sense'—the applicant was not able to move freely around Iran and was confined to a particular area.[204] The fact that he was also discriminated

---

[200] *Ouda* (n 174) 454.
[201] *SZTFX* (n 24) [52] (the applicant was a Faili Kurd born in Iran).   [202] ibid, [47].
[203] The Australian *Migration Act 1958* (Cth) s 5J(5) provides that 'being persecuted' requires 'serious harm' and that: 'Without limiting what is serious harm for the purposes of paragraph (4)(b), the following are instances of *serious harm* for the purposes of that paragraph: '(a) a threat to the person's life or liberty; (b) significant physical harassment of the person; (c) significant physical ill-treatment of the person; (d) significant economic hardship that threatens the person's capacity to subsist; (e) denial of access to basic services, where the denial threatens the person's capacity to subsist; (f) denial of capacity to earn a livelihood of any kind, where the denial threatens the person's capacity to subsist'.
[204] Australia: *SZSVT v Minister for Immigration* [2014] FCCA 768 (17 April 2014) [15] (hereafter *SZSVT*); *071454724* [2007] RRTA 200 (30 August 2007) (hereafter *071454724*)—being held at 'checkpoints is discriminatory and harassment which delayed the applicant going to play sport or

against in education, health care, and other areas did not alter this assessment.[205] The Court furthermore agreed with the Australian Tribunal that the applicant had been seriously harmed in the past on two occasions for reasons of his ethnicity, but considered these incidents to have happened in the past and to have been the result of random encounters.[206] Hence, no well-founded fear of persecution was found to exist.

The absence of physical injury, arrest, detention, or questioning is a powerful factor against a finding of persecution, even if discrimination and harassment exist.[207] Sometimes even credible evidence of physical mistreatment (e.g. being hit and spit at, and being used as a human shield when searching neighbours' houses) was not enough to amount to persecution; the treatments in question being described as 'minor injuries' and periods of detention as 'brief'.[208]

In many respects, the assessment of whether certain violations are sufficiently serious so as to amount to persecution requires a similar analysis in every refugee claim, regardless of whether or not the applicant is stateless. However, one key issue that differentiates the claims of stateless applicants from those with a nationality is an explicit or implicit assumption by some decision-makers that because an applicant is stateless, he or she is not entitled to enjoy certain rights in the country of former habitual residence; hence on this reasoning the denial of such rights cannot amount to persecution.

In some cases in which harm is not considered sufficiently serious so as to amount to persecution, there appears to be an implicit assumption that stateless persons are not entitled to enjoy the same rights as citizens in their country of origin; hence some differential treatment is expected to be tolerated.

In other cases, the analysis is more explicit, in some instances following from an earlier conclusion that the lack of nationality is not itself persecutory because it is the result of non-discriminatory nationality laws. The reasoning appears to be that if an applicant is not entitled to obtain the nationality of the country of origin, he or she is equally devoid of an entitlement to rights protection in the home state. For example, in *Ahmed v Ashcroft*, the US Court of Appeals for the Third Circuit rejected the claim of a Palestinian man who had submitted that in Saudi Arabia—his country of birth and former habitual residence—he was subjected to a variety of restrictions including those on owning property or a business, unequal work rights, and restrictions on tertiary study, and security of residence. Rather than assessing the claim on the basis of whether these harms were human rights violations that constituted persecution, the Court affirmed the views previously expressed by courts in other US circuits that because the restrictions applied not just to ethnic Palestinians but more broadly to all foreigners, this was not a risk of being persecuted, since '[t]o find

his work but it is not significant nor is it so serious': at [67]. Canada: *Khalifeh v Canada (Minister of Citizenship and Immigration)*, 2003 FC 1044—constant harassment at checkpoints between Jericho and Jerusalem, delays, but no detention or arrest.

[205] *SZSVT* (n 204) [16].   [206] ibid, [17].
[207] *Pavlovich v Gonzales*, 476 F 3d 613 (8th Cir, 2007).
[208] *Aburuwaida v US Attorney General*, 446 Fed Appx 207 (11th Cir, 2011) (stateless Palestinian from the West Bank and Gaza) (hereafter *Aburuwaida*).

persecution under these circumstances would require a finding that *jus sanguinis* is persecution *per se*'.[209]

Yet these are not at all synonymous points. Rather, as observed in Chapter 3, international human rights law is unequivocal in requiring states to respect and guarantee rights even in relation to non-citizens. In other words, the fact that a state may not be required to grant nationality to a particular individual does not remove all responsibility for the rights of that individual. Rather, Article 2 of the *ICCPR* obligates states to respect and ensure the rights in the *Covenant* to all people within a state's territory and subject to its jurisdiction, 'without distinction of any kind, such as race, colour, sex, language, religion, political or other opinion, national or social origin, property, birth or other status', which the Human Rights Committee has clarified means that rights in the *ICCPR* are 'not limited to citizens of States Parties but must also be available to all individuals, regardless of nationality or statelessness, such as asylum seekers, refugees, migrant workers and other persons, who may find themselves in the territory or subject to the jurisdiction of the State Party'.[210] A person who has 'found themselves' in the territory by virtue of birth and/or long-standing residence is undoubtedly entitled to equal access to the rights in the *Covenant*.[211] Importantly, the relevance of such widely ratified human rights treaties to the persecution analysis is sound notwithstanding that the home state in question may not be party to the relevant treaty. This is because reference to such treaties in the refugee context is for the purpose of illuminating the terms in the *Refugee Convention*, not in order to enforce other international treaties.[212]

4.2 Generalized harm

Another challenge that emerges in claims by stateless applicants is that courts have a tendency to conclude that 'generally harsh conditions shared by many other persons' does not amount to persecution, such as the treatment of Palestinians during the 1967 war and the destruction of thousands of their homes in 1976.[213] Treatment

---

[209] *Ahmed v Ashcroft*, 341 F 3d 214 (3rd Cir, 2003). This is not an isolated example: see also United States: *Aboushehata v United States AG*, 143 Fed Appx 302 (11th Cir, 2005) 7–8; *El Bitar v Ashcroft*, 109 Fed Appx 179 (9th Cir, 2004) 6–7.

[210] UN HRC, 'General Comment No 31: The Nature of the General Legal Obligation Imposed on States Parties to the Covenant' (26 May 2004) UN Doc CCPR/C/21/Rev.1/Add.13, para 10.

[211] Of course, there are limited exceptions, as some are explicitly granted to citizens (right to vote). The fact that there is such a distinction tends to confirm rather than undermine the position that in general *ICCPR* rights are not confined to citizens.

[212] Hathaway and Foster, *The Law of Refugee Status 2* (n 3) 5–12.

[213] United States: *Al-Fara v Gonzales*, 404 F 3d 733, 740 (3rd Cir, 2005)—in this case, the US Court of Appeals Third Circuit cited Congress's (erroneous) interpretation that a refugee and a displaced person are two very different categories: the latter but *not the former* includes 'individuals who flee widespread conditions of indiscriminative violence resulting from civil war or military strife in a country': at 740. United Kingdom: *YL* (n 151)—applicant of Eritrean ethnicity claiming to be of Ethiopian nationality or stateless: detention in 'circumstances close to persecution' was not persecution; *E-Ali v Secretary of State for the Home Department* [2002] UKAIT 00159: in rather outdated reasoning, the then UK Asylum and Immigration Tribunal found that despite having been detained and investigated by the Lebanese authorities, this treatment did not constitute persecution for a *Refugee Convention* reason (the appellant was a stateless Palestinian born in Kuwait but living in Lebanon).

that affects all Palestinians or all non-nationals (i.e. generalized violence) is used in some jurisdictions to deny refugee status (e.g. Canada, United Kingdom) whereas in other jurisdictions the lack of a pattern of widespread treatment may be used against applicants (e.g. United States, United Kingdom).

Yet such interpretation is difficult to reconcile with accepted refugee law doctrine. The conventional approach is exemplified in the UNHCR Guidelines on International Protection No 12 on claims for refugee status related to situations of armed conflict and violence, which clearly contemplate persecution against whole communities or civilians generally.[214]

Finally, in terms of nexus, in cases where denial of civil and political rights was found to amount to persecution, one of the five grounds of the *Refugee Convention* was relied on (sometimes in combination) and accepted by courts, namely (imputed) political opinion, race, nationality/ethnicity (e.g. Palestinian), membership of a particular group, and religion. Hence this is an issue that rarely raised much discussion in the case law.[215]

Part 5: Denial of Socio-Economic Rights as Persecution

It has been observed that statelessness 'may well be the most important factor making for economic harm'.[216] There is clear and well-documented evidence of discrimination against and exclusion of stateless populations globally in the context of access to work, financial ownership, access to the housing market, social security and public education, and the frequently experienced social ostracism that is visited upon stateless people.[217]

Yet refugee claims by stateless persons rarely focus primarily, or even in some cases at all, on the socio-economic harm to which they would likely be subjected on return. Where socio-economic deprivation is raised in refugee claims by stateless applicants, it is most often combined with denials of civil and political rights, as is the case in many other contexts. One of the most common claims across multiple

---

[214] UNHCR, 'Guidelines on International Protection No 12' (2 December 2016) UN Doc HCR/GIP/16/12, paras 17–18.

[215] See e.g., *BA* (n 16), where the UK Tribunal found that '[s]ince the Bedoon have a tribal identity and are not simply a collection of (mainly) stateless persons, they face persecution by reason of a Refugee Convention ground of race. They can also be seen to form a particular social group': at [90]. While it is well accepted that persecution for reasons of statelessness may constitute persecution on the grounds of nationality for the purposes of the *Refugee Convention* (see Hathaway and Foster, *The Law of Refugee Status 2* (n 3) 397–98), this was questioned in a 1998 Federal Court decision, *Husein Ali Harris v Minister for Immigration and Multicultural Affairs* [1998] FCA 78 (12 February 1998) (Moore J). However, the Australian Tribunal in *1114181* (n 3) observed that 'With respect, this judgment appears to be at odds with the approach taken to other Convention grounds such as religion, as there is authority for the proposition that persecution "for reasons of religion" can also include persecution because the applicant does *not* have a particular religion': at [79]. Ultimately, the claim was successful on the basis that 'the Bidoons of Kuwait do appear to the Tribunal to constitute a particular social group': at [82].

[216] William E Conklin, *Statelessness: The Enigma of the International Community* (Hart 2014) 126 (hereafter Conklin, *Statelessness*).

[217] ibid, 126–34.

jurisdictions relates to Palestinians living in refugee camps in, for example, Lebanon, where the threat of ill-treatment at checkpoints, arbitrary arrest, and detention, combined with severe discrimination, significant economic hardship, employment restrictions, extreme poverty, bans on buying property, and no access to public social services has been found to amount to persecution in several jurisdictions.[218] Other successful cases have involved stateless Kurds from Syria, where denial of both civil and political rights and socio-economic rights taken cumulatively were found to amount to persecution.[219]

5.1 Socio-economic deprivation

In cases involving stateless Bidoon born in Kuwait, decision-makers have generally found *undocumented* (but not documented[220]) Bidoon to suffer treatment amounting to persecution on the ground that without documents, they cannot access *any* form of social services, including education, health care and benefits.[221] Indeed in a decision of the UK Tribunal intended as a 'country guideline' decision, the Tribunal found that in Kuwait, 'the authorities, having acted to exclude most Bedoon from Kuwaiti nationality and from lawful residence status, have then confined access to basic civil, political, social, economic and cultural rights to those having either Kuwaiti nationality or (as lawful residents) foreign nationality'.[222]

The Tribunal insisted on the importance of assessing state policy in relation to stateless populations in an historical context.[223] In the case of Kuwait, the Tribunal found that the 'steps taken by the Kuwaiti authorities to marginalize the Bedoon have been part of a deliberate state policy to drive large numbers of the Bedoon out of

---

[218] Australia: *1010968* [2011] RRTA 203 (9 March 2011) [52]–[55]; 1005911 [2010] RRTA 923 (20 October 2010) [110]–[117]. Canada: *X (Re)*, 2002 CanLII 52679 (CA IRB); *X v Canada (Immigration and Refugee Board)*, 2001 Can LII 26883 (CA IRB); *X v Canada (Immigration and Refugee Board)*, 2001 Can LII 26842 (CA IRB) (threat of arbitrary arrest of detention together with deprivation of medical care, employment opportunities, and adequate housing and food amount to persecution, taken cumulatively).

[219] Bulgaria: Върховен административен съд [Bulgarian Supreme Administrative Court], *Madjid v Head of the State Agency for Refugees*, 11261/2009, 28 October 2010 (applicant belongs to the group 'maktumen'—'second-class' Kurds in Syria without recognized citizenship and without recognition of their birth on the territory of Syria—who do not have any rights in Syria). See in another context, *VO3/16458* (n 101) 5.

[220] Those with documents are generally denied refugee status on the ground that the restrictions imposed on their employment, political expression, and access to services represent mild discrimination that does not amount to persecution or serious harm (even if taken cumulatively): Australia: *BZADW* (n 38) [31], [33]; *1303526* [2013] RRTA 815 (19 November 2013) [25]–[26] (hereafter *1303526*). New Zealand: *Refugee Appeal No 74449* (n 46) [49].

[221] New Zealand: *Refugee Appeal No 76506* (n 124) [83]; *Refugee Appeal No 74880* (n 10) [21]–[23]. United Kingdom: *NM* (n 47); *Queen on the application of (ZA) (Kuwait) v Secretary of State for the Home Department* [2011] EWCA Civ 1082 (the degree of discrimination faced by undocumented Bidoon is sufficient to amount to persecution); *HE v Secretary of State for the Home Department* [2006] UKAIT 00051 (hereafter *HE*) (the level of discrimination faced by undocumented Bidoon in so many aspects of their lives in Kuwait amounts to persecution); *BA* (n 16) (the treatment of undocumented Bidoon amounts to persecution based on the denial of their civil and political rights as well as socio-economic rights).

[222] *BA* (n 16) [64].   [223] ibid, [66].

the country',[224] and that the 'dramatic fall' in the number of Bidoon in Kuwait over preceding decades with 'some 120,000 persons having left in circumstances often tantamount to forced deportation—speaks for itself'.[225] The Tribunal bore in mind 'that at international law the prohibition of forced deportation is widely considered to have the status of *ius cogens*'.[226] In a more recent decision, the tribunal maintained that the treatment—mainly in the form of socio-economic deprivation—of undocumented Bidoon amounts to persecution, finding that the definition of persecution in Article 9 of the EU Qualification Directive accommodates discrimination,[227] where measures involve 'persistent and serious ill-treatment without just cause',[228] are 'of a substantially prejudicial nature', and 'affect a significant part of the individual's or group's existence'.[229] A similar analysis has been adopted in other jurisdictions in assessing identical claims, including in New Zealand, where the RSAA concluded that the accumulation of discriminatory measures against the Bidoon in Kuwait 'effectively rendered [the applicant] a non-person in his own country' and was clearly persecution.[230]

While the level of segregation and exclusion described by the UK Tribunal above in relation to undocumented Bidoon is not present in relation to every stateless population, it is also not confined to the situation of the Bidoon. Others include the response of Kuwait to the Gulf War, which entailed 'embarking on a systematic effort to decrease its population of non-Kuwaiti residents',[231] with 'Palestinians in particular ... targeted',[232] notably through severe economic discrimination.[233] A particularly poignant contemporary example is the treatment of the Rohingya in Myanmar, in which there is 'an inextricable link between the serious discrimination, marginalization, denial of a wide range of basic rights, and the deprivation of citizenship',[234] and the forced deportation from August 2017.

One key challenge for stateless applicants is that often the very heart of the claim is founded on the deprivation of socio-economic rights yet, as has been analysed in previous scholarship, decision-makers have a tendency to undervalue the impact and significance of such harm on applicants as a general matter.[235] Cases in this category are sometimes dismissed on the basis that the treatment feared is simply discrimination and/or harassment, rather than persecution.[236]

---

[224] ibid. [225] ibid. [226] ibid. [227] *NM* (n 47) [93]. [228] ibid.
[229] ibid.
[230] *Refugee Appeal No 74467* (n 38) [103]. See also *Refugee Appeal No 74880* (n 10) [84].
[231] *El Himri v Ashcroft*, 378 F 3d 932 (9th Cir, 2004) 936 (hereafter *El Himri*).
[232] ibid. See also Anker, *Law of Asylum* (n 179).
[233] See also *Ouda* (n 174), involving a stateless Palestinian in Kuwait after the Gulf War.
[234] UN High Commissioner for Refugees (UNHCR), *Statelessness and the Rohingya Crisis* (10 November 2017) <https://www.refworld.org/docid/5a05b4664.html> accessed 9 December 2018.
[235] Michelle Foster, *International Refugee Law and Socio-Economic Rights: Refuge from Deprivation* (CUP 2007) Chapter 3 (hereafter Foster, *International Refugee Law and Socio-Economic Rights*).
[236] In countries such as Bangladesh, although Biharis are considered to be an impoverished group, it has been found in some cases that they are not *significantly* more impoverished than Bangladeshi in general: New Zealand: *Refugee Appeal No 72024* [2000] NZRSAA 281 (13 July 2000) [28]. See also Canada: *X (Re)*, 2005 CanLII 77811 (CA IRB) (Tibetan in India). In New Zealand, the RSAA is of the view that: 'Discrimination *per se* does not amount to persecution ... The discrimination must result in some form of serious harm in respect of which it can be said there is also a failure of state protection': *Refugee Appeal No 73958* [2005] NZRSAA 151 (26 May 2005) [72] (hereafter *Refugee Appeal*

For example, in cases involving stateless Palestinians living in refugee camps in Lebanon who suffer discrimination across a wide range of socio-economic rights but nonetheless have enough to eat, accommodation, access to basic education, and some health care, some decision-makers have found that they do not qualify for refugee status.[237] In the words of the UK Upper Tribunal: 'There has to be shown to be a severe deprivation with denial of shelter, food and the most basic necessities of life for the appeal to succeed.'[238]

In a different case, the UK Upper Tribunal considered that '[t]he difficulties faced by Palestinians in the Occupied Territories (economic situation, food insecurity travel restrictions etc) taken cumulatively are not such that the minimum level of severity for persecution or serious harm is reached';[239] this applies even in the case of a Palestinian male between sixteen and thirty-five who would have to endure greater travel restrictions and possible violence; for the Tribunal, the risk of being 'stopped and subjected to persecutory ill-treatment remains speculative'.[240]

On the other hand, in some instances the assessment that severe socio-economic harm amounts only to discrimination and not persecution has been overturned on appeal.[241] For example, in a refugee claim by a husband and wife who claimed

---

No 73958). The US Court of Appeals for the Sixth Circuit also held: 'Economic deprivation may rise to the level of persecution, though it may do so "only when the resulting conditions are sufficiently severe" ... that they "constitute a threat to [the] individual's life or freedom" ': *El Assadi v Holder*, 418 Fed Appx 484 (6th Cir, 2011) [5]–[6] (hereafter *El Assadi*) (stateless Palestinian woman, living in Saudi Arabia). See also *Asad v Ashcroft*, 135 Fed Appx 839 (6th Cir, 2005) (not being able to find a job because of one's gender or ethnicity 'is not sufficient objectively to establish a well-founded fear of future persecution': at [17]); *Elfarra* (n 67) ('Persecution is the infliction or threat of death, torture, or injury to one's person or freedom, on account of race, religion, nationality, membership in a particular social group, or political opinion.... being denied the right to pursue the educational goals of one's choice and having economic or professional hardship is not persecution': at [3]). In this case, it concluded that 'these reports do not suggest that women cannot work at all or that they face economic deprivations of sufficient severity to rise to the level of persecution'; hence asylum was not granted: *El Assadi*, [6]–[7].

[237] Canada: *Younes v Canada (Citizenship and Immigration)*, 2013 FC 1122 (hereafter *Younes*) (stateless Palestinian from Lebanon receiving assistance from the United Nations Relief and Works Agency for Palestine Refugees in the Near East (UNWRA), faces harassment and discrimination but not persecution). See also *X (Re)*, 2012 CanLII 100060 (CA IRB) [24]–[28]; *X (Re)*, 2010 CanLII 96825 (CA IRB); *X (Re)*, 2008 CanLII 88011 (CA IRB). United Kingdom: *JA v Secretary of State for the Home Department* [2005] UKIAT 00045 (27 January 2005) (Palestinian living in Iraq; nothing to suggest that Palestinians are being targeted by Iraqi citizens: at [13]); *KK* (n 68): 'discriminatory denial of third category rights in Lebanon for the Palestinians ... does not amount to persecution': at [106], 'though poor, the appellants would not be destitute in Lebanon': at [107].

[238] United Kingdom: *HS* (n 154) [224], see also [222]–[223]: problems of access to electricity and clean water as well as products are encountered by other residents of Gaza; these problems do not reach the level of risk of persecution or serious harm. The risk to their life or person is minimal—it is not exceptional; *NA v Secretary of State for the Home Department* [2005] UKIAT 00094 (hereafter *NA* 2005).

[239] *MA v Secretary of State for the Home Department* [2007] UKAIT 00017 [127]–[129].

[240] ibid, [140]. See also *JA v Secretary of State for the Home Department* [2005] UKIAT 00045—no immediate danger at the point when the Adjudicator was considering the evidence: at [13].

[241] For instance, the Canadian Tribunal held, in relation to a stateless person from Saudi Arabia, descended from a displaced nomadic tribe, that the Refugee Protection Division had been in error because it 'should have considered whether the Appellant will face discrimination in his access to medical care in the future due to his lack of employment, which may result in a lack of medical insurance': Immigration and Refugee Board of Canada, Refugee Appeal Division, RAD File No MB6-00677 (27 October 2016) at [72].

refugee protection based on their fear of persecution in Lebanon as stateless Palestinians, the Federal Court of Canada agreed with the appellant's submission that 'the stateless-Palestinians of Lebanon have been and continue to be the beneficiaries of an on-going cycle of exclusion, suffering, deplorable neglect, misery, insecurity and despair',[242] and were living in 'abject poverty'.[243] Yet it was 'clear that the Panel simply did not carefully analyze the overwhelming documentary evidence in light of the particular circumstances of the Applicants', and hence the decision was set aside by the Court.[244]

There are relatively few cases where the denial of socio-economic rights has been found to amount to persecution, individually or cumulatively, for this reason alone. This is partly due to the fact that, as mentioned above, most cases in reality involve a range of rights violations. However, it is also explained by a general failure across many jurisdictions adequately to understand the nature and importance of socio-economic rights.[245] And yet the centrality of the denial of socio-economic rights to the plight of stateless persons in many contexts today is clear and indisputable. As the New Zealand Removal Review Authority has recognized, a person without a nationality may be 'forced to lead a marginalised, impoverished and insecure existence'.[246] Indeed, the UNHCR explains that the impact of such an existence may have intergenerational impacts, in observing 'the fact of their marginalization—from education and livelihood, as well as restrictions on movement—may constitute the worst of the daily persecution [stateless persons] suffer, because they may create intergenerational extreme poverty and prevent stateless people from achieving any sort of economic stability'.[247]

A negative determination in cases involving socio-economic persecution in refugee law is sometimes based on the view that such rights are 'third category rights',[248] a concept that mistakenly implies that socio-economic rights are normatively inferior, and hence their violation less significant, than 'category 1 and 2' civil and political rights.[249] Yet this categorical and hierarchical approach to rights is out of step with contemporary international human rights norms that recognize the interdependence of all rights and the lack of a normative hierarchy.[250] Indeed, the hierarchical approach to determining persecution in refugee law has been explicitly criticized in refugee jurisprudence in some jurisdictions.[251]

---

[242] *Younes* (n 237) [12].   [243] ibid, [13].   [244] ibid, [12].

[245] See e.g., Foster, *International Refugee Law and Socio-Economic Rights* (n 235); Hathaway and Foster, *The Law of Refugee Status 2* (n 3) Chapter 3.2.3.

[246] *Removal Appeal No 45942* [2007] NZRRA 69 (31 August 2007) [30]. This determination did not involve the *Refugee Convention*, but rather a claim to remain based on 'exceptional humanitarian considerations': see at [3].

[247] UNHCR, 'Guidelines on Representing Stateless Persons' (n 142) 18.

[248] *KK* (n 68) [106].

[249] There also appears to be an element of 'floodgates' reasoning in some cases; see e.g., *HS* (n 154) [224].

[250] Foster, *International Refugee Law and Socio-Economic Rights* (n 235) 136–41.

[251] In *Refugee Appeal No 75221* [2005] NZRSAA 289 (23 September 2005), the New Zealand RSAA observed that 'overly rigid categorization of rights in terms of hierarchies are therefore to be avoided': at [81].

There are, of course, numerous examples of progressive decision-making in which the potentially devastating consequences of the denial of socio-economic rights has been recognized and acknowledged. For instance, in *El Himri v Ashcroft*, the US Court of Appeal for the Ninth Circuit noted that, following the Gulf War, Palestinians who remained in Kuwait were 'denied the right to work, to go to school, or even obtain drinking water'.[252] Accordingly,

[e]ven if the El Himris were fortunate enough to avoid violent persecution upon their return to Kuwait, they would not be able to avoid the state-sponsored economic discrimination that has been enacted against Palestinians living in Kuwait since the end of the Gulf War. This court has held that extreme economic discrimination constitutes persecution.[253]

In another positive decision involving the same situation, the US Court of Appeals for the Sixth Circuit observed that following the Gulf War, the applicant's father 'was not allowed to return to work because he was a Palestinian who was perceived as supporting Iraq when he continued teaching during the war. Indeed, the Kuwaitis engaged in a general campaign to prohibit Palestinians from working, attending school, buying food, obtaining water or obtaining drivers' licenses.'[254]

While as indicated above, decisions regarding Palestinians, whether residing in refugee camps or in an urban environment, produce mixed outcomes, there are numerous decisions that rely heavily on the socio-economic deprivation suffered by such applicants in concluding that refugee status is warranted. For example, refugee status was granted in Australia to a Palestinian from Lebanon because of the restrictions placed on his 'ability to work in Lebanon which would cause him significant economic hardship and which ... would impact on his ability to financially support himself, and also the other severe discriminatory measures imposed upon him because of his Palestinian ethnicity'.[255] The Australian Tribunal found that the labour situation in Lebanon for Palestinians had not improved following the lifting of the ban of jobs available to Palestinians in 2005: '[a]lthough the applicant was able to get some education in Lebanon in the camp with the financial assistance of the UNRWA ... [his] employment opportunities are/will be severely limited in his country'.[256]

Similarly, the Canadian Tribunal found that the stateless Palestinian applicant would experience in Lebanon 'such concerted and severe discrimination, including deprivation of medical care, employment opportunities and adequate housing and food, so as to amount to persecution'.[257]

---

[252] *El Himri* (n 231) 937.
[253] ibid, citing *Baballah v Ashcroft*, 367 F 3d 1067, 1075–76 (9th Cir, 2004).
[254] *Ouda* (n 174) 453–54.   [255] *1100132* [2011] RRTA 246 (29 March 2011) [62].
[256] ibid, [60].
[257] *X v Canada (Immigration and Refugee Board)*, 2001 CanLII 26842 (CA IRB) 7. On the other hand, similar cases are found in Canada, where the Board does not accept that discrimination with regard to education, employment, or medical care, as a result of being stateless amounts to persecution, even if taken cumulatively. *X (Re)*, 2014 CanLII 81883 (CA IRB) [37] (Bidoon born and living in Kuwait); *X (Re)*, 2013 CanLII 99979 (CA IRB) [18]–[19] (stateless Palestinian in Lebanon; changes made to the employment legislation in August 2010 meant that they could make a living, at least in theory); *Canada (Minister of Citizenship and Immigration) v Hamdan*, 2006 FC 290 (6 March 2006) (Palestinian spouse of a Jordanian; foreigners, including the respondent, can obtain temporary residence permits, which

In a different context in a case decided by the US Court of Appeals for the Sixth Circuit, it was the 'sweeping limitations' on the applicant's profession as a paediatrician (i.e. the invalidation of her Russian diplomas), particularly where that profession is a highly skilled one in which the person invested education or training, that was considered to be persecution.[258]

In many cases, however, denial of socio-economic rights has not been found to amount to persecution. For instance, in a number of cases concerning stateless Faili Kurds in Iran, Australian courts have acknowledged that discrimination against Iran's Kurdish minority is widespread. However, they concluded that no matter how difficult their life might be, the threshold of persecution is not met if evidence exists of access to education and health care in Iran, to some work albeit informally (e.g. as a shepherd), and to some finances (e.g. being able to fund travel to Australia).[259] Thus, for the Australian courts/tribunals, one needs to establish that denial of social and economic rights would in the future result in 'significant economic hardship, denial of access to basic services and denial of a capacity to earn a living', threatening the applicant's capacity to subsist.[260] 'Denial' in this context is understood to mean a total lack of access to private health care,[261] education,[262] and employment (including unlawful employment).[263]

Even where an applicant may have been subjected to violations of civil and political rights as well as socio-economic deprivation, claims are not always successful. For example, in one case the applicant experienced detention and on a separate incident violence, yet these were dismissed as 'isolated acts' that did not indicate a 'pattern of human rights abuses against ethnic Russians in Estonia'.[264] In fact, 'programs existed for integrating ethnic Russians into Estonia' and no evidence existed that 'the Estonian government would decline to protect their rights because

---

give them the right to work in Jordan and travel; claims to the contrary are purely speculative: at [28], [41]); *X (Re)* 2000 (n 173).

[258] *Stserba* (n 112) 27.

[259] *SZTEO v Minister for Immigration* [2015] FCCA 2228 (21 August 2015) [8]; *SZSVT* (n 204) [12]. See also *1008868* [2011] RRTA 3 (3 January 2011) (stateless Palestinian in Lebanon who never lived in the Palestinian camps, who had access to the Lebanese education system and who was employed as a butcher).

[260] *WZAPN* (n 184) [96].

[261] *WZAPK v Minister for Immigration* [2013] FMCA 19 (22 January 2013) [23].

[262] *Poorvadi v Minister for Immigration & Multicultural Affairs* [2002] FCA 234 (13 March 2002) (stateless person with no right to live in Iran, her marriage to an Iranian was not officially recognized, her children were considered illegitimate; faced constant discrimination and harassment but the children were able to enrol at school; no persecution). See also NZ: *Refugee Appeal No 73958* (n 236) (both the father and his brother were educated to tertiary education; the children were also able to obtain education; no persecution).

[263] *SZPZI* (n 4) [37]. See also *071454724* (n 204) (stateless Palestinian in Lebanon who worked illegally in his trade for a number of years).

[264] *Protsenko v US Attorney General*, 149 Fed Appx 947 (11th Cir, 2005) [12]–[13] (hereafter *Protsenko*). United Kingdom: *S v Secretary of State for the Home Department* [2001] UKIAT 00019 ('human rights abuses committed by the police are limited in number and whilst the judicial system is still relatively weak, there is no evidence of significant corruption or bias': at [15]; legislation exists to protect the human rights of ethnic minorities, including ethnic Russians); *NA* 2005 (n 238) [24] (ethnic Palestinians are not persecuted or treated in breach of Article 3 *ECHR*, although they may be discriminated against).

of their Russian ethnicity'.[265] Hence, the treatment they feared was not persecution and refugee status was denied.

In sum, socio-economic deprivation is often the most devastating consequence of statelessness; hence refugee law's historical failure adequately to accommodate claims anchored in socio-economic deprivation has been particularly detrimental to stateless persons seeking refugee protection. However an increasing willingness by many decision-makers to fully assess such claims, particularly in light of a more sophisticated and contemporary understanding of the nature and importance of socio-economic rights, suggests that there is yet capacity for refugee law to better protect stateless persons on the move.

5.2 The impact of statelessness on children

One particularly glaring gap in analysis is in relation to the impact of statelessness on children. Although statelessness 'impacts especially negatively upon women and children',[266] in most refugee claims involving a stateless family, decision-makers fail to consider the impact of return on children independently of the adult family members. While research into the causes and ramifications of statelessness globally has increasingly identified childhood statelessness as a particularly urgent issue, this has received almost no recognition in the refugee context. The UNHCR's research reveals that for children 'not being recognized as a national of any country can create insurmountable barriers to education and adequate health care and stifle job prospects',[267] and a recent report highlights the 'devastating psychological toll of statelessness'[268] for young people. Similarly, an extensive study on stateless children by the Institute on Statelessness and Inclusion outlines in compelling detail the fact that for children the absence of nationality 'is strongly correlated with serious rights violations and profound human suffering'.[269] The impact of such deprivation is particularly acute in the case of children in light of their unique developmental needs and the often irreversible and enduring impact of childhood deprivation. As Laura van Waas and Amal de Chickera observe, 'to be stateless as a child can stunt opportunity, erode ambition and destroy the sense of self-worth'.[270] Yet, while it is increasingly accepted in refugee law jurisprudence that a child may 'apprehend a level or degree of physical or psychological harm that will not qualify as persecution in the case of an adult but which may amount to persecution when considered from

---

[265] *Protsenko* (n 264) [14].

[266] Conklin, *Statelessness* (n 216) 117. See also 118–21 for specific examples of the impact of statelessness on children.

[267] UNHCR, 'I Am Here, I Belong' (n 137) 1.

[268] ibid. See also Institute on Statelessness and Inclusion ('ISI'), *The World's Stateless: Children* (Wolf Legal Publishers 2017) (hereafter ISI, *The World's Stateless: Children*).

[269] Jacqueline Bhabha, 'The Importance of Nationality for Children' in ISI, *The World's Stateless Children* (Wolf Legal Publishers 2017) 112, 118.

[270] Laura van Waas and Amal de Chickera, 'Chapter 7: Introduction' in ISI, *The World's Stateless: Children* (Wolf Legal Publishers 2017) 109.

the perspective of a child',[271] this insight has generally not been applied to refugee claims by stateless persons and in this regard represents an anomalous approach that is ripe for reconsideration by refugee decision-makers.

There is some limited guidance available, for example, the UNHCR's 'Guidelines on International Protection: Child Asylum Claims' includes in its list of child-specific forms of persecution, 'stateless children as a result of loss of nationality and attendant rights'.[272] The Guidelines further observe that 'a violation of an economic, social or cultural right may amount to persecution'[273] and that this 'could for instance, be the case where children with disabilities or stateless children lack access to birth registration and, as a result, are excluded from education, health care and other services'.[274] This analysis was applied in a recent Australian Tribunal decision that overturned the initial rejection of the application for refugee status of a stateless woman from Lebanon and her stateless son. The Tribunal observed that due to Lebanon's discriminatory nationality laws, the mother was unable to pass on her nationality to her son, who was thus stateless. The Tribunal found that the child 'will be denied education, health care, residence, and work rights in Lebanon, as well as civil rights associated with nationality, such as the right to vote'.[275] The Tribunal found that 'the denial of health care and a right to work in Lebanon threaten the [child's] capacity to subsist (the test in Australian law for persecution)'.[276] The Tribunal further found that 'the discrimination and restrictions the [child] will face in Lebanon amount to an intolerable situation for him there and should be considered serious harm [and hence persecution]'.[277]

In our view, consistent with this progressive Australian decision, closer attention needs to be paid by advocates and decision-makers to the distinct position of stateless or potentially stateless children should they be returned to their own or their parents' country of origin.

5.3 Stateless persons as rights holders

Another particular challenge that has presented in some cases involving socio-economic rights deprivation in relation to stateless persons is reminiscent of the challenge identified earlier in relation to civil and political rights, namely the notion that as non-citizens, stateless applicants do not have an entitlement to socio-economic rights in their country of origin, and hence cannot claim to fear persecution on that basis.

---

[271] Jason Pobjoy, *The Child in International Refugee Law* (CUP 2017) 117. See also Hathaway and Foster, *The Law of Refugee Status 2* (n 3); Foster, *International Refugee Law and Socio-Economic Rights* (n 235) 201–14. For a particularly compelling articulation of the correct approach in refugee law, see *Canada (Minister of Citizenship and Immigration) v Patel* [2009] 2 FCR 196.
[272] UNHCR, 'Guidelines on International Protection: Child Asylum Claims under Articles 1(A)2 and 1(F) of the 1951 Convention and/or 1967 Protocol relating to the Status of Refugees' (22 December 2009) UN Doc HCR/GIP/09/08, para 18.
[273] ibid, para 35.   [274] ibid.   [275] *1617142* (n 62) [63].   [276] ibid, [66].
[277] ibid. The Tribunal found that the reason for the harm was membership 'of two particular social groups, namely Lebanese children with a foreign father, and children born out of wedlock in Lebanon': at [71].

In some cases, decision-makers have queried, but not reached a definitive view on the scope of protection that should be afforded to stateless persons in their home country. For example, in assessing the refugee claim of a stateless Palestinian family from Jordan, the New Zealand RSAA observed, in relation to the children, that 'being the dependent children of a Gaza-Palestinian, [they] do not have any right to acquire the citizenship status of their mother', a Jordanian citizen,[278] hence they would remain stateless. The refugee claim was based on the fact that, inter alia, 'as stateless Palestinians in Jordan, each will face discrimination in accessing public services such as health and education'.[279] However, the Tribunal observed that 'caution here is warranted',[280] because '[t]he question arises as to what is the obligation of Jordan under the ICESCR [*International Covenant on Economic, Social and Cultural Rights*] towards the husband and the children as non-nationals'.[281] The Tribunal cited academic authority that suggested that 'the ICESCR does not embody a general norm of non-discrimination against aliens',[282] although also observed that '[t]his is not to say that foreign nationals are without any rights whatsoever'.[283] Ultimately, the Tribunal found it was not necessary to 'resolve the extent to which State parties owe obligations under the ICESCR to non nationals',[284] on the basis that the claim in relation to such rights was 'entirely speculative' in the case of the children.

In other cases, decision-makers have reached firmer (negative) conclusions, in some cases relying on Article 2(3) *ICESCR*, which provides that, '[d]eveloping countries, with due regard to human rights and their national economy, may determine to what extent they would guarantee the economic rights recognized in the present Covenant to non-nationals'. In the United Kingdom, the Tribunal has applied this provision in the context of Lebanon to conclude that 'the treatment of aliens or stateless persons different from and less favourable than that accorded by the state to its own citizens, does not of itself amount to persecution'.[285] This decision is open to criticism, however, on the basis that the correct interpretation of Article 2(3) was not analysed by the UK Tribunal at all, other than to call into question the applicant's reliance on a UN Special Rapporteur's view that 'Article 2(3) must be narrowly construed'.[286] The Tribunal observed that it was 'not sure to what extent a report of the UN Special Rapporteur can be said to qualify or give binding guidance on the meaning of a provision in an international agreement',[287] yet did not consider the views of the UN Committee that *can* give such guidance or otherwise examine the issue.

---

[278] *Refugee Appeal No 73952* [2005] NZRSAA 145 (26 May 2005) [63] (hereafter *Refugee Appeal No 73952*).
[279] ibid, [66].   [280] ibid, [67].   [281] ibid, [69].
[282] ibid, [70], citing Richard B Lillich, *The Human Rights of Aliens in Contemporary International Law* (Manchester University Press 1984) 47–48.
[283] *Refugee Appeal No 73952* (n 278) [71].   [284] ibid, [72].
[285] *KK* (n 68) [104]. This reasoning was applied also in *MM and FH* (n 68) [143]–[144].
[286] *KK* (n 68) [103].   [287] ibid, [104].

The Committee on Economic, Social and Cultural Rights has strongly affirmed the overarching principle of non-discrimination, in noting, in its General Comment No 20 on non-discrimination in economic, social, and cultural rights, that:

The ground of nationality should not bar access to Covenant rights, e.g. all children within a State, including those with an undocumented status, have a right to receive education and access to adequate food and affordable health care. The Covenant rights apply to everyone including non-nationals, such as refugees, asylum-seekers, *stateless persons*, migrant workers and victims of international trafficking, regardless of legal status and documentation.[288]

While this is clearly subject to Article 2(3), the *travaux préparatoires* of the *ICESCR*— a legitimate source of treaty interpretation[289]—reveals that Article 2(3) was inserted 'to allow former colonies which had recently gained independence, and whose economies were consequently dominated by the influence of non-nationals, to protect the position of their nationals'.[290] Hence it is indeed well accepted, as indicated by the UN Special Rapporteur cited above, that it 'should be interpreted narrowly'.[291] On its terms it is limited to economic rights—essentially employment—and, in any event, has never sought to be invoked by any country.[292]

In our view therefore, Article 2(3) cannot legitimately be relied upon to reject the refugee applications of stateless persons whose claim involves a violation of socio-economic rights regardless of the economic status of their country of origin. In other words, any assessment of the well-founded fear of persecution on return should be assessed in the same way as in any case—that is by reference to whether the potential harm amounts to persecution—and not by reference to an (incorrect) assumption that stateless persons are not entitled to enjoy human rights in their own country and therefore cannot be at risk of persecution for the purposes of refugee law.

In sum, in our view, the *Refugee Convention* is capable of accommodating a wider range of claims by stateless applicants than has been accepted by national courts to date. A greater understanding of the discrimination at the heart of the predicament of many stateless applicants, and that they are indeed rights holders at international law, would produce a more principled and inclusive application of the *Convention*.

In the final Part of this chapter we turn briefly to consider claims by stateless applicants for protection under complementary protection regimes that are based not on the *Refugee Convention* but other *non-refoulement* obligations at international law.

---

[288] UN Committee on Economic, Social and Cultural Rights, 'General Comment No 20: Non-Discrimination in Economic, Social and Cultural Rights (Art. 2, Para. 2, of the International Covenant on Economic, Social and Cultural Rights)' (2 July 2009) UN Doc E/C.12/GC/20 , para 30 (emphasis added). The General Comment footnotes Article 2(3) *ICESCR*, noting that this is an exception.

[289] *Vienna Convention on the Law of Treaties* (adopted 22 May 1969, entered into force 27 January 1980) 1155 UNTS 331, art 32.

[290] See Ben Saul, David Kinley, and Jacqueline Mowbray, *The International Covenant on Economic, Social and Cultural Rights: Commentary, Cases and Materials* (OUP 2014) 215 (hereafter Saul, Kinley, and Mowbray, *The International Covenant on Economic, Social and Cultural Rights*).

[291] UN Commission on Human Rights, 'Note Verbale Dated 5 December 1986 from the Permanent Mission of the Netherlands to the United Nations Office at Geneva Addressed to the Centre for Human Rights' (8 January 1987) UN Doc E/CN.4/1987/17, para 43.

[292] Saul, Kinley and Mowbray, *The International Covenant on Economic, Social and Cultural Rights* (n 290) 214.

Part 6: Complementary/Subsidiary Protection[293]

Several jurisdictions, including Member States of the European Union, Australia, New Zealand, the United States, and Canada, have in place provisions for complementary or subsidiary protection alongside those provisions for refugee status incorporating the 1951 *Refugee Convention*; these are based on the *ICCPR*, the *Convention Against Torture* ('*CAT*'), the *ECHR*, or codifying state practice.[294] How these provisions apply to stateless asylum applicants has so far remained largely unexplored. This section examines the relatively scarce case law on the subject and identifies areas for future judicial exploration and application.

With the exception of one case in which the Australian Tribunal considered that 'the complementary protection provisions did not apply to the applicant' because he was stateless,[295] the general position of tribunals and courts is that stateless persons are eligible for complementary/subsidiary protection provided the necessary requirements are met.

In some respects, these requirements are less stringent than under the *Refugee Convention*. Indeed, a *Refugee Convention* nexus or reason for the harm feared is not required for complementary protection.[296] Thus, in France subsidiary protection status for stateless persons is used where a risk of treatment contrary to Article 3 *ECHR* upon return exists but there is no *Convention* ground.[297]

Furthermore, the threshold of 'degrading treatment or punishment' in the *ECHR* and *ICCPR* appears to be lower (at least in theory) than that of persecution, as it includes, for instance, hardship.[298] However, in practice, persecution (under the *Refugee Convention*) and serious harm (under complementary/subsidiary protection) is often equated, which can lead to two results: (1) undocumented Bidoon from Kuwait, Kurds from Syria, or stateless Palestinians from Iraq, having their

---

[293] The EU and its Member States use the term 'subsidiary', whereas in other parts of the world the term 'complementary' is preferred.

[294] EU: Qualification Directive 2011/95/EU 2011 (n 36) art 15. Australia: *Migration Act 1958* (Cth), s 36. New Zealand: *Immigration Act 2009*, s 131. United States: two grounds (withholding of removal under the Immigration and Nationality Act 1965, and withholding of removal under the *Convention Against Torture* (adopted 10 December 1984, entered into force 26 June 1987) 1465 UNTS 85) (hereafter *CAT*). Canada: *Immigration and Refugee Protection Act*, SC 2001, c 27, s 97(1).

[295] Australia: *1311115* [2013] RRTA 822 (25 November 2013) [29], [68]. Note that no explanation was given as to why complementary protection provisions should not apply to a stateless person. However, in *1407022 (Refugee)* [2015] AATA 3606 (6 November 2015) (hereafter *1407022*), the Administrative Appeals Tribunal of Australia explained, 'The Tribunal is not satisfied that the applicant is stateless, and therefore it is not satisfied there is a real risk of the applicant facing significant harm *on this basis*': at [52] (emphasis added).

[296] Australia: *SZSFK v Minister for Immigration* [2013] FCCA 7 (16 May 2013) [90], [92], [97]. In the UK, a clear sequential approach is applied: the courts first consider applications on the basis of refugee protection, and if this fails, they move on to consider the application against human rights law, see e.g., *KA v Secretary of State for the Home Department* [2008] UKAIT 00042.

[297] Commission de Recours des Réfugiés (CRR)—which was the former CNDA, decision no°567575, 30 August 2006. In other cases, statelessness status was granted instead: Conseil d'État [French Administrative Court] ('CE'), decision no°216121, 29 December 2000.

[298] Canada: *Abeleira v Canada (Citizenship and Immigration)*, 2015 FC 1340.

appeals against decisions refusing them refugee status and subsidiary protection status normally allowed;[299] or (2) some tribunals struggling to recognize that the criteria for complementary/subsidiary protection are met once the refugee criteria have failed (e.g. in Australia[300] or in the United Kingdom[301]). And indeed, scarce are the cases granting complementary/subsidiary protection where refugee protection has failed.

The requirements for complementary/subsidiary protection are also more stringent than those for refugee 'protection. Indeed, removal must be imminent before a violation of a provision of the *ICCPR, CAT,* or the *ECHR* upon return can be found (i.e. the applicant needs to be a 'victim').[302] As a result, the issue of whether serious obstacles exist to re-admission remains central to the question of whether there is a real risk of serious harm.[303] This is not the case in refugee law, where an inability to return does not, in the case of a stateless person, exclude the possibility of protection under the *Refugee Convention.*[304]

Finally, it is important to remember that complementary protection provides protection against *refoulement* only; it does not guarantee a legal status (e.g. refugee status under the *Refugee Convention* or subsidiary protection status under the EU Qualification Directive[305]), unless this exists in domestic law.

Be that as it may, protection against *refoulement* in international human rights law is absolute, which means that no contracting parties to the *ECHR, ICCPR,* or *CAT* can return a stateless person to a country where they may be tortured (or subjected to other ill-treatment), even if they constitute a risk to the national security or public order of the country or community in which they seek protection. In contrast, Article 1F of the *Refugee Convention* (or Article 12 of the 2011 EU Qualification Directive) allows for exclusion from refugee status on certain grounds. Article 33(2) further permits states to '*refouler*' a person to a country where their life or freedom

---

[299] *NM* (n 47) [100], [116]; *HE* (n 221); *SA* (n 192); *NA* 2008 (n 192).

[300] *1407022* (n 295) [52]–[55].

[301] *MA (Palestinian Territories)* (n 154) [52]; *Secretary of State for the Home Department v AS* [2002] UKIAT 05943 [4]. Note that British courts and tribunals follow the lead of the European Court of Human Rights ('ECtHR') on the interpretation of inhuman or degrading treatment in art 3 *ECHR*; this interpretation has considerably evolved in recent years and now applies to asylum seekers (as vulnerable people wholly dependent on state support) and children (as extremely vulnerable people) in situations of extreme poverty, serious deprivation, or want incompatible with human dignity, see *MSS v Belgium* (2011) 53 EHRR 2; *Tarakhel v Switzerland* (2015) 60 EHRR 28.

[302] *Optional Protocol to the International Covenant on Civil and Political Rights* (adopted 16 December 1966, entered into force 23 March 1976) 999 UNTS 171, art 1; *CAT* (n 294) art 22(1); *Convention for the Protection of Human Rights and Fundamental Freedoms* (adopted 4 November 1950, entered into force 3 September 1953) 213 UNTS 221, art 34(1) (hereafter *ECHR*). UN Human Rights Committee, 'Communication No 35/1978: *Aumeeruddy-Cziffra v Mauritius*' (9 April 1981) UN Doc CCPR/C/OP/1 at 67, para 9.2; UN Committee Against Torture, 'Communication No 96/1997: *AD v Netherlands*' (12 *November* 1999) UN Doc CAT/C/23/D/96/1997, paras 6.2, 7.3; *Vijayanathan v France* (1993) 15 EHRR 62, applied in *BA* (n 16) [48]. See also Adrienne Anderson, Michelle Foster, Hélène Lambert, and Jane McAdam, 'Imminence in Refugee and Human Rights Law: A Misplaced Notion for International Protection (2019) 68 *International and Comparative Law Quarterly* 111.

[303] *YL* (n 151) [64].

[304] See Chapter 4, Part 1.2 'Inability to return as exclusion from refugee status?'.

[305] Note that the *ECHR* has been interpreted as guaranteeing protection against *refoulement* but not necessarily a status akin to that under the Qualification Directive 2011/95/EU (n 36).

may be threatened if they constitute a danger to the security of the country or the community of that country. No such limitations exist in international human rights law treaties.[306] For instance, in *Auad v Bulgaria*, a case involving a stateless person of Palestinian origin who had been granted humanitarian protection but was subsequently issued with an order for expulsion for being a suspected terrorist, the European Court of Human Rights ('ECtHR') noted that national security considerations were irrelevant; the relevant issue was whether his expulsion would give rise to a real risk of ill-treatment.[307]

Thus, provisions protecting against torture, inhuman or degrading treatment, or punishment are highly relevant in the context of the expulsion of stateless persons. The Austrian Constitutional Court has ruled that where a person is stateless and his only real ties are with the country in which he was born and has lived all his life, legislation and/or practice that would allow the expulsion of such a person, on grounds of criminal conviction, to the country of nationality of his mother or father would violate Article 3 *ECHR*, and would remain unlawful until such a time as the person concerned has managed to acquire the nationality of another country.[308] Similar rulings exist in Belgium, where orders to leave the territory have been annulled on the ground that being stateless constitutes 'exceptional circumstances' against the rule that a person must normally apply for a residence permit from their country of origin or residence abroad.[309]

In most cases where complementary/subsidiary protection was discussed, the treatment faced by stateless applicants was found not to meet the requisite threshold, namely real risk of serious harm. These cases can be grouped into three categories.

The first group concerns cases in Australia where the treatment feared must amount to 'extreme humiliation', which is defined in s 5(1) of the *Migration Act 1958* (Cth) as '[a]n act or omission that causes, and is intended to cause, extreme humiliation which is unreasonable'.[310] As a result, the discriminatory treatment faced by stateless Bidoon in Iraq or Kuwait was found not to amount to 'significant harm', even when taken cumulatively.[311] The Federal Circuit Court of Australia further accepted that '*in some circumstances* discrimination on the grounds of race could be inherently degrading and capable of amounting to extreme humiliation',[312] begging

---

[306] Although art 17 of the EU Qualification Directive 2011/95/EU (n 36) provides for exclusion clauses similar to those in the *Refugee Convention* (art 1F) for persons seeking subsidiary protection (e.g. on grounds similar to *ECHR* grounds)—thereby contradicting the very nature of art 3 *ECHR*.

[307] ECtHR: *Auad v Bulgaria*, Application No 46390/10 (11 January 2012) [100]–[101]. The Court concluded that in view of 'the lack of a legal framework providing adequate safeguards ... there are substantial grounds for believing that the applicant risks a violation of his rights under Article 3': at [107].

[308] Verfassungsgerichtshof [Austrian Constitutional Court], decision n°U2131/2012, 6 March 2014.

[309] CCE, *X v l'Etat belge*, arrêt n°157845, 8 December 2015; CCE, *X v l'Etat belge*, arrêt n°155732, 29 October 2015; CCE, *X v l'Etat belge*, arrêt n°142096, 27 March 2015; CCE, *X v l'Etat belge*, arrêt n°134185, 28 November 2014.

[310] *SZSVT* (n 204) [24].

[311] *MZZQN v Minister for Immigration* [2014] FCCA 2886 (10 December 2014) (no fear of arbitrary deprivation of life); *1303526* (n 220) (no real risk of the death penalty); *1218580* [2013] RRTA 279 (2 April 2013) (verbal abuse or a restriction on his access to Sunni mosques did not amount to cruel or inhuman treatment or punishment, or to degrading treatment or punishment).

[312] *SZSVT* (n 204) [82] (emphasis added).

the question why it failed to recognize this to be the case in *all* circumstances, considering that the norm against racial discrimination has been recognized by the International Court of Justice to be an obligation *erga omnes*.[313]

The second group concerns stateless applicants who are found not to meet the requisite threshold to constitute serious harm in the event of an expulsion because they fled a situation of generalized violence.[314] In Europe, only the most extreme cases of general violence would give rise to such treatment.[315]

The third group concerns applicants in the United States who, if they fail in their application for asylum, then necessarily fail to satisfy the more stringent standard of proof for withholding of removal under the *Immigration and Nationality Act* (which corresponds to Article 33 of the *Refugee Convention*).[316] In addition, because applicants usually rely on the same evidence to support their claim of protection under the *CAT* (i.e. risk of torture), these also fail because the US courts require that 'it is "more likely than not" that [the applicant] herself would be subject to such treatment'.[317]

A particularly important point is that, as highlighted in Chapter 3, no international court has so far recognized arbitrary deprivation of nationality itself or indeed statelessness, as amounting to inhuman or degrading treatment under Article 3 *ECHR*.[318] Rather, related acts such as detention or risk of expulsion that could be connected to statelessness have been found to violate Article 3 *ECHR*.[319] The same is true of national courts.[320] This is surprising in light of the increasing recognition both of the international human rights law constraints on state discretion in relation to the denial or deprivation of nationality and the very significant consequences of being denied or deprived of a nationality. Hence, in our view, there is great scope for strategic litigation based on Article 3 *ECHR*, for example to explore the ambit of protection that may be afforded stateless persons from return under complementary protection regimes.

---

[313] *Case concerning the Barcelona Traction, Light and Power Company, Limited (Belgium v Spain)* (Second Phase) [1970] ICJ Rep 3, 32 [33]–[34].

[314] Canada: *X (Re)*, 2015 CarswellNat 4673; *X (Re)*, 2013 CanLII 100828 (CA IRB)—appellant not personally targeted.

[315] France: CE, decision no°363181, 5 November 2014; United Kingdom: *HS* (n 154) [219], referring to *NA v United Kingdom* (2009) 48 EHRR 15.

[316] *Aburuwaida* (n 208); *Maksimova* (n 102).

[317] *Almuhtaseb v Gonzales*, 453 F 3d 743, 749 (6th Cir, 2006) [22]; *Agha v Holder*, 743 F 3d 609 (8th Cir, 2014) [19]; *El Assadi* (n 236) 487.

[318] As discussed in Chapter 3, the ECtHR has so far preferred to assess such acts under art 8 *ECHR* (private and family life): See Chapter 3, Part 2.3.1.2 'Arbitrary deprivation of nationality'.

[319] See Chapter 3, Part 2.3.1.2 'Arbitrary deprivation of nationality'.

[320] For instance, in *AK* (n 153) '[i]t was submitted that the denial of re-entry to the Occupied Territories by reason of the appellant's Palestinian identity was capable of constituting degrading treatment contrary to Article 3'. However, Mr Williams (acting on behalf of the Appellant) accepted that 'the point would stand or fall with that under the Refugee Convention' and that it was not argued before the UK Tribunal, hence the Court did not pursue the point: at [49].

Part 7: Conclusion

In this chapter we have examined in depth the question that is widely understood to constitute the heart of the refugee claim, namely whether the harm feared on return constitutes persecution for the purposes of the *Refugee Convention*. We have analysed both harm that is particular to stateless persons, connected to the lack of nationality itself, and harm that also befalls a wider range of applicants, analysing the latter through the prism of the particular challenges that stateless applicants face in litigating their refugee claims. Our analysis of jurisprudence across a wide range of jurisdictions suggests that while some courts have taken into account wider developments in international law, especially human rights law, to assess properly the predicament of stateless persons, there has been a tendency in many cases for decision-makers to dismiss claims based on incorrect assumptions about the entitlement of stateless persons to enjoy a wide range of human rights. There is therefore in our view great scope for more progressive and principled application of the *Refugee Convention* to stateless persons, consonant both with developments in the wider system of international law and with the international community's greater understanding and insight into the human rights violations faced by stateless persons today.

6

Denial of Refugee Protection for Stateless Persons

Cessation of and Exclusion from Protection

In previous chapters we examined various elements of the 'inclusion clause' in the *Convention relating to the Status of Refugees* ('*Refugee Convention*') from the perspective of stateless applicants seeking recognition of refugee status. This chapter, by contrast, investigates the potential grounds on which a stateless person may be denied refugee protection because (1) protection is no longer required (Article 1C); (2) protection is not necessary, due to alternative protection options (Articles 1D and 1E); or (3) protection is not warranted due to the previous conduct of the applicant (Article 1F).

These issues of cessation and exclusion have been the subject of voluminous jurisprudence and refugee law scholarship over recent years. However, there is very little case law or literature that has examined these issues specifically from the perspective of stateless persons. In some respects, this is because similar issues may arise regardless of the nationality of the applicant. For example, if the reasons for the original fear of persecution have 'ceased to exist', and the refugee is able safely to return home, then refugee status may no longer be warranted regardless of the nationality of the applicant. Similarly, where there are serious reasons for considering that an applicant has committed a war crime, then again nationality is irrelevant to the conclusion that they must not benefit from refugee protection.

Accordingly, this chapter does not attempt to traverse in any comprehensive manner the various debates and controversies that remain in relation to the cessation and exclusion clauses. Rather, we highlight those issues that may be particularly relevant to claims by stateless persons. In Part 1 we consider the circumstances in which a stateless person's need for refugee protection may cease. In Part 2 we turn to Article 1D of the *Refugee Convention*, which in light of its intended application to Palestinians is highly pertinent in any discussion of stateless refugees. That Part also briefly considers Article 1E, while Part 3 examines the relevance of Article 1F to the refugee claims of stateless persons.

International Refugee Law and the Protection of Stateless Persons. Michelle Foster and Hélène Lambert.
© Michelle Foster and Hélène Lambert 2019. Published 2019 by Oxford University Press.

Part 1: The Cessation of Refugee Status for Stateless Persons

Refugee status is not conceived as necessarily permanent; rather, it is intended to provide transitional (or surrogate) protection until a permanent solution can be found (through voluntary repatriation, resettlement, or local integration).[1] In the context of the *Refugee Convention*, Article 1C lists (exhaustively) six clauses for cessation of refugee status.[2] The first four are premised upon changes in the individual refugee's circumstances: (1) re-availment of national protection; (2) re-acquisition of nationality; (3) acquisition of a new nationality; and (4) re-establishment in the country of origin. The final two clauses, (5) and (6), involve fundamental changes in the country of origin's circumstances that have the effect of removing the fear of persecution and of guaranteeing protection on return to that country.

Not all of the cessation clauses in the *Refugee Convention* are relevant to stateless persons; according to the United Nations High Commissioner for Refugees ('UNHCR'), both clauses (4) and (6) in Article 1C apply to stateless persons.[3] We nevertheless start by discussing briefly the clauses in Article 1C which are unlikely to apply to stateless persons and why that is so, namely clauses (1), (2), (3), and (5),[4] before examining the two clauses that apply squarely to persons without a nationality.

Article 1C(1) applies to persons who have voluntarily re-availed themselves of the protection of their country *of nationality*,[5] hence it is generally not applicable

---

[1] United Nations High Commissioner for Refugees (UNHCR), 'The Cessation Clauses: Guidelines on Their Application' (Geneva April 1999) para 1 (hereafter UNHCR, 'Guidelines on Cessation').

[2] Note that cessation clauses also exist in the Statute of the Office of the UNHCR and the *1969 Organisation of African Unity ('OAU') Convention Governing the Specific Aspects of Refugee Problems in Africa*—to read about these issues, see Joan Fitzpatrick and Rafael Bonoan, 'Cessation of Refugee Protection' in Erika Feller, Volker Türk, and Frances Nicholson (eds), *Refugee Protection in International Law: UNHCR's Global Consultations on International Protection* (CUP 2003) 491 (hereafter Fitzpatrick and Bonoan, 'Cessation of Refugee Protection').

[3] UNHCR, 'Handbook and Guidelines on Procedures and Criteria for Determining Refugee Status' (Geneva December 2011) UN Doc HCR/1P/4/ENG/REV.3, paras 133, 137 (hereafter UNHCR, 'Handbook on Refugee Status').

[4] These clauses are nevertheless important in compelling states of origin and other states 'to address any problems of statelessness in the context of attaining a durable solution, be it voluntary repatriation, local integration or resettlement': Laura van Waas, *Nationality Matters: Statelessness under International Law* (Intersentia 2008) 182.

[5] A consensus exists that art 1C(1) is not to apply when a refugee returns to her or his country. According to James Hathaway and Michelle Foster, 'The purpose of Art. 1C(1) is to withdraw refugee status where there is evidence of diplomatic or consular protection'; return is insufficient. Hence, art 1C(1) will rarely be applicable: James Hathaway and Michelle Foster, *The Law of Refugee Status* (2nd edn, CUP 2014) 469–70 (hereafter Hathaway and Foster, *The Law of Refugee Status 2*). Guy Goodwin-Gill and Jane McAdam, on the other hand, recognize that possession of a national passport *and* a visit in the country of origin may suffice but that account must be taken of 'All the circumstances of the contact between the individual and the authorities of the country of origin': Guy S Goodwin-Gill and Jane McAdam, *The Refugee in International Law* (3rd edn, OUP 2007) 136–37 (hereafter Goodwin-Gill and McAdam, *The Refugee in International Law*). As for Atle Grahl-Madsen, what matters is 'the normalization of the relationship between the State and individual': Atle Grahl-Madsen, *The Status of Refugees in International Law*, vol 1 (A W Sijthoff 1966) 384.

to stateless persons. Likewise, Article 1C(5) does not apply to stateless persons as it expressly refers to 'the protection of the country *of his nationality*'.[6]

Article 1C(2) is similar to Article 1C(1) and covers 'a narrow subset of refugees' who 'having lost' their nationality whilst enjoying refugee status, decide to 'voluntarily re-acquire it'.[7] Whilst the terms 'having lost' are sufficiently vague to include at least withdrawal of nationality occurring by operation of the law,[8] the term 'has … re-acquired it' are unambiguous: Article 1C(2) only applies once the individual in question *has* the nationality that s/he had lost,[9] and therefore excludes possible scenarios of inchoate nationality.[10] The reference to the acquisition occurring 'voluntarily' ensures that a nationality that is imposed on an individual against her or his will cannot form the basis of a cessation of refugee status.[11]

As in the case of Article 1C(2), Article 1C(3) contemplates situations where the individual '*has* acquired a new nationality, and enjoys the protection of the country of his new nationality'[12] and is therefore no longer in need of international protection.[13] Once again, the use of the past tense ('has acquired') dictates that an individual *has been* granted nationality, not that he or she may possess a mere entitlement to such nationality. In addition, any such new nationality must be effective, i.e. it must guarantee at least the right to return to and reside in the 'new' country.[14] Only once the individual *has* acquired the new nationality (most commonly that of her country of refuge through naturalization) and *enjoys* the protection of her or his new country, may cessation of refugee status apply.[15]

---

[6] *Convention relating to the Status of Refugees* (adopted 28 July 1951, entered into force 22 April 1954) 189 UNTS 137 art 1C(5) (emphasis added) (hereafter *Refugee Convention*).

[7] Hathaway and Foster, *The Law of Refugee Status 2* (n 5) 471.

[8] See *Convention relating to the Status of Stateless Persons* (adopted 28 September 1954, entered into force 6 June 1960) 360 UNTS 117, art 1 (hereafter *1954 Convention*); *Convention on the Reduction of Statelessness* (adopted 30 August 1961, entered into force 13 December 1975) 989 UNTS 175, arts 7–8 (hereafter *1961 Convention*).

[9] Eric Fripp, *Nationality and Statelessness in the International Law of Refugee Status* (Hart 2016) 336 (hereafter Fripp, *Nationality and Statelessness*).

[10] See Chapter 4, Part 2.6.1.

[11] UNHCR, 'Handbook on Refugee Status' (n 3) para 128. Goodwin-Gill and McAdam, *The Refugee in International Law* (n 5) 138.

[12] *Refugee Convention* (n 6) art 1C(3) (emphasis added).

[13] UNHCR, 'Handbook on Refugee Status' (n 3) para 129.

[14] Goodwin-Gill and McAdam, *The Refugee in International Law* (n 5) 138; Hathaway and Foster, *The Law of Refugee Status 2* (n 5) 498.

[15] It is interesting to note that in the context of the *1954 Convention*, a person ceases to be entitled to protection as a stateless person if they 'are recognized by the competent authorities of the country in which they have taken residence as having the rights and obligations which are attached to the possession of the nationality of that country': *1954 Convention* (n 8) art 1(2)(ii). The UNHCR 'Handbook on Protection of Stateless Persons' does not address art 1(2); however, it does explain that: 'If an individual recognised as stateless subsequently acquires or re-acquires the nationality of another State, for instance because of a change in its nationality laws, he or she will cease to be stateless in terms of the 1954 Convention': UNHCR, 'Handbook on Protection of Stateless Persons' (Geneva 2014) para 149 (hereafter UNHCR, 'Handbook on Stateless Persons'). See also Budislav Vukas, 'International Instruments Dealing with the Status of Stateless Persons and of Refugees' (1972) 8 Revue Belge de Droit International 143: 'statelessness occurs and ceases not on the ground of mere change of circumstance, but because an internal legal order designates some facts as legally relevant to the loss or acquisition of nationality': at 143; Carol Batchelor, 'The 1954 Convention relating to the Status of

In our view, the lack of the word 'voluntarily' in Article 1C(3) should not distract from the purposive and compelling interpretation that a new nationality should not generally be considered as being acquired if it was against the will of the individual in question. This is confirmed by the words '*and enjoys the protection* of the country of his new nationality',[16] pointing to the existence of a genuine link between the host country and the stateless refugee that would assume consent on the part of the recipient of nationality. This is the position of most commentators[17] and the UNHCR 'Guidelines on Cessation',[18] and is supported by the drafting history of Article 1C(3),[19] and the text of Article 34 of the *Refugee Convention* (which merely imposes on states a duty to promote naturalization, not to impose it on refugees).

In our view, while the text does not on its face require that the acquisition be 'voluntary', an interpretation that permitted withdrawal of refugee status where a nationality has been imposed would be overly harsh in a cessation context, where the stakes are clearly very high for the individual concerned and where voluntariness is required in the cognate circumstances in Articles 1C(1), (2), and (4).[20] Furthermore, practices of automatic acquisition of nationality are traditionally found in countries where women automatically acquire their husband's nationality upon marriage; such practices have become questionable under the international human rights law framework, including prohibitions on gender discrimination, as discussed in Chapter 3.[21] The 'right to opt' for a nationality for persons who have appropriate connections with a state and who would otherwise be stateless is further entrenched in the International Law Commission (ILC) *Draft Articles on Nationality of Natural Persons in Relation to the Succession of States*.[22] In short, fair process, the high stakes involved, and principles of international human rights law

---

Stateless Persons: Implementation within the European Union Member States and Recommendations for Harmonization' (2005) 22 Refuge 31, 38 (hereafter Batchelor, 'The 1954 Convention').

[16] *Refugee Convention* (n 6) art 1C(3) (emphasis added).

[17] Goodwin-Gill and McAdam, *The Refugee in International Law* (n 5) 138. We note that Hathaway and Foster argue against the acquisition of a new nationality needing to be voluntary, 'except to the extent that volition is required in a given context to ensure the lawfulness of the grant of nationality': *The Law of Refugee Status 2* (n 5) 499.

[18] UNHCR, 'Guidelines on Cessation' (n 1) para 17: 'The enjoyment of the protection of the country of new nationality is the crucial factor. Two conditions must be fulfilled ... (i) the new nationality must be effective, in the sense that it must correspond to a genuine link between the individual and the State; and (ii) the refugee must be able and willing to avail himself or herself of the protection of the government of his or her new nationality'. See also para 18.

[19] See Hathaway and Foster, *The Law of Refugee Status 2* (n 5) 496–97.

[20] Fitzpatrick and Bonoan, 'Cessation of Refugee Protection' (n 2) 514–17, 523–27. In particular, they emphasize the importance of the process of cessation of refugee status being as formal as the process for grant of refugee status, 'given the stakes for the individual' (at 515) and that the assessment of cessation pursuant to all four clauses (1–4) must be guided by the elements of voluntariness, intent, and effective protection.

[21] ibid, 527. Such practices can indeed lead to new forms of persecution.

[22] ILC, *Draft Articles on Nationality of Natural Persons in relation to the Succession of States with Commentaries* (ILC 1999) art 11(2): 'Each State concerned shall grant a right to opt for its nationality to persons concerned who have appropriate connections with that State if those persons would otherwise become stateless as a result of the succession of States.'

(e.g. prohibition of gender discrimination),[23] all seem to mitigate against the non-voluntary, non-intentional acquisition of a nationality *in the context of cessation* of refugee status.

In the final cessation provision relating to conduct on the part of the applicant, Article 1C(4) contemplates the situation where a refugee (including a stateless refugee) 'has voluntarily re-established himself in the country which he left or outside which he remained owing to fear of persecution'. As Eric Fripp observes, reference to 'the country' without further specifying 'of nationality' or 'of former habitual residence' would be capable of including a 'territory' without a requirement of statehood.[24] However, the key point here is that in order to fall within Article 1C(4), 'the individual must have settlement on a permanent basis'.[25] As explained by the UNHCR, 'voluntary re-establishment' must be understood as 'return to the country of nationality or former habitual residence with a view to permanently residing there'; the return must be voluntary.[26] Hence, a temporary visit will not cease an individual's refugee status. The terms 'voluntarily' and 're-established' would suggest that state practices of incentivizing refugees to return may not be grounds for cessation of refugee status unless the individual's decision to return home (the country which she or he left owing to fear of persecution) was truly voluntary, and the individual becomes fully resettled in that country and able to access all basic services available to nationals (i.e. she or he is able to live a 'normal' life).[27]

In the final section of Part 1, we consider cessation where the circumstances surrounding the original need for protection have ceased. Indeed, this is the most common context in which cessation is considered by states of asylum.[28] Article 1C(6) stipulates that refugee status will cease if '[b]eing a person who has no nationality he is, because of the circumstances in connexion with which he has been recognized as a refugee have ceased to exist, able to return to the country of his former habitual residence'. Article 1C(6) is the only cessation clause dealing *exclusively* with stateless persons (Article 1C(4) contemplates persons with and without a nationality); it is the mirror of Article 1C(5) but uses language specific to stateless refugees, namely 'country of former habitual residence' instead of country of nationality, and 'return' to that country instead of protection of the country of nationality. Most of the literature and case law about change of circumstances have focused on refugees with a nationality—namely Article 1C(5)—and very little indeed has been written on Article 1C(6).[29] James Hathaway and Michelle Foster explain that for

[23] See also Chapter 4, Part 2.4, which observes that there is a trend towards non-recognition where a nationality has been imposed without consent.
[24] Fripp, *Nationality and Statelessness* (n 9) 337.
[25] Goodwin-Gill and McAdam, *The Refugee in International Law* (n 5) 139.
[26] UNHCR, 'Handbook on Refugee Status' (n 3) para 134.
[27] Hathaway and Foster, *The Law of Refugee Status 2* (n 5) 474–75.
[28] This is most commonly discussed in relation to art 1C(5), which applies to those with a nationality.
[29] The most comprehensive analysis of art 1C(6) to date can be found in Hathaway and Foster, *The Law of Refugee Status 2* (n 5) 476–99. Whilst the discussion covers both clauses (5) and (6), it provides useful insight into art 1C(6). A useful discussion can also be found in Lindsey N Kingston, 'Bringing Rwandan Refugees "Home": The Cessation Clause, Statelessness, and Forced Repatriation' (2017) 29 IJRL 417 (hereafter Kingston, 'Bringing Rwandan Refugees "Home" ').

Article 1C(6) to apply to a stateless refugee, two essential requirements must be met: first, there must be a change in circumstance ('the circumstances in connexion with which he has been recognised as a refugee have ceased to exist'); second, as a consequence of this change or because of this change, the individual in question is now 'able to return to the country of his former habitual residence'.[30]

With regard to the first requirement, it is now widely accepted that the change in circumstances must be 'fundamental, stable, and durable',[31] 'substantial and significant',[32] or of 'a significant and non-temporary nature',[33] and that it must have 'eradicated the basis for the original risk' of persecution.[34] In one rare case from Australia,[35] these issues were analysed in the context of a refugee claim by a stateless Palestinian born in Syria. The fundamental issue relating to Article 1C(6) concerned the meaning of 'ceased to exist'. The Refugee Review Tribunal sought guidance from the UNHCR 'Guidelines on International Protection' relating to cessation as well as the writing of eminent scholars, including Guy Goodwin-Gill and James Hathaway, and concluded that 'for cessation clauses to apply, the changes in circumstances that gave rise to the refugee status need to be of a fundamental nature such that the refugee can no longer continue to refuse to avail themselves of the protection of the relevant country'.[36] The Tribunal went on to explain that 'Article 1C(6) would at least require material, or substantial changes in circumstances in the country'.[37] It considered that although there had been a change in the Syrian presidency resulting in some improvements, the evidence was that there remained serious concerns about the treatment of political opponents. Hence, it could not be said that there had been substantial and fundamental changes in the Syrian regime, such that the circumstances that led to the applicant's recognition as a refugee had ceased to exist. Whether or not he had a right to return to Syria, the cessation clause does not apply to him. This cautious attitude is echoed in academic writing. For instance, Joan Fitzpatrick and Rafael Bonoan observe that 'formal regime change does not necessarily erase deep-seated prejudices, nor eliminate the risk that persecution will continue at the hands of rogue officials and non-State actors',[38] and that '[p]olitical change, whether democratic or violent, may simply substitute a new risk of persecution for a recognized refugee'.[39]

It is also worth noting that despite the existence of clause (6) in Article 1C of the *Refugee Convention*, judicial practice (at least in Australia) indicates a preference for applying Article 1C(5) even in cases where the applicant claims to be stateless and the court or tribunal does not dispute it. For instance, in one case, the applicant was from Iran and claimed to be stateless.[40] Although the Australian Refugee Review

---

[30] Hathaway and Foster, *The Law of Refugee Status 2* (n 5) 476–94.
[31] UNHCR, 'Conclusions Adopted by the Executive Committee on the International Protection of Refugees' (December 2009) No 69 (XLIII) Cessation of Status (1992).
[32] Hathaway and Foster, *The Law of Refugee Status 2* (n 5) 494.
[33] Joined Cases C-175/08, C-176/08, C-178/08 and C-179/08 *Abdulla v Germany* [2010] ECR I–1532 [76]—this case was about art 1C(5).
[34] Hathaway and Foster, *The Law of Refugee Status 2* (n 5) 487.
[35] *N04/48633* [2004] RRTA 481 (29 June 2004).   [36] ibid, 21.   [37] ibid, 22.
[38] Fitzpatrick and Bonoan, 'Cessation of Refugee Protection' (n 2) 516.   [39] ibid, 517.
[40] *N05/52051* [2005] RRTA 257 (4 October 2005).

Tribunal did not specifically address this issue, it assessed his claim for refugee status by reference to his 'country of former habitual residence', thereby implying that he was stateless. However, when considering issues of cessation, the Tribunal applied Article 1C(5) rather than Article 1C(6). It found no evidence before it that the political circumstances in Iran had changed so substantially that the circumstances in connection with which he had originally been recognized as a refugee no longer existed, and therefore Article 1C(5) did not apply. In another case, an interesting question arose as to whether recognition of refugee status by Switzerland, of an applicant from Vietnam claiming to be stateless, required the Australian Tribunal to assess her claim on the basis that she was a recognized refugee (by Switzerland) and hence could only be denied an Australian protection visa if Article 1C(5) applied.[41] The Australian Federal Magistrates Court considered the recognition of refugee status by Switzerland to be non-binding on Australia or even persuasive, hence consideration of Article 1C(5) was not appropriate.[42] In other words, the application had been appropriately assessed *de novo* according to the situation prevailing at the time of adjudication.

With regard to the second requirement in Article 1C(6), namely that, as a consequence of the changed circumstances, she is now able to return to the country of her former habitual residence, assumptions should not be made that because the first requirement is met, the second requirement is automatically met.[43] Hathaway and Foster argue that 'a consequential ability of the stateless refugee "to return to the country of his former habitual residence"—predicates cessation upon the stateless refugee's ability to resume the bond to which she is most clearly entitled under international law',[44] for instance through the possession of a valid re-entry permit, protection against expulsion, and the ability to live a normal life there. Such an interpretation would be in harmony with the wording of Article 1C(5), which requires that the refugee be able 'to avail himself of the protection of the country of his nationality', understood to mean that 'protection must … be effective and available' not just in terms of physical security and safety, but also in terms of basic infrastructure and livelihood.[45]

A final important point in relation to cessation is that a careful assessment must be made of whether invocation of the cessation clause would itself engender a risk of statelessness independent of the original reasons for flight. For instance, Lindsey Kingston argues that many Rwandans whose refugee status has been revoked due to the UNHCR-invoked cessation clause which came into effect in 2013[46] 'essentially face either forced repatriation or serious vulnerabilities to de jure or de facto statelessness'.[47] Specifically in relation to de jure statelessness she observes that 'denationalization seems to have already occurred for some exiles whose citizenship was revoked as punishment for their criticism of the Rwandan government'.[48]

---

[41] *SZCZJ v Minister for Immigration* [2006] FMCA 1583 (25 October 2006) [36].
[42] ibid, [55]–[59] (Scarlett FM).
[43] Hathaway and Foster, *The Law of Refugee Status 2* (n 5) 487.   [44] ibid, 488–89.
[45] UNHCR, 'Guidelines on Cessation' (n 1).
[46] Kingston, 'Bringing Rwandan Refugees "Home"' (n 29) 418.   [47] ibid, 434.
[48] ibid.

Cessation processes cannot create situations of statelessness and threaten the right to a nationality.[49]

To conclude, states have rarely invoked the cessation clauses in Article 1C of the *Refugee Convention* vis-à-vis stateless refugees.[50] As a result, global jurisprudence on cessation of refugee status in a statelessness context is extremely scarce, although some guidance may be sought in the academic literature and UNHCR Guidelines. It is generally accepted that return to the country of origin does not cease refugee status. In the context of a stateless refugee, cessation of refugee status only occurs if the person in question voluntarily acquires a new nationality and enjoys the protection of the country of new nationality, re-establishes herself in the country which she left because of a fear of persecution (Article 1C(4)), or if a fundamental change of circumstances in that country means that the facts upon which refugee status was recognized no longer exist and the stateless person can return safely to her country of former habitual residence and enjoy a normal life there (Article 1C(6)).

Cessation of refugee status may justify cancellation of a residence permit obtained on the basis of recognition of refugee status, and the loss of other rights attached to refugee status. It may also result in the individual being returned to her or his country of origin. However, considerations of proportionality and necessity in relation to acquired rights under international human rights law may need to be taken into account, for example whether the individual has established a private and family life in the country of refuge.[51]

Part 2: Exclusion Based on the Availability of Protection Elsewhere

Separately from, and unrelated to issues of cessation, are considerations of exclusion from refugee status. In this Part we consider the circumstances in which an applicant for refugee status may be excluded from refugee protection on the basis that he or she has protection from another entity, specifically in relation to (1) persons already receiving UN protection and assistance (Article 1D); or (2) persons who are entitled to de facto nationality elsewhere (Article 1E). It is interesting to observe at the outset that these two provisions, as well as the exclusion clauses set out in Article 1F for persons undeserving of international protection considered in Part 3, are reproduced word for word in the 1954 *Convention relating to the Status of Stateless Persons* ('*1954 Convention*') (Article 1(2)(i)(ii)(iii)). However, their interpretation was left out of the scope of the UNHCR 'Handbook on Protection of Stateless Persons', and these provisions have generally not been the subject of extensive judicial or scholarly

---

[49] ibid.

[50] They are, however, 'frequently considered by UNHCR' in armed conflict situations: Fitzpatrick and Bonoan, 'Cessation of Refugee Protection' (n 2) 512. Although one might assume that, in the context of refugee protection from armed conflict, states would soon (re)discover art 1C(5)(6) should a conflict end, temporary protection and subsidiary protection regimes mitigate against such an assumption, as well as considerations of international human rights law and administrative costs.

[51] Hélène Lambert, 'The European Court of Human Rights and the Right of Refugees and Other Persons in Need of Protection to Family Reunion' (1999) 11 IJRL 427.

scrutiny.[52] In any event, since the *1954 Convention* does not deal with a fear of being persecuted, we shall also not refer to those provisions here.[53]

2.1 Persons already receiving UN protection and assistance

Article 1D (first sentence) excludes from the benefit of the rights and obligations in the *Refugee Convention* 'persons who are at present receiving from organs or agencies of the United Nations other than the United Nations High Commissioner for Refugees protection or assistance'. On its face one clear purpose of the provision is the avoidance of 'overlapping competencies between UNRWA and UNHCR'.[54] Although a literal reading could result in its application to other situations, for example, in the past to persons benefiting from protection or assistance from the former UN Korean Reconstruction Agency,[55] the drafting history and accepted doctrine is clear that Article 1D is solely directed to the exclusion of the Palestinian refugee population.[56] Hence today it applies *exclusively* to refugees from Palestine who, in particular areas of the Middle East (namely, Lebanon, Syria, Jordan, the Gaza Strip, and the West Bank), benefit from protection or assistance from the UN Relief and Works Agency for Palestine Refugees ('UNRWA').[57] Mutaz Qafisheh and Valentina Azarova argue that the reason for excluding Palestinian refugees from the benefits of the 1951 *Refugee Convention* through Article 1D of that treaty was 'to facilitate the international community's administration of the refugee problem'; thus for a purely 'procedural reason'.[58] Should such protection or assistance cease

---

[52] One exception is Katia Bianchini's book, which examines art 1(2)(i) of the *1954 Convention* and its similarity to art 1D of the 1951 *Refugee Convention*: Katia Bianchini, *Protecting Stateless Persons: The Implementation of the Convention relating to the Status of Stateless Persons across EU States* (Brill Nijhoff 2018) 86–96.

[53] For a brief overview, see Batchelor, 'The 1954 Convention' (n 15) 37–38. See also Belgium: Cour de Cassation de Belgique [Court of Cassation Belgium], *AMM v Procureur General Près de la Cour D'Appel de Bruxelles*, arrêt no°C.06.0427.F, 22 January 2009 (stateless Palestinian who left Lebanon to study in Belgium; was found to be excluded from protection as a stateless person under the *1954 Convention* (art 1(2)(i)) because his stay in Belgium was only temporary and nothing prevented him from returning to Lebanon and resuming assistance from the United Nations Relief and Works Agency for Palestine (UNRWA)). France: Conseil d'État ('CE') [French Administrative Court], decision no°277373, 22 November 2006 (stateless Palestinian born in Syria but living in France since 1985 can no longer benefit from the protection or assistance of UNRWA, and can therefore benefit from the *1954 Convention* regime).

[54] UNHCR, 'Revised Note on the Applicability of Article 1D of the 1951 Convention relating to the Status of Refugees to Palestinian Refugees' (2009) 28 Refugee Survey Quarterly 657, para 2 (hereafter UNHCR, 'Revised Note').

[55] This was the position in the UNHCR 'Handbook on Refugee Status' (n 3) 28 para 142. The UNHCR has revised this position in its 'Revised Note' (n 54).

[56] See the drafting history and scholarly authority discussed by the New Zealand Immigration and Protection Tribunal decision in *AD (Palestine)* [2015] NZIPT 800693–695 (23 December 2015) (hereafter *AD (Palestine)*).

[57] Hathaway and Foster, *Law of Refugee Status 2* (n 5) 510. See also in Ireland, *MA v Refugee Appeals Tribunal* [2013] IEHC 36: 'Such special arrangements are currently in place, for example, in relation to stateless persons of Palestinian origin who are under the protection of the [UNRWA]': at [20]; 'Article 1D presently has no applicability other than to Palestinian refugees': at [21].

[58] Mutaz M Qafisheh and Valentina Azarova, 'Article 1 D 1951 Convention' in Andreas Zimmermann, Felix Machts, and Jonas Dörschner (eds), *The 1951 Convention relating to the Status of Refugees and its 1967 Protocol: A Commentary* (OUP 2011) 536, 550 (hereafter Qafisheh and Azarova,

'for any reason', Article 1D specifies that 'these persons shall *ipso facto* be entitled to the benefits of this [the Refugee] Convention'; thereby it 'ensures the continuity of protection and assistance to Palestinian refugees as necessary'.[59]

The *raison d'être* and exact meaning of the terms in Article 1D of the *Refugee Convention* have been much discussed in the academic literature,[60] but with no real focus on statelessness,[61] despite the fact that Palestinian refugees are for the great majority stateless.[62] Below therefore we concentrate our analysis on the case law and how it tackles statelessness. Judicial decisions commonly refer to *stateless* Palestinians, be they from Syria, Lebanon, or the Gaza, who have had to leave their *country of former habitual residence*.

Courts and tribunals in Europe have, for the most part, construed the exclusion clause in Article 1D narrowly so as to maximize the opportunities for protection guaranteed under the *Refugee Convention* and therefore access to refugee status. The driving force for this liberal jurisprudence appears to be the Court of Justice of the European Union ('CJEU'), in particular its rulings in *Bolbol*[63] and *El Kott*,[64] which are binding on the national courts and tribunals of European Union Member States.[65]

Although the CJEU has not accepted the position that Article 1D has no current relevance because it is applicable only to those Palestinians who were receiving the relevant protection or assistance from UNRWA on 28 July 1951,[66] it has otherwise

---

'Article 1 D 1951 Convention'). For a thorough description of the background and drafting history of art 1D, see *AD (Palestine)* (n 56) [79]–[100].

[59] UNHCR, 'Revised Note' (n 54) para 2.

[60] See in particular, Hathaway and Foster, *Law of Refugee Status 2* (n 5) 509–23; Goodwin-Gill and McAdam, *The Refugee in International Law* (n 5).

[61] For instance, Fripp's book, *Nationality and Statelessness* (n 9) does not discuss art 1D.

[62] Qafisheh and Azarova, 'Article 1D 1951 Convention' (n 58) make the case, based on the *travaux préparatoires* of the *Refugee Convention*, that 'although Palestinian refugees were not specifically mentioned in Art. 1 D, this group of refugees was in the mind of the drafters of the 1951 Convention': at 544. They further observe that '[i]t is estimated that only slightly over 2.5 million out of about 6.5 million Palestinian refugees have been granted citizenship somewhere in the world. The denial of citizenship to Palestinian refugees by Arab countries is mainly due to the fact that their admission into their territories was expected to be on a temporary basis until a solution based on self-determination and repatriation could be achieved': at 548.

[63] Case C-31/09 *Bolbol v Bevándorlási és Állampolgársági Hivatal* [2010] ECR I–05539 (hereafter *Bolbol*).

[64] Case C-364/11 *El Kott v Bevándorlási és Állampolgársági Hivatal* [2012] ECR (hereafter *El Kott*).

[65] This is the case with regard to twenty-seven Member States, but not Denmark (not bound by the Common European Asylum System ('CEAS')); the United Kingdom and Ireland, however, although bound by the first phase of CEAS (e.g. Qualification Directive), are not bound by the second phase of CEAS (e.g. Recast Qualification Directive).

[66] *Bolbol* (n 63). There is some support for this position in the drafting history. For instance, the UK delegate, Mr Hoare, in discussing art 1D (at that stage art 1C) emphasized that he 'wished to make it quite clear that he understood paragraph C to exclude persons who were defined as those who at the time when the Convention came into force were receiving protection or assistance from United Nations organs or agencies': Conference of Plenipotentiaries on the Status of Refugees and Stateless Persons, 'Summary Record of the Nineteenth Meeting' (26 November 1951) UN Doc A/CONF.2/SR.19, 20. A compelling case for this position is put by Hathaway and Foster in *Law of Refugee Status 2* (n 5) at 513–15; however, it must be acknowledged that this has generally not been accepted in the majority of jurisdictions. See the summary on this issue in *AD (Palestine)* (n 56) [120]–[125]. It was also rejected by the New Zealand Immigration and Protection Tribunal *in AD (Palestine)*: see [147]–[149].

adopted a closely circumscribed approach to the circumstances in which Article 1D applies to exclude Palestinians today. As the CJEU emphasized in *Bolbol*, Article 1D must 'be construed narrowly'.[67]

The resulting case law reveals that once persons fall within the second sentence of Article 1D, they are 'automatically' (i.e. 'ipso facto') entitled to refugee protection.[68] The *reasons* for cessation of protection or assistance by UNRWA are key elements in the assessment of eligibility for Article 1A(2) protection, and may include no longer being in the relevant geographical area and thereby ceasing to receive protection or assistance for reasons beyond one's control and independent of one's volition.[69] Thus, being forced to leave the place where UNRWA was operating due to a serious threat to personal safety, or where UNRWA lacked the ability to guarantee the living conditions its duties demand are all determinant factors.[70] Furthermore, mere entitlement or being eligible to such protection or assistance does not suffice to trigger Article 1D; the person must be in a position to avail herself or himself of that protection and UNRWA must actually be providing protection or assistance, such as guaranteeing living conditions.[71] If the country of former habitual residence obstructs the return of the Palestinian, that person should be recognized as a refugee without further examination of Article 1A(2) of the *Refugee Convention*.[72] Once the protection or assistance by UNRWA has ceased, it must be substituted by equivalent protection under the 1951 *Refugee Convention*, unless Article 1E or Article 1F applies.[73]

Thus, in Europe at least, the predicament of stateless Palestinian refugees who received or were entitled to the protection or assistance of UNRWA and who lost it involuntarily has been recognized to be the same as that of refugees under the

[67] *Bolbol* (n 63) [51].

[68] Belgium: Conseil du Contentieux des Etrangers ('CCE') [Belgian Council for Alien Law Litigation], *X v de Commissaris-generaal voor de vluchtelingen en de staatlozen*, arrêt no°37.912, 29 January 2010 (hereafter Arrêt no°37.912); France: Cour Nationale du Droit d'Asile ('CNDA') [French National Court of Asylum], decision nos°04020557, 04020558, 24 May 2013 (hereafter Decision nos°04020557, 04020558); CNDA, decision no°493412, 14 May 2008 (hereafter Decision no°493412); Sweden: Migrationsöverdomstolen [Swedish Migration Court of Appeal], mål nr UM 1590-13, 26 November 2013 (hereafter UM 1590-13) (where the Migration Court of Appeal quashed a decision of the Migration Board to grant the stateless Palestinian applicant subsidiary protection instead of refugee status).

[69] *El Kott* (n 64); *Bolbol* (n 63). France: Decision nos°04020557, 04020558 (n 68). A contrario, a person cannot rely on the 'automatic inclusion clause' if she or he left the area of protection or assistance by UNRWA voluntarily: France: CE, decision no°318356, 23 July 2010; Hungary: Fővárosi Közigazgatási és Munkaügyi Bíróság ('Budapest Administrative and Labour Court') [Budapest Metropolitan Court of Administration and Labour], *HAI v Bevándorlási és Állampolgársági Hivatal*, 3.K.30.602/2013/15, 29 August 2013 (hereafter *HAI*); Budapest Administrative and Labour Court, *KKF v Bevándorlási és Állampolgársági Hivatal*, 15.K30.590/2013/5, 21 March 2013; Budapest Administrative and Labour Court, *AAA v Bevándorlási és Állampolgársági Hivatal*, 6.K.30.092/2013/12, 7 March 2013.

[70] United Kingdom: *Said v Secretary of State for the Home Department* [2012] UKUT 00413 (IAC) [12], [13] (hereafter *Said*). Note that in the United Kingdom, *El-Ali v Secretary of State for the Home Department* [2002] EWCA Civ 1103 (hereafter *El-Ali*) no longer stands following *Bolbol* (n 63) and *El Kott* (n 64). Sweden: UM 1590-13 (n 68). Belgium: CCE, *X v Commissaire général aux réfugiés et aux apatrides*, arrêt no°103.509, 27 May 2013 (hereafter Arrêt no°103.509); CCE, *X v de Commissaris-generaal voor de vluchtelingen en de staatlozen*, arrêt no°102.283, 2 May 2013 (hereafter Arrêt no°102.283).

[71] *Bolbol* (n 63) [51], [53]. Belgium: Arrêt no°103.509 (n 70); Arrêt no°102.283 (n 70).

[72] Belgium: Arrêt no°37.912 (n 68).   [73] France: Decision no°493412 (n 68).

Refugee Convention, and hence they have been granted refugee status. It is acknowledged that these persons 'were entitled to receive highly preferential and special treatment … [this] was itself a recognition of the particular responsibility borne by the United Nations towards Palestinian Arabs who had been displaced'.[74]

In many jurisdictions, Article 1D is not routinely considered or invoked. For example, in the case of Canada, the jurisprudence largely fails to mention Article 1D in any of the cases involving registration with UNRWA,[75] and indeed the numerous cases involving stateless Palestinians, many of which have been analysed in previous chapters, are adjudicated without reference to Article 1D but rather solely by reference to Article 1A(2).

In other jurisdictions outside Europe there appears to be a trend towards convergence in interpretation in line with the position adopted by the CJEU. For example, in the case of New Zealand, a precedent decision of the Immigration and Protection Tribunal in 2015 examined in great depth the history, scholarship, and global jurisprudence relating to Article 1D to determine New Zealand's approach.[76] Although it critiqued some elements of the CJEU's approach,[77] ultimately the position put forward was largely consistent, viz, 'the individual circumstances of a claimant giving rise to a lack of effective protection or assistance may also, in principle, constitute a *de facto* cessation under the inclusionary second paragraph of Article 1D in cases of involuntary departures or stay from an UNRWA field of operation'.[78] The Tribunal cited the factors identified by the UNHCR as relevant to the assessment of cessation of protection, including threats to life, physical security or freedom, or other serious protection-related reasons, and practical, legal, or safety barriers to return.[79]

By contrast, Australia's position appears more restrictive and thus seems to run counter to the intention of the drafters that Palestinian refugees should 'be ensured *heightened* protection'.[80] In *WABQ* in 2002, the Full Federal Court of Australia held: 'Almost every element of Article 1(D) is pregnant with ambiguity. So much

[74] United Kingdom: *El-Ali* (n 70) [36]. Note that in *Said* (n 70) the UK Upper Tribunal stated that '*Bolbol* clearly overrules *El-Ali*': at [23]. Furthermore, at paras 24–25 of the *Said* judgment, the UK Tribunal indicate their preference for Advocate General Sharpston's construction of art 1D in *Bolbol* (n 63).

[75] Canada: *Abu-Fahra v Canada (Minister of Citizenship and Immigration)*, 2003 FC 860 (10 July 2007); *Kukhon v Canada (Minister of Citizenship and Immigration)*, 2003 FCT 69 (23 January 2003); *X (Re)*, 2000 CanLII 21408 (16 February 2000). This may mainly be due to the fact that the Canadian legislation on refugee protection does not incorporate art 1D—*Immigration and Refugee Protection Act*, SC 2001, c 27.

[76] The previous authority in New Zealand, *Refugee Appeal No 73873* [2006] NZRSAA 77 (28 April 2006), appeared to suggest a construction of art 1D similar in some respect to that of the CJEU and EU Member States: 'It is clear from the terms of Article 1 D itself that it applies only to those who are currently receiving protection or assistance from the UN and that where such protection and assistance ceases "for any reason" the benefits of the Convention are then engaged': at [50]. The Tribunal further held, '[t]he conclusion the Authority has reached is consistent with the approach taken by the Authority in previous decisions … [where] it was held that Article 1D was primarily concerned with the status of persons receiving *or potentially able to receive* assistance from UNWRA': at [51] (emphasis added).

[77] See *AD (Palestine)* (n 56) [150]–[153].   [78] ibid, [177].

[79] UNHCR, 'Revised Note' (n 54), cited in *AD (Palestine)* (n 56) [189]–[190].

[80] Qafisheh and Azarova, 'Article 1 D 1951 Convention' (n 58) 550 (emphasis in original). It also runs counter to UNHCR, 'Revised Note' (n 54).

is apparent, not only from the different views which have been expressed by Judges of this Court at first instance, but also from the different approaches that have been adopted in Courts and Tribunals around the World.' [81] The Court then considered the first sentence of Article 1D to be applicable to a class of persons (i.e. Palestinians) who were receiving protection or assistance from UNRWA as at 28 July 1951.[82] In the case of a stateless Palestinian applicant, Article 1D applies because 'Palestinians as a group were as at 28 July 1951 receiving protection or assistance'.[83] While that position is not controversial, the difficulty is that this class-based approach is also applied, at least in theory, to the question whether protection or assistance has ceased. In *WABQ*, the Full Court held that in order for the second paragraph to apply, it 'will not be sufficient that protection or assistance has ceased in relation to an individual member of the class'.[84] Rather, protection or assistance must have 'ceased for any reason in respect of the class'.[85] However, in practice the Refugee Review Tribunal of Australia has 'in other cases for several years now ... taken the view that protection can be said to have ceased'[86] in the particular context of the case. There is clearly a need for further review and clarity at the appellate level on this issue. Finally, when protection or assistance has ceased, the Australian position is that the class of persons does not automatically become refugees; rather, their application for refugee status must be considered and they must satisfy the requirements of the refugee definition.[87] This interpretation is based on a reading of the second sentence of Article 1D ('shall ipso facto be entitled to the benefits of this Convention') that considers 'those benefits, such as the non-expulsion provisions of Article 32 and the non-refoulement provisions of Article 33 ... [to be] available only to those persons who are refugees. They are not available to anyone else.'[88] In our view, this interpretation is erroneous because as stated by the UNHCR, the terms 'the benefits of this Convention' are clear and plain, and they include the rights and obligations in Articles 2–34, and not just 32 and 33.[89] Hence, in our view, the Australian position is ripe for reconsideration.

In sum, Article 1D is highly relevant to the potential refugee claims of one of the world's largest stateless populations, namely Palestinians. However, rather than operating as a bar to refugee status, in cases where an applicant no longer enjoys protection from UNRWA due to UNRWA's inability to adequately offer such protection for that individual, she or he is automatically (ipso facto) entitled to refugee status.

---

[81] *Minister for Immigration and Multicultural Affairs v WABQ* [2002] FCAFC 329 (8 November 2002) [18] (Hill J) (hereafter *WABQ*).

[82] ibid.

[83] See decision of the Refugee Review Tribunal of Australia ('RRT') in *0904796* [2010] RRTA 1005 (15 November 2010) [15] (hereafter *0904796*).

[84] As discussed in the RRT in ibid, [60].		[85] ibid.

[86] RRT decision *1108899* [2012] RRTA 133 (7 March 2012) [49] (hereafter *1108899*).

[87] *WABQ* (n 81). See also *1108899* (n 86); *WAJB v Minister for Immigration and Multicultural Affairs* [2002] FCA 1443 (22 November 2002) (hereafter *WAJB*).

[88] *WABQ* (n 81) [69] (Hill J). Also held in *WAJB* (n 87) [37]; *WACG v Minister for Immigration and Multicultural Affairs* [2002] FCAFC 332 (8 November 2002); *WACH v Minister for Immigration and Multicultural Affairs* [2002] FCAFC 338 (8 November 2002).

[89] UNHCR, 'Revised Note' (n 54) para 9.

2.2 Persons not considered to be in need of international protection

Article 1E of the *Refugee Convention* excludes from the scope of protection of the *Convention* 'a person who is recognized by the competent authorities of the country in which he has taken residence as having the rights and obligations which are attached to the possession of the nationality of that country'. As stated by UNHCR, '[t]his provision relates to persons who might otherwise qualify for refugee status and who have been received in a country where they have been granted most of the rights normally enjoyed by nationals, but not formal citizenship'.[90] In this regard, the Federal Court of Canada noted that it 'is not dissimilar to the cessation provisions', in particular Article 1C(3) (he has acquired a new nationality, and enjoys the protection of the country of his new nationality).[91] Ultimately, 'Article 1E is intended to prevent asylum shopping.'[92]

The *Constitution of the International Refugee Organization* ('IRO') and earlier drafts of the 1951 *Refugee Convention* excluded 'members of former German minorities outside of Germany who [following the fall of the Nazi regime] returned to, sought refuge in, or were expelled to Germany, and who are living there'.[93] Indeed, it was clearly felt at the time, that these persons were the responsibility of the German government and not that of the UN (Mr Henkin, United States representative), and that a number of them had probably worked for the Nazis (Mr Robinson, Israel representative).[94] The final text of Article 1E abandoned any references to German minorities, focusing instead on a general formulation,[95] and today Article 1E applies to individuals as well as groups, refugees with a nationality as well as stateless persons.

Although the academic literature and UNHCR 'Handbook and Guidelines on Procedures and Criteria for Determining Refugee Status' refer to 'persons' or 'refugees' when examining Article 1E, there are a few cases dealing specifically with stateless refugees, as distinct from refugees with a nationality, in the context of Article 1E. The analysis below focuses on these cases, as well as on general academic and UNHCR writing.

Considering the nature of Article 1E as an exclusion clause, it is generally accepted that the requirements in Article 1E are stringent and not easily satisfied. First, the person or persons must have 'taken residence' in a country where they do not have nationality; '[t]his implies continued residence and not a mere visit',[96] and she or he must have *already* taken residence.[97] In the same way as Article 1E does not

---

[90] UNHCR, 'Handbook on Refugee Status' (n 3) para 144.

[91] Canada: *Thabet v Canada (Minister of Citizenship and Immigration)* [1998] 4 FC 21 (11 May 1998) (Linden JA) (the case involved a stateless Palestinian, born in Kuwait, who studied in the United States, and whose application for asylum was rejected there, then he came to Canada).

[92] *Canada (Citizenship and Immigration) v Alsha'bi*, 2015 FC 1381 (14 December 2015) [62] (hereafter *Alsha'bi*); *Canada (Citizenship and Immigration) v Zeng*, 2010 FCA 118 (10 May 2010) [19].

[93] Hathaway and Foster, *The Law of Refugee Status 2* (n 5) 501 n 245. See also Goodwin-Gill and McAdam, *The Refugee in International Law* (n 5) 161.

[94] Hathaway and Foster, *The Law of Refugee Status 2* (n 5) 500 n 244.

[95] Goodwin-Gill and McAdam, *The Refugee in International Law* (n 5) 161–62.

[96] UNHCR, 'Handbook on Refugee Status' (n 3) para 146.

[97] Hathaway and Foster, *The Law of Refugee Status 2* (n 5) 502–3.

apply to a refugee's country of origin or nationality, Article 1E does not apply to a stateless person's country of former habitual residence. Rather, Article 1E relates to a *third country* where a person has acquired what might be determined 'de facto nationality', and where they could safely go to avoid the harm feared in their country of reference.[98] The drafting history supports this reading of Article 1E as requiring a status akin to nationality. As the representative of the UNHCR at the Conference of Plenipotentiaries explained in describing the purpose of Article 1E (at that stage paragraph D of Article 1), it required that 'a person had the status of *de facto* citizenship, that was to say, if he really had the rights and obligations of a citizen of a given country'.[99]

Second, the requirement that the individual is recognized by the authorities of that country as 'having the rights and obligations which are attached to the possession of the nationality of that country', means that 'the focus of [the] analysis must . . . be on the substance of rights and obligations' rather than on a particular formal status.[100] Indeed, Article 1E requires a 'guarantee of rights at a very high level', well beyond protection against persecution or even protection of refugee rights.[101]

In *Alsha'bi*, the Canadian Federal Court of Appeal, recognizing the special situation of stateless refugees, held: 'A claimant who is acknowledged to be stateless does not have a country of nationality or status in any country that is substantially similar to nationality and, for that reason, would not fall within the application of the exclusion.'[102]

For the Federal Court,

Unless such a person has substantially the same rights as a national of their country of former habitual residence they may lack that [state] protection. The lack of state protection is a key element of a stateless person's claim of refugee status and its availability is a key element of the potential exclusion of a claimant under Article 1E.[103]

---

[98] Australia: *N01/37373* [2001] RRTA 610 (29 June 2001) (hereafter *N01/37373*); *N00/35614* [2001] RRTA 34 (15 January 2001); *N00/35689* [2001] RRTA 40 (16 January 2001)—all three cases involved a stateless Palestinian, formerly in Syria.

[99] Conference of Plenipotentiaries on the Status of Refugees and Stateless Persons, 'Summary Record of the Twenty-Third Meeting' (26 November 1951) UN Doc A/CONF.2/SR.23, 11 (van Heuven Goedhart) (emphasis added).

[100] Hathaway and Foster, *The Law of Refugee Status 2* (n 5) 503.

[101] ibid, 504. For instance, in Australia, the RRT recognized that Palestinians in Syria receiving assistance from UNWRA do not have the same rights and obligations as Syrian nationals: *N01/37373* (n 98). In Canada, stateless Palestinians on a temporary status in the United Arab Emirates do not have the right to citizenship; they are subject to (arbitrary) deportation and are denied the right to return, hence they do not have the same rights and obligations as nationals: *Alsha'bi* (n 92). In the United Kingdom, the Upper Tribunal (Immigration and Asylum Chamber) held that a Tibetan exile from China 'does not have the rights and obligations which are attached to Indian nationality or rights and obligations equivalent to those and accordingly he benefits from the Refugee Convention': *TG (Interaction of Directives and Rules)* [2016] UKUT 00374 (IAC) (18 May 2016) at [32] (hereafter *TG (Interaction of Directives and Rules)*).

[102] *TG (Interaction of Directives and Rules)* (n 101) [66]. See also discussion of art 1E in the context of the discussion of 'country of former habitual residence' in Chapter 4, Part 3.2.

[103] *Alsha'bi* (n 92) [80].

Thus, the rights and obligations in the proposed country of residence must be as close as possible to those of nationals of that country; however, opinion diverges on the exact scope of the rights to be guaranteed. It is generally accepted that Article 1E regards the following rights as essential: the right to diplomatic protection; the right of entry to the country, to remain, to return, and protection against deportation and expulsion, as well as economic rights.[104] It is nevertheless unclear whether 'rights' under Article 1E also include political rights, i.e. the right to vote.[105]

Hathaway and Foster argue that political rights should be included under Article 1E because 'any deviation from the rights of nationals renders Art. 1(E) inapplicable'.[106] However, Goodwin-Gill and McAdam consider that Article 1E 'do[es] not require that the individuals in question should enjoy the full range of rights incidental to citizenship'.[107] The latter position is further endorsed by the UNHCR[108] and Reinhard Marx.[109] As discussed above, the case law has focused exclusively on the key rights inherent in state protection (e.g. freedom of movement, including the right to return, protection against deportation, and economic rights); the right to vote is not mentioned in any of the cases. The formulation in the existing case law that status be substantially *similar or the same* to that of nationals would suggest that both views will continue to be advocated.

In sum, the requirements for a stateless person or persons to be excluded from refugee status are onerous. There is some support in the case law (*Alsha'bi*) for the proposition that stateless refugees may not be caught by Article 1E altogether on the ground that they lack nationality and therefore state protection and the guarantee of essential rights required for Article 1E to apply. However, such interpretation is based on the formality of status and ignores the reality that citizenship is not always a reliable indicator of the enjoyment of rights, or that international human rights law has extended the rights of non-citizens to include, for instance, the right to enter and remain in one's own country. Nevertheless, it will be an extremely rare case in

---

[104] For instance, the US courts require that an applicant be 'firmly resettled in another country prior to arriving in the United States' before he or she be denied asylum. *Mengstu v Holder,* 560 F 3d 1055 (9th Cir, 2009) [9] (although the case does not mention art 1E, it addresses similar issues in relation to US legislation, finding that firm resettlement in Sudan was not supported by substantial evidence as her entry visa was issued by the Ethiopian government, not the Sudanese, and it was never stamped; her two-year stay was in a refugee camp; she and her husband had no employment, funds, or other social or economic ties to Sudan). See also *Maharaj v Gonzales,* 450 F 3d 961 (9th Cir, 2006) 976 and *Ali v Ashcroft,* 394 F 3d 780 (9th Cir, 2005) 789–90 (finding that an alien who resided in Ethiopia for five years but who never received any aid or legal status was not firmly resettled); *Camposeco-Montejo v Ashcroft,* 384 F 3d 814 (9th Cir, 2004) 820–21 (finding that petitioner had not firmly resettled despite living in Mexico for sixteen years because he was not offered permanent status and his movements were restricted).

[105] See also R Marx, 'Article 1 E 1951 Convention' in Andreas Zimmermann, Felix Machts, and Jonas Dörschner (eds), *The 1951 Convention relating to the Status of Refugees and its 1967 Protocol: A Commentary* (OUP 2011) 571, 574 (hereafter Marx, 'Article 1 E 1951 Convention'). Generally, on the subject, see Ruvi Ziegler, *Voting Rights of Refugees* (CUP 2017).

[106] Hathaway and Foster, *The Law of Refugee Status 2* (n 5) 505 (emphasis omitted).

[107] Goodwin-Gill and McAdam, *The Refugee in International Law* (n 5) 162.

[108] The UNHCR is satisfied that 'the exclusion operates if a person's status is largely assimilated to that of a national of the country': 'Handbook on Refugee Status' (n 3) para 145.

[109] Marx, 'Article 1 E 1951 Convention' (n 105) 574.

which Article 1E can legitimately be applied to exclude a stateless applicant from refugee status.

Part 3: Persons Undeserving of International Protection

Article 1F excludes from the protection of the *Refugee Convention,*

any person with respect to whom there are serious reasons for considering that:
(a) he has committed a crime against peace, a war crime, or a crime against humanity . . .;
(b) he has committed a serious non-political crime outside the country of refuge prior to his admission to that country as a refugee;
(c) he has been guilty of acts contrary to the purposes and principles of the United Nations.[110]

There is nothing in these provisions indicating that a stateless person should be treated any differently from someone with a nationality, or indeed that Article 1F should be interpreted differently in cases involving stateless persons.[111] Thus, unlike Article 1A(2) (the 'inclusion clause') or Article 1C (the 'cessation clauses'), nationality (old or new) does not appear to play any role in exclusion from refugee status. Whilst case law on Article 1F as it applies to persons with a nationality is relatively substantial and well established, there is scant case law on exclusion of stateless persons from refugee status.

Noteworthy is a decision of the New Zealand Refugee Status Appeals Authority concerning a Bidoon (meaning 'without a nationality') born in Kuwait who, although not directly involved in torturing and executing prisoners, was frequently present during these acts, willingly watching, over a period of eight years.[112] The Tribunal found him to be excluded from refugee protection by application of Article 1F(a). It held:

We are not required by the Refugee Convention to make a final determination whether the appellant has committed a crime against humanity. We are only called upon to decide whether there are serious reasons for considering that he has. We are satisfied that as a matter of law torture is a crime against humanity. We are further satisfied on the facts that the appellant has, over a period of eight years voluntarily placed himself at the scene of torture and that he thereby intended to encourage and did in fact encourage those perpetrating the crime

---

[110] *Refugee Convention* (n 6) art 1F. Geoff Gilbert summarizes the two aims of the exclusion clauses to be: 'protection of only the "deserving" refugee; and the need to ensure that serious international criminals do not escape punishment': Geoff Gilbert, 'Current Issues in the Application of the Exclusion Clauses' in Erika Feller, Volker Türk, and Frances Nicholson (eds), *Refugee Protection in International Law: UNHCR's Global Consultations on International Protection* (CUP 2003) 425, 429 (hereafter Gilbert, 'Current Issues in the Application of Exclusion Clauses'). See also Andreas Zimmermann and Philipp Wennholz, 'Article 1 F 1951 Convention' in Andreas Zimmermann, Felix Machts, and Jonas Dörschner (eds), *The 1951 Convention relating to the Status of Refugees and its 1967 Protocol: A Commentary* (OUP 2011) 579.
[111] This might be one of the reasons why Fripp, in his book *Nationality and Statelessness* (n 9), does not discuss or indeed even mention Article 1F.
[112] *Refugee Appeal No 72635* [2002] NZRSAA 344 (6 September 2002).

of torture. There was personal and knowing participation, a shared common purpose and a failure to dissociate or withdraw at the earliest safe opportunity.[113]

The Tribunal thus concluded 'there are serious reasons for considering that the appellant has committed a crime against humanity. As a result he is excluded from the Refugee Convention by virtue of Article 1F(a).'[114]

This interpretation of Article 1F(a) is well entrenched in cases involving refugees with a nationality.[115] Thus, there does not appear to be any difference in interpretation between cases involving applicants for refugee status who have a nationality and those who do not. The fact that the applicant in this case was stateless did not, appropriately, have a bearing on the court's decision.

In another decision from the Hungarian Metropolitan Court of Budapest concerning a Palestinian stateless person living in a refugee camp in Lebanon and working for the Fatah, the Court recalled that Article 1F's list of exclusion clauses is exhaustive and cannot be added to arbitrarily, and that in all cases, including cases involving national security, an effective judicial remedy must be provided (referring to the judgment of the European Court of Human Rights in *Al Nashif v Bulgaria*).[116] The Court held the objection of the Office of Immigration and Nationality concerning a matter of national security to be unverifiable by documents and hence unfounded, and recognized the applicant as a refugee. Again, the fact that the applicant was stateless did not have a bearing on the decision made by the Court.

There is nevertheless a context in which statelessness and exclusion may overlap, namely, that of withdrawal of nationality in the context of security concerns, i.e. in relation to legislation aimed at depriving of their nationality 'foreign fighters' who have fought for a foreign country or group, most notably in recent years in Syria.[117] As explained in Chapter 5, there has been a resurgence of democratic states adopting the penalty of denationalization for those who have or are suspected of having been involved in fighting for another country or entity when that activity is deemed contrary to the interests of the state withdrawing nationality. In Chapter 5

---

[113] ibid, [209].   [114] ibid, [210(d)].
[115] Gilbert, 'Current Issues in the Application of Exclusion Clauses' (n 110) 425–78.
[116] Hungary: *HAI* (n 69).
[117] Instances of withdrawal of nationality, which were used during the First World War and the Second World War, have recently re-emerged following 11 September 2001. See Sangeetha Pillai and George Williams, 'Twenty-First Century Banishment: Citizenship Stripping in Common Law Nations' (2017) 66 ICLQ 521, 526–28 (hereafter Pillai and Williams, 'Twenty-First Century Banishment'). See also Michelle Foster, 'An "Alien" by the Barest of Threads—the Legality of the Deportation of Long-Term Residents from Australia' (2009) 33 MULR 483. For instance, in the United Kingdom, s 40(4A) of the *British Nationality Act 1981* provides that the Secretary of State may deprive a naturalized British citizen of their citizenship where he or she believes this would be 'conducive to the public good', even if that person would become stateless as a result. Three conditions are attached to this provision:
   (a) the citizenship status results from the person's naturalisation,
   (b) the Secretary of State is satisfied that the deprivation is conducive to the public good because the person, while having that citizenship status, has conducted him or herself in a manner which is seriously prejudicial to the vital interests of the United Kingdom, any of the Islands, or any British overseas territory, and
   (c) the Secretary of State has reasonable grounds for believing that the person is able, under the law of a country or territory outside the United Kingdom, to become a national of such a country or territory.

we considered briefly whether denationalization in such a context is a violation of human rights and thus relevant to the assessment of persecution. In this chapter, the question is whether an applicant who has engaged in such activity, at least as assessed by a state that has subsequently withdrawn his or her nationality on that basis, can legitimately be excluded from refugee status in a third state by virtue of that activity in accordance with Article 1F.

We note that while there has been much recent scholarship exploring this phenomenon of denationalization on security grounds, and some emerging jurisprudence dealing with the domestic validity of such provisions,[118] the question of the relevance of such legislation to refugee law is at this stage largely theoretical. This may be partly due to the fact that as international law generally prohibits withdrawal of nationality where it would render a person stateless,[119] most domestic regimes pertain only to dual nationals. Hence even where a person is denationalized, they retain an alternative nationality that would in any event exclude them from refugee protection should they seek protection in another state.[120]

However, it is theoretically possible that a person who once had dual nationality but whose nationality in state A has been withdrawn on security grounds may be unable to avail themselves of the protection of their remaining state (B) due to a genuine well-founded fear in the state, for example arising out of his or her involvement in the very activity that gave rise to their denationalization by state A. Could a putative state of asylum, state C, reject an applicant's claim in relation to state B on the basis that their conduct falls within the exclusion clauses of Article 1F?[121]

The provision most relevant to his question is Article 1F(b),[122] which provides that the *Refugee Convention* shall not apply to any person with respect to whom there are serious reasons for considering that 'he has committed a serious non-political crime outside the country of refuge prior to his admission to that country as a refugee'. In this regard we observe that there are a number of important questions that would need to be considered and assessed before Article 1F(b) could be relied upon in this context.

---

[118] See e.g., in the United Kingdom: *Secretary of State for the Home Department v Al-Jedda* [2013] UKSC 62; *B2 v Secretary of State for the Home Department* [2013] EWCA Civ 616; *Pham v Secretary of State for the Home Department* [2015] UKSC 19.

[119] Article 8 of the *1961 Convention* (n 8), although we note the exception in art 8(3), which has been relied on by the United Kingdom. See Michelle Foster and Hélène Lambert, 'Statelessness as a Human Rights Issue: A Concept Whose Time Has Come' (2016) 28 IJRL 564 (hereafter Foster and Lambert, 'Statelessness as a Human Rights Issue').

[120] Article 1A(2) provides that, 'In the case of a person who has more than one nationality, the term "the country of his nationality" shall mean each of the countries of which he is a national, and a person shall not be deemed to be lacking the protection of the country of his nationality if, without any valid reason based on well-founded fear, he has not availed himself of the protection of one of the countries of which he is a national.'

[121] We note that art 1F is not concerned with the security interests of the asylum state; rather, that is the role of art 33(2), which may also be relevant in these contexts: see Hathaway and Foster, *The Law of Refugee Status 2* (n 5) 538–41.

[122] We assume that art 1F(a) is unlikely to be relevant in such scenarios ('he has committed a crime against peace, a war crime, or a crime against humanity'), nor is art 1F(c), which should be interpreted narrowly ('he has been guilty of acts contrary to the purposes and principles of the United Nations'): see the discussion in Hathaway and Foster, *The Law of Refugee Status 2* (n 5), 586–98.

First, it is arguable that the purpose of Article 1F(b) is to exclude from refugee protection 'fugitives from justice', and hence in order for Article 1F(b) to apply the 'crime' must remain justiciable.[123] Where the applicant has already been 'punished' in the form of denationalization, then it is arguable he or she should not be excluded under 1F(b).[124] However, given that this is not a universally held position, in some jurisdictions the expiation is not a bar to reliance on Article 1F(b).[125]

The second question is whether the crime is deemed 'serious'. As an aside, this assumes that the relevant conduct has indeed been criminalized, rather than subject only to the administrative penalty of denationalization. Assuming it is appropriately considered a crime, we observe that while, as currently framed, much domestic legislation in this area may well meet a seriousness criterion, a more difficult question may be whether there are 'serious reasons for considering' that a crime has been committed. This is because the procedural safeguards to ensure an adequate fact-finding exercise is undertaken, including opportunities for review, are deficient in some domestic regimes in the context of denationalization.[126]

Third, there could be an argument in some cases about whether the crime is *political* and therefore outside the ambit of the 'non-political crime' exception in Article 1F(b). It is now generally accepted that most terrorism offences are non-political crimes.[127] In particular, Article 1F would apply to exclude a person from refugee status, including a person whose nationality was withdrawn for reasons of involvement in terrorist activities.[128] However, assessing whether conduct giving rise to denationalization was political would require examination of the nature of the conduct, the intention or political objective (if any) of the applicant in carrying out such conduct, and the extent of harm caused and whether it was disproportionately harmful.[129]

As this brief overview suggests, it cannot be assumed that Article 1F is immediately and straightforwardly applicable to the context of denationalization for security reasons. Rather, if such a case were presented to a refugee decision-maker, a careful analysis of the relevant elements of Article 1F would need to be undertaken before any conclusion could be reached on the facts in a particular case.

Finally, even if Article 1F were appropriately applied in this context, such persons would remain protected against *non-refoulement* under instruments of international

[123] Hathaway and Foster, *The Law of Refugee Status 2* (n 5), 543.   [124] ibid.
[125] ibid, 544.
[126] See Foster and Lambert, 'Statelessness as a Human Rights Issue' (n 119). This is particularly true of Australia: see Michelle Foster, Jane McAdam, and Davina Wadley, 'Part Two: The Prevention and Reduction of Statelessness in Australia—An Ongoing Challenge' (2016) 40 MULR 456.
[127] Sarah Singer, *Terrorism and Exclusion from Refugee Status in the UK: Asylum Seekers Suspected of Serious Criminality* (Brill Nijhoff 2015). See also, Hathaway and Foster, *The Law of Refugee Status 2* (n 5) 558–62, 591–98 for a critical assessment of the use of art 1F(c) instead of art 1F(b). Whether they also qualify as acts contrary to the principles of the UN is more controversial.
[128] Article 33(2) further permits states to '*refouler*' a person to a country where their life or freedom may be threatened if they constitute a danger to the security of the country or the community of that country.
[129] Hathaway and Foster, *The Law of Refugee Status 2* (n 5).

human rights law.[130] For instance, in *Auad v Bulgaria*, a case involving a stateless person of Palestinian origin who had been granted humanitarian protection but was subsequently issued with an expulsion order for being a suspected terrorist, the European Court of Human Rights noted that national security considerations were irrelevant; the relevant issue was whether his expulsion would give rise to a real risk of ill-treatment.[131] Thus, once a decision on Article 1F has been made, provisions against torture, inhuman or degrading treatment, or punishment are very relevant in the context of expulsion of stateless persons. In another instance, the Austrian Constitutional Court ruled that where a person is stateless and his only real ties are with the country in which he was born and has lived all his life, legislation and/ or practice that would allow the expulsion of such a person, on grounds of criminal conviction, to the country of nationality of his mother or father would violate Article 3 *European Convention on Human Rights*, and would remain unlawful until such a time as the person concerned has managed to acquire the nationality of another country.[132] Similar rulings exist in Belgium, where orders to leave the territory have been annulled on the ground that being stateless constitutes 'exceptional circumstances' against the rule that a person must normally apply for a residence permit from their country of origin or residence abroad.[133] Hence, the practice of some states (e.g. the United Kingdom) to strip a naturalized citizen of his or her citizenship (usually when he or she is abroad), coupled with a cancellation or refusal of passport, or a temporary exclusion order, to prevent the undesirable individual from returning, may well be unlawful under international human rights law, even if Article 1F (and/or Article 33(2)) of the *Refugee Convention* do not prohibit such scenarios.[134]

Part 4: Conclusion

As this chapter has analysed, some of the provisions on cessation and exclusion in the Refugee Convention are distinctly applicable to stateless persons; this is the case in particular for Article 1C(4) and (6) and Article 1D. However, other provisions have been shown to apply indistinctly to both persons with a nationality and stateless persons, e.g., Article 1C(1), (2), (3), (5), Article 1E, and Article 1F. Whilst doctrinal engagement with these provisions in a stateless refugee context has been very limited indeed, a small body of case law exists. Overall, this jurisprudence illustrates

---

[130] It is therefore puzzling that art 17 of the EU Qualification Directive 2011 provides exclusion clauses similar to those in the *Refugee Convention* (art 1F) but for persons seeking subsidiary protection (i.e. on grounds similar to *ECHR* grounds).

[131] European Court of Human Rights (ECtHR): *Auad v Bulgaria*, Application No 46390/10 (11 January 2012) [100]–[101]. The Court concluded that in view of '[t]he lack of a legal framework providing adequate safeguards … there are substantial grounds for believing that the applicant risks a violation of his rights under Article 3': at [107].

[132] Verfassungsgerichtshof [Constitutional Court of Austria], U2131/2012, 6 March 2014.

[133] CCE, arrêt n°157845, 8 December 2015; CCE, arrêt n°155732, 29 October 2015; CCE, arrêt n°142096, 27 March 2015; CCE, arrêt n°134185, 28 November 2014.

[134] Pillai and Williams, 'Twenty-First Century Banishment' (n 117) 537–38.

a particularly cautious attitude by judicial decision-makers for two reasons: first, cessation and exclusion clauses impose limits on the inclusion clauses, hence they have to be interpreted restrictively; second, courts and tribunals accept stateless persons as particularly vulnerable because of their statelessness and consequential lack of state protection and denial of access to key rights. As a result, provisions on cessation and exclusion have scarcely been applied to stateless refugees.

7

Conclusion

The 1951 *Convention relating to the Status of Refugees* ('*Refugee Convention*') is clearly relevant to the protection of de jure stateless persons on the move. As this book has established, its pertinence has increased steadily over the years and is endorsed in a gradually more progressive reading of the *Refugee Convention* by senior courts, legal practitioners, and scholars.

The background to this modern interpretation is an international refugee law regime informed and enriched by the significant developments in international law that post-date its formulation. A comprehensive web of human rights treaties, including the 1954 *Convention relating to the Status of Stateless Persons* ('*1954 Convention*') and the 1961 *Convention on the Reduction of Statelessness* ('*1961 Convention*'), as well as soft law and jurisprudence, are relevant to and appropriately relied upon in refugee decision-making across a wide range of jurisdictions. This evolutionary interpretation of the *Refugee Convention* means that its ambit extends beyond that envisaged by the drafters. An examination of the *travaux préparatoires* of both the 1951 *Refugee Convention* and the *1954 Convention* as well as the contemporaneous literature, in Chapter 2, uncovers a notional engagement with the root causes of statelessness. At the time, it was clear who were 'unprotected persons' as a result of the Second World War, and consensus existed that they should be protected and able to access and enjoy certain rights. However, the reasons for their statelessness were not yet fully appreciated in human rights terms.

Chapter 3 thus examined the changing significance of nationality in international law over time. From being merely viewed as a technical legal issue, statelessness has emerged as an important human rights issue. State discretion in matters of nationality has come to be limited by the right to a nationality, the prohibition on arbitrary deprivation of nationality, the prevention of statelessness, the rights of children, and crucially in the context of this book, the role of non-discrimination, which provides a critical link to the definition of a refugee and, in particular, the concept of persecution.

Notwithstanding these developments, there remains room for further evolution. For instance, there is still today no *universally* guaranteed right to a nationality that is enforceable against a particular state (except in the case of children). Nevertheless, all main *regional* instruments guarantee the right of everyone to a nationality as part of one's legal identity or legal status. Some of these regional instruments also contain provisions for the elimination of statelessness. Yet, no court or supervisory body appears to have recognized statelessness per se and/or the act of depriving arbitrarily

International Refugee Law and the Protection of Stateless Persons. Michelle Foster and Hélène Lambert. © Michelle Foster and Hélène Lambert 2019. Published 2019 by Oxford University Press.

someone of their nationality as a form of inhuman or degrading treatment. This is particularly noteworthy in the context of the *Convention for the Protection of Human Rights and Fundamental Freedoms*, where the interpretation of inhuman and degrading treatment in recent years has evolved to apply to asylum seekers (as vulnerable people wholly dependent on state support) and children (as extremely vulnerable people) in situations of extreme poverty, serious deprivation, or want incompatible with human dignity. We observed that there is scope for legal arguments to be put forward by representatives of stateless persons relating to the consequences of being stateless (i.e. pointing to tangible detriment), particularly in cases where there is nowhere else to go for the applicant and he or she would otherwise live in a state of limbo.[1]

Our overall argument is that while there is scope for further evolution in establishing the right to a nationality, human rights law today imposes significant constraints on states in the formulation and application of their nationality laws that ought to be considered by refugee decision-makers. In the second half of Chapter 3 we examined the impact that international human rights law has had in terms of expanding obligations on states to protect all those within territory or jurisdiction, including stateless persons. This understanding is vital for an accurate assessment of whether deprivation of rights in a stateless person's country of former habitual residence amounts to persecution for the purposes of refugee law.

When it comes to accessing the *Refugee Convention*, Chapter 4 discussed the complex legal and factual issues that stateless persons face. The first issue concerned the legal definition of a refugee and whether this requires persons without a nationality to meet the same criteria as those set for persons with a nationality. With rare exceptions, legal scholars and senior courts across the world have rejected any distinction between refugees with and without a nationality in favour of a single test for refugee status. Indeed, neither statelessness per se nor the inability to return *automatically* confers refugee status on a stateless person, nor does it automatically deprive a stateless person from refugee status. The second issue concerned the meaning of 'not having a nationality' in the refugee definition. Following an analysis based on the *travaux préparatoires* of the 1951 *Refugee Convention* and the *1954 Convention*, the rules of treaty interpretation and case law globally, we concluded that 'not having a nationality' (Article 1A(2) *Refugee Convention*) means 'not considered as a national by any State' (Article 1(1) *1954 Convention*). We clarified that a state's illegal withdrawal or refusal of nationality is a pertinent question in establishing a well-founded fear of persecution, but that it has no bearing on the question of the country of reference. We also argued for a rejection outright of the principle of inchoate nationality based on the ordinary meaning of the text of the refugee definition (Article 1A(2)) and a contextual reading of the *Refugee Convention*. Finally, on the meaning of the

---

[1] We are grateful to Judith Carter for this insight. See also, Hélène Lambert, 'Nationality and Statelessness before the European Court of Human Rights: A Landmark Judgment but What About Article 3 ECHR?' (*Strasbourg Observers*, 16 May 2018) <https://strasbourgobservers.com/2018/05/16/nationality-and-statelessness-before-the-european-court-of-human-rights-a-landmark-judgment-but-what-about-article-3-echr/> accessed 16 November 2018.

key phrase 'country of former habitual residence', the *travaux préparatoires* and the case law are clear that 'residence' does not mean 'domicile'; it simply means residence 'of some standing and duration'. In situations where an applicant has more than one country of habitual residence, he or she only needs to establish a well-founded fear of persecution in relation to one of those countries.

Chapter 5 interrogated the distinction often made in the case law between state-less persons and refugees by focusing on the concept of persecution, the core of refugee claims. It is here, in the case law pertinent to persecution, that we found the clearest evidence of statelessness having evolved from a mere technical issue to a human rights issue. This is particularly visible in cases of withdrawal of nationality (or denationalization) leading to statelessness, on a ground protected by the *Refugee Convention*, where courts have generally accepted these acts to amount to persecu-tion. However, in instances of denial of nationality decision-makers have been less willing to interrogate or question state sovereignty in nationality laws. In our view, closer attention to the discrimination potentially underlying nationality legislation, an issue that has received greater attention from researchers and policy makers in recent years, would result in a more sophisticated refugee law jurisprudence on this issue. In terms of the impact of statelessness, as this book has explored, stateless-ness is much more than a technical legal issue; it has a social significance by way of affecting the everyday lives of millions of persons without a nationality. However, there is still resistance on the parts of national courts and tribunals assessing refugee claims to fully engage with what it means to be stateless. Only then will the full po-tential of the legal definition of a refugee in the *Refugee Convention* be reached for stateless persons.

Chapter 5 also argued for a more robust consideration of the 'right to return' for stateless persons, especially by reference to Article 12(4) of the *International Covenant on Civil and Political Rights*. Correctly applied, Article 12(4) can be grounds for arguing that prohibiting someone from returning to his or her own country due to that person's statelessness can amount to persecution on ground of (lack of) nationality. Finally, in Chapter 5 we observed that differential treatment between citizens and stateless persons is further entrenched in the case law con-cerning denial of rights as a consequence of statelessness, with senior courts often as-suming (wrongly) that stateless persons are not entitled to enjoy the whole gamut of human rights in their own country, and therefore cannot be at risk of persecution for the purpose of refugee law. In our view, such reasoning and resulting jurisprudence fails to understand the discrimination at the heart of the predicament of many state-less applicants, as well as the impact that statelessness has on children in particular and the enjoyment of rights more generally.

Finally, Chapter 6 examined the provisions on cessation and exclusion in the *Refugee Convention* that apply distinctly to stateless persons as well as those that do not call for any distinctions to be made between applicants with a nationality and those without. It noted the existence of a small body of case law illustrative of a liberal application of these provisions to stateless persons and considered the the-oretical relevance to refugee law of newly adopted legislation on denationalization for security reasons.

Our analysis of each independent element of the *Refugee Convention*, in light of existing jurisprudence and parallel relevant developments in international law, supports our hypothesis that there is far greater capacity for the protection of stateless persons pursuant to the 1951 *Refugee Convention* than has been assumed to date.

However, regardless of the progressiveness of an interpretation of the *Refugee Convention*, many stateless persons outside their country will not meet the refugee definition. In the many countries in which there is no alternative form of protection, and in particular, that required by the *1954 Convention*, they are likely to find themselves 'stateless and in limbo',[2] as recognized by domestic judges across multiple jurisdictions, who have expressed great concern about the plight of such stateless persons.[3] Judges have acknowledged that the twin consequences of inability to be returned to any other country and the lack of status in the host country can leave stateless persons vulnerable to other human rights violations, such as indefinite detention,[4] and relegation to destitution.[5] In one decision of the Full Federal Court of Australia that dismissed an appeal against a decision to reject the refugee claim of a stateless individual of 'Western Saharan' origin, Justice Wigney acknowledged that the 'end result' for the applicant is 'uncertain',[6] and that having been in immigration detention for over five years at the date of the decision, he 'remains in detention'[7] in Australia with no right to a protection visa, nor any right to return to any other country.

This points to the need for *both* a more informed assessment of refugee status in the case of stateless persons and also implementation of the *1954 Convention* in those states that are party to both treaties. The UNHCR recommends that States consider 'combining statelessness and refugee determination in the same procedure'.[8] However, due to the higher level of protection accorded by the 1951 *Refugee Convention*, refugee claims must be prioritized in such a case. In particular, '[c]onfidentiality requirements for applications by asylum seekers and refugees must be respected regardless of the form or location of the statelessness determination procedure'.[9] In practice this means that '[e]very applicant in a statelessness determination procedure is to be informed at the outset of the need to raise refugee-related

---

[2] *Al-Shimeary v Secretary of State for the Home Department* [2011] EWHC 564 (17 January 2011) at [29] (hereafter *Al-Shimeary*).

[3] In *Al-Shimeary*, ibid, Judge Kaye expressed 'some sadness' about the predicament that the applicant was left in once his claim for protection was dismissed: at [34]. In the decision of the Full Federal Court of Australia in *SZUNZ v Minister for Immigration and Border Protection* [2015] FCAFC 32 (13 March 2015) (hereafter *SZUNZ*), Justice Wigney observed that the case 'shows how a stateless person is prone to end up in a potential immigration limbo when he (or she) has no right or entitlement to enter any other country': at [77]. Similarly, in *Abeleira v Minister of Immigration, Refugees and Citizenship Canada* (2017) FC 1008 (7 November 2017), the stateless applicant for permanent residence on humanitarian and compassionate grounds 'faces an indefinite period of legal limbo in Canada': at [57].

[4] For instance, the applicant in *SZUNZ* (n 3), had been in immigration detention over five years at the date of the decision.

[5] In *Al-Shimeary* (n 2), the judge noted that the claimant is 'now at a complete impasse' because he 'cannot legitimately get entry into the United Kingdom and he cannot legitimately get back to Kuwait': at [29]. In addition, he 'appears to be destitute': at [29].

[6] *SZUNZ* (n 3) [128]. [7] ibid, [128].

[8] UNHCR, 'Handbook on Protection of Stateless Persons' (Geneva 2014) [66]. [9] ibid.

concerns, should they exist',[10] and 'the identity of a refugee or an asylum-seeker must not be disclosed to the authorities of the individual's country of origin',[11] for example in the course of seeking clarification of nationality. In this way, a comprehensive approach to protecting stateless persons outside their own country can be developed which ensures full compliance with the two core treaties: the *Refugee Convention* and the *1954 Convention*.

This book has pointed to the need for a better understanding of the causes and consequences of statelessness in the context of refugee status determination, meaning that the analysis has particular implications for refugee advocates and decision-makers. Yet we believe it also has implications for scholars, researchers, and advocates interested in the protection of stateless persons more broadly. Our analysis has suggested a need for more research across multiple disciplines, but particularly that which bridges the social, economic, and philosophical understandings of statelessness with legal obligations. In particular, recent research that reveals the very strong connection between minority status and statelessness suggests scope for further exploration of the ramifications of the norm of non-discrimination on the basis of race—widely understood to have *jus cogens* status—for international law standards that (in relation to nationality) are predicated in part on state sovereignty. The potential for refugeehood to lead to statelessness—discussed in Chapter 1—is another example of an issue in need of further research.

It is certainly the case that statelessness has 'arrived' as an area of academic study,[12] and it is hoped that this volume contributes to and further inspires a rich scholarship to continue to develop which will complement and support the international community's efforts to identify and protect stateless persons, and ultimately eliminate statelessness.

---

[10] ibid, [79].   [11] ibid.

[12] Mark Manly and Laura van Waas, 'The State of Statelessness Research: A Human Rights Imperative' (2014) 19 Tilburg Law Review 3, 3.

Bibliography

BOOKS AND MONOGRAPHS

Anker, D E, *Law of Asylum in the United States* (Thomson Reuters 2013)

Anker, D E, *Law of Asylum in the United States* (Thomson Reuters 2017)

Arendt, H, *The Origins of Totalitarianism* (Schocken Books 1951)

Battjes, H, *European Asylum Law and International Law* (Brill 2006)

Bianchini, K, *Protecting Stateless Persons: The Implementation of the Convention relating to the Status of Stateless Persons across EU States* (Brill Nijhoff 2018)

Blitz, B K and Lynch, M (eds), *Statelessness and Citizenship: A Comparative Study on the Benefits of Nationality* (Edward Elgar 2011)

Clapham, A, *Brierly's Law of Nations* (7th edn, OUP 2012)

Cohen, G D, *In War's Wake—Europe's Displaced Persons in the Postwar Order* (OUP 2012)

Conklin, W E, *Statelessness: The Enigma of the International Community* (Hart 2014)

Crawford, J, *Brownlie's Principles of Public International Law* (8th edn, OUP 2012)

Crock, M and Berg, L, *Immigration Refugees and Forced Migration: Law, Policy and Practice in Australia* (The Federation Press 2011)

Dembour, M-B, *When Humans Become Migrants: Study of the European Court of Human Rights with an Inter-American Counterpoint* (OUP 2015)

Edwards, A and Ferstman, C (eds), *Human Security and Non-Citizens: Law, Policy and International Affairs* (CUP 2010)

Edwards, A and van Waas, L (eds), *Nationality and Statelessness under International Law* (CUP 2014)

Foster, M, *International Refugee Law and Socio-Economic Rights: Refuge from Deprivation* (CUP 2007)

Fripp, E, *Nationality and Statelessness in the International Law of Refugee Status* (Hart 2016)

Goodwin-Gill, G S, *The Refugee in International Law* (2nd edn, OUP 1996)

Goodwin-Gill, G S and Lambert, H (eds), *The Limits of Transnational Law: Refugee Law, Policy Harmonization and Judicial Dialogue in the European Union* (CUP 2010)

Goodwin-Gill, G S and McAdam, J, *The Refugee in International Law* (3rd edn, OUP 2007)

Grahl-Madsen, A, *The Status of Refugees in International Law*, vol 1 (A W Sijthoff 1966)

Harris, D J, *Cases and Materials on International Law* (5th edn, Sweet & Maxwell 1998)

Hathaway, J, *The Law of Refugee Status* (Butterworths 1991)

Hathaway, J and Foster, M, *The Law of Refugee Status* (2nd edn, CUP 2014)

Higgins, R, *Problems and Process: International Law and How We Use It* (Clarendon Press 1994)

Hirsch Ballin, E, *Citizens' Rights and the Right to Be a Citizen* (Brill Nijhoff 2014)

Holborn, L, *The International Refugee Organization: A Specialized Agency of the United Nations, Its History and Work, 1946–1952* (OUP 1956)

Howard-Hassmann, R E and Walton-Roberts, M (eds), *The Human Right to Citizenship: A Slippery Concept* (University of Pennsylvania Press 2015)

Institute on Statelessness and Inclusion, *The World's Stateless* (Wolf Legal Publishers 2014)

Institute on Statelessness and Inclusion, *The World's Stateless: Children* (Wolf Legal Publishers 2017)

International Law Commission (ILC), *Draft Articles on Nationality of Natural Persons in relation to the Succession of Sates with Commentaries* (ILC 1999)

Jennings, R and Watts, A (eds), *Oppenheim's International Law*, vol I ('Peace') (9th edn, Longman 1992)

Jones, J M, *British Nationality Law and Practice* (Clarendon Press 1947)

Kesby, A, *The Right to Have Rights: Citizenship, Humanity, and International Law* (OUP 2012)

Lauterpacht, H, *International Law Collected Papers: The Law of Peace Part I International Law in General*, vol 2 (CUP 1975)

Lillich, R B, *The Human Rights of Aliens in Contemporary International Law* (Manchester University Press 1984)

Macartney, C A, *Refugees: The Work of the League* (League of Nations Union 1931)

Mutharika, A P, *The Regulation of Statelessness under International and National Law* (Oceana Publications 1977)

Perry, C and Fitzmaurice, G (eds), *British Digest of International Law Part VI: The Individual in International Law*, vol 5 (Stevens & Sons 1965)

Pobjoy, J, *The Child in International Refugee Law* (CUP 2017)

Robinson, N, *The Universal Declaration of Human Rights: Its Origin, Significance, Application, and Interpretation* (Institute of Jewish Affairs 1958)

Robinson, N, *Convention relating to the Status of Stateless Persons: Its History and Interpretation, A Commentary* (UNHCR 1997)

Salomon, K, *Refugees in the Cold War: Toward a New International Refugee Regime in the Early Postwar Era* (Lund University Press 1991)

Saul, B, Kinley, D, and Mowbray, J, *The International Covenant on Economic, Social and Cultural Rights: Commentary, Cases and Materials* (OUP 2014)

Simpson, J H, *The Refugee Problem: Report of a Survey* (OUP 1939)

Singer, S, *Terrorism and Exclusion from Refugee Status in the UK: Asylum Seekers Suspected of Serious Criminality* (Brill Nijhoff 2015)

Singh Juss, S, *International Migration and Global Justice* (Ashgate 2006)

Sjöberg, T, *The Powers and the Persecuted: The Refugee Problem and the Intergovernmental Committee on Refugees (IGCR), 1938–1947* (Lund University Press 1991)

Skran, C M, *Refugees in Inter-War Europe: The Emergence of a Regime* (Clarendon Press 1995)

Ssenyonjo, M, *Economic, Social and Cultural Rights in International Law* (Hart 2016)

Symes, M and Jorro, P, *Asylum Law and Practice* (2nd edn, Bloomsbury Professional 2010)

van Waas, L, *Nationality Matters: Statelessness under International Law* (Intersentia 2008)

Weis, P, *Nationality and Statelessness in International Law* (Steven & Sons 1956)

Weis, P, *Nationality and Statelessness in International Law* (2nd edn, Sijthoff & Noordhoff 1979)

Ziegler, R, *Voting Rights of Refugees* (CUP 2017)

ARTICLES, CHAPTERS, REPORTS, AND OCCASIONAL PAPERS

Albarazi, Z and van Waas, L, 'Statelessness and Displacement: Scoping Paper' (Norwegian Refugee Council and Tilburg University 2016)

Alexander, H and Simon, J, '"Unable to Return" in the 1951 Refugee Convention: Stateless Refugees and Climate Change' (2014) 26 Fla J Int'l L 531

Anderson, A, Foster, M, Lambert, H, and McAdam, J, 'Imminence in Refugee and Human Rights Law: A Misplaced Notion for International Protection' (2019) 68 ICLQ 111

Baluarte, D C, 'Life after Limbo: Stateless Persons in the United States and the Role of International Protection in Achieving a Legal Solution' (2015) 29 Geo Immigr L J 351

Batchelor, C A, 'Stateless Persons: Some Gaps in International Protection' (1995) 7 IJRL 232

Batchelor, C A, 'Statelessness and the Problem of Resolving Nationality Status' (1998) 10 IJRL 156

Batchelor, C A, 'The 1954 Convention relating to the Status of Stateless Persons: Implementation within the European Union Member States and Recommendations for Harmonization' (2005) 22 Refuge 31

Batchelor, C A, 'Transforming International Legal Principles into National Law: The Right to a Nationality and the Avoidance of Statelessness' (2006) 25 Refugee Survey Quarterly 8

Beck, R J, 'Britain and the 1933 Refugee Convention: National or State Sovereignty?' (1999) 11 IJRL 597

Berry, A, 'Who Are You? Fraud, Impersonation and Loss of Nationality Without Procedural Protection' (*European Network on Statelessness*, 25 June 2014) <www.statelessness.eu/blog/who-are-you-fraud-impersonation-and-loss-nationality-without-procedural-protection> accessed 10 November 2018

Bhabha, J, 'The Importance of Nationality for Children' in Institute on Statelessness and Inclusion (ISI), *The World's Stateless Children* (Wolf Legal Publishers 2017) 112

Blitz, B K and Lynch, M (eds), 'Statelessness and the Benefits of Citizenship: A Comparative Study' (Geneva Academy of International Humanitarian Law and Human Rights and the International Observatory on Statelessness 2009)

Bradsher, G, 'The Nuremberg Laws: Archives Receives Original Nazi Documents that "Legalized" Persecution of Jews' (2010) 42 *Prologue Magazine* <https://www.archives.gov/publications/prologue/2010/winter/nuremberg.html> accessed 12 November 2018

Byrne, R, 'James C. Hathaway and Michelle Foster. The Law of Refugee Status' (2015) 26 EJIL 564

Campbell, J, 'The Enduring Problem of Statelessness in the Horn of Africa: How Nation-States and Western Courts (Re)Define Nationality' (2011) 23 IJRL 656

Carter, J and Woodhouse, S, 'Statelessness and Applications for Leave to Remain: A Best Practice Guide' (Immigration Law Practitioners' Association, 3 November 2016)

de Castro, F, 'La nationalité' in *Recueil des cours*, vol 102 (Académie de Droit International 1961) 523

Chetail, V, 'The Transnational Movement of Persons under General International Law— Mapping the Customary Law Foundations of International Migration Law' in V Chetail and C Bauloz (eds), *Research Handbook on International Law and Migration* (Edward Elgar 2014) 1

de Chickera A and Whiteman, J, 'Discrimination and the Human Security of Stateless People' (2014) 46 Forced Migration Review 56

de Chickera, A and Whiteman, J, 'Addressing Statelessness through the Rights to Equality and Non-Discrimination' in L van Waas and M J Khanna (eds), *Solving Statelessness* (Wolf Legal Publishers 2016) 99

Choudhury, T, 'The Radicalisation of Citizenship Deprivation' (2017) 37 Critical Social Policy 225

Committee on Feminism and International Law, 'Final Report on Women's Equality and Nationality' (International Law Association Conference, London, 2000)

Costello, C, 'On Refugeehood and Citizenship' in A Shachar, R Bauböck, I Bloemraad, and M Vink (eds), *The Oxford Handbook of Citizenship* (OUP 2017)

Costello, C and Foster, M, 'Non-Refoulement as Custom and Jus Cogens? Putting the Prohibition to the Test' (2015) 46 NYIL 273

Council of Europe, 'Explanatory Report to the European Convention on Nationality' (Strasbourg, 6 November 1997)

Council of Europe, Committee of Ministers' Rec (2000) (Strasbourg, 13 September 2000) 15

Council of Europe, 'Explanatory Report to the Protocol No 12 to the Convention for the Protection of Human Rights and Fundamental Freedoms' (Strasbourg, 4 November 2000)

Council of Europe, Parliamentary Assembly Res 1989 (Strasbourg, 9 April 2014)

Council of Europe, Recommendation 2042 (Strasbourg, 9 April 2014)

Council of Europe, 'Chart of Signatures and Ratifications of Treaty 177' (*Council of Europe*, 30 June 2018) <http://www.coe.int/en/web/conventions/search-on-treaties/-/conventions/treaty/177/signatures?p_auth=0Kq9rtcm> accessed 12 November 2018

Darling, K, 'Protection of Stateless Persons in International Asylum and Refugee Law' (2009) 21 IJRL 742

Dembour, M-D, 'Ramadan v Malta: When Will the Strasbourg Court Understand that Nationality is a Core Human Rights Issue?' (*Strasbourg Observers*, 22 July 2016) <https://strasbourgobservers.com/2016/07/22/ramadan-v-malta-when-will-the-strasbourg-court-understand-that-nationality-is-a-core-human-rights-issue/> accessed 10 November 2018

Department of Immigration and Border Protection, *Procedures Advice Manual 3: Refugee and Humanitarian—Protection Visas—All Applications—Common Processing Guidelines* (16 February 2016)

Dhillon, A, 'India: 4 Million Excluded from Assam's Draft List of Citizens' *The Guardian* (London, 30 July 2018) <www.theguardian.com/world/2018/jul/30/four-million-excluded-from-indian-states-assam-draft-list-of-citizens> accessed 10 November 2018

Dörr, O, 'Article 31: General Rule of Interpretation' in O Dörr and K Schmalenbach (eds), *Vienna Convention on the Law of Treaties: A Commentary* (Springer-Verlag 2012) 521

Dowd, R, 'Dissecting Discrimination in Refugee Law: An Analysis of its Meaning and its Cumulative Effect' (2011) 23 IJRL 28

Edwards, A, 'The Meaning of Nationality in International Law in an Era of Human Rights: Procedural and Substantive Issues' in A Edwards and L van Waas (eds), *Nationality and Statelessness under International Law* (CUP 2014) 11

Einarsen, T, 'Drafting History of the 1951 Convention and the 1967 Protocol' in A Zimmermann (ed), *The 1951 Convention relating to the Status of Refugees and its 1967 Protocol: A Commentary* (OUP 2011) 37

Ferris, E, 'Displacement and Statelessness' in *A World on the Move: Migration and Statelessness*, vol 1 (International Affairs Forum 2016) 79

Fitzmaurice, G, 'The General Principles of International Law Considered from the Standpoint of the Rule of Law' in *Recuil des cours*, vol 92 (Académie de Droit International 1957) 198

Fitzpatrick, J and Bonoan, R, 'Cessation of Refugee Protection' in E Feller, V Türk, and F Nicholson (eds), *Refugee Protection in International Law: UNHCR's Global Consultations on International Protection* (CUP 2003) 491

Forbes, S E, ' "Imagine There's No Country": Statelessness as Persecution in Light of *Haile II*' (2013) 61 BuffLR 699

Foster, M, 'An "Alien" by the Barest of Threads—the Legality of the Deportation of Long-Term Residents from Australia' (2009) 33 MULR 483

Foster, M and Lambert, H, 'Statelessness as a Human Rights Issue: A Concept Whose Time Has Come' (2016) 28 IJRL 564

Foster, M, McAdam, J, and Wadley, D, 'Part Two: The Prevention and Reduction of Statelessness in Australia—An Ongoing Challenge' (2017) 40 *MULR* 456

François, J-P-A, 'Le problème des apatrides' in *Recueil des cours*, vol 53 (Académie de Droit International 1935) 283

Fripp, E, 'Deprivation of Nationality, "the Country of His Nationality" in Article 1A(2) of the Refugee Convention, and Non-Recognition in International Law' (2016) 28 IJRL 453

Fullerton, M, 'Without Protection: Refugees and Statelessness—A Commentary and Challenge' (Brooklyn Law School Legal Studies Paper No 351, 8 August 2013) 29 https:// papers.ssrn.com/abstract_id=2307531 accessed 13 November 2018

Fullerton, M, 'The Intersection of Statelessness and Refugee Protection in US Asylum Policy' (2014) 2 JMHS 144

Fullerton, M, 'Comparative Perspectives on Statelessness and Persecution' (2015) 63 UKanLRev 863

Gamboa, L and Harrington Reddy, J, 'Judicial Denationalisation of Dominicans of Haitian Descent' (2014) (46) Forced Migration Review 52

Gibney, M, ' "A Very Transcendental Power": Denaturalisation and the Liberalisation of Citizenship in the United Kingdom' (2013) 61 Political Studies 637

Gibney, M, 'Should Citizenship Be Conditional? The Ethics of Denationalization' (2013) 75 Journal of Politics 646

Gibney, M, 'Denationalization' in A Shachar, R Bauböck, I Bloemraad, and M Vink (eds), *The Oxford Handbook of Citizenship* (OUP 2017) 359

Gilbert, G, 'Current Issues in the Application of the Exclusion Clauses' in E Feller, V Türk, and F Nicholson (eds), *Refugee Protection in International Law: UNHCR's Global Consultations on International Protection* (CUP 2003) 425

Gillan, S, 'Refugee Convention: Whether Deprivation of Citizenship Amounts to Persecution' (2007) 21 JIANL 347

Goldschmidt, H, 'Recent Applications of Domestic Nationality Laws by International Tribunals' (1959) 28 Fordham LRev 689

Goodwin-Gill, G S, 'Nationality and Statelessness, Residence and Refugee Status: Issues Affecting Palestinians' (March 1990) <http://repository.forcedmigration.org/show_metadata.jsp?pid=fmo:567> accessed 9 December 2018

Goodwin-Gill, G S, 'Stateless Persons and Protection under the 1951 Convention or Refugees, Beware of Academic Error!' (Colloque portant sur 'Les récents developpements en droit de l'immigration', Barreau de Québec, 22 January 1993)

Goodwin-Gill, G S, 'The Rights of Refugees and Stateless Persons' in K P Saksena (ed), *Human Rights Perspective and Challenges* (Lancers Books 1994) 378

Goodwin-Gill, G S, '*Revenko v Secretary of State for the Home Department:* Report on Behalf of the Appellant' (UK Court of Appeal Civil Division, 23 July 2000)

Goodwin-Gill, G S, 'Convention relating to the Status of Refugees; Protocol relating to the Status of Refugees' (United Nations Audiovisual Library of International Law 2008)

Goodwin-Gill, G S, 'Convention relating to the Status of Stateless Persons' (United Nations Audiovisual Library of International Law 2010)

Goodwin-Gill, G S, 'Mr Al-Jedda, Deprivation of Citizenship, and International Law' (Seminar, Middlesex University, 14 February 2014)

Goodwin-Gill, G S, 'Deprivation of Citizenship Resulting in Statelessness and its Implications in International Law' (Opinion Piece, 12 March 2014)

Goodwin-Gill, G S, 'Deprivation of Citizenship Resulting in Statelessness and its Implications in International Law: Further Comments' (6 April 2014) <https://www.law.oxoac.u/research-and-subject-groups/human-rights-law/publications?page=10> accessed 9 December 2018

Goodwin-Gill, G S, 'Deprivation of Citizenship Resulting in Statelessness and its Implications in International Law: More Authority (If It Were Needed . . .)' (5 May 2014) (unpublished paper)

Goodwin-Gill, G S, 'International Refugee Law: Yesterday, Today, but Tomorrow?' (January 2017) (paper on file with authors) <https://www.blackstonechambers.com/documents/306/GSGG-PastPresentFuture.pdf > accessed 11 February 2019

de Groot, G-R, 'Children, their Right to a Nationality and Child Statelessness' in A Edwards and L van Waas, *Nationality and Statelessness under International Law* (CUP 2014) 144

Hailbronner, K, 'Nationality in Public International Law and European Law' in R Bauböck, E Ersbøll, K Groenendijk, and H Waldrauch (eds), *Acquisition and Loss of Nationality: Policies and Trends in 15 European Countries*, vol 1 (Amsterdam University Press 2006) 35

Hall, S, 'The European Convention on Nationality and the Right to Have Rights' (1999) 24 ELRev 586

Hamann, K, 'Statelessness Determination: The Swiss Experience' (February 2017) 54 FMR 96

Hanley, W, 'Statelessness: An Invisible Theme in the History of International Law' (2014) 25 EJIL 321

Hathaway, J C, 'The Evolution of Refugee Status in International Law: 1920–1950' (1984) 33 ICLQ 348

Holborn, L W, 'The Legal Status of Political Refugees, 1920–1938' (1938) 32 AJIL 680

Hudson, M O and Flournoy Jr, R W, 'The Law of Nationality' (1929) 23 AJIL Supplement: Codification of International Law 1

Immigration and Refugee Board of Canada, 'Interpretation of the Convention Refugee Definition in the Case Law' (December 2010) Legal Refeences, Ch 2 para 2.2 <http://wwwirb-cisr.gc.ca/Eng/BoaCom/references/LegJur/Pages/RefDef02.aspx> accessed 15 November 2018

Imseis, A, 'Statelessness and Convention Refugee Determination: An Examination of the Palestinian Experience at the Immigration and Refugee Board of Canada' (1997) 31 UBC Law Rev 317

Institute on Statelessness and Inclusion, 'Addressing the Right to a Nationality through the Convention on the Rights of the Child: A Toolkit for Civil Society' <www.institutesi.org/children> accessed 10 November 2018

Inter-American Commission on Human Rights, 'Situation of Human Rights in the Dominican Republic' (31 December 2015) OEA/Ser.L/V/II Doc 45/15

Intergovernmental Committee on Refugees, 'Statelessness and Some of Its Causes: An Outline' (IGCR 1946)

International Association for Refugee Law Judges European Chapter, 'Qualification for International Protection (Directive 2011/95/EU): A Judicial Analysis' (European Asylum support Office December 2016)

International Law Association, 'Final Report on Women's Equality and Nationality in International Law' (2000) 69 ILA Rep Conf 257

Isay, E, 'De la nationalité' in *Recueil des cours*, vol 5 (Académie de Droit International 1924) 429

Jeffers, K, Honohan, I, and Bauböck, R, 'Comparing Citizenship across Europe: Laws, Implementation and Impact, CITLAW Indicators: How to Measure the Purposes of Citizenship Laws' (EUDO 2012)

Jennings, R Y, 'Some International Law Aspects of the Refugee Question' (1939) 20 BYBIL 98

Joseph, S and Castan, M, *The International Covenant on Civil and Political Rights: Cases, Materials, and Commentary* (3rd edn, OUP 2013)

Keetharuth, S, 'The African Charter and the Right to a Nationality' (Report of a Meeting Held in Banjul, The Gambia, 14 May 2010)

Kim, K, 'Lack of State Protection or Fear of Persecution? Determining the Refugee Status of North Koreans in Canada' (2016) 28 IJRL 85

Kingston, L N, 'Bringing Rwandan Refugees "Home": The Cessation Clause, Statelessness, and Forced Repatriation' (2017) 29 IJRL 417

Lambert, H, 'The European Court of Human Rights and the Right of Refugees and Other Persons in Need of Protection to Family Reunion' (1999) 11 IJRL 427

Lambert, H, 'Transnational Judicial Dialogue, Harmonization and the Common European Asylum System' (2009) 58 ICLQ 519

Lambert, H, 'Comparative Perspectives on Arbitrary Deprivation of Nationality and Refugee Status' (2015) 64 ICLQ 1

Lambert, H, 'Nationality and Statelessness before the European Court of Human Rights: A Landmark Judgment but What About Article 3 ECHR?' (*Strasbourg Observers*, 16 May 2018) <https://strasbourgobservers.com/2018/05/16/nationality-and-statelessness-before-the-european-court-of-human-rights-a-landmark-judgment-but-what-about-article-3-echr/> accessed 10 November 2018

League of Nations, 'Armenian Refugees: Report by Dr Fridtjof Nansen High Commission for Refugees' (31 May 1924) LN Doc C 237 1924

Lepoutre, J, 'Les États membres de l'Union peuvent-ils vendre la citoyenneté européenne?' (2015) 19 Petites affiches 6

'Letter of Resignation of James G McDonald, High Commissioner for Refugees (Jewish and Other) Coming from Germany addressed to the Secretary General of the League of Nations' (27 December 1935) LN Doc C.B.M.12.1936.XII v

Lori, N A, 'Statelessness, "In-Between" Statutes and Precarious Citizenship' in A Shachar, R Baubock, I Bloemraad, and Maarten Vink (eds), *The Oxford Handbook of Citizenship* (OUP 2017)

Macklin, A, 'Who Is the Citizen's Other? Considering the Heft of Citizenship' (2007) 8 Theo Inq Law 333

Macklin, A, 'Citizenship Revocation, the Privilege to Have Rights and the Production of the Alien' (2014) 40 Queens LJ 1

Macklin, A, 'Introduction' in A Macklin and R Baubock (eds), *The Return of Banishment: Do the New Denationalisation Policies Weaken Citizenship* (EUI Working Papers 2015)

Macklin, A, 'Sticky Citizenship' in R E Howard-Hassmann and M Walton-Roberts (eds), *The Human Right to Citizenship: A Slippery Concept* (University of Pennsylvania Press 2015) 231

Manly, M, 'UNHCR's Mandate and Activities to Address Statelessness' in A Edwards and L van Waas (eds), *Nationality and Statelessness under International Law* (CUP 2014)

Manly, M and van Waas, L, 'The Value of the Human Security Framework in Addressing Statelessness' in A Edwards and C Ferstman (eds), *Human Security and Non-Citizens: Law, Policy and International Affairs* (CUP 2010) 49

Manly, M and van Waas, L, 'The State of Statelessness Research: A Human Rights Imperative' (2014) 19 Tilburg Law Review 3

Mantu, S, '"Terrorist" Citizens and the Human Right to Nationality' (2018) 26 Journal of Contemporary European Studies 28

Marx, R, 'Article 1 E 1951 Convention' in A Zimmermann, F Machts, and J Dörschner (eds), *The 1951 Convention relating to the Status of Refugees and its 1967 Protocol: A Commentary* (OUP 2011) 571

Montecler, M-C de, 'Office de la CNDA pour determiner la nationalité d'un demandeur d'asile' (2014) (20) AJDA 1128

Mortenson, J D, 'The *Travaux* of *Travaux*: Is the Vienna Convention Hostile to Drafting History?' (2013) 107 AJIL 780

Noll, G, 'Evidentiary Assessment in Refugee Status Determination and the EU Qualification Directive' (2006) 12 EPL 295

Pillai, S and Williams, G, 'Twenty-First Century Banishment: Citizenship Stripping in Common Law Nations' (2017) 66 ICLQ 521

Policek, N, 'Turning the Invisible into the Visible: Stateless Children in Italy' in M O Ensor and E M Goździak (eds), *Children and Forced Migration* (Springer 2017)

Preuss, L, 'International Law and Deprivation of Nationality' (1935) 23 GeoLJ 250

Qafisheh, M M and Azarova, V, 'Article 1 D 1951 Convention' in A Zimmermann, F Machts, and J Dörschner (eds), *The 1951 Convention relating to the Status of Refugees and its 1967 Protocol: A Commentary* (OUP 2011) 536

Quintana, F, 'Inter-American Court Condemns Unprecedented Situation of Statelessness in the Dominican Republic' (*European Network on Statelessness*, 27 October 2014) <https:// www.statelessness.eu/blog/inter-american-court-condemns-unprecedented-situation-statelessness-dominican-republic> accessed 20 November 2018

Reynolds, S and Duoos, T, 'A Generation of Syrians Born in Exile Risk a Future of Statelessness' (*European Network on Statelessness*, 15 July 2015) <http://www.statelessness.eu/blog/ generation-syrians-born-exile-risk-future-statelessness> accessed 10 November 2018

Robinson, N, 'Convention relating to the Status of Stateless Persons: It's History and Interpretation: A Commentary' (World Jewish Congress, Institute of Jewish Affairs, 1955)

Rubinstein, M J L, 'The Refugee Problem' (1936) 15 International Affairs 716

Seet, M, 'The Origins of the UNHCR's Global Mandate on Statelessness' (2016) 28 IJRL 7

Sironi, A, 'Nationality of Individuals in Public International Law— A Functional Approach' in A Annoni and S Forlati (eds), *The Changing Role of Nationality in International Law* (Routledge 2013) 54

Skran, C M, 'Historical Development of International Refugee Law' in A Zimmermann (ed), *The 1951 Convention relating to the Status of Refugees and its 1967 Protocol: A Commentary* (OUP 2011) 2

Sloane, R D, 'Breaking the Genuine Link: The Contemporary International Legal Regulation of Nationality' (2009) 50 Harv Int'l LJ 1

Spiro, P J, 'A New International Law of Citizenship' (2011) 105 AJIL 694

Spiro, P J, 'Citizenship, Nationality, and Statelessness' in V Chetail and C Bauloz (eds), *Research Handbook on International Law and Migration* (Edward Elgar 2014) 281

Stark, B and Ziesemer, J, 'The Right to Have Rights: Loss of Citizenship, Asylum, and Constitutional Principles' (2016) 30 GeoImmigLJ 429

Sturkenboom, I and van Waas, L, 'How Real is the Risk of a "Stateless Generation" in Europe?: Reflections on How to Fulfil the Right to a Nationality for Children Born to Refugee and Migrant Parents in the European Union' (14 October 2016) <https://papers. ssrn.com/sol3/papers.cfm?abstract_id=2877368> accessed 9 December 2018

Thwaites, R, 'The Security of Citizenship?: Finnis in the Context of the United Kingdom's Citizenship Stripping Provisions' in F Jenkins, M Nolan, and K Rubenstein (eds), *Allegiance and Identity in a Globalised World* (CUP (2014) 243

UK Home Office, 'Asylum Policy Instruction: Statelessness and Applications for Leave to Remain' (Home Office, 18 February 2016)

UK Home Office, 'Nationality: Doubtful, Disputed and Other Cases' (Home Office, 2 October 2017)

UNHCR, 'Revised Note on the Applicability of Article 1D of the 1951 Convention relating to the Status of Refugees to Palestinian Refugees' (2009) 28 Refugee Survey Quarterly 657

UN Treaty Collection, 'Chapter V: Refugees and Stateless Persons, 4. Convention on the Reduction of Statelessness' (UN Treaty Collection, 12 July 2018) <https://treaties.un.org/Pages/ViewDetails.aspx?src=IND&mtdsg_no=V-4&chapter=5&clang=_en> accessed 12 November 2018

Verdross, A, 'Les règles internationales concernant le traitement des étrangers' in *Recueil des cours*, vol 37 (Académie de Droit International 1931) 339

Vermeer-Künzli, A, 'Diplomatic Protection and Consular Assistance of Migrants' in V Chetail and C Bauloz (eds), *Research Handbook on International Law and Migration* (Edward Elgar 2014) 265

Vichniac, M, 'Le statut international des apatrides' in *Recueil des cours*, vol 43 (Académie de Droit International 1933) 119

Viel, C, 'Détermination de la nationalité du demandeur d'asile: le Conseil d'Etat encadre l'office de la CNDA' (2004) (235) Dictionnaire permanent—Droit des étrangers 10

Volpp, L, 'Feminist, Sexual and Queer Citizenship' in A Shachar, R Bauböck, I Bloemraad, and M Vink (eds), *The Oxford Handbook of Citizenship* (OUP 2017) 53

Vukas, B, 'International Instruments Dealing with the Status of Stateless Persons and of Refugees' (1972) 8 Revue Belge de Droit International 143

van Waas, L, 'The UN Statelessness Conventions' in A Edwards and L van Waas (eds), *Nationality and Statelessness under International Law* (CUP 2014) 64

van Waas, L and de Chickera, A, 'Chapter 7: Introduction' in ISI, *The World's Stateless: Children* (Wolf Legal Publishers 2017) 109

Waldron, J, 'Supersession and Sovereignty' (Julius Stone Address, University of Sydney, 3 August 2006)

Weis, P, 'Statelessness as a Legal-Political Problem' in P Weis and R Graupner, *The Problem of Statelessness* (British Section of the World Jewish Congress 1944)

Weis, P, 'The International Protection of Refugees' (1954) 48 AJIL 183

Weis, P, 'The United Nations Convention on the Reduction of Statelessness, 1961' (1962) 11 ICLQ 1073

Williams, J F, 'Denationalization' (1927) 8 BYBIL 45

Zedner, L, 'Citizenship Deprivation, Security and Human Rights' (2016) 18 EJML 222

Ziemele, I, 'State Succession and Issues of Nationality and Statelessness' in A Edwards and L van Waas (eds), *Nationality and Statelessness under International Law* (CUP 2014) 217

Zimmermann, A and Mahler, C, 'Article 1 A, Para 2' in A Zimmermann (ed), *The 1951 Convention relating to the Status of Refugees and its 1967 Protocol: A Commentary* (OUP 2011) 280

Zimmermann, A and Wennholz, P, 'Article 1 F 1951 Convention' in A Zimmermann, F Machts, and J Dörschner (eds), *The 1951 Convention relating to the Status of Refugees and its 1967 Protocol: A Commentary* (OUP 2011) 579

SELECTED UNITED NATIONS DOCUMENTS

Ad Hoc Committee on Refugees and Stateless Persons, 'A Study of Statelessness' (1949) E/1112

Ad Hoc Committee on Refugees and Stateless Persons, 'Belgium: Proposal for Article I paragraph A.2 of Document E/AC.32/L.6/Rev.1' (31 January 1950) UN Doc E/AC.32/L.18

Ad Hoc Committee on Refugees and Stateless Persons, 'Summary Record of the Forty-Third Meeting' (28 September 1950) E/AC.32/SR.43

Ad Hoc Committee on Refugees and Stateless Persons, 'Draft Convention relating to the Status of Refugees, Decisions of the Working Group Taken on 9 February 1950' (9 February 1950) UN Doc E/AC.32/L.32

Ad Hoc Committee on Statelessness and Related Problems, 'Status of Refugees and Stateless Persons: Memorandum by the Secretary-General' (3 January 1950) UN Doc E/AC.32/2

Ad Hoc Committee on Statelessness and Related Problems, 'Elimination of Statelessness: Memorandum prepared by the Secretary-General' (17 January 1950) UN Doc E/AC.32/4

Ad Hoc Committee on Statelessness and Related Problems, 'United Kingdom: Draft Proposal of Article 1' (17 January 1950) UN Doc E/AC.32/L.2

Ad Hoc Committee on Statelessness and Related Problems, 'Provisional Draft of Parts of the Definition: Article of the Preliminary Draft Convention relating to the Status of Refugees, Prepared by the Working Group on this Article' (23 January 1950) UN Doc E/AC.32/L.6

Ad Hoc Committee on Statelessness and Related Problems, 'Summary Record of the First Meeting' (23 January 1950) UN Doc E/AC.32/SR.1

Ad Hoc Committee on Statelessness and Related Problems, 'Summary Record of the Second Meeting' (26 January 1950) UN Doc E/AC.32/SR.2

Ad Hoc Committee on Statelessness and Related Problems, 'Summary Record of the Third Meeting' (26 January 1950) UN Doc E/AC.32/SR.3

Ad Hoc Committee on Statelessness and Related Problems, 'Summary Record of the Fourth Meeting' (26 January 1950) UN Doc E/AC.32/SR.4

Ad Hoc Committee on Statelessness and Related Problems, 'First Session: Summary Record of the Eighth Meeting Held at Lake Success, New York, on Monday, 23 January 1950, at 3 p.m' (30 January 1950) UN Doc E/AC.32/SR.8

Ad Hoc Committee on Statelessness and Related Problems, 'Memorandum from the Secretariat of the International Refugee Organization' (30 January 1950) UN Doc E/AC.32/L.16

Ad Hoc Committee on Statelessness and Related Problems, 'Decisions of the Committee on Statelessness and Related Problems Taken at the Meetings of 31 January 1950' (31 January 1950) UN Doc E/AC.32/L.20

Ad Hoc Committee on Statelessness and Related Problems, 'First Session: Summary Record of the Ninth Meeting Held at Lake Success, New York, on Tuesday, 24 January 1950, at 11 a.m.' (3 February 1950) UN Doc E/AC.32/SR.9

Ad Hoc Committee on Statelessness and Related Problems, 'Draft Convention relating to the Status of Refugees, Decisions of the Working Group Taken on 9 February 1950' (9 February 1950) UN Doc E/AC.32/L.32

Ad Hoc Committee on Statelessness and Related Problems, 'Comments of the Committee on the Draft Convention' (10 February 1950) UN Doc E/AC.32/L.32/Add.1

Ad Hoc Committee on Statelessness and Related Problems, 'Summary Record of the Twenty-Second Meeting' (14 February 1950) UN Doc E/AC.32/SR.22

Ad Hoc Committee on Statelessness and Related Problems, 'Summary Record of the Twenty-Fifth Meeting' (17 February 1950) UN Doc E/AC.32/SR.25

Ad Hoc Committee on Statelessness and Related Problems, 'Summary Record of the Twenty-Sixth Meeting' (23 February 1950) UN Doc E/AC.32/SR.26

Ad Hoc Committee on Statelessness and Related Problems, 'Summary Record of the Twenty-Seventh Meeting' (23 February 1950) E/AC.32/SR.27

Ad Hoc Committee on Statelessness and Related Problems, 'Summary Record of the Twenty-Eighth Meeting' (23 February 1950) UN Doc E/AC.32/SR.28

Ad Hoc Committee on Statelessness and Related Problems, 'Summary Record of the Twenty-Ninth Meeting' (23 February 1950) UN Doc E/AC.32/SR.29

African Commission on Human and Peoples' Rights, '234: Resolution on the Right to Nationality' (23 April 2013)

African Committee of Experts on the Rights and Welfare of the Child (ACERWC), 'General Comment on Article 6 of the African Charter on the Rights and Welfare of the Child' (16 April 2014) ACERWC/GC/02

Committee on the Protection of the Rights of All Migrant Workers and Members of their Families and Committee on the Rights of the Child, 'Joint General Comment No 3 (2017) of the CMW and No 22 (2017) of the CRC on the General Principles regarding the Human Rights of Children in the Context of International Migration' (16 November 2017) UN Doc CMW/C/GC/3–CRC/C/GC/22

Committee on the Protection of the Rights of All Migrant Workers and Members of their Families and Committee on the Rights of the Child, 'Joint General Comment No 4 (2017) of the CMW and No 23 (2017) of the CRC on State Obligations regarding the Human Rights of Children in the Context of International Migration in Countries of Origin, Transit, Destination and Return' (16 November 2017) UN Doc CMW/C/GC/4–CRC/C/GC/23

Conference of Plenipotentiaries on the Status of Refugees and Stateless Persons, 'Final Act and Convention relating to the Status of Refugees' (2–25 July 1951) UN Doc A/CONF.2/108

Conference of Plenipotentiaries on the Status of Refugees and Stateless Persons, 'Summary Record of the Second Meeting' (29 September 1954) UN Doc E/CONF.17/SR.2

Conference of Plenipotentiaries on the Status of Refugees and Stateless Persons, 'Summary Record of the Third Meeting' (29 September 1954) UN Doc E/CONF.17/SR.3

Conference of Plenipotentiaries on the Status of Refugees and Stateless Persons, 'Summary Record of the Sixth Meeting' (29 September 1954) UN Doc E/CONF.17/SR.6

Conference of Plenipotentiaries on the Status of Refugees and Stateless Persons, 'Summary Record of the Seventh Meeting' (29 September 1954) UN Doc E/CONF.17/SR.7

Conference of Plenipotentiaries on the Status of Refugees and Stateless Persons, 'Summary Record of the Eighth Meeting' (29 September 1954) UN Doc E/CONF.17/SR.8

Conference of Plenipotentiaries on the Status of Refugees and Stateless Persons, 'Summary Record of the Ninth Meeting' (30 September 1954) UN Doc E/CONF.17/SR.9

Conference of Plenipotentiaries on the Status of Refugees and Stateless Persons, 'Summary Record of the Tenth Meeting' (6 October 1954) UN Doc E/CONF.17/SR.10

Conference of Plenipotentiaries on the Status of Refugees and Stateless Persons, 'Summary Record of the Twelfth Meeting' (12 October 1954) UN Doc E/CONF.17/SR.12

Conference of Plenipotentiaries on the Status of Refugees and Stateless Persons, 'Summary Record of the Third Meeting' (12 October 1954) UN Doc E/CONF.17/SR.13

Conference of Plenipotentiaries on the Status of Refugees and Stateless Persons, 'Summary Record of the Sixteenth Meeting' (23 November 1951) UN Doc A/CONF.2/SR.16

Conference of Plenipotentiaries on the Status of Refugees and Stateless Persons, 'Summary Record of the Nineteenth Meeting' (26 November 1951) UN Doc A/CONF.2/SR.19

Conference of Plenipotentiaries on the Status of Refugees and Stateless Persons, 'Summary Record of the Twenty-Third Meeting' (26 November 1951) UN Doc A/CONF.2/SR.23

Conference of Plenipotentiaries on the Status of Refugees and Stateless Persons, 'Summary Record of the Thirty-First Meeting' (29 November 1951) UN Doc A/CONF.2/SR.31

Conference of Plenipotentiaries on the Status of Refugees and Stateless Persons, 'Summary Record of the Thirty-Fourth Meeting' (30 November 1951) UN Doc A/CONF.2/34

Edwards, A, 'Displacement, Statelessness and Questions of Gender Equality under the Convention on the Elimination of All Forms of Discrimination Against Women' (Background Paper, UNHCR Legal and Protection Policy Research Series, April 2009)

European Commission, 'Communication from the commission to the European Parliament, The European Council, the Council and the European Investment Bank on Establishing a New Partnership Framework with Third Countries under the European Agenda on Migration' (Strasbourg, 7 June 2016) COM (2016) 385 final

Hudson, M O, 'Report on Nationality, Including Statelessness' (12 February 1952) UN Doc A/CN.4/50

Immigration and Naturalization Service Officer of the General Counsel, Memorandum 'Legal Opinion: Your Memorandum of June 6, 1992: Palestine Applicants' to Margaret Ramos, Supervisory Asylum Officer, Houston Asylum Office (19 August 1992)

International Law Commission, 'Report on Nationality, Including Statelessness by Mr. Manley O. Hudson, Special Rapporteur' (21 February 1952) UN Doc A/CN.4/50

Inter-Parliamentary Union, and UNHCR, *Nationality and Statelessness: A Handbook for Parliamentarians No 22* (2014)

Lambert, H, 'Refugee Status, Arbitrary Deprivation of Nationality, and Statelessness within the Context of Article 1A(2) of the 1951 Convention and its 1967 Protocol relating to the Status of Refugees' (UNHCR Legal and Protection Policy Research Series PPLA/2014/01, October 2014)

Massey, H, 'UNHCR and De Facto Statelessness' (UNHCR Legal and Protection Policy Research Series, April 2010)

Office of the High Commissioner for Human Rights, 'General Comment No 17: Article 24 (Rights of the Child)' (7 April 1989) UN Doc HRI/GEN/1/Rev.1

Statute of the Office of the United Nations High Commissioner for Refugees, UNGA Res 428 (V) (14 December 1950)

UN Commission on Human Rights, 'Report of the Working Party on an International Convention on Human Rights' (11 December 1947) UN Doc E/CN.4/56

UN Commission on Human Rights, 'Report of the Drafting Committee to the Commission on Human Rights' (21 May 1948) UN Doc E/CN.4/95

UN Commission on Human Rights, 'Summary Record of the Fifty-Ninth Meeting' (10 June 1948) UN Doc E/CN.4/SR.59

UN Commission on Human Rights, 'Report to the Economic and Social Council on the Seventh Session of the Commission, held at the Palais des Nations, Geneva, from 16 April to 19 May 1951' (24 May 1951) UN Doc E/1992

UN Commission on Human Rights, 'Note Verbale Dated 5 December 1986 from the Permanent Mission of the Netherlands to the United Nations Office at Geneva Addressed to the Centre for Human Rights' (8 January 1987) UN Doc E/CN.4/1987/17

UN Committee Against Torture, 'Communication No 96/1997: *AD v Netherlands*' (12 November 1999) UN Doc CAT/C/23/D/96/1997

UN Committee on Economic, Social and Cultural Rights, 'General Comment No. 20: Non-Discrimination in Economic, Social and Cultural Rights (Art. 2, Para. 2, of the International Covenant on Economic, Social and Cultural Rights)' (2 July 2009) UN Doc E/C.12/GC/20

UN Committee on the Elimination of All Forms of Discrimination Against Women (CEDAW), 'General Recommendation No 21: Equality in Marriage and Family Relations' (1994) UN Doc A/49/38

UN Committee on the Elimination of All Forms of Discrimination Against Women (CEDAW), 'Declarations, Reservations, Objections and Notifications of Withdrawal of

Reservations relating to the Convention on the Elimination of All Forms of Discrimination against Women' (10 April 2006) UN Doc CEDAW/SP/2006/2

UN Committee on the Elimination of Racial Discrimination (CERD), 'General Recommendation 21: Equality in Marriage and Family Relations' (1994) UN Doc A/49/38

UN Committee on the Elimination of Racial Discrimination (CERD), 'General Recommendation 30: Discrimination against Non-Citizens' (23 February–12 March 2004) UN Doc CERD/C/64/Misc.11/rev.3

UN Committee on the Elimination of Racial Discrimination, 'Concluding Observations on the Combined Twenty-First to Twenty-Fourth Periodic Reports of Kuwait' (19 September 2017) UN Doc CERD/C/KWT/CO/21-24

UN Economic and Social Council, 'Report of the Ad Hoc Committee on Statelessness and Related Problems' (17 February 1950) UN Docs E/1618, E/AC.32/5

UN Economic and Social Council, 'Summary Record of the 160th Meeting' (2 August 1950) UN Doc E/AC.7/SR.160

UN Economic and Social Council, 'Compilation of the Comments of Governments and Specialized Agencies on the Report of the Ad Hoc Committee on Statelessness and Related Problems' (10 August 1950) UN Doc E/AC.32/L.40

UN Economic and Social Council, 'Refugees and Stateless Persons: Resolutions Adopted by the Economic and Social Council on 11 August 1950' (12 August 1950) UN Doc E/1818

UN Economic and Social Council, 'Report of the Ad Hoc Committee on Refugees and Stateless Persons' (25 August 1950) UN Docs E/1850, E/AC.32/8

UN Economic and Social Council, 'Comments Received from Governments on the Subject of the Draft Protocol relating to the Status of Stateless Persons: Belgium' (27 February 1953) UN Doc E/2373

UN Economic and Social Council, 'Comments Received from Governments on the Subject of the Draft Protocol relating to the Status of Stateless Persons: Finland' (15 April 1953) UN Doc E/2373/Add.2

UN Economic and Social Council, 'Comments Received from Governments on the Subject of the Draft Protocol relating to the Status of Stateless Persons: France' (27 April 1953) UN Doc E/2373.Add.4

UN Economic and Social Council, 'Comments Received from Governments on the Subject of the Draft Protocol relating to the Status of Stateless Persons: United States' (5 May 1953) UN Doc E/2373.Add.5

UN Economic and Social Council, 'Comments Received from Governments on the Subject of the Draft Protocol relating to the Status of Stateless Persons: South Africa' (14 July 1953) UN Doc E/2373.Add.9

UN Economic and Social Council, 'Comments Received from Governments on the Subject of the Draft Protocol relating to the Status of Stateless Persons: Pakistan' (3 August 1953) UN Doc E/2373/Add.10

UN Economic and Social Council, 'Comments Received from Governments on the Subject of the Draft Protocol relating to the Status of Stateless Persons: United Kingdom of Great Britain and Northern Ireland' (3 August 1953) UN Doc E/2373/Add.11

UN Economic and Social Council, 'Comments Received from Governments on the Subject of the Draft Protocol relating to the Status of Stateless Persons: Switzerland' (10 August 1953) UN Doc E/2372/Add.12

UN Economic and Social Council, 'Comments Received from Governments on the Subject of the Draft Protocol relating to the Status of Stateless Persons: Netherlands', UN Doc E/2372/Add.13

UN Economic and Social Council, 'Comments Received from Governments on the Subject of the Draft Protocol relating to the Status of Stateless Persons: Norway', UN Doc E/2372/Add.14

UN Economic and Social Council, 'Comments Received from Governments on the Subject of the Draft Protocol relating to the Status of Stateless Persons: Netherlands' (26 January 1954) UN Doc E/2373/Add.13

UN Economic and Social Council, 'The Draft Protocol relating to the Status of Stateless Persons: Memorandum by the Secretary-General' (6 August 1954) UN Doc E/CONF.17/3

UN Economic and Social Council, 'General Comment 20: Non-Discrimination in Economic, Social and Cultural Rights' (2 July 2009) UN Doc E/C.12/GC/20

UN Executive Committee of the High Commissioner's Programme, 'Conclusion of the Executive Committee on International Cooperation from a Protection and Solutions Perspective' (6 October 2016) Conclusion No 112 (LXVII) 2016

UN Executive Committee of the High Commissioner's Programme, 'Conclusion of the Executive Committee on Youth' (6 October 2016) Conclusion No 113 (LXVII) 2016

UNGA, 'Statute of the Office of the United Nations High Commissioner for Refugees' (14 December 1950) UN Doc A/RES/428(V)

UNGA, 'Draft Convention relating to the Status of Refugees: Amendment to Article 1/United Kingdom' (3 July 1951) UN Doc A/CONF.2/27

UNGA, 'Draft Convention relating to the Status of Refugees: Amendment to Article 1/Israel' (17 July 1951) UN Doc A/CONF.2/82/Rev.1

UNGA, 'Draft Protocol relating to the Status of Stateless Persons. Draft Final Clauses (Prepared by the Secretariat on the Request of the President of the Conference)' (19 July 1951)

UNGA, 'Report of the Third Committee' (5 December 1957) UN Doc A/3764

UNGA, 'Report of the Third Committee' (10 December 1957) UN Doc A/3764/Add.1

UNGA, 'Report of the Third Committee' (17 December 1962) UN Doc A/5365, para 25

UNGA, 'Third Committee, 1261st Meeting' (12 November 1963) UN Doc A/C.3/SR.1261

UNGA, 'Third Committee, 1262nd Meeting' (13 November 1963) UN Doc A/C.3/SR.1262

UNGA, 'Third Committee, 1263rd Meeting' (14 November 1963) UN Doc A/C.3/SR.1263

UNGA, 'Third Committee, 1265th Meeting' (15 November 1963) UN Doc A/C.3/SR.1265

UNGA, 'Third Committee, 1266th Meeting' (18 November 1963) UN Doc A/C.3/SR.1266

UNGA, 'Report of the Third Committee' (10 December 1963) UN Doc A/5655

UNGA Res 2200A(XXI) (16 December 1966) UN Doc A/RES/2200A(XXI)

UNGA Res 50/152 (9 February 1996) UN Doc A/RES/50/152

UNGA, 'Report of the International Law Commission on the Work of its Fifty-Third Session' UN GAOR Fifty-Third Session Supp No 10 UN Doc A/56/10 (Commentary on Draft Article 26 on Responsibility of States for Internationally Wrongful Acts (2001) chIV(E)(2))

UNGA, 'Report of the International Law Commission: Fifty Eighth Session' UN GAOR Sixty-First Session Supp No 10 UN Doc A/61/10 (Draft Articles on Diplomatic Protection with Commentaries (2006) chIV(E)(1))

UNGA Res 71/1 (3 October 2016) UN Doc A/RES/71/1

UNHCR, 'The Cessation Clauses: Guidelines on Their Application' (Geneva, April 1999)

UNHCR, 'Guidelines on International Protection: Gender-Related Persecution within the Context of Article 1A(2) of the 1951 Convention and/or its 1967 Protocol relating to the Status of Refugees' (7 May 2002) UN Doc HCR/GIP/02/01

UNHCR, 'Annotated Comments on the EC Council Directive 2004/83/EC of 29 April 2004 on Minimum Standards for the Qualification and Status of Third Country Nationals or Stateless Persons as Refugees or as Persons Who Otherwise Need International Protection and the Content of the Protection Granted' (30 September 2004) OJ L 304/12

UNHCR, 'Conclusion on the Provision on International Protection Including through Complementary Forms of Protection No. 103 (LVI)—2005' (7 October 2005) UN Doc A/AC.96/1021

UNHCR, 'Guidelines on International Protection: The Application of Article 1A(2) of the 1951 Convention and/or 1967 Protocol relating to the Status of Refugees to Victims of Trafficking and Persons at Risk of being Trafficked' (7 April 2006) UN Doc HCR/GIP/06/07

UNHCR, 'Guidelines on International Protection: Child Asylum Claims under Articles 1(A)2 and 1(F) of the 1951 Convention and/or 1967 Protocol relating to the Status of Refugees' (22 December 2009) UN Doc HCR/GIP/09/08

UNHCR, 'Conclusions Adopted by the Executive Committee on the International Protection of Refugees' (December 2009) No 69 (XLIII) Cessation of Status (1992)

UNHCR, 'Note on International Protection: Report of the High Commissioner' (28 June 2011) UN Doc A/AC.96/1098

UNHCR, 'Handbook and Guidelines on Procedures and Criteria for Determining Refugee Status' (Geneva December 2011) UN Doc HCR/1P/4/ENG/REV 3

UNHCR, 'Global Action Plan to End Statelessness 2014–24' (November 2014)

UNHCR, 'Handbook on Protection of Stateless Persons' (Geneva, 2014)

UNHCR, 'I Am Here, I Belong: The Urgent Need to End Childhood Statelessness' (November 2015)

UNHCR, 'Guidelines on International Protection No 12' (2 December 2016) UN Doc HCR/GIP/16/12

UNHCR, Executive Committee of the High Commissioner's Programme, 'Update on Statelessness' (7 June 2017) UN Doc EC/68/SC/CRP.13

UNHCR, 'Representing Stateless Persons before U.S. Immigration Authorities' (August 2017)

UNHCR, 'Statelessness and the Rohingya Crisis' (November 2017) <https://www.refworld.org/docid/5a05b4664.html> accessed 9 December 2018

UNHCR, ' "This is Our Home": Stateless Minorities and their Search for Citizenship' (November 2017)

UNHCR, 'Background Note on Gender Equality, Nationality Laws and Statelessness 2018' (8 March 2018)

UNHCR, 'Global Compact on Refugees, Advance Version', (20 July 2018) para 83 <www.unhcr.org/en-au/5b51fd587> accessed 10 November 2018

UN HRC, 'Concluding Observations of the Human Rights Committee: Israel' (18 August 1998) UN Doc CCPR/C/79/Add 93

UN HRC, 'Human Rights and Arbitrary Deprivation of Nationality: Report of the Secretary-General' (14 December 2009) UN Doc A/HRC/13/34

UN HRC, 'Human Rights and Arbitrary Deprivation of Nationality: Report of the Secretary-General' (19 December 2011) UN Doc A/HRC/19/43

UN HRC, 'Human Rights and Arbitrary Deprivation of Nationality: Report of the Secretary-General' (19 December 2013) UN Doc A/HRC/25/28

UN HRC, 'Communication No 35/1978: *Aumeeruddy-Cziffra v Mauritius*' (9 April 1981) UN Doc CCPR/C/21/OP/1

UN HRC, 'CCPR General Comment No 15: The Position of Aliens under the Covenant' (11 April 1986) UN Doc HRI/GEN/1/Rev.1 at 18 (1994)

UN HRC, 'CCPR General Comment No 25: Article 25 (Participation in Public Affairs and the Right to Vote) The Right to Participate in Public Affairs, Voting Rights and the Right of Equal Access to Public Service' (12 July 1996) UN Doc CCPR/C/21/Rev.1/Add.7

UN HRC, 'Communication No 586/1994: *Adam v Czech Republic*' (23 July 1996) UN Doc CCPR/C/57/D/586/1994

UN HRC, 'Communication No 538/1993: *Stewart v Canada*' (1 November 1996) UN Doc CCPR/C/58/D/538/1993

UN HRC, 'Concluding Observations of the Human Rights Committee: Israel' (18 August 1998) UN Doc CCPR/C/79/Add.93

UN HRC, 'CCPR General Comment No 27: Article 12 (Freedom of Movement)' (2 November 1999) UN Doc CCPR/C/21/Rev.1/Add.9

UN HRC, 'Communication No 675/1995: *Taola v New Zealand*' (2 November 2000) UN Doc CCPR/C/70/D/675/1995

UN HRC, 'Communication No 859/1999: *Vaca v Colombia*' (15 April 2002) UN Doc CCPR/C/74/D/859/1999

UN HRC, 'General Comment No 31: The Nature of the General Legal Obligation Imposed on States Parties to the Covenant' (26 May 2004) UN Doc CCPR/C/21/Rev.1/Add.13

UN HRC, 'Communication No 1463/2006: *Gratzinger v Czech Republic*' (25 October 2007) UN Doc CCPR/C/91/D/1463/2006

UN HRC, 'Communication No 1557/2007: *Nystrom v Australia*' (1 September 2011) UN Doc CCPR/C/102/D/1557/2007

UN HRC, 'Communication No 1959/2010: *Warsame v Canada*' (1 September 2011) UN Doc CCPR/C/102/D/1959/2010

UN HRC, 'Communication No 2001/2010: *Q v Denmark*' (19 May 2015) UN Doc CCPR/C/113/D/2001/2010

UN Secretary General, 'Text of Articles Adopted by the Third Committee at the Tenth to Seventeenth Sessions of the General Assembly' (24 September 1963) UN Doc A/C.3/L.1062

Index

Printed and bound by CPI Group (UK) Ltd, Croydon, CR0 4YY